TAKEN CAPTIVE

TAKEN CAPTIVE
A Japanese POW's Story

Ōoka Shōhei

Translated from the Japanese and edited by
Wayne P. Lammers

John Wiley & Sons, Inc.

New York • Chichester • Brisbane • Toronto • Singapore

English Language translation copyright © 1996 by Pacific Basin Institute
Published by John Wiley & Sons, Inc.

Originally Published in 1952 as *Furyoki*
copyright © 1952 by Harue Ōoka
A Pacific Basin Institute Book

Major funding for the English translation of Ōoka Shōhei's text was provided by the Japan Foundation, the Sumitomo Foundation, the Japan-U.S. Friendship Commission, and the Sasakawa Peace Foundation.

Library of Congress Cataloging-in-Publication Data

Ōoka, Shōhei
    [Furyoki. English]
    Taken captive : a Japanese POW's story / Ōoka Shōhei : translated from the Japanese and edited by Wayne P. Lammers.
      p. cm.
    Includes index.
    ISBN 0-471-14285-9 (alk. paper)
    I. Lammers, Wayne P. II. Title.
  PL835.O5F813   1996
  940.54'7273'092—dc20   95-35865
  [B]

Printed in the United States of America

10 9 8 7 6 5 4 3 2 1

[It is] reasonable to represent one kind of imprisonment by another.

Daniel Defoe,
Preface to Volume III of *Robinson Crusoe*

Contents

Foreword

by Frank B. Gibney

Shortly after New Year's Day, 1944, a thirty-five-year-old literary critic named Ōoka Shōhei* was called to serve in the Japanese Imperial Army. His summons was typically terse and admitted no appeal. Upon reporting to a regimental depot in Tokyo, he was given rudimentary training and shipped off with a newly formed infantry battalion to join the garrison troops on the Japanese-occupied island of Mindoro, then nervously awaiting the expected American landing in the Philippines.

There were few more improbable soldiers. A graduate of Kyoto Imperial University but born and raised in Tokyo, Ōoka was part of a small but vigorous group of young intellectuals who were attracted to the study of European, in particular French, literature. By that time, he had translated several works by Stendhal. In fact, translating Stendhal's detached descriptions of nineteenth-century French battlefields was as close as Ōoka had come to experiencing the horrors of war.

To become a private soldier in the brutal Japanese army of those days was a sudden introduction to the real thing—and in Ōoka's case, under the most adverse possible conditions. Predictably, he was repelled by army life. In February, he wrote a caption for a photograph taken of him in uniform: "Second Class Private—and not very happy about it. I must try to keep my hatred for the military from turning into hatred for humankind."

On December 15, 1944, two U.S. regimental combat teams landed on Mindoro, as a prelude to the larger attack on Luzon. There were fewer than a thousand Japanese troops on the island at the time. They were unsupplied and unsupported, written off as expendable by General Yamashita Tomoyuki's headquarters. Ōoka's unit was soon scattered. Hundreds were killed by the advancing Americans. Those who were left, hungry and wounded, wandered through the hills in small groups, scavenging in the inhospitable jungle. Some offered last-ditch resistance. Others committed suicide, following the stated Japanese military doctrine that to be taken prisoner meant ultimate disgrace for a soldier and his family.

In the end, many were in fact taken prisoner as the fighting entered its final stages. Ōoka was one of these. After his capture, he was brought to an American prisoner-of-war camp on Leyte. There he remained until he was repatriated to Japan at the end of 1945.

---

* All Japanese names in this book are given in Japanese order, surname first.

This experience changed Ōoka's life. On returning home, he began to sort out what he had felt and thought—the reflections of a sophisticated and cosmopolitan observer thrown with his companions into a desperate, primitive struggle for life. *Taken Captive (Furyoki)* was published in separate parts between 1948 and 1951, and it established Ōoka's postwar reputation. In 1951, he published a second war book, the novel *Fires on the Plain (Nobi)*, which won the Yomiuri Prize for Literature and was later made into a prize-winning film. Although he wrote other highly regarded books over the years, the war experience dominated his thinking. One of his last books, *A Record of the Battle of Leyte (Reite senki)*, was characterized by the critic Katō Shūichi as "the finest work of war literature since the [medieval] *Heike Monogatari*."

Although international and rather Western-oriented in his outlook—for example, he often makes use of Christian images and references—Ōoka adheres to the tradition of autobiographical fiction so beloved by Japanese intellectuals. Ōe Kenzaburō, Japan's 1994 Nobel Prize–winning author, is a great admirer of Ōoka, who died in 1988 at the age of seventy-nine after a lifetime of literary activity. Ōe ranks Ōoka with Japan's great early-twentieth-century novelist, Natsume Sōseki. In one of his essays, Ōe called on younger writers to learn as much as they could from Ōoka if they wished to bring literature to life.

Although loosely called a novel by Japanese critics, *Taken Captive* is heavily autobiographical, rooted as it is in Ōoka's own wartime experience. Yet he makes a conscious effort to see the plight and conduct of himself and his fellow prisoners as something of an allegory of the human condition. Following an idea common to the immediate postwar period, he envisions the prison camp as a microcosm of Japan itself, a nation in a sense taken prisoner after its defeat.

The book basically consists of two parts. The first concentrates on Ōoka's personal struggle and the reflections of a man who suddenly found himself a hunted fugitive. The latter part of the book, which deals with the behavioral quirks of people forced to live in confinement, brilliantly dissects the rootlessness of Japanese prisoners. Some comparisons can be made to James Clavell's novel *King Rat*, which pungently describes the conduct of British and American prisoners of war in a similar situation. For all that they rationalized their situation, most Japanese POWs had difficulty coming to terms with the idea that they incurred everlasting disgrace by being captured. Ōoka himself is not totally free of this concern, even though he denounces the militarist propaganda that held being taken prisoner as dishonorable.

I had considerable personal experience of these Japanese attitudes during my own service in World War II. As a navy intelligence officer specializing in prisoner-of-war interrogation, I found myself, so to speak, on the other side of the fence from Ōoka. Although I stopped only briefly in the Philippines, I did spend a great deal of time in Peleliu (1944) and Okinawa (1945), as well as at our base camp in Pearl Harbor, working with Japanese prisoners, most of them from army units like Ōoka's. Very few of them wanted their families to be advised of their capture; in fact, at the outset most gave us hastily assumed false names. Disillusionment with the war was pervasive. Many actively denounced the government of the military high command that had deceived them about wartime realities.

Yet, for the Japanese the normal discomfort of being a POW was intensified by their depression at having somehow broken with their comrades who had, according to custom, either died in battle or taken their own lives by way of compensation. Despite the good treatment they generally received, despite their sense of betrayal in a war founded on false premises, many continued to feel that their capture had sundered them from their tight island society. Their very alienation reflected the power of the massive groupthink that had thrown an ancient, cultured nation into a suicidal war.

Ōoka describes this in a masterful way. He also shows us how individuals can bear up under unspeakable hardships and then somehow put their lives back together for what at the time seemed like an appallingly bleak future.

His Japanese shows the hand of a great stylist as well as a talented observer. That it comes out so well in English is a tribute to Wayne Lammers, the translator. Translation from one European language to another is difficult enough. In the case of Japanese—so internally rich, yet so totally different from Western languages in its moods and manner of expression—the translator must often break down and reassemble the structure to convey both art and meaning. Bilingual since his school days in Japan, Dr. Lammers has taught Japanese in several American universities, and over the years he has produced a variety of translations whose ease and naturalness of expression belie the difficulty of doing them. As a classic of postwar Japanese literature, *Taken Captive* justly deserves its selection as the sixth book in the Library of Japan series. First appearing in 1992, these volumes represent an effort to offer the best of modern Japanese fiction and nonfiction to an English-speaking readership. They were developed under the aegis of the U.S.–Japan Conference on Cultural and Educational Exchange (CULCON).

On behalf of the Pacific Basin Institute, I would like to thank the Sasakawa Peace Foundation, the Sumitomo Foundation, the Japan–U.S. Friendship Commission, and the Japan Foundation for their support in the translation and editing of *Taken Captive*.

Translator's Note

The chapters of this book originally appeared independently in nine different journals between February 1948 and January 1951. These separate pieces were then brought together and published as a unified book by Sōgensha in December 1952. The working text used for the present translation was the Shinchō Bunko paperback, first issued in 1967, based directly on the Sōgensha edition.

Though Ōoka made a number of corrections and minor alterations when producing the unified book, he chose for the most part to leave the chapters as they were, making no discernible effort to excise redundancies arising from the chapters' original publication as separate works. In the interest of faithfulness, I initially translated all such passages in full, but I found, as many other translators have before me, that the tolerable level of repetition in English is considerably below that in Japanese. I have therefore edited the English text to eliminate unnecessary duplication as well as to reconcile inconsistencies of fact and remove other vestiges of the individual chapters' original form. In conjunction with these alterations, I have also chosen to excise a small amount of material that related mainly to events during the Occupation period, when Ōoka was writing the work, rather than to his POW experience, feeling that for readers half a century later it would detract from the more universal and timeless themes Ōoka develops through his account of life in captivity. The result is a manuscript that reads like a single, integrated work and is approximately 7 to 8 percent shorter than my initial, more faithful English rendering. All editorial adjustments were based on the content of the original, and I do not believe the fundamental historical authenticity of Ōoka's account has been compromised in any way. Nevertheless, as always, students and scholars who wish to study Ōoka's work closely are advised to seek out the original text.

In acknowledging the many debts I have acquired in bringing this translation to completion, I would first like to express my gratitude to Frank Gibney and the Pacific Basin Institute, both for the opportunity to undertake the work and for their unflagging support of the project even when the initial publication plans had to be altered. For help on the manuscript itself, I am especially indebted to my wife Cheryl and fellow translator David Olson for reading through the entire work at different stages and offering me their invaluable editorial advice. I am grateful to Connie Prener, Hiroaki Sato, and Kyoko Selden for helping to cast light on a number of particularly troublesome references, and to Antoon Postma of Mindoro Island in the Philippines for advising me on the orthography of several obscure place names. Subscribers of the Internet newsgroups and mailing lists soc.culture.filipino, sci.lang.translation, MILHST-L, and honyaku responded to a host of queries regarding the culture and geography of the Philippines, military terminology, subtleties of Japanese and English usage, and so forth, often going the second and third mile in their effort to aid a faceless stranger; they are too numerous to name individually, but their willingness to offer a hand, along with the technology that made it possible, proved to be a vital complement to the often limited local resources I had to draw on. And finally, I am grateful to Mary Ray Worley at Impressions Book and Journal Services, Inc. for her careful and perceptive editing.

In so many ways, large and small, the help extended by these individuals improved the translation beyond my own capabilities, and I thank them all. At the same time, I alone must bear the burden for any lingering errors or infelicities that remain.

—Wayne P. Lammers

Aparri

Tuguegarao

LUZON

Baguio

Lingayen Gulf

Rosales

Lingayen

Central Luzon Plain

Iba Tariac

Cabanatuan

Plaridol

○MANILA

Cavite

Batangas

Philippine Sea

Legaspi

MINDORO

SAMAR

Tacloban

Tagauayan

PANAY

LEYTE

CUYO IS.

CEBU

NEGROS

Mindanao Sea

Cagayan

☐ DEL MONTE FIELD

MINDANAO

Davao

Davao Gulf

Paluan

Calapan

Pinamalayan

Sablayan

Bongabong

MINDORO

Bulalacao

San Jose

0   100
Statute Miles

The Philippines

⌐ 1 ⌐

My Capture

It is not from goodness of heart that you do not kill.
—Tannishō[1]

On January 25, 1945, I was captured by American forces in the mountains of southern Mindoro in the Philippines.

The island of Mindoro, situated to the southwest of Luzon, is about half the size of our Shikoku. It had no military facilities to speak of, and the forces deployed there comprised but two companies of infantry nominally occupying and patrolling six strategic points along the coastline.

My unit had been assigned to patrol the southern and western portions of the island in August 1944, and my own platoon was stationed together with the company command at San Jose in the far southwest. Two other platoons were stationed respectively at Bulalacao in the southeast and Paluan in the northwest. The western coastline between San Jose and Paluan—which is to say, virtually the entire hundred-mile length of the island—remained open, and local guerrilla forces could freely obtain supplies from American submarines. Fortunately, they did not attack our San Jose post.

On December 15, 1944, an American task force of some sixty ships had landed near San Jose. We immediately retreated into the hills and cut across the island through the southern mountains to join up three days later with the Bulalacao platoon, now bivouacked on a ridge overlooking that town. American forces had not come ashore there, but the platoon had

---

1 A Japanese Buddhist treatise from the thirteenth century.

heard the roar of the bombardment at San Jose and had taken refuge preemptively, bringing with them their food stores and radio gear. The food supply was quite ample—sufficient to last more than three months even after our numbers swelled to nearly two hundred with the arrival of some survivors from a seaplane base near San Jose, a group of marooned shipping engineers, and a number of noncombatants. This expanded company remained encamped at that location for some forty days, until an attack by American forces on January 24 sent us scattering in every direction.

U.S. warplanes flew back and forth in the skies overhead day in and day out, but the Americans were in no hurry to pursue us.

"Those bastards are obviously too lazy to come after us all the way out here," one of the noncoms said, as he supervised the construction of the crude huts that were to become our barracks. "And if they're not coming after us, why should we go out looking for trouble? The war'll probably be over pretty soon, anyway."

His remark put in plain words the hope that many of us held silently in our hearts. That is to say, since it seemed quite apparent that the enemy regarded Mindoro merely as a stepping-stone to Luzon, so long as we stayed put in the hills, there was a good chance the fighting would leapfrog right over us and leave us untouched for the duration of the war, making our position one of the so-called forgotten fronts. For a small, isolated force like ours, cut off from any possibility of further supplies or reinforcements, this was our only hope for survival.

Unfortunately, it soon became impossible for us not to "go out looking for trouble": We received orders from the battalion command at Batangas on Luzon to report on enemy activities in the San Jose area. Detachments of a dozen or more men were sent by turns to scout the hills in back of San Jose for periods of a week or ten days. One of those detachments was discovered and fired upon by an American patrol.

Eventually, the full Bulalacao platoon moved to a ridge overlooking San Jose and began sending back daily reports of what they had observed through their telescopes. We then relayed the information to battalion headquarters. The lookouts frequently spied convoys of several dozen vessels bearing northward past San Jose, and they saw squadrons of massive bombers taking off from newly constructed airstrips. The bay where we had previously anchored our boats to fish was now crisscrossed by the foamy wakes of American outboards.

At the beginning of the new year, battalion headquarters sent word that 150 commandos were being dispatched to Mindoro. As luck would have it, though, American troops landed at several points along the island's east coast on the very day the commandos were scheduled to arrive, and we were unable to make contact with the boat transporting the special unit.

To be sure, the news of their impending arrival was not entirely welcome, for it inevitably meant that several of our own number would have to accompany them as guides—a virtual suicide mission. We had no illusions about the success of 150 commandos against an American force brought to shore in a task force of sixty warships.

Subsequent orders took us back down to Bulalacao to meet the promised shock troops, but again to no avail. We looted the abandoned homes and took captive a local man unfortunate enough to have come back at the wrong moment to retrieve his belongings. In this way we recklessly went on multiplying cause for the local population to wish us eradicated.

Despite the utter hopelessness of our situation, we, the enlisted men, remained quite undisturbed. The company was made up entirely of reservists called into active duty in early 1944 and sent to the front directly from three months of boot camp, so we were too green to genuinely understand how dire the situation had become. Yet, even if we had understood the true nature of our situation, it would have done us no good to spend the days paralyzed in fear of impending attack by an impossibly superior foe, so perhaps you could say our ignorance was a blessing. The great majority of my cohorts were, like myself, over thirty, and we had no desire to force a speedy resolution of our predicament.

To begin with, life in the hills was not so uncomfortable. The dry season had begun, so we did not have to contend with rain, and even during the worst of the daytime heat, it remained cool in the shade. It was the perfect sort of weather for camping out with nothing but the shirts on our backs; we faced no immediate shortage of rations; and since each squad had its own separate hut, discipline was quite naturally relaxed, freeing us from the stiff decorum that normally dominates military life. We cooked our meals with water drawn from a nearby stream, just as we might have done on a camping trip back home, and we bartered with the friendly Mangyans nearby to obtain potatoes, bananas, and tobacco in exchange for red fabric and aluminum coins. (These highlanders, darker skinned and belonging to an altogether different tribe from the Tagalog people who lived down by the sea, were completely indifferent to the war.) Now and then we descended from the hills to shoot a free-roaming carabao and feast on its meat.

Trouble arrived, however, from an unexpected quarter: malaria.

Mindoro was said to harbor the most virulent strains of malaria in the Philippines, but by taking the appropriate precautions, we had never had more than a handful of cases during our occupation of San Jose. Unfortunately, the medical officer had left behind our supply of quinine when we fled into the mountains, and the disease spread rapidly through our ranks after that. By the time the American forces attacked on January 24, fewer than thirty men remained with the legs to fight. During the final two weeks of that period, malaria claimed an average of three men a day.

The stricken went quietly to their deaths. Their loss of spirit was swift and complete, standing in eerie contrast to the easygoing mood that otherwise prevailed.

Our commanding officer, a first lieutenant, made daily rounds of the squad huts. As he came to each hut, he would stand somberly in the doorway, gazing in on the ailing soldiers crowding the floor.

The sergeant commanding my own squad bitterly assailed the lieutenant for failing to immediately order a headlong dash to the northern end of the island, where we could have crossed over to Luzon, as soon as the American forces had landed. We would never have been ordered by battalion headquarters to report on enemy activities, he groused, nor would we have been immobilized by an outbreak of malaria, if the lieutenant had not kept us dawdling around in these mountains.

It was the voice of noncom egotism. Underlying his position was the myopic presumption that the island of Luzon remained, and would continue to remain, an invulnerable safety zone. The lieutenant, on the other hand, was a seasoned veteran who had seen action at Nomonhan,[2] and his view of the fate of Japanese forces in the Philippines could hardly have been so sanguine.

The young lieutenant had gained his rank by way of the reserve officer training corps. He was only twenty-seven, but he had a taciturn, mournful air that made him look no less than thirty. Never once did he speak of what he had seen or experienced at Nomonhan, but I daresay it showed in the expression of his eyes, of his face. Sometimes I even thought I could smell the stench of his dead comrades still clinging to his person.

"A garrison must think of its post as its final resting place," he often repeated, and I cannot believe that he was merely mouthing a commonplace.

The lieutenant took no special precautions to keep our position concealed from the Americans. Contrary to the usual custom, he paid the guides who had shown us the way through the mountains from San Jose with food and allowed them to return home. A note of resignation manifested itself in everything he did or said. His movements were languidly deliberate, and his occasional smile appeared weakly on his lips, as though he had just barely managed to squeeze it from between his teeth.

In a way, he seemed to yearn for death. On punitive expeditions conducted during our occupation of San Jose, he always fought in the vanguard,

---

2 On the border between Outer Mongolia and Manchuria where, in a 1939 clash, Soviet troops routed a division of Japan's Guandong Army.

making no effort to shield himself from danger. He had been cast in the mold of the sensitive commander—the kind who accepted the dictates of the war as his highest calling, yet felt a deep sense of personal responsibility when it came to passing those dictates on to his subordinates. As a rule, men like him find it difficult to justify what they ask of their subordinates with anything other than their own deaths.

When the Americans finally attacked our mountain encampment, the lieutenant strode forward alone to survey the American positions and became the first to die, taking the direct hit of a mortar shell. It was no doubt exactly the way he had wished to go.

I identified closely with this young CO and was privately very fond of him. Though in a considerably different sense from him, I, too, lived in the face of my own certain death.

I had long since given up believing in a Japanese victory. I held nothing but contempt for the General Staff who had dragged our country into such a hopeless fight. Yet, since I had not had the courage to take any action toward preventing that fight, I did not feel I could claim any right, at so late a stage, to protest the fate to which they had consigned me. This reasoning, which placed a single powerless citizen on an equal footing with the massive organization by which an entire nation exercises its violent power, seemed almost comical to me; and yet, had I not taken such a view, I could not have kept from laughing at the absurdity of the predicament in which I found myself, traveling rapidly toward a meaningless death.

All the same, this reasoning did nothing to efface the disemboweling wretchedness I experienced as my comrades and I, herded aboard like a cargo of slaves, stood on the deck of a transport ship in Moji and peered down at the red and green lights of toylike ferries plying the waters below while waiting for the ship to get us under way on our voyage to death.

Until the day we shipped out for the front, I had lightheartedly resigned myself to joining my own fate to my country's, wherever that might lead, and I had scoffed alike at the wartime opportunists so full of lies and the defeatists with their fruitless dissents. The moment I boarded that transport, however, I was struck utterly dumb by the looming figure of Death sitting squarely before me.

At thirty-five, I could not yet say I had lived a full life, and there were farewells to be said, loved ones with whom I found it indeed painful to part. But the act of boarding the transport ineluctably pushed all that behind me. The future held nothing but death, which we humans can envision only as absolute nothingness; yet, if I could be transported to that nothingness as easily as I had been brought aboard that ship, then what possible good would fretting do? I reminded myself of this again and again. Even so, the idea of death continually returned to assault my consciousness in everything

I did as I went about my daily activities. Eventually I realized it was not the nature of death that troubled me; it was simply living with my own certain extinction so close at hand.

In fact, the proximity of death brought with it elements of pleasure. The vibrant colors of the Philippine sunrises and sunsets, of the islands' palm and flame trees, were a delight to behold. Though my eyes saw the shadow of death in every direction, they also feasted greedily on the tropical landscape in which the flora so overpowered the fauna. I thanked the fates for bringing me into the midst of such a lushness of life in the time before my death. After we retreated into the mountains, the palm trees were missing, and the teeming, luxuriant growth of the lowlands was replaced by the more temperate landscape of the highlands, but to me it seemed only the more beautiful. I became convinced that the ever-increasing pleasure I experienced in the embrace of nature was a certain sign that my time was drawing near.

Yet, once we had lost our only route of escape and my brothers in arms began dying one after the other, a peculiar transformation came over me: I suddenly believed in the possibility of my survival. The 99 percent certainty of death was abruptly swept aside in my mind. I found myself imagining instead a medley of ways by which I might actually ensure my survival, and I determined to pursue them. At the very least I would exercise all due care in everything I did. It seemed senseless to do otherwise.

Clearly, the deepening shadows of death that surrounded me had triggered an inborn determination to survive. What our instincts compel us to do in the face of extremity is always highly pragmatic; the schemes they make us dream up, on the other hand, are typically quite preposterous.

I had one particular friend whom I shall call S. He was my own age, and like myself a married man with children. His father sat on the board of directors of a large fisheries firm, but S had "had it up to here" (as he put it) with the self-serving egotism of the capitalists on the home islands, and he dreamed of going to the front to fight as a common soldier instead of becoming an agent of the capitalists' greed. During our training back in Japan, he had concealed the likelihood of his being sent to the front from his father, who had high connections in the military—thereby deliberately severing all chance of remaining safely in Japan. Once he had actually seen conditions in the war zone, however, his dreams were shattered. Finding the manner in which our forces were conducting the war utterly witless, he declared it would be a pure and simple waste to die on such a battlefield.

His words came as a revelation to me. Suddenly I could see the patent self-deception in proudly insisting to myself that I had chosen this path of death at my own volition. To die helplessly in these faraway mountains as the victim of some foolishly conceived war plan was indeed a "pure and simple waste" and nothing more.

We developed a plan for escape together. Since there could be no doubt that the Americans would eventually force us from our refuge, we would somehow make our way through enemy positions to the island's west coast. There we would commandeer a sailboat and, catching the prevailing winds, steer a course that skirted the string of islands leading to Borneo (sailing techniques I had learned on trips to the beach would come in handy at this point). When I questioned whether Borneo would be safe and suggested instead that we cut across the South China Sea to Indochina, S convinced me that our limited food supply and navigational skills required us to settle for the next best plan.

If we could not obtain a sailboat, we would return to the mountains and subsist on roots and whatever else we could forage while we waited for the war to end. Recalling some of the details of *Robinson Crusoe*, which we had both read as young boys, we got some tribesmen to show us how to start a fire with bamboo.

The plan was a sheer fantasy, but not for a moment did we doubt that it would succeed.

Even as three more of our comrades continued to die each day, we rehearsed our survival plan over and over, like a pair of cheerful grave diggers. (And, in fact, we did dig graves.) We contemplated, too, the threat of malaria, our most immediate enemy at the time, and we adopted the only means at our disposal for staving off the disease: striving our utmost to maintain what reserves of strength we had. We voraciously devoured any rice gruel left uneaten by the sick, and we did not hesitate even to eat spilled rice we had retrieved from the ground.

Though we thought we had prepared ourselves for every eventuality, we had failed to consider the possibility that the Americans would arrive at the precise moment when the disease had struck the two of us. Almost as if by appointment, S and I both came down with fevers on January 16. My temperature stayed relentlessly at 104 degrees, rendering me completely unable to stand on the second day and slurring my speech on the third. S's symptoms were milder, but his temperature, too, remained above 102 degrees.

I now faced my first genuine battle. "Take up your arms," I commanded my heart. I was not particularly robust in physique, but I knew that I had a relatively high resistance to disease. Observing my symptoms carefully, I devised my own strategy for treatment. Since the onset of my fever had led immediately to diarrhea, I decided to avoid all unnecessary stress on my digestive system—this was how I reasoned at the time—by not eating anything. I felt confident that I had enough reserves of energy to go without food for a week or two without it affecting my constitutional strength.

In the mountains, the medics had invented a truly bizarre prescription for malaria: no water. Though I had blindly followed their instructions before, this time I abandoned my docility. Objecting strenuously, I presented argument after argument as to why such a prohibition was misguided, but I succeeded only in angering my sergeant, who forbade my squad mates from bringing me water. The only way I managed to keep my canteen filled was by waiting for men from other squads to pass by and secretly soliciting their aid, or by dragging myself on hands and knees to the spring about sixty feet away.

I had noticed that death struck the sick with precipitous speed, so I constantly monitored my physical state to reaffirm that I had not yet reached the fateful threshold. Since I had seen many of the sick become incontinent before they died, I made a point of crawling outside to urinate whenever I began feeling the least bit worse.

One of my squad mates died, and his body was hauled away over my chest. Since the entire squad was afflicted to one degree or another, those with relatively light symptoms were called upon to help with the burial. A fellow whose long siege of fever had at length eased a bit was sent to deliver the deceased man's equipment and personal effects to our company HQ a hundred yards or so up the mountain. Reentering the hut on his return, he looked to be suffering. The next morning he, too, was dead.

That man died on January 22. My fever eased a bit the same day, and in the evening I ate a small amount of rice gruel for the first time since falling ill. As I was eating, a report came that the lookout had spied three American ships entering the bay at Bulalacao.

Our sergeant went to the command post and remained there for quite some time. When he finally returned, he lay down sullenly without a word. We learned from a passing soldier that a party of four scouts had been dispatched to investigate.

I remember feeling surprised when I awoke the next morning and saw the light of day fully risen and our little hut still intact. I had vaguely expected the Americans to attack at dawn. Another day passed without incident. The scouts sent out the night before failed to return.

"I wonder if they didn't attack today because they want to surround us first?" I speculated to my sergeant that evening.

"Aw, shut up," he snarled. "What would an invalid like you know?"

The next day, January 24, a second party of scouts left at dawn, this time with an officer in command. One of the scouts returned around 7:00 A.M. to report that they had met an ambush at the foot of the mountain and that the officer had been killed.

Our sergeant was summoned to the command post again, but this time he returned without delay. The sick were to evacuate along with all noncombatants to the position of the platoon on the ridge overlooking San Jose. Everyone capable of walking was to prepare to march immediately, he said, and he quickly began gathering up his gear. He, too, had recently joined the ranks of the sick.

I had finally recovered enough strength to walk to the latrine, but I doubted I could manage the fifteen kilometers to where the detached platoon was camped. Even if I made it that far, there was no telling how much farther I would have to walk next. I resigned myself to dying there in that hut.

The original complement of my squad was twelve privates, but we had lost two, leaving ten. Four of those ten decided to stay behind, including myself. As S packed his gear, I went outside and slowly worked my way around the hut on my feet.

"I won't be going," I told S.

He had recovered much of his former strength. Now he thrust his arm under mine and said, "You can do it. I'll help you. Come with us."

I decided I should at least go with him until my legs gave out, and I told my sergeant I had changed my mind. He said nothing.

The men went about their preparations in silence. No one exchanged farewells.

The time came to move out. As I started to fall in after the others, the sergeant turned toward me, though avoiding my eyes, and said, "Ōoka, you think maybe you should stay?"

His words made me realize how much of a hindrance I was likely to become to the others, as well as how my present condition must have looked to the eyes of a professional soldier. I replied, "Yes, Sir," and lowered my rifle from my shoulder.

For some reason S had been one of the first to move out and had already climbed out of sight. Under the circumstances, I could not bring myself to call him back. I parted from the buddy with whom I had planned to escape without even saying good-bye.

Those of us remaining behind had received no orders, but we wrapped our gaiters and laced up our boots to prepare for combat and then lay down to rest.

In my case, there should never have been any question that I would stay, since my fever was worse than anyone else's, but I was surprised by the other three who chose not to go. They seemed no worse off than the men who had gone.

One was an office worker named K, the son of a famous *rakugo* critic of the Taishō Era.[3] His ever-phlegmatic response to orders, exerting himself not the slightest bit in excess of the minimally required effort, did not sit well with his superiors. Since K is a relatively unusual surname, I asked him one day if he was related to Dr. K.

"Give me a break," he spat out between gritted teeth.

---

3 The Taishō Era spanned from 1912 to 1926. *Rakugo* refers to comic monologues recited by professional storytellers.

Something in his tone made it difficult for me to take this as meaning, "No, we're unrelated," and I felt quite certain that he must be Dr. K's son. Put off by his manner, though, I chose not to pursue the matter. Later, when I had my first bout of fever just before the Americans landed at San Jose, he happened to be confined to quarters at the same time by a leg injury, and he kindly fetched water for me in my mess tin and put cool compresses on my forehead. His nursing had a curiously feminine gentleness, which seemed rather sharply at odds with the egotistic and standoffish attitude he usually displayed. I repeated my earlier question, and this time he answered straightforwardly that he was Dr. K's second son. Without further prompting, he went on to detail his family's history since his father's untimely death in the Great Tokyo Earthquake of 1923. We became friendly after that, but he laughed scornfully at the escape plan S and I formulated in the mountains.

K's symptoms were so mild that some suspected he was only feigning illness. At the very least, there could be no question that he was in far better shape than S, who had chosen to evacuate with the others.

"It won't make a whit of difference whether we go or stay," he said with a sneer. He had a gentle spirit, but he apparently did not apply it to himself.

Another of those remaining behind was a civil engineer. He impressed his superior officers with his efficiency during our stint at San Jose, and he often drew assignments that would normally have gone to PFCs. I disliked him because he struck me as a bootlicker, but even after we had retreated into the mountains where rank and promotions could no longer be anyone's concern, he continued to work just as hard, volunteering to carry the heaviest loads and so on. No doubt it was owing to these exertions that he became the first in our squad to fall ill. Inwardly, I felt ashamed that even at my age I remained such a poor judge of character. He had now emerged from his long bout with the fever, but the illness had perhaps taken a greater toll on his strength than was readily apparent.

The last was a taciturn farmer from a village west of Tokyo. He had given no clear sign of whether he would evacuate or stay, but when I looked around after the others had gone, he was still there. Appearing on the verge of tears, he rolled over to face the other way and went to sleep without even doing up his gaiters.

Since none of us had a watch, I do not know what time the evacuees departed. A short while later, a passing soldier kindly brought me some water in my mess tin, and I made several attempts to pour it into my canteen before giving up. Complete silence settled over the mountain. No one else came by.

Three dull reports sounded somewhere farther down our canyon. Moments later we heard three sharp explosions in the vicinity of the command post on the ridge above us.

This, obviously, was not small arms fire. I had never heard the sound of mortars before, but for some reason I instinctively knew that was what the reports were. I surmised these first three rounds were test shots for measuring the range.

We all immediately sat up. No one showed any emotion.

"I guess this is it," I said. "Maybe we'd better head up top."

"Yeah," they said, as they moved into action.

I tried again to transfer the water from my mess tin into my canteen, but my hands shook too much and the water spilled down over the sides.

"What do I need water for when I'm about to die anyway?" I muttered, and I hurled the mess tin away as far as I could.

Friends have often criticized me for being too quick to give up, but in this case I would never have returned home alive, and I would not be writing these words today, had I not recklessly thrown that water away.

I wanted to avoid weighing myself down with unnecessary items, so I took only a single cartridge belt. At that point I could not imagine surviving long enough to use even those thirty rounds.

My three companions were still rustling around inside the hut. Our command post was not much more than a hundred yards up the hill, but I lacked confidence whether I could make it even that far.

"I'm going on ahead," I called out, and began walking.

"Aren't we going together?" K asked as if in protest.

"I don't know how far my legs'll hold up, so I thought I'd get a head start," I said. "You'll probably catch up to me when I'm resting somewhere along the way."

Using my rifle as a walking stick, I started up the narrow path winding up the side of the mountain. It turned out to be the last time I saw those three men. They took too long getting ready and never made it out of that canyon, which presently became the main target of the American mortar barrage.

I surprised myself with my strength and managed to climb all the way without resting. The mountaintop was alive with activity. Tense-faced soldiers hurried back and forth in twos and threes without a word. I staggered into a squad hut just over the ridgeline and sat down to rest. Several sick men lay inside, hugging their rifles and looking unspeakably grim.

The roar of an explosion shook the hut. Reflexively, I dashed outside and threw myself to the ground in the direction from which the shells were coming—which is to say, in the direction of the canyon from which I had ascended only moments before. More explosions followed one after another.

"Move forward! Move forward!" someone started yelling. A guard post located about ten yards behind me had been hit, and one of the sentries had gotten a leg blown off. Still hugging the ground, I slowly pulled myself ahead a short distance, but a series of shattering explosions in that direction made me stop. The voice still yelled, "Move forward!"

Our CO emerged from the command hut. His helmet dangled at the back of his neck, and he had pulled his coat on over it, making him look like a hunchback.

"Isn't this great?" he said, his face beaming. "We're finally seeing some action." Holding a pair of binoculars in his hands, he moved across my field of vision toward the explosions like a man striding dramatically across a movie screen. It was the last I saw of him.

About twenty other men remained flattened on the ground around me. I looked at the fellow next to me. His pale, puffy pallor revealed instantly that he was in the grip of the fever, but his face, like the lieutenant's, was beaming.

Another, more concerted barrage of shells came, still falling some distance ahead of us. Then the shelling stopped.

"The CO's been hit!" someone yelled. "Medic!" (The medic I met later at the prison camp said he had been unable to find a single part of the lieutenant's body.)

A sergeant came by and ordered, "Everyone who's not in condition to fight, get down into the canyon!"

I returned to the hut where I had rested a few minutes before and prodded the men there to come with me. They had not moved a muscle since the first time I came in. Whether or not they heard me now, they made no effort to comply with my urgings.

A file of men started down into the canyon on the other side of the ridge. Perfectly healthy men joined the column as well. I walked right behind the sergeant.

"The CO's been hit!" someone shouted again. The sergeant walked on, paying no attention. I watched him from behind, feeling as though I were gazing at some mysterious life form.

"Sergeant, Sir. They're saying the CO's been hit," I said.

"Yeah?" he said, neither turning around nor slackening his steps. "I wonder."

Another sergeant sat beside the path at the bottom. The first sergeant halted.

"They say the CO got hit. I wonder if it's true?" he said.

"Hmm, I wonder if it's true?" the other parrotted.

I did not care to listen to their inane exchange, so I moved on.

"Assemble over there and wait for orders," the first sergeant called to everyone within hearing, pointing toward a break in the trees on the far side of the canyon floor.

Some thirty men had already gathered in the clearing. Fever-stricken men had collapsed on both sides of the path. Some lay face down with every appearance of being dead; others lay curled on their sides, hugging their rifles, resting. One man had his right hand on a cartridge pushed halfway into his magazine, apparently having reached the end of his strength right in the middle of loading. More cartridges lay scattered about on the ground. I pushed the cartridge in place for him and shook his shoulder, but he failed to open his eyes.

Among the men gathered in the clearing was a corporal. I told him the sergeant had said to wait there for orders.

"Cripes! Who's got time to wait for orders? I know a way out. Come on, men, follow me." He started up another path at a fast clip. I followed mechanically. The uphill climb was a severe strain for me, and I soon fell behind. As I was catching my breath some fifty or sixty yards up, the others came rushing noisily back down.

"It's no good," the corporal said with bloodshot eyes. "They're shooting over this way, too. Let's try that way. If that doesn't work either, then, hey, we'll just have to dig in at the gun emplacement and fight to the finish." He slipped by me and proceeded on down the path.

A navy man I had never seen before looked me in the face as he started after the sergeant. "Pull yourself together, man," he said.

I gazed blankly after their receding figures. I had exhausted all my strength climbing to that spot. Should I follow them? *Could* I follow them? Uncertain what to do, I sank to the ground. The file of men reached the bottom of the hill, then veered off to the left and disappeared into the forest. A little farther up the canyon in that direction, there was supposed to be another path that led up the next rise in the mountain and eventually merged with the path the men had just come back down. I had never gone that way.

Another file of men marched quickly across the clearing and disappeared into the forest. I thought I spied among them the figure of a young soldier who had befriended me and had come by now and then to chat. He, too, had been battling malaria. Seeing him going with the others reawakened in me the desire to follow. I mustered enough strength to get to my feet and started back down the path.

The clearing now stood empty except for the men who had collapsed. There was no obvious track leading into the forest. At first I could hear the fleeing men calling back and forth in the distance, but their voices moved quickly away, becoming mere murmurs, then fading altogether. I knew from the speed with which they receded that I had no hope of catching up.

I sat down again. "Okay, okay," I mumbled aloud, "I give up." (After I was left alone I fell into the habit of thinking out loud like this. I suppose

it was my way of making sure I knew what was going on in my own mind.)
Hadn't I already decided I would die here anyway? I had surprised myself
with my own strength and managed to get this far, but there really had
never been any chance that I'd be able to keep up with the others. So, okay,
I accept my fate. That was what I meant when I said "Okay, okay."

Lowering myself against the foot of a huge tree resembling a Japanese
oak, I carefully detached the hand grenade from my belt and placed it on
the ground beside me. This had now become my sole friend, my one and
only hope. Its powerful explosive force would transport me painlessly into
the afterworld.

Curiously, I did not think of the Americans who would be coming that
way soon. I suppose I was too overwhelmed by the realization that my final
moment was at hand. Or perhaps subconsciously I assumed I still had ample
time before the Americans made their appearance. Though the corporal
had mentioned gunfire, I had heard no reports myself.

I felt no emotion. I had already exhausted every possible thought about
death. From the time my unit shipped out of Moji, fate had led me in a
single straight line that offered no escape. I had simply come to the final
point on that line. "Well, then. Water for a dying man's lips," I mumbled,
and lifted my canteen. It was empty.

I recalled how I had cast my water-filled mess tin aside as I prepared
to leave the squad hut. Scarcely had I imagined then that I would have time
later for a leisurely drink of water. Maybe I had been too hasty. A sour smile
of chagrin came to my lips. My thirst multiplied.

I told myself it hardly mattered whether I had a drink of water when
I was preparing to put an end to my existence momentarily. Even as I tried
to persuade myself of this, however, my thirst continued to intensify.

There was no source of potable water nearby. The stream running
down that canyon had already stopped flowing by the time we bivouacked
in the area, and its bed had continued to dry up as the rainless season
advanced. Now, only a few muddy pools remained here and there. If I
wanted water, I would have to climb back up to the command post and
then down the other side to the spring near my squad hut. I doubted I had
the strength to travel such a distance anymore.

Then I remembered that I had once crossed a stream farther up this
canyon—probably the upper reaches of this same stream—and the pools of
water there had not yet turned black. In this case, too, getting there by the
familiar route required a climb back up to our command post, but if that
stream was indeed this stream, then all I needed to do was follow the
streambed up the canyon and I would eventually reach the same spot. It
would be a level path, so I could probably still make it there with the
strength I had left.

After reattaching the hand grenade to my belt, I rose to my feet and pushed my way through some underbrush to step down into the dry streambed.

I wrote before that I am alive today solely because I threw my water away at the squad hut. First, that action allowed me to quit, in the barest nick of time, the place that became the main target of the American mortar barrage. And second, my waterless canteen now made me abandon the first spot I chose as my final resting place. As I learned later, a scout from the platoon near San Jose penetrated as far as that clearing the next morning and found the soldier who had collapsed in the midst of loading his rifle shot through the chest. One prong of the Americans' attack came straight up that canyon, so if I had remained in that spot much longer, regardless of whether I had tried to put up a fight, my life would most surely have come to an end at the hands of an American GI.

The stream held even less water than I remembered. Every fifty feet or so there was a muddy pool perhaps five or six feet across.

Discovering a narrow path beside the stream, I started mechanically placing one foot before the other. My thirst was intensifying moment by moment, and soon I could endure it no longer. I had not gone this long without water since first coming down with the fever.

I stared at the blackened liquid before me. A foul smell rose to where I stood. A dark insect of some kind crawled along beneath the surface. Dropping to my knees, I scooped up a handful of water and drew it into my mouth, but a terrible bitterness stabbed at my tongue and I could not swallow it.

I came to a larger pool where four or five carabao were soaking. They had served as our pack animals when we came here from San Jose.

One of them looked up at me suspiciously. We stared at each other for several moments. The more I stared at him, the more human he looked, and I felt a strange sense of confusion come over me. Then the carabao turned away as though suddenly embarrassed, lowed once, and started up out of the pool. Water splashed off his huge body into the pool. Needless to say, I could not drink this water, either.

The carabao climbed from the streambed onto the bank and made his way into the forest. As I followed him with my eyes, I noticed how just above the pool the two banks of the stream formed low cliffs that pressed in from both sides and my path turned away from the stream into the forest where the carabao had gone. Beyond the cliffs the streambed took an abrupt turn and disappeared from sight.

I could not bring myself to wade through the pool between the other carabaos. Guessing that the path through the forest would most likely rejoin the stream somewhere farther on, I decided to stay on the path.

The gently sloping path was on the opposite side of the stream from the hill I had most recently descended—which is to say, it was on the side of the ridge atop which our command post was located. By this time I had to support myself by grabbing hold of branches on both sides of the path. The path continued to angle away from the stream and before long emerged from the forest into an open meadow. At that point it curved even farther away from the stream.

I realized then that I was not on a path that followed the stream, but a path that led to our stronghold. (We had not in fact constructed anything that could truly be called a stronghold, but some fifty or sixty yards from the command post, at the point where the trails from Bulalacao and San Jose met, we had dug an emplacement for our one and only machine gun and called it our stronghold; this was what the corporal referred to when he said we would dig in at the gun emplacement.) If I wanted to make it to where I had once crossed the upper reaches of the stream, I would apparently first have to climb all the way up to the emplacement and proceed from there along the path I had taken before.

Once again, I had exhausted my strength. I began to wonder whether the water at my destination would be sufficient to reward the effort involved in getting there. Considering how much drier the streambed had become down here, did I not have to assume that the same had happened farther upstream? I stumbled to the ground at the edge of the forest.

The meadow before me was only about a hundred feet across, hemmed in by dense foliage on the stream side to my left as well as straight ahead, but it spread open to the right, sloping gently up the mountainside toward the stronghold. It was covered with the same tall cogon grass, rather like Japanese kaya grass, that brought such a soft, dreamy green to hills and meadows throughout the Philippines.

Silence reigned all around. I do not know how long I lay motionless in that spot. Nor do I know whether I spent that time contemplating my suicide or merely suffering from unquenchable pangs of thirst, for the event that followed erased from my memory all recollection of anything not directly related to it.

I do know that I contemplated what action I would take if an American GI appeared before me. I decided I would hold my fire.

Whether I shot an enemy soldier in that place could in no way alter my own fate or that of my brothers in arms. Its only effect would be to change the fate of the man I shot. I did not wish to stain the waning moments of my life with another man's blood.

I envisioned the encounter: A GI appears. We stand facing each other with our rifles poised. An eternity goes by but I do not shoot, and finally, impatiently, the GI pulls his trigger. I crumple to the ground. He dashes up, wondering what to make of my strange behavior.

A real encounter could not possibly have followed such a script, but I am recording the scene here exactly as it played out in my imagination at the time. Hand in hand with the final moral decision I had made came the desire to have someone else know of my benevolent intentions. Deep in the mountains of the Philippines, that someone could be none other than the man who would kill me.

It did not take long for my decision to be put to the test.

A shout rang out high up on the other side of the canyon. "Yes, something or other," a second voice responded—in English, but with a Philippine accent. The voices reverberated through the crisp forest air. This was my first direct contact with the opposing force of violence against which my outfit had for so long remained at a distant standoff, and I felt oddly cleansed by it. I rose to my elbow.

The voices said nothing more. In their place I heard the rustling of footsteps in the grass, and I turned my head in that direction. A lone GI had come into view, still some distance away.

I had no desire to shoot.

The GI was a tall youth of about twenty, his cheeks red beneath the deep-set steel helmet covering his head. Standing erect and holding his rifle at an angle before him, he advanced toward me with the gentle stride of someone on a pleasure outing in the mountains.

His lack of caution astonished me. The possibility that an enemy soldier might be lying in wait for him along his path seemed the farthest thing from his mind. A soldier across the canyon shouted something I couldn't make out, and this young GI gave a clipped reply. Probably some simple exchange like: "Finding anything?" "Negative." The youth continued to approach.

My breath caught in my throat. I, too, was a soldier. Though not particularly deft in my motor skills, I had held great confidence in my marksmanship ever since scoring well in live-fire target drills as a student. No matter how drained I might be in strength, I had seen him first, and he was standing at full height completely in the open: I could not miss. My right hand moved instinctively to release the safety on my rifle.

When the GI had traversed approximately half the distance between us, a sudden burst of machine-gun fire broke out at the stronghold.

His head spun around. The rattle of guns continued. He stood motionless for several moments as though taking measure of the racket, then slowly swung about and started walking in its direction. His stride quickly gained speed, and soon he had exited my field of vision.

I heaved a sigh of relief. "Well, well," I said with a wry smile. "A mother somewhere in America should be thanking me right now."

Since then I have often reflected on this encounter, and the decision that preceded it.

I am surprised, first of all, by my own humanity. I had never borne any real hatred for the enemy, but as one of Stendhal's characters says, "So long as your opponent holds your life in his hands, you have every right to kill him." Since any enemy I met on the battlefield would have the power if not the desire to kill me, I had wholly anticipated showing no mercy in return, however innocent the man might otherwise be of any offense for which I might wish him dead. Never had it occurred to me that I might choose to hold my fire in such an encounter.

What led me to discard my "Kill or be killed" cynicism at that fateful moment was without doubt linked to the fact that I could no longer entertain any hope of survival. If my own death was a fait accompli, then the logic of "Kill or be killed" no longer applied. I had subconsciously recognized this new truth.

Yet this recognition does not in itself explain my decision to refrain from killing. The conclusion "Since I'm going to die anyway, I won't kill" makes eminent sense when premised on the proposition "Kill or be killed," but it does not follow *necessarily*. The knowledge that one is going to die anyway can lead just as easily to the opposite conclusion—that it makes no difference whether one kills or not. Nothing dictated a decision not to kill.

In my repeated contemplations of the maxim "Kill or be killed," I have discovered that it also subsumes the ethic "Avoid killing if possible." That is why, when the either/or logic of the maxim broke down, I so readily resolved not to kill. The seemingly Machiavellian dictum was not so cynical as I once believed.

In essence, then, my reflections bring me to the universal human prohibition against killing—though this is not to say that my decision derived from "love for all humanity." I know my spirit is far too mean, and my temper too hot, for me to lay claim to such a sublime and rarefied ideal.

To the contrary, when I reflect on how I drew back from the shedding of human blood, I see at work only a kind of visceral instinct. Our universal abhorrence of killing is in all likelihood merely an inversion of our desire not to be killed ourselves. Consider, for example, that the abhorrence we feel when we imagine ourselves killing another person and the abhorrence we feel when we imagine someone else killing another person are exactly the same. Whether one does the deed with one's own hands makes no difference in our perception of the deed.

Not that this is the only response the human animal can have to the killing of his own kind. This particular response gained primacy only because we humans learned how to maintain our existence without killing one another, at least within our own communities. Recognition that each individual's continuing existence was beneficial to the entire group made "Thou shalt not kill" one of the earliest laws. Yet to this day the religions of the world sanction killing in the context of war when the interests of communities collide.

That is to say, our abhorrence of killing is an instinct that belongs to peacetime, and my response to the GI in the meadow shows that I had already ceased to be a soldier at war. Separation from my comrades had facilitated this transformation. War is an act of collective violence, and the behavior of each participant in the violence is constrained on the one hand and incited on the other by the collective consciousness of the group. If at the time of my fateful encounter I had had even one of my fellows at my side, I no doubt would have fired my rifle without hesitation, quite without regard for what I expected to happen to my own life.

Whatever the ultimate reasons—whether love of humanity or something closer to animal instinct—I had resolved not to shoot. And indeed, I did not shoot. But an important question remains: Can I truly claim to have carried out my resolve?

I can certainly confirm that I experienced no impulse to shoot when the young GI first came into view. But if he had continued his steady advance in my direction and finally caught sight of me lying there at a distance of, say, twelve or fifteen feet, would I still have chosen to hold my fire even after I knew that he had seen me?

When I recall how my hand moved reflexively to release the safety on my rifle, I confront the fact that the only thing *compelling* me to remain faithful to my resolve was the eruption of machine-gun fire at the top of the hill, which caused the GI to turn his steps away from me. That is to say, it was pure accident. At the very least, my physical reflexes seem to have been incomplete in their compliance with my earlier resolve.

As I replay images of the encounter through my mind, many questions remain.

My first reaction when I saw the GI standing tall and fully exposed was one of apprehension, not for myself but for him. I recall how astonished I was at his lack of caution—a response that reveals my soldierly instincts and demonstrates that despite the cursory nature of my training, I had indeed acquired a warrior's habits of mind. Indeed, on the obverse side of my apprehension and astonishment lay the awareness: "It is in my power to kill this man." Where would those instincts have led me if the encounter had lasted any longer than it did?

The grim intensity of the GI's gaze remains etched in my memory, suggesting that my restraint may have come not from a deep resolve within my own heart but from what I discerned in my adversary. My adversary was none other than the vanguard of a massive force of violence bent on my destruction, and this meant that I must exercise every caution in facing him. Could it be that I actually held back out of simple cowardice?

I recall vividly, too, the rosy glow of the youth's cheek when he turned to answer the shout from across the canyon. It moved something deep in my heart.

The beauty of his face struck me with wonder. From the contrast between his pure white skin and the bright red of his cheeks to the individual features of his face so different from our own, I gazed upon a simple yet undeniable beauty—a beauty whose sudden appearance before me held a particular freshness because the world it represented had been banished from my sight since Pearl Harbor. During that brief moment of rest when the soldier paused in his advance toward me, this beauty seems to have reached into my heart and switched off the warrior's instinct that had been awakened when I first spied him.

At the same time, I was struck anew by his extreme youth. That he was quite young I had noticed at first sight. But now, several steps closer, when he abandoned the posture of his steady advance to raise his head and bring the full length of his face out from under the shade of his helmet, the tenderness of his age became all too apparent. I doubted he had seen his twentieth birthday.

Though the words he shouted escaped me, his voice was a clear tenor, matching his youthful countenance, and when he finished speaking he pinched the corners of his mouth in the manner of a child. Then, lowering his head, he turned his gaze farther down the other side of the canyon as though surveying the path his buddies would take. (What he really ought to have been surveying, of course, was what lay ahead along his own path.)

The movement of my heart upon seeing the GI's extreme youth resembled feelings I had experienced from time to time, since becoming a father, at the sight of young children or of nearly grown children who still carried an air of adolescent innocence. This may not be sufficient grounds for claiming that it was the GI's youth that stayed my hand from shooting him, but I believe his youth can explain why my first thought after he disappeared from sight was of his mother somewhere in America and the gratitude she owed me. Clearly, that turn of mind could have come only after I had actually seen the soldier. Earlier, when I first resolved not to shoot, I could not anticipate the age of the soldier I would face, so I had no reason to think of his mother.

Though not from love for all humanity, might I have held my fire out of love for the young soldier as an individual? Absent any clear sign that the decision I had made beforehand determined my actions, I am drawn to the hypothesis that my feelings as a father forbade me to shoot, even though I cannot remember consciously feeling anything of the kind at the time. Both the image of youthfulness preserved in my memory and the nature of the thought that came to mind immediately after the soldier disappeared seem to bear this hypothesis out.

Next, however, I encounter an unexplained blank. I can recall a turbulent, suffocating feeling of tension growing within me, something closely akin to terror, but I can conjure no images to accompany it. Though I know he must have turned to face me and resume his advance, no such frames appear in the motion picture of my memory. Apparently, something deep down inside me does not wish to remember those events. Instead, the next frame in my memory is of the GI turned the other way, in response to the sound of the machine guns. And my own rifle is poised with the safety released: During those moments of building tension, I had taken up my weapon.

Had I decided to shoot after all? Or was this merely an instinctive act of defense, with no more significance than reflexively closing my eyes when an insect flies in my face?

Then the machine guns rattled, blasting away both the oppressive tension and the threatened confrontation. The encounter was over. Today, too, the shattering gunfire rings in my ears and brings all my pondering to a halt.

Whatever the deeper truths may have been, the young American ultimately moved away without ever catching sight of me, and I smugly congratulated myself for the "good deed" of having spared him.

This self-congratulation did not come without a certain bitter aftertaste when I immediately realized that the man I had spared would join the battle at the stronghold and thereby increase the burden on my comrades. It was a painful realization, but I rationalized that the undeniable superiority of the American forces doomed my comrades to certain death in any event, and the same held for me. This had become my convenient way of absolving myself no matter what happened.

The rattling of the guns continued. One sustained burst was followed by another, as if in reply, and the exchange was repeated several times. It sounded exactly like opposing forces answering each other's fire.

Since the GI had approached from the other side of the meadow, I could but guess that the men led by the corporal had failed to escape in that direction as well and had returned to the stronghold where they were now engaged in their anticipated fight to the finish. I listened to the gunfire as though monitoring the pulse of a dying man.

The shooting went on for quite some time but finally came to an end with a single shot that left a long lingering echo.

A short while later shots were fired down in the canyon, in the general direction of the spot where the two sergeants had debated our CO's death. This shooting stopped right away but was followed by an explosion—most likely a hand grenade. That was the last of the reports I heard.

With the return of quiet, I was left once more to stare death in the face alone. I removed my belt, unwound my gaiters, and slowly lay back down. Scarcely had I done this when violent thirst assailed me again.

Kill myself and I could simultaneously kill that thirst, my mind argued. But my parched throat adamantly objected, insisting that I first quench its burning thirst and only after that proceed with extinguishing my existence.

This did not seem unreasonable. The theme appealed to me: the suicide who craves a drink of water before he dies. It affirmed the appetites of the flesh.

I revisited the question of where and how I might obtain some water. With the closest sources ruled out by the American occupation of the ridge, the next alternative meant a substantially longer journey, following the dry stream running through this canyon all the way down to where it joined another, larger river. This would require retracing my steps past the spot where those two sergeants had earlier had their little debate—which is to say, I had to cross the main artery traversing the canyon. The risk of discovery would be exceedingly high, at least until nightfall. I remembered, though, that the moon would be rising late, so I decided to wait for it to appear and attempt this alternative plan, gambling everything on whether the Americans chose to occupy that position overnight.

I waited impatiently for the sun to set and the moon to emerge. My body had become a single throbbing bundle of thirst. I gave myself over to visions of stretching out on the bank of the larger river with my face in the water, gulping down as much as I could possibly hold. During the daytime I would hide nearby in the underbrush with a full canteen, and at night I would return to lie on the riverbank and slake my thirst some more. Two or three days later, after my thirst had been fully satisfied, I would choose my own moment to end my life. I regretted ever having left the canyon where my squad hut had stood near a plentiful spring.

The moon finally made its appearance.

I cast aside my rifle and sword. Even if I were to come upon some GIs, I knew I would have no desire to fight. I also discarded my haversack after transferring a fistful of rice into each of my pockets. I was not hungry then, but I would likely crave it later if I spent two or three days in slaking my thirst. I took with me only my hand grenade, attached securely to my belt, and my canteen, looped over my shoulder.

Reaching for some branches, I pulled myself upright and onto my feet. I started to black out and clung desperately to the branches to keep from falling. Five or six halting steps brought me back to the path, but as soon as I released my hold on the branches, my spine and legs went limp and I fell flat on my face.

I had experienced this exact same sensation before. I knew at once that the day's exertions had rudely reverted me to the condition I was in at the height of my fever, when I could not walk a single step.

Lying on my elbows like a wounded animal, I contemplated my predicament. For the first time, the dark premonition that I might not be able to fulfill my final wish crossed my mind. But I refused to give up hope. Neither then nor later, no matter how hopeless my situation seemed to become, did I ever grow so discouraged that I stopped considering what my next step should be. To judge from this experience, I would conclude that the two parts of the word *hopeless* comprise an oxymoron and that the word is merely hyperbole for a state of mind that cannot actually exist.

I reexamined my plan. Obviously, I was in no condition to walk at present, but since I had indeed been able to walk several hours before, it seemed fair to conclude that this condition was temporary. Even so, given how I had collapsed a moment ago, I had to assume it would take at least until morning for me to recover my strength. Once daylight returned, I could no longer hope to make my way safely down the canyon through American lines. That meant I had to find a source of water in the opposite direction.

I remembered another large river I had once seen when delivering a message to the platoon near San Jose. It was about eight kilometers away— normally a two-hour hike—by a path that went along the ridge on the other side of the canyon. I imagined that all the American troops converging on our command post had by now gone past my position and that I was therefore outside their perimeter. If I could start out at dawn, I should be able to make it to the river by noon at the latest. Compared to the time I had already endured my thirst, it did not seem so terribly long.

My hope now rested on being able to walk again by daybreak. Clearly, the most important thing for me to do was to get some sleep.

I returned to the spot where I had lain before, where some protruding tree roots and soft grass made a cozy little bed just big enough for one person. I lay down and closed my eyes.

Sleep refused to come. Suddenly I heard a voice whispering in my ear—a voice like that of a draper's head clerk (that was the image that came to mind), calm and self-possessed, warning me that at any minute my internal organs would go out on strike; they were demanding redress for my failure to make my legs carry me to a source of water forthwith. I knew, of course, that this voice was a hallucination brought on by my fever. I laughed.

"Oh, shut up," I shouted, "I know very well you don't really exist. You're just a figment of my fever."

The next moment I realized that even to berate the voice like this was to acknowledge its existence. I pursed my lips.

At the same time it occurred to me that the voice was like the specter that haunts the delirious Ivan in *The Brothers Karamazov*. I found it a bitter realization—having to acknowledge that even my own private hallucinations in the final moments of my life were in fact derivative of my predecessors. Nor did I care for the pseudointellectual air of the specter threatening me with "internal organs out on strike"; I would have much preferred a good old-fashioned ogre or demoness to appear before me. There was no pleasure in discovering that the part of my consciousness responsible for producing hallucinations was filled with such useless pretensions to knowledge.

The whispering voice also set off a rush of fresh anxiety, for it was in fact my first hallucination of any kind since coming down with the fever. Even when my fever had stayed at 104 degrees for a full week, I could not recall ever having lapsed into delirium. My mind had always remained lucid, fully conscious not only of my own condition but of what was going on around me as well. This hallucination, then, loomed as a distinctly ill omen. I attempted to quiet my mind and drive it away, but on and on the equable voice of the admonitory draper's clerk murmured strings of words I can no longer recall.

A breath of damp air rustled through the trees. I slowly raised myself to my elbow as a sudden new hope burned within me. That wind, I knew, was the wind native superstition blamed for bringing sudden death to livestock, but I knew also that in this season it was a precursor of rain.

Presently the rain came. A refreshing patter filled the air, and before long, droplets of water began to drip from the lower leaves of the trees.

I opened my mouth to catch the falling droplets, but they instantly dissipated in my parched throat, creating scarcely the slightest sensation. The rain let up a little, and the space between droplets grew longer. Thinking it silly to remain in the brush waiting for water to collect on the leaves when the rain fell steadily out in the open, I dragged myself into the meadow and rolled onto my back. Unfortunately, the raindrops falling directly into my open mouth came no faster than the droplets from the leaves.

Now the rain stopped completely. I turned to look upwind. This was the direction of the stronghold, and above the gentle slope of the meadow I could see a familiar stand of trees hazy in the moonlight. With surprise, I discovered that I was much closer to the stronghold than I had realized.

A dense fog descended on the stand of trees. The night came alive with sounds again, the moist breeze cooled my cheeks, and a fresh shower of raindrops fell from the depths of the sky. I opened my mouth with my hands cupped on either side to help gather the raindrops, but the rain ceased without even moistening my palms. The clouds near the top of the sky began to break up, revealing a misshapen moon whose brightness stabbed painfully at my eyes. No more rain came after that.

How long could it have been from then until daybreak? I returned to my comfortable bed among the trees. The whispering voice had departed, but I was now gripped by an excruciating oppression in my chest such as I had never experienced before. Turning one way and another, I tried every manner of contortion to ease the pain. I cried aloud in torment; I discovered that tearing at one's chest in agony was more than a figure of speech.

Slowly the moon descended over the towering trees across the meadow and then seemed to hesitate as it touched the treetops. The moonlit night gave way imperceptibly to a milky twilight as the moon disappeared. The day had broken.

A carabao lumbered down the slope—no doubt the same one that had led me up this way the day before. Seeing me, he stopped to study me for a few moments but then swung his pendulous neck forward again and proceeded on his way.

Watching his slow, plodding steps gave me new energy. The pain in my chest subsided, and I experienced something of the exhilaration that comes to a sick man who has made it through a difficult night. I ceremonially chewed on a few grains of rice and prepared to set out on my journey.

Just then I heard a report on the other side of the canyon, precisely in the direction I was making ready to go.

As I later learned, the San Jose platoon had sent some scouts to investigate our position that morning. Spying enemy troops on this side of the canyon, the scouts beat a hasty retreat, but not before one of them had fired at the Americans. When I later met that man at the POW camp, he told me he had fired three shots, but I can remember only one, and I find it a telling lapse of memory: In essence, under the circumstances at the time, the difference between one shot and three was immaterial; all that mattered was that I had heard gunfire. Because I could not imagine friendly troops returning to the area, this gunfire signified to me that I still remained within the circle of American troops and that it would therefore be impossible for me to escape by my planned route. Furthermore, lacking any clue as to when the Americans might withdraw, there was no telling how long I would remain pinned down in that spot with no water.

I finally accepted that I would die thirsty. And since death was inevitable in any case, what point could there be in hopelessly prolonging my life? It would merely prolong my suffering.

Arriving at my decision calmly, I smiled commiseratively at myself for having failed to come to it sooner.

I removed the hand grenade from my waist and set it on the ground before me. I studied it carefully. Known as a Model 99, it was a six-sided steel cylinder with a grid of grooves running all around its sides and painted a reddish brown. The pieces of steel roughly one-third of an inch square formed by the grooves were apparently intended to fragment in all directions when the charge inside exploded.

I pulled on the safety pin stuck sideways through the fuse assembly. The pin clung tenaciously to its place and refused to budge by hand. As I pried at it with the tip of my sword I began to worry that I might fail to dislodge it and, for no more reason than that, fail to die. To some degree, that may in fact have been my hope. As if in willful betrayal of any such hope, however, my hands continued their efforts and ultimately succeeded in extracting the pin.

I do not intend to belabor the question of why I failed to kill myself. The psychology of a suicide is of minimal interest, and the psychology of the man who fails in his attempt is of less interest still. In essence, his substantial will to undertake an act that contravenes nature is met by the altogether normal response of his flesh in opposition to that will. What then actually determines the outcome is in most cases an entirely extraneous, accidental factor. My life today owes itself to the accident that the hand grenade I carried was a dud. Of course, since they say that 60 percent of the hand grenades issued to Japanese troops in the Pacific were duds, my good fortune cannot be considered an especially rare stroke of luck.

The relative ease with which I was able to cross over the line that should have marked the end of my life probably owed to my physical infirmity at the time.

In my mind I tried to picture the faces of all those I had loved, but I could not bring any of their images into focus with the clarity of a picture. Feeling a little sorry for them as they milled vaguely about in the depths of my consciousness, I smiled, said "So long," and struck the head of the fuse against a nearby rock. The fuse assembly flew off, but the grenade failed to explode.

I examined the grenade minus its fuse. A hole ran down the middle of the grenade from its now exposed top, and at the bottom of this hole was a small round protuberance—obviously the detonator. I looked at it and shuddered. This was the only time during my day and night alone in the woods that I consciously experienced genuine terror.

I gathered up the pieces of the fuse assembly and put them back together. The slender rod that fit down into the hole appeared too short to reach the detonator inside. I struck the assembly against the rock again, but the grenade remained intact.

I had to smile. The irony of fate that refused to grant me even a quick and easy death seemed funny to me somehow. Everything that had befallen me in the last twenty-four hours had been altogether one great irony. I clicked my tongue in irritation and hurled the grenade deep into the forest.

I had guessed that pushing on the protuberance at the bottom of the hole would detonate the grenade, but oddly enough, I never thought to try setting it off with anything other than the original fuse assembly—such as with a twig. Whether this would have worked is another matter. What is significant here is that the possibility never entered my mind.

Suicides succeed or fail by the means fixed upon at the outset. The person focuses his mental energies solely on carrying out the chosen means; he does not waste his energies second-guessing them. This explains why certain methods of suicide seem to enjoy vogues.

I had placed my hopes on the hand grenade because I had imagined it to be the best means of assuring the instantaneous annihilation of my vital organs. It was supposed to snuff out my suffering as summarily as the flick of a light switch. I was not prepared for that simple flick to be hindered by complications, which only the exercise of creative ingenuity could overcome.

I had in fact exhausted the greater part of my mental energies just in the very first strike of the grenade against the rock.

My failure to think of pushing the protuberance with something else may no doubt be attributed to the extremity of my bewilderment and debilitation. I continued to show the same lack of inventiveness in subsequent events as well.

I next attempted to kill myself with my rifle. Sitting up, I removed my right boot and then held the barrel to my forehead with both hands as I tried to push the trigger with my big toe. (I had learned this arrangement from the veterans during basic training back in Japan. In this, too, I followed the example of my predecessors.) To my chagrin, I immediately lost my balance and rolled over onto my side. I'm sure to botch it up this way, I thought. Recalling a story I had read about a man who shot himself twice in the mouth but succeeded only in blowing away his cheek, I decided it would be wiser to wait until my fever had subsided at least a little.

In this case, too, if I had been more determined, I would surely have thought to push the trigger with a stick. Even if I persisted in using my toe, I could have leaned against a tree or figured out a way to do it on my side. Instead, I behaved like a man who only halfheartedly wished to kill himself. At the same time, I must ultimately consider myself fortunate that the rifle barrel in my hands moved away from my forehead when I lost my balance and fell over, thus preventing me from realizing that I could in fact shoot myself in that position.

I laid the rifle down beside me. Instead of putting my right boot back on, I took off my left boot as well and lay down again. I seem to remember the sun having climbed quite high into the sky by this time. I had apparently been contemplating and going through the motions of my suicide in an extremely dilatory fashion. My thirst must have remained, but I have no recollection of it.

I do not know whether I dozed off or passed out, but the next thing I remember is gradually becoming aware of a blunt object striking my body over and over. Just as I realized it was a boot kicking me in the side, I felt my arm being grabbed roughly, and I returned to full consciousness.

One GI had hold of my right arm, and another had his rifle pointed at me, nearly touching me.

"Don't move. We're taking you prisoner," the one with the rifle said.

I stared at him and he stared at me. A moment passed. I saw that he understood I had no intention of resisting.

Later, at the POW camps, the Americans often asked me: "Did you give yourself up, or were you taken prisoner?" No doubt they wanted to see if it was true that we Japanese would kill ourselves rather than give ourselves up.

I made a point of answering proudly, "I was taken prisoner."

"Did you think we killed our prisoners?" they asked next.

"I'm not fool enough to believe that kind of propaganda," I answered.

"Then why didn't you give yourself up?"

"It's a question of honor. I have nothing against surrendering as such, but my own sense of pride would not let me submit voluntarily to the enemy."

Now that I am no longer a prisoner trying desperately to hold onto my self-respect, I can take a different view of the event. Since I gave up all resistance quite willingly when faced with that rifle, I can admit that I did, after all, give myself up. The difference between surrendering to the enemy with white flag raised and casting down one's arms when surrounded is merely a matter of degree.

The first GI gathered up my rifle and sword while the second kept his weapon trained on me.

"Get up and start walking," he said.

"I can't walk."

"Walk, walk," they both repeated.

We went down the path I had come up the day before. I stumbled from one tree to the next as far as the dry streambed and then sank to my knees with nothing left to hold onto. One of the GIs put his arm through mine to help me along.

Noticing the canteen at his waist, I said, "Water?"

He shook his canteen to show me it was empty and said, "No." He turned to look at his companion.

"No," he said.

We reached the clearing of the day before, where I had first descended into this canyon. Helmets, a mess kit, a pot of half-cooked rice, a crushed gas mask, and sundry other items lay strewn about. I saw no blood, but I did not doubt that many men from my unit had died there. One of the sergeants had been carefully ripening some bananas. Seeing them scattered on the ground made my heart weep.

The climb to our former command post was arduous. As we neared the hut, the GI who was helping me walk shouted continually, "Don't shoot. Don't shoot."

At the hut, they turned me over to four or five other GIs, who checked me carefully for hidden weapons. I was then escorted along the ridgeline to a plateau cultivated by the Mangyans. A force of some five hundred American troops had set up camp there.

I do not know how I got it into my head that they were taking me to my execution, but that is what I thought. Still craving a drink of water before I died, I looked for men who had canteens at their sides.

"Water! Please, some water!" I cried, hoping one of them might step forward on a whim.

As we continued on through the camp, my eyes roved over the Americans all around me with greedy curiosity. When that young GI had turned aside the previous day, I had assumed he would probably be the last person I saw before I died. Now I presumed these troops would be the last.

It was a long march. When we passed what appeared to be the center of the encampment with still no order to halt, I became even more certain that they were leading me to a firing squad somewhere on the far edge of the camp. Here and there holes had been dug in the ground, about the right size for a person to lie in. I guessed they were graves for burying me and my comrades. (I had no means of knowing that I was the only prisoner taken at that location.)

"Sit down," I was finally commanded.

I fell forward onto my hands and knees. "Water!" I cried again. Picking out a man who looked important, I fixed him straight in the eye and repeated my plea as politely as I could.

"I'll see what I can do," he said, and went away.

He did not return for a long time. With the advent of hope, my thirst once again grew unbearable. I cried out repeatedly. Finally the man's face reappeared behind the wall of figures around me. He had no water. After fidgeting about and looking embarrassed for a time, he moved away with a wave of his hand. My hope was crushed.

I went on begging for water. Suddenly someone threw an Imperial Army–issue canteen down in front of me. It was about half full. I drained it in a single draft. The water lacked any taste.

Two bespectacled GIs came and ordered me to take off my clothes. They told me to remove my underpants, too. When I pulled them down and started to step out of them, they said, "That's enough." It was a strip search.

Two more soldiers came. One of them had a U.S. Army helmet filled with water. I leaped for it. He stopped me with his hand and transferred the water to the canteen they had given me. The other soldier, a thin, middle-aged man, helped as he poured, kindly holding back the little pieces of grass floating in the water.

After I took several long drafts, this older man looked at me and demanded, "What's your name?" The sharp look in his eyes and the tone of his voice told me he must be the commanding officer.

Prisoners of war in fiction often refuse to say anything besides "I am a common soldier," but I did not follow their example. Without the least hesitation, I gave my name, rank, and unit. It seemed easiest to simply tell the truth about such routine things.

Another soldier pulled a stack of papers from an Imperial Army haversack. They had presumably found it abandoned somewhere in the vicinity. Among other things, the papers included our company CO's maps, organizational charts of our platoons and squads, and individual soldiers' private papers. The Americans seemed to accept my assertion that none of the documents was of any importance.

I sucked at my canteen continually even as the interrogation progressed. I still believed they would shoot me after they were through asking me questions, so when a soldier came up and whispered something in the commander's ear, I imagined he was bringing word that preparations had been completed for my execution. In a great hurry, I guzzled down the rest of my water. I had drunk a large American helmetful of water in less than thirty minutes.

They gave me a cigarette, but the first puff set my head spinning. I could not smoke it.

The sun had climbed high overhead. We were under the only tree in the immediate area, but it was a tree with scant leaves clinging like a crown high up on its branches, casting a shade almost too pale to be called shade. I lay with my head in this shade (they permitted me to remain lying on the ground during my interrogation), periodically adjusting my position as the shade shifted.

The interrogation must have taken at least an hour. The commander repeated certain important questions several times. Trying to be sure I gave the same answer every time made me tense. The effort exhausted me.

The commander took out a Japanese soldier's diary and told me to translate what it said. I welcomed this respite from the barrage of questions and set about translating the diary line by line. It was written in a childish hand, and the opening entry was from when our company had been stationed in San Jose. The author declared he had stopped keeping a diary after joining the army, but since he could not find anything else to do for diversion, he had decided that setting things down in a diary when off duty would in no way compromise the discharge of his responsibilities. Still, spending time on his diary meant he would have to devote himself more diligently to his military duties at all other times. The entry went on and on in this jejune vein—words placed there in case the diary fell into the hands of his superior officer, no doubt. That was all, however. There were no further entries.

The author had not inscribed his name, and I did not recognize the hand, but I knew it had to have belonged to one of our young reservists from the class of 1943. Though these greenhorns had all proved themselves to be utterly ignorant of anything, they were also kind and generous and worked hard to cover for the cunning and indolence of us older men. They knew nothing about pacing themselves to conserve their strength, so when they fell ill they were quick to die.

I looked up from the diary. The commander was looking at me with eyes that seemed to hold both sympathy and familiarity. We spoke at the same moment.

"That's all."

"That's enough."

This brought my interrogation to an end.

The commander turned sideways and said in a low murmur, "We'll get you something to eat, now. Someday you'll be able to go home." I lay there vacantly, my spirit too tired to respond.

One of the soldiers returned the papers to the haversack. The owner's name stitched into the flap flashed before my eyes.

It had belonged to K, the *rakugo* critic's son, the fellow who had protested "Aren't we going together?" when we were preparing to evacuate the squad hut and I decided I would get a head start. My shock was immense. I turned my face away and screamed, "Kill me! Shoot me now! How can I alone go on living when all my buddies have died?"

"Be glad to," I heard someone say. I turned toward the voice to find a man leveling his automatic rifle at me.

"Go ahead," I said, spreading my chest, but my face twisted into a frown when I saw the playful gleam in his eye.

The commander walked away as though he had never even heard my cries.

A package of cookies fell on my chest. I looked up to see a ruddy young soldier with a dark stubble of a beard standing over me. His face was a blank. When I thanked him, he silently shifted the rifle on his shoulder and walked away.

I resumed my observation of the American troops around me. Never before had I seen men of such varied skin tones and hair color gathered together in a single place. Most of them seemed to be off duty—though a few had work to do. A man with a mobile radio unit on his back stopped near me with the entire sky spread out behind him. He adjusted something and then moved on. One group of men was taking turns peering through what looked like a surveyor's telescope on a tripod. Far away in the direction the telescope pointed rose a range of green mountains. Somewhere among those mountains was the ridge over San Jose where our detached platoon was camped. I gazed off at the distant range, caressing each beautiful peak, each gentle mountain fold with my eyes. The platoon could be under attack even now, I thought. I mentally reviewed everything I had said during my interrogation, trying to reassure myself I had said nothing that could be harmful to them.

A burly, middle-aged soldier approached and took my picture. Coming closer he said, "What're you sick with?"

"Malaria," I answered.

He felt my forehead with his hand. "Open your mouth," he commanded. When I obeyed, he tossed in five or six yellow pills and said, "Now take a drink." After watching me wash the pills down he explained, "I'm the doctor," and then walked off.

Flames rose from the hut that had housed our command post, as well as from the squad hut with the sick soldiers where I had first rested the day before. I had never seen columns of flame rise so high. Perhaps the huts had been doused with gasoline to help burn the corpses of the dead.

Evening approached. The American troops built fires in the holes I had thought might be graves and started preparing dinner. An amiable-looking youth brought me some food. I had no appetite. I merely nibbled at a cookie.

A young Mangyan tribesman I recognized happened by. Never before nor since have I seen a face so filled with pity—which is to say, in all my life, I have never been in a more pitiable circumstance than I was at that moment. In accord with their custom, the Mangyan youth wore his hair down to his shoulders and had a red cloth wrapped around his head. His beautiful face could easily have been mistaken for a girl's.

Except for being awakened several times during the night to take more pills, I slept soundly.

The next morning the commander said, "Today we return to San Jose. The troops will board ship directly south of here, but you will go from Bulalacao. Can you walk?"

"I'll do my best."

With GIs supporting me on either side, I managed to stay on my feet all the way down the mountain. Several Filipinos carried me by stretcher from there to Bulalacao, ten kilometers away. Once they had hoisted the stretcher onto their shoulders, all I could see from where I lay was the bright sky and the leafy treetops lining both sides of the road. Watching the beautiful green foliage flow by me on and on as the stretcher moved forward, it finally began to sink in that I had been saved—that the duration of my life now extended indefinitely into the future. It struck me, too, just how bizarre an existence I had been leading, facing death at every turn.

∼ 2 ∼

San Jose Field Hospital

When we reached Bulalacao, my captors took me to a jail cell in the town hall on the waterfront. A detachment from my company had previously billeted in the same building, but they had gotten along quite well with the locals, and the jail had always remained empty.

I was exhausted. Although I had had it easy once they loaded me onto the stretcher, the strain of the climb down two kilometers of mountain path had left me with a persistent aching in my chest. I lay alone on the wooden floor of the small, iron-barred cell taking long, deep breaths.

A cutout of the sky hung in the window high up on the wall, replete with the glow of the late afternoon sun. The glow seemed to penetrate the sky to its very depths, reflecting the color of the sea spread out below. I had long lived with death as my companion in the mountains; this descent to the sea signified my return to the world of the living.

Soon a nisei soldier appeared, a well-favored man of twenty-four or five. I could hardly believe that I would meet a Japanese man in such excellent health at this place, only a few miles removed from where my outfit had been so ravaged by disease. Never did I feel more painfully the meaning of defeat than when I saw this man of Japanese blood dressed in an American uniform.

I suppose my eyes must have tendered a plea for his goodwill. He smiled warmly before beginning a brief interrogation. To my surprise, he knew a great deal about the state of our troops.

"Have you ever seen one of these?" he asked, handing me a flier. The sheet urged Japanese troops to surrender and showed a picture of POWs somewhere in the South Pacific, their heads shaded by large sun hats, weaving nipa fronds and tilling fields. White rectangles masked their eyes, but their lips were spread in broad smiles.

34

"Let's all stop this senseless fighting," the message said, "and enjoy the rest of the war under the generous protection of the American forces."

I suspect my interrogator intended the flier to assuage any fears I might have had about my future, but I already knew from the way I had been treated that I was in the hands of a civilized nation. In fact, as the sick are wont to demand of their caretakers anywhere, I seemed to have already come to expect the Americans to wait on me hand and foot like an honored guest. At any rate, between the disease-ravaged condition of my body and this swollen-headed perception of my status in the hands of the Americans, the picture of prisoners happily engaged in empty tasks of menial labor failed to generate any particular feelings of gratitude within me.

"No, this is the first time," I said truthfully, and handed the flier back.

I asked my interrogator his name and where he had been born.

"I am not permitted to tell you things like that here," he said brusquely, and then went away. "Here" presumably meant "on the field of battle."

After that, the cell door of iron bars remained unlocked. The guard sitting beside it handed me a candy bar and some sugar cubes through the bars. Their wondrous sweetness lingers on my tongue even today. Next he offered me a big chunk of cheese. When I turned it down, he promptly hurled it out the window.

A stretcher arrived and I was carried outside again. We wended our way among some palm trees down to the beach, where they laid me in the bottom of a small sailboat. With crimson clouds flowing across the evening sky at his back, the shirtless boatman raised a shout and set to work. The sail came round and the sound of the bow cutting through the waves began to lap pleasantly at my ears. The boat headed straight out into the offing.

Presently the steel hull of a patrol boat loomed across my field of vision, and the boat carrying me drew up along side it. My stretcher was hoisted up. As it cleared the side of the larger craft, an American seaman abruptly lifted me in his arms, circled around the bow, and lay me down on top of the doors to the hold. I was astonished. When we had taken Filipinos captive in San Jose, I had sneaked them food or cigarettes and did them other small favors, but whatever the need, I doubt I would ever have been willing to actually touch their unclean bodies.

I had worn the same pair of army pants for the last forty days, and all I had for a shirt was a raincoat, cut off at the waist, which the Americans had given me in their camp. (The coat had a label saying "Made in London," but I cannot imagine how such a garment would have come to be on that mountain.) Around my neck hung a POW tag bearing my name, date of birth, place of capture, and so forth. Without a word the seaman removed this tag and pushed it into the pocket of my raincoat. Then he went away.

To my mind, the goodwill expressed in this gesture went beyond the usual generosity of spirit expected of the victorious. The American form of government, together with her economic prosperity, allowed each individual to act in whatever benevolent fashion he saw fit. We certainly need not regard such qualities with suspicion.

My nisei interrogator had apparently been assigned to escort me to San Jose, and after a while he came to check on me.

The patrol boat began to move, bearing southward along the coast. I recalled that the trip from Bulalacao to San Jose had taken eight hours on the small motor launch my company had used to transport men and supplies—a fishing boat from back home pressed into military service. Darkness fell and the moon appeared shortly after.

Gazing in turns at the mountains enveloped in shadow and the sea glistening in the moonlight, I savored once again the joy of survival. At the same time, the realization that I had become a prisoner of war began to weigh heavily on my heart.

I did not regard capture by the enemy as the heinous disgrace our drill instructors had painted it. Because modern advances in weaponry had dramatically reduced the importance of manpower among the numerous elements affecting the outcome of battle, I believed our military leaders were themselves to blame for any disparities in fighting strength at the front. Soldiers in the field had every right to abandon hopeless resistance. Yet once I had actually fallen captive, how discomfiting, how reprehensible it felt to be idly enjoying a renewed life among the enemy while my brothers in arms continued to die in battle.

I experienced a sudden urge to throw myself into the ocean and kill myself. It was not an impulse that came from the heart, however. As when I had screamed "Kill me!" upon recognizing my dead comrade's haversack the day before, it was a false desire that did not flow from the true center of my being. Even though no guard had been posted nearby, I did not in fact move a muscle.

Once the urge had passed, it left behind only a deep sense of sadness. I pitied myself for the circumstances that had made it necessary for me to experience such a false impulse.

Having eventually dropped off to asleep, I later awoke to the approaching sound of voices. We had arrived. The same seaman lifted and carried me down the steps to the stern, but the only way to get into the launch that would take me ashore was to leap under my own power. I gathered my strength and jumped. Falling forward onto my stomach as I landed on the launch's flat rear section, I ended up with my head and chest hanging over the side but somehow managed to keep from tumbling on over into the sea.

The beach was illuminated with bright floodlights, and each of the indentations left by the constant foot traffic held a small shadow. A newly constructed radio tower filled the air with transmission sounds. The town of San Jose, several kilometers inland, already had a tower the Americans had put up when they were here before, but with their ample resources they could simply erect another one wherever they wished. Seeing so plainly the extent of American abundance made my heart ache.

This was not the beach my unit had used as our landing for San Jose. The town itself was located in the middle of a small plain that spread out from the coast, requiring a four-kilometer trip inland no matter where you came ashore.

My nisei escort helped me across the beach to a waiting jeep, which immediately drove off down a broad, smooth highway toward San Jose. Every so often its headlights picked out another concrete pillbox lying low at the side of the road.

Turning toward me, the nisei asked, "How about it? Are you impressed?"

I could but acknowledge the truth. When he relayed my surprise to the driver, they both burst out laughing. I felt a sensation of pleasure swelling up within me at having made them laugh, and I quickly bit my lip in self-reproach. For the first time since capture, I had to stanch the impulse to toady to my captors. In the year that followed, during which I lived under the care of American troops and spent much of my time working as an interpreter, I tried vigilantly to remain on guard against such temptations, but even so I could not completely banish the feelings of gratification that arose within me when I saw the pleasure my captors took at a flattering or self-deprecating remark I had made. What I find noteworthy is not that I suppressed those feelings, but rather that I could not prevent them from arising in the first place. I cannot help but wonder why.

I caught sight of the building that had been our barracks—a grade school the Americans had built to provide English language education for the islanders. The long, single-story building stood quietly in the moonlight with all of its windows closed up tight, offering nary a hint of what it had been through. As I craned my neck to get a better view, the jeep swung around a corner and the building disappeared from sight.

I had expected to pass through a small hamlet on the way from the beach but had missed it. Now, when we turned the corner, I discovered that the woods and the sunken hollow that used to lie there had vanished without a trace, replaced by a flat expanse of numberless tents stretched out in rows. Agape, I marveled all over again at the U.S. Army's engineering resources.

The jeep came to a halt in front of one of these tents, and I was helped inside to a canvas cot. A doctor came over to examine me and gave me some tablets to take. The nisei explained that I was to recuperate there for two or three days until I had recovered enough strength to walk; then I would be transferred to a POW hospital on the island of Leyte.

More than a dozen beds lined the two sides of the rectangular tent, each one hidden within its own mosquito net. The time was apparently quite late, for the lights had already been extinguished. The nisei went away with the doctor, leaving behind a lone soldier to stand guard.

The black outline of mountains arching gracefully from one sharply pointed peak to the next rose up over my pillow. It seemed strange that I could not remember ever having seen them like that before. I had been stationed here for half a year and thought I had gotten to know every aspect of the local terrain, yet here was a spot where the mountains took on an altogether different shape. A vague sense of melancholy came over me.

I experienced a recurrence of the oppressive pain that had made me tear at my chest in the woods two nights before. Apparently the strain of the day's journey was showing its effect. I groaned and pressed my fingers against my ribs trying to somehow relieve the pain. That unfamiliar view of the mountains remained constantly within sight, lurking over me as if to startle or mock as I tossed about.

"Could you try to keep it down?" the GI in the next bed called out in a loud whisper.

My guard spoke with the medic on duty, who went to get the surgeon. When he arrived, I described the pain and asked for a camphor injection along with some sleeping pills (I was still trying to prescribe my own treatment, as I had done in the absence of doctors in the mountains). The surgeon tried to calm me, gave me a foul-smelling pill to swallow, and went away.

The pain did not stop, and I could not fall asleep. Thinking I must be about to die, I stewed angrily over the doctor's refusal of the camphor shot I had requested.

This same pain two nights before had brought no thoughts of death. At that point, I had already accepted the inevitability of my impending demise, and the excruciating pressure in my chest merely represented a condition that had to be endured if I wished to quench my thirst one last time. Now, however, I lay in the tranquil surroundings of an American field hospital, and I had regained hope for my future. As a result, I thought immediately of death, and I feared it.

(I know now that I did indeed spend that night on the very verge of death. In the days to come, I saw more than a few patients die on their first nights in the hospital. I also learned that a camphor injection under my condition at the time would only have aggravated my symptoms.)

I managed, in time, to fall asleep. When I awoke, daylight had returned and my mosquito net was gone. Most of the other patients, all Americans, were sitting up in their beds. The pain in my chest had abated.

My bed was at one end of the tent. Immediately next to the tent lay a broad clearing spread with gravel, and beyond that was another long row of tents. To my considerable surprise, I realized it was the roofs of those tents that had formed the peaks and valleys of the mountains I thought I had seen the night before.

A young orderly went from bed to bed serving a breakfast of pancakes and coffee. I still had no appetite, so I just sipped at some coffee.

The man in the bed next to me rose to his feet and started getting dressed. I gathered he was being discharged back to his unit.

"Sorry about all the noise last night," I said.

"Oh, never mind that," he said. "It wasn't so bad." He took out a candy bar. "Would you like this?"

"No thanks," I said, but he nevertheless insisted on leaving it beside my pillow as he departed. It turned out to be the only food that passed my lips that day.

"Hey, Tōjō," a voice called from a bed some distance away, and I felt the blood rise to my head.[1] I hated that name bitterly and could hardly have wished to be addressed by it. I pretended not to hear and held my tongue.

"I guess he doesn't know English," the man muttered in a lower voice, then said nothing more.

When I later read in an American magazine that "Tōjō" was GI slang for Japanese troops in general, I realized the man had not intended it as an insult; he was merely trying to get my attention. I had gotten angry for nothing.

Four or five GIs gathered noisily about my bed and started bombarding me with questions about "Fujiyama" and "geesha girls." I wanted the man who called me Tōjō to know that he had jumped to the wrong conclusion about my command of English, so even though every word took great effort, I answered each of their questions in as much detail as I could muster.

"Why did you guys treat the American wounded you captured in Bataan so ruthlessly?" they wanted to know.

I had heard about the Bataan Death March from a press corps friend stationed in the Philippines at the time, and I found myself hard put for an answer. It would have been easy to blame the events entirely on the military high command, but since I had tacitly supported the military by my silence, I could not in good conscience do that. For much the same reason I had felt personally insulted at being called Tōjō, I now felt personally implicated in the circumstances that had made the Death March possible. The words that presently emerged from my lips were ones I myself had found utterly without credibility in statements issued by the General Staff at the time.

"I heard that Americans were not hurt in Bataan," I said. "Didn't you

---

1 Tōjō Hideki became prime minister in 1941 and chief of the General Staff in 1944.

just supervise from behind the lines while the Filipinos fought the battle up front?"

The GIs collapsed into fits of laughter. Laugh though they might, however, I had effectively escaped having to give a straight answer to their awkward question.

One of the men thrust a flier written in Japanese at me. The sheet was about one-fourth the size of a newspaper page and bore the masthead "Parachute News"—obviously a propaganda flier intended for air-dropping over Japanese positions. The photo at the top showed B-29s taking off from a base in Saipan, and the accompanying article described recent bombing runs to Japan along with the battle situation on Luzon. Overleaf were a political cartoon caricaturing the General Staff and an old "Little Fuku" comic strip. The GIs made me translate some of the flier, but when I read that it had been published by the Southwest Pacific GHQ, they took it away, saying, "Oh, it's our own propaganda."

"You guys aren't supposed to talk to him," my guard broke in, and they all went back to their beds.

I let my eyes roam the tent. More than half of the GIs sat with their mosquito nets hanging down around them even in daytime. The tent was evidently a malaria ward.

A golden-haired young soldier sat hugging his knees and talking through his net with the fellow across the aisle. He had the relaxed and easy manner of one born to wealth, and he seemed in no way different from a patient in a well-to-do civilian hospital. If the men in this army could fight a war as if it were merely a natural extension of their civilian life, it was indeed the ideal army.

One of the men sat up and raised a Japanese wicker lunchbox over his head, smiling as he tried to catch my attention. When our eyes met, he shook the box and asked, "Whadda ya use this for?"

"It's for carrying your lunch," I said.

Nodding as though satisfied with my answer, he lay back down.

I recognized him as the fellow who had called me Tōjō, but his innocent curiosity disarmed me.

I wondered if I should be concerned about where and how he had come into possession of the lunch box, but I told myself it was not the sort of thing a soldier carried, so he had probably just picked up what some evacuating Japanese civilian had left behind. At the time I did not have the strength to consider the matter any further.

They took an X ray of my chest and drew blood from my finger. A short while later a nurse came to hang my mosquito net.

"You need to stay covered," she said. The lab had found malarial parasites in my blood.

The day drew to a close. I continued to suffer discomfort from my elevated temperature, but the chest pains of the previous night did not return. I slept well.

The next morning, I still had no appetite. The tall orderly who brought breakfast demanded, "Whadda ya mean, you don't want any? It'll go down real easy," and he made me take a plate. I did not wish his kindness to be for naught, but I simply could not bring myself to eat the breakfast of powdered eggs.

"You seem to like tea, so I'll leave you some in this," a nurse said as she poured some black tea into a large aluminum cup. She set it under my cot.

The surgeon came to examine me. "You're doing much better," he said. "I think we can transfer you to the hospital on Leyte tomorrow."

Another nurse ducked under the mosquito net at the head of my bed and crouched next to my pillow, facing the other way as she busied herself with something for a moment. I sensed an uneasy tension in her movements even from behind. When she finally turned around, I saw a distinctly unattractive middle-aged woman with small eyes, a dark complexion, and a prominent, heavily creased brow. She fixed her fierce brown eyes firmly on mine, and I realized she had come expressly to talk to me.

"Are you from the Tenth?" she blurted out.

Though her tone made it clear the question was very important to her, I failed to grasp what she was asking. "Excuse me?" I said.

She merely repeated the same question, this time with a note of irritation creeping into her voice. I still did not understand.

The surgeon ambled over. "She wants to know if you were among the troops at Bataan," he enlightened me, then stood waiting expectantly for my answer. His manner puzzled me. I had already told him that I had not been called up for active duty until 1944. Why was he trying to make me go through all that again?

When I repeated what I had said before, he and the nurse exchanged words for a few moments, both of them speaking too rapidly for me to follow. Then he turned back to me and said, "When our men surrendered at Bataan, why did your troops treat them the way they did?"

That question again. Now I understood. This nurse was no doubt married to a GI missing in action at Bataan, and she had volunteered for frontline duty in hopes that she might eventually learn something about what had happened to her husband. When word spread to her tent that the new Japanese prisoner in the malaria ward spoke English, she had hurried over to make her usual inquiries. Her "Tenth" had been a reference to Japan's Tenth Army Division.

But what if I *had* participated in the events on Bataan? What would she have asked of me then? And why had she taken such a strong interest in me in particular, so much so that the doctor felt obliged to make me deny my involvement with my own tongue? Her eyes when she first fixed her gaze on mine had held something far removed from hopeful optimism. Quite possibly, she had already given up all hope of discovering her husband alive, and what she wanted of me was to find out whether I was the one who had killed him.

Once again I was at a loss for an answer. My interlocutors yesterday had asked the same question out of a more general curiosity, which had permitted me to brush aside their nationalistic indignation by simply playing dumb. This time, however, I was faced with the wife of a Death March victim, and all I could honestly do was say nothing.

The surgeon spoke again. "Even though you people mistreated our POWs, we are providing for your POWs in strict accord with international conventions. That is our official policy, handed down from above. But when it comes to members of your Tenth and Sixteenth Divisions, those of us who have actually seen action in the Philippines are not so willing to forgive and forget."

(I subsequently concluded that this doctor was merely speaking on behalf of the Bataan widow next to him, or else expressing an essentially personal opinion, for I found that the majority of POWs I met in the camps on Leyte came from the Sixteenth Division. The Sixteenth was the division defending Leyte at the time of the American landing.)

The surgeon's words finally gave me an opening.

"But the men who make up the Tenth today can't all be charged with the Bataan excesses," I said. "Most of them would be replacements."

"We can check them out one by one," the doctor scowled.

I wanted to say more. I wanted to declare that it was wrong of them to blame the individual men who had engaged in the brutalities. Those individuals' most evil instincts had been loosed by execrable orders from above, and as such, they, too, must be considered pitiable victims. They knew not what they did. Yet there before me stood one of the victims of these victims. Could there be any greater insult than to look this ultimate victim straight in the eye and argue that the executioners, too, were victims? The argument that the perpetrators were victims really applied only when speaking of the state of affairs within our own house. I held my tongue.

Grasping at the possibility that the nurse's husband might have survived and been sent to Japan, I decided to tell them about some American POWs I had seen in Kobe. They listened in obvious disbelief as I described how the POWs had been held in European-style buildings in what used to be the foreign settlement there and how I had seen them playing catch in the street.

I told them, too, how word had leaked out that the American POWs were being served meat every day even though the ration for Japanese civilians was only slightly more than a pound of meat per month. The city council had subsequently passed a resolution of protest, but the government refused to change its policy.

"And what year was that?" the doctor asked sarcastically.

Unfortunately, I had to admit that it was 1942. "But even in 1944," I hastened to add, "we were doing everything we could for your POWs. We gave them work to do in our shipyards and places like that, and we served them fried rice instead of plain steamed rice for their meals."

"Did you see these men yourself?"

"I know about them firsthand because I worked in the front office at one of the shipyards in Kobe. The prisoners arrived at eight in the morning and left at four in the afternoon. We gave them simple, physical jobs. You Americans are all so big and strong, you know. . . . Oh, yes, there were some black men, too."

This last detail, which I had tacked on as an afterthought, seemed to make a genuine impression on them. They looked at each other and sighed. The presence of blacks among the well-treated POWs I had seen proved beyond any doubt that they were indeed Americans.

The fierceness had vanished from the nurse's eyes, but she still did not look especially comforted when she presently thanked me and went away.

I had told her no lies, but neither had I revealed everything I knew. I was aware that untold numbers of prisoners had died at one particular shipyard on the continent. And I could well imagine the reprisals the POWs in Japan might be suffering at the hands of our militarists now that B-29s had begun carpet bombing our cities. My reason for not speaking of such things had more to do with saving my own skin than with any desire to minimize the nurse's distress.

A black man was carried in. He groaned and sweated all night long as he suffered through an attack of the fever. I was glad to have beside me someone on whom even I could take pity.

The next morning, January 29, I was informed again that I would be airlifted to Leyte that day. To accommodate my 11:00 A.M. departure time, the orderly made a special trip to the mess tent to bring me an early lunch, but I left most of the food sitting on my plate, including a generous portion of meat. After helping me into the hospital transport, he stood waiting for me to look at him again so he could say good-bye, but I obstinately kept my head turned the other direction, and he eventually just gave an awkward wave and walked away. I still cannot explain what made me return his generosity with such blatant rudeness.

We drove past my former barracks again. Today, too, the building stood quietly with all its windows closed up tight. With the water tanks and sandbag barriers we had erected remaining exactly as they had been before, the school seemed to stand forgotten amid the dramatic changes that had taken place all around. The comrades with whom I had spent six months of my life here had now mostly perished. Though I continued to gaze at the building for as long as it remained in sight, the feeling in my heart was actually something close to indifference.

They had died, and I had survived. There could be no two ways of understanding this inexorable fact. Beneath the mournful, funereal mask of all survivors lies a powerful egotism. It has nothing to do with sentiment; it is a simple matter of fact.

The airstrip was one of the newly built strips where our men camped on the ridge overlooking San Jose had observed B-24s coming and going. While I waited my turn to board a twin-engine Douglas displaying the red cross, I rested in the shade of its wing. Out on the wide runway, all manner of aircraft were taking off and landing one after another. To sit among enemy troops and watch them carry on the war against one's brothers in arms is to experience something very close to physical pain.

Eventually my turn came, and I boarded the plane with the GI assigned to escort me. This was to be my first plane ride. A young woman with a colorful scarf wrapped around her head like a turban directed me to a seat. I had not seen such feminine beauty since leaving Japan. A brunette, she wore heavy makeup in the American style, and she looked rather chic in a jumpsuit with a pocket below one knee. She was apparently responsible for taking care of the sick during the flight.

"How's this guy look?" my escort asked her.

"He doesn't look bad," she said, glancing at me out of the corner of her eye. Her eyes overflowed with maidenly compassion, but the curl of her penciled eyebrows and painted lips gave her a grotesque effect. Contemporary styles of makeup seem wholly ill-suited to the female character.

The engines roared into action and the plane began to move. The long, ovoid space that held me rushed forward at a speed faster than I had ever experienced before. The cabin vibrated noisily, and the gravel on the ground outside the window dashed by in myriad white streaks. I waited expectantly to feel the gentle liftoff and see the earth drop away, but when the plane kept racing endlessly forward along the runway, I tired of waiting and turned my eyes back inside.

A few moments later I looked out the window again to a bird's-eye view of the island aglare in the bright sunlight. Long stretches of beach etched a twisted white line along the shore, and miniature trucks plied the highway between San Jose and the coast. The deep green verdure of the forests stood out in ill-complexioned relief against the fields, and the ocean glistened in the sun. Far in the distance the horizon seemed to lift up and fold back over me. Then the scene tilted and began to rotate, and the glare of sunlight reflecting off the ocean gradually spread across my window.

The plane tossed about erratically, and the recurring sensation of sudden short drops made me very uncomfortable. When I asked if I could lie down in the aisle between the seats, the woman went to get a stretcher from a storage compartment in the tail and laid it on the floor for me. Soon the others on board started getting airsick, too, one after another.

A GI complained about me taking up too much space with my stretcher. "The guy's only pretending to be sick," he said, not caring that I could hear.

"I can get up," I told my guard.

"It's okay. Just stay as you are," the woman said from nearby.

I lay like that for perhaps two hours, intending to return to my seat when the plane started its descent so I could watch out the window as we approached the landing strip. Suddenly the woman called to me as if in admonishment, "Maybe you should get up." Not quite sure what to make of her tone, I slowly started to rise, but then she put out her hand as if to hold me back and said, "Never mind, never mind." The next moment a series of sharp jolts hit the plane from below, quickly giving way to a noisy, bumpy ride like our takeoff run. We had landed.

The airstrip at Tacloban did not seem particularly different from the one at San Jose. We climbed into a small hospital transport, which made its way to a coastal highway lined with palm trees and drove on for some distance.

On Mindoro the weather had been clear, but on Leyte it was overcast. The bay appeared gray and muddy, with choppy, triangular waves; I could almost feel their chill. The palm trees along the way grew taller and ganglier than those on Mindoro, their leaves much sparser; a layer of dust darkened their trunks.

I saw the American forces' superior weaponry on display everywhere. Though I had imagined as much, to now actually observe with my own eyes the massive power represented by this profusion of steel made me ask once again whether this reckless war could not have been avoided. The answer, unfortunately, was negative.

The guard escorting me was a high-spirited fellow, dark-skinned and not very tall. His preference for slang proved no small headache for me.

"Do you like war?" I asked him.

"Shit, no. But I'm one helluva fighter," he said, raising his rifle and pretending to take aim.

"What are they going to do to me when we arrive?" I asked next.

"They're gonna string you up," he said, spitting the words out between clenched teeth. I still cannot imagine what possessed him to make a joke of that nature.

It was quite some distance to the hospital. At long last the transport left the coastal highway behind and started making turns, the roads becoming muddier and muddier as we went. Just beyond a sign that said U.S. Army Field Hospital, we finally pulled to a halt.

Separated from the road by a stretch of green stood a large chalkstone building. A GI came out to meet us, and without so much as a glance at me, my escort started walking back toward the building with him shoulder to shoulder. As I stood wondering whether I should follow, I heard a voice call out in Japanese, "Hey, you there! You belong over here."

Turning toward the voice, I looked across the road at a fenced compound surrounded by barbed wire. Next to a palm-log gatepost stood a nisei GI beckoning to me.

Right. I had forgotten about the fences that loomed in my future.

A bridge of planks had been placed over the muddy roadway, and I slowly made my way across them to the gate. Inside the enclosure stood several tents, their rows of beds filled with Japanese men wearing the close-cropped military haircuts I knew so well.

I experienced a searing surge of shame. These were the first of my compatriots I had encountered since being captured, and like me, they were all men who had allowed themselves to be taken prisoner. The shame I experienced was the shame shared by partners in crime.

My eyes met those of a man near the entrance. His expression seemed to convey the same inner shame I was feeling. In a fluster, I hastily shifted my gaze away. Unable to look any of them in the eye, I fixed my focus high up on the far end of the tent and walked into their midst as though stumbling blindly into a bank of clouds.

3

Rainy Tacloban

What did you go out into the wilderness to behold?
A reed shaken in the wind?
—Matthew 11:7

The many turns had made me lose my sense of direction, but I gathered that the transport had brought us through the outskirts of Tacloban to the inland edge of the city, where it extended into a narrow valley connecting the coast with the hinterland. A two-lane road wound its way along the foot of the hills on one side of the valley, and marshlands filled the two hundred odd yards from there to the hills rising opposite. The chalkstone building stood in the hollow of a hill that had a lookout post on its summit. The structure had apparently been a public building of some kind before being converted into a surgical hospital by the Americans. Across the road, a section of the marsh had been filled in to make room for a small power plant that supplied electricity to the hospital facilities. A barbed-wire enclosure about twenty yards wide and forty yards front-to-back stood next to the power plant. This was the Leyte POW hospital to which I had been sent.

Approximately 250 prisoners were being cared for there when I arrived on January 29, 1945. The hospital comprised eight tents of varying sizes, five for surgery and three for internal medicine. Many of the patients in the internal medicine wards were men who remained hospitalized for beriberi and other secondary ailments after recovering from battle wounds.

The nisei interpreter showed me to a bed right by the entrance of the tent nearest the gate. It being almost sundown by now, the doctors had

47

already departed. The medic in charge consulted with the interpreter and gave me five or six yellow pills to take, telling me they were a quinine substitute. Exhausted by the half-day's journey from San Jose, I lay down for some much-needed rest. The air in the tent shook ceaselessly with the rumble from the generator next door.

My tent held about thirty beds separated by an aisle down the middle. They were occupied by Japanese POWs in ill-fitting light blue pajamas, some sitting, some reclining. The pressure of all their eyes, trained curiously in my direction, seemed to burn my cheeks.

I felt wretched. Even though the circumstances had undeniably been beyond my control, now that I was surrounded by these Japanese faces, I felt a deep sense of shame at having been taken alive.

During the five days I had lived entirely amongst Americans, I had received clear enough indications that I would soon be sent to a place where I would meet and pass the days with others who had suffered the same fate as myself. But I found such comfort in what seemed like pampered-guest treatment in the hands of my civilized captors that I had forgotten to prepare my heart for the barbed-wire fences standing athwart my future. I had forgotten, too, the compatriots whom I would meet within those fences. The sudden wave of shame I now experienced caught me completely off guard.

To begin with, I had never been persuaded that becoming a POW was as shameful as the military taught, and the manner in which the Americans had treated me served to corroborate this view. Besides that, there was the question of why I should have felt any shame before others who had allowed themselves to be captured just like myself.

One hypothesis might be that I had subconsciously internalized the lessons taught in grade school about the Homeland and Honor, but I find this untenable. In the years since my school days, in the privacy of my own thoughts, I have had a long and broad-ranging history of rejecting the tenets of those indoctrinations, and it would be highly irrational to suppose that the prejudices of my grade-school teachers had remained permanently imprinted in the depths of my subconscious quite in spite of all subsequent events. Much less do I place any store in mystical beliefs about race or blood.

I ultimately concluded that my shame derived from coming into the midst of my compatriots *lately* and *singly*. They were many, and I was one. I feared that they might regard me as a disgrace. To be concerned about others' opinions of oneself is one of the most basic of social instincts, but in this case, my fears had been raised by my own presumption that the others, too, felt pangs of the same shame: the shame of shared guilt in a crime.

Perhaps I had avoided thinking about our impending meeting because some subconscious mechanism had made me anticipate their shame. If so, it was out of respect for them.

I could not remember ever having experienced such a shame before. I should have realized, however: It was essentially the same emotion I had experienced upon discovering that I could not love my country in the same blind way my brothers in arms did, and so had to assuage the pangs of self-reproach by telling myself that the others were in fact merely deceiving themselves. I should also have realized that, from then on, for however long I remained within barbed-wire fences, any relationship between myself and the others would have to be built on top of my fears. If I had indeed realized these things, then I might have learned a great deal in captivity. Instead, my heart gradually retreated into its inherent arrogance. Shame is not a sentiment that endures.

I cannot recall the first words I spoke to the patient next to me. I do remember that I spoke first and that I had a great deal of difficulty enunciating my words. Until that moment, I was not aware that the slurred speech from my fever remained with me.

He was a young soldier in his mid-twenties, and his slender, somewhat dark-skinned face gave a personable impression. Perhaps I asked him to get me some water; that would explain the picture I have of him in my mind, limping toward me with a dripping tin can in his hand. He also stabilized my cot for me by wedging scraps of wood and stones under the legs. I still cringe to remember how he avoided looking me in the eye as he experimented one way and another.

"Where did they bring you in from?" he asked in barely a whisper as he lay back down.

"Mindoro," I said. "This malaria did me in. How about you?"

"Right here, near Ormoc," he said. "The Yanks wouldn't kill me, you know, so what could I do?"

I studied his face from where I lay. His transparent eyes remained fixed on the roof of the tent. I could not doubt that those words represented his true feelings. These candid words from my first neighbor in the POW hospital subsequently became the yardstick against which I measured every POW I met. I still believe that they all experienced those sentiments at one point or another.

Presently we commenced the conversation that inevitably took place when two captured soldiers met for the first time—which is to say, we exchanged accounts of the military careers that had brought us there. This simple exchange proved a tremendous comfort to me. After four days of having to communicate constantly in an alien tongue, I was starving for some Japanese conversation.

He had belonged to the Eighth Division, redeployed from the Soviet-

Manchurian border to Luzon in October 1944. After helping to build defensive positions at several sites in the south of that island, his unit was ordered to Leyte in mid-November. Of three small transport vessels, two were sunk en route, and then the troops on the third vessel came under aerial bombardment as they made their landing on the island's west coast, reducing their strength by half. He had himself sustained a wound in the knee. He hid in an islander's home while his unit went on a raid to Ormoc but was discovered by American ground troops. As he fled the house, he was hit again, this time in the thigh, and taken into custody.

My company had also been under the command of the Eighth Division at the end, but his detachment had had no connection with our battalion headquartered at Batangas. Though he was a corporal, his attitude toward me did not change when he learned I was a private. Perhaps the shame of captivity had equalized our ranks.

Once we had each briefly detailed the events leading to our capture, our conversation came to a halt.

An indefinable feeling of anguish took hold of me as the awareness sank in that I was not the only prisoner there. Every man in sight was a prisoner.

A dark green tent stretched over our heads, and taut canvas cots held us suspended off the ground. We wore dapper light blue pajamas, and we had each been issued our own private mosquito net and two blankets. Not only were conditions far better than in the mountains, but we also could be grateful that our lives were no longer threatened. Yet what did it mean for us to be gathered here, each with his own shame, spending our days in idle tranquility?

An American orderly roved the aisle between the two rows of beds, pausing here and there to greet the prisoners he knew, joking with them in a combination of hand gestures and simple words. Perhaps it was only my imagination, but I thought his manner lacked the unrestrained cheerfulness of the Americans I had seen at the field hospital on Mindoro. This orderly acted more like a jailer. From his point of view, too, it must have been an unpleasant role to fill, but at least for him a life of freedom awaited him back at his barracks. Our lives, on the other hand, were confined entirely to this one place.

I gazed out absentmindedly through the barbed-wire fence that stretched across my field of vision just five or six paces from my pillow. When the sun had descended low in the western sky, GIs of all sizes and in sundry attire rambled by, carrying shiny mess kits. A helmeted guard sat on a chair in front of the gate, puffing a cigarette. Suddenly he rose to his feet, paced forward a few steps, spun around on his heels, whistled, marched back to his chair, sat down, and immediately crossed his legs.

Moments later, a man whom I took to be an NCO approached. The guard remained seated but tilted his rifle forward as if for inspection. The other man grasped the barrel and gave it a cursory glance, then moved away.

I could see that I had come into the midst of a military machine of fairy-tale efficiency. However, I had also entered a life of captivity that seemed as unreal as a fairy tale, and I found myself at an utter loss what to make of it. Most distressing of all was realizing that I was not alone in my captivity and that I could not even begin to guess how long we might all continue to be confined together.

A truck pulled up and the driver stuck his head out the window.

"Chow!" he shouted.

I later learned that "chow" meant "mealtime" in American military parlance. The word was relayed to the back of the tent, where four or five muscular men rose to their feet and came trotting forward (the men had been tapped to work as food servers after recovering from their ailments). They lowered several metal boxes from the truck and carried them into the tent on stretchers. As the boxes were hauled by, I spied on their sides the two letters that would become such a familiar sight over the next ten months: "PW." Our meals were brought to us like this from the main mess hall.

In a sudden commotion that began at the back of the tent, patients rose from their beds and lined up in the center aisle like a bucket brigade. Only those who did not have the strength to stand remained as they were.

Square plates came down the line one after the other. My neighbor brought one to me. The plates were large, more like trays, really, made of a metal alloy of some kind and having several molded indentations that held servings of canned meat, vegetables, fruit, dessert, and so forth. The bread was delicious, the best I had tasted since Pearl Harbor. One of the servers came round with a large container from which he ladled coffee into the cups the patients held out.

I still had very little appetite. After taking a few bites of the bread and fruit, I turned to my neighbor.

"Excuse me, but would you like the rest of my food?" I said.

I realized as the words left my lips that it was the first time I had begun a sentence with "Excuse me, but . . ." since entering the army. That the words now rolled so naturally off my tongue showed how far I had come toward shedding my military mentality since being captured.

After the trays were stacked and sent back, my neighbor took a half-smoked cigarette from under his pillow and placed it in a small pipe he had fashioned from a piece of tin. He offered me a puff, but I declined. I did not think my body was quite ready for tobacco yet.

My neighbor explained that cigarettes were doled out every third day at the rate of one per person per day. Since U.S. Army shipments for the POWs did not include cigarettes, Red Cross care packages were the only source, and that was why the ration was so small. Sympathetic GIs made a point of tossing their cigarette butts where the patients could easily reach them.

It remains a point of some considerable pride to me that I never once picked up any of those cigarette butts, even after I had recovered my health and regained my craving for tobacco. Being both a heavy smoker and un-accustomed to curbing any of my appetites, this was the first time I had adopted such a discipline for myself, and I feel a measure of contentment at having successfully carried it through to the end. I must admit, however, that I gladly accepted a number of puffs on my neighbor's pipe from ciga-rette butts he had picked up. The accommodations a prisoner makes in order to sustain his pride can verge on the comical.

Darkness descended. An orderly brought me a pair of the same light blue pajamas everyone else wore. I asked him to lower my mosquito net and prepared to go to sleep. All lights but one in the middle of the tent went out. A patient nearing full recovery served night watch to help the more seriously ill patients with their bedpans. The American medics on duty played cards in their own separate tent. Intermittently breaking through the noise of the generator, which now seemed to have grown louder, came the moans and groans of patients suffering from serious injuries in tents farther away.

The next day it rained. Spilling from the sky in sheets, the rain poured off the roof into a drain gutter that had been dug around the tent and flowed rapidly off toward the back of the compound. The din of the rain pounding on the roof and dripping from the eaves drowned out the noise of the gen-erator, but I could still feel its low rumble coming to me through the ground beneath the moist air. We prisoners had to shout at one another to be heard.

There could hardly have been more ways of sporting a simple pair of pajamas. Following the form taught in the Japanese military, everyone tucked his shirt into his pants, but whereas some fastened their buttons all the way to their throats, others folded their collars back like the lapels of a suit jacket. Some rolled their shirt cuffs up just to the wrist, others all the way to their elbows, and pants cuffs got much the same treatment. Some donned their tops from the front like smocks, and asked their neighbors to help them with the buttons down their back. Some chose not to wear their pajama tops at all, using them instead like covers pulled snugly to their chins, or folding them in half vertically and laying them on their chests. One characteristic they all had in common was that they tied the draw-strings of their pants very tight. Some of the men felt uncomfortable with the bagginess around their loins and pulled their pants up as high as they could, bringing the drawstring all the way up to their chest; they walked about with the fabric stretched tight over their rounded stomachs, looking like potbellied kids.

Two doctors came on rounds in the morning, an internist and a surgeon, each with a medic and nisei interpreter in tow. Several Japanese interpreters and orderlies joined them. Like the food servers, these were men who had recovered from their ailments or wounds.

It need come as no surprise that "the Japanese staff" (as the orderlies, food servers, and interpreters called themselves) considered themselves the guardians of many of the Japanese military's worst traditions, taking advantage of every opportunity to throw their weight around, behaving callously toward their fellow prisoners and misappropriating supplies for their own use. I do not intend to catalog their offenses here; I fear I could not portray the utter depravity of their behavior without seeming mean-spirited myself. They may merely have been displaying a weakness we Japanese all share in regard to special privileges—those who have them inevitably abuse them; those who do not have them fawn on those who do—from having grown too accustomed to absolutism.

One and all, the American doctors and medics treated us kindly. I need not detail these actions either. I should note, however, that the POWs did not respond especially well to the Americans' kindness.

To receive such kindness from "the enemy" was bewildering to them. Some returned the incomprehensible generosity with an unseemly obsequiousness; others regarded it with suspicion, as an attempt to appease us and win us over. Still others accepted it with a cynical "Hey, I won't complain" attitude. As time passed, all became desensitized to it and vacantly gave themselves over to the stunned state of abstraction that I will call "POW's daze."

Their confusion, it seems to me, was quite understandable. Their military indoctrination prevented them from accepting the Americans' warmheartedness with simple gratitude. Whereas they saw themselves as dishonorable captives, the Americans treated them as human beings, and this excessive kindness, so to speak, confounded them completely.

For the Americans to provide the same clothing and food to POWs as they did their own servicemen need not have been perceived as an act of inordinate generosity. It merely reflected the spirit of the Red Cross, which is rooted in the concept of individual human rights first voiced by Jean-Jacques Rousseau. Our Japanese consciousness of human rights having been historically quite dim, however, the POWs naturally could not comprehend this. At the same time, from the perspective of a POW, there is much about the spirit of the Red Cross that is puzzling in and of itself.

The notion of caring for sick and wounded combatants without regard to their nationalities arose at a time in history when the development of modern weapons brought about dramatic increases in the number of battle-field casualties, and the new character of military service under the modern state meant that the vast majority of those casualties were commoners. I do not doubt that Lady Florence Nightingale of Britain, who felt such sorrow at the suffering she witnessed on the battlefield, and the philanthropist Jean Henri Dunant of Switzerland were both motivated by a deep love of humanity; but the zeal these two crusaders showed for the cause, and the quickness with which numerous heads of state embraced it, are two quite different matters. The chief executives realized that if they wanted to order large segments of their populations onto the battlefield, there could be pragmatic benefits in making agreements with one another that provided those populations with certain guarantees. However, it was mainly their wives who bore the burden of implementing the new ideals, for that work proved too awkward for the chiefs themselves to undertake. The spirit of the Red Cross, like other charity enterprises, embodies a contradiction: It treats the symptom without removing the cause.

The Japanese POWs, innocent of the concept of human rights, had instinctively sensed this contradiction. Their insight was a by-product of the self-deprecating conviction that they had forever forfeited their personal honor the moment they allowed themselves to be taken captive.

These men believed that the army and navy military codes expressly prescribed the execution of captives who later returned home. This belief had no basis in fact, but it came from both their ideological indoctrination in school and their training in the military itself. Since a man cannot live with such a consequence as the only prospect for his future, the POWs also believed that some kind of extraordinary pardon would be forthcoming. Widespread credence was given the rumor that Japanese men taken captive in the 1932 Shanghai Incident had upon repatriation been sent to labor camps in Manchuria, and the POWs in the Philippines imagined they would likely have to walk the same path. Then after two or three years of atoning for their crime, they would be allowed to return to society.

Ultimately, of course, everything depended on whether Japan won or lost the war, but they were not yet prepared to consider the possibility of Japan's defeat when envisioning their own futures.

Many of the POWs went by assumed names. Navy men used the names of their ships; army men, the names of their outfits. Some borrowed the names of places or friends back home. The largest number adopted common surnames they had simply picked out of the air, resulting in a disproportionately large number of Kobayashis, Tanakas, and Suzukis on the POW rolls. This led to unfortunate consequences at the time of repatriation, when orders came down for all men of certain surnames to remain behind for questioning because the locals had mentioned them in connection with war crimes. Those who had only recently adopted the unhappy surnames rued their senseless precaution.

I had given my true name from the start. At the time of my capture, I, like everyone else, had believed I would be killed, and I did not wish to preclude the possibility that information about when and where I died might somehow reach my family. When I exulted over my honesty and ridiculed those who had brought misfortune on themselves out of misguided vanity, I was standing next to a man using an assumed name that had not yet been implicated.

"You can't really say which was the better course," he said. "Some guys wanted their families to know where they'd died, but others didn't want anyone to find out they'd died as prisoners and not in action. They feared negative repercussions for their families back home."

Indeed, these prisoners were concerned about safeguarding not only their families' honor, but also the condolence money paid to the families of soldiers who died in combat; the interests of their family came first. In retrospect, I must admit that this instinctive concern for the welfare of others demonstrated by those who falsified their names seems far superior to my own silly egotism in trying to preserve a trace of my own demise. Their actions came from a self-effacing altruism quite removed from the fight-to-the-death mentality drummed into them by the military.

Today, long after the fact, all such responses to the realities of wartime are dismissed as simpleminded foolishness. However, nothing demeans one's present more than denying the facts of one's past.

Of course, the generalizations I make here about the POWs reflect only my own personal interpretations of what I experienced and saw. Understanding any human entity is an act of interpretation. The validity of that interpretation is confirmed or denied by the entity's subsequent movements or the ultimate effects of those movements. If an entity remains utterly static, one has no means of gaining perspective; but to therefore force a perspective is inevitably to err—the failure of the Realist movement in the latter half of the nineteenth century provides a case in point. That is to say, any effort to comprehend a particular human entity entails elements not only political but prophetic. Yet I must admit that I am not entirely certain what I would prophesy through my observations of the prisoners' behavior.

One thing I can report with complete certainty is that every man, without exception, wore the glassy-eyed look of POW's daze. I cannot pretend to have understood all that lay beneath that look. Outwardly, in their identity as a group, these captured soldiers still manifested a substantially martial mentality, while inwardly, as individuals who had fallen (or been liberated) from the glory of fighting for their country, they had already begun to go their separate ways. In the midst of the prisoners' idleness, chaotic fragments of those separate ways came spilling out, as from an upended toy box, but to piece those fragments together into a coherent whole was a task that exceeded my capabilities—especially at a time when I myself suffered from POW's daze.

The vacant gaze of a dazed man suggests emptiness, but inside that person is anything but empty.

One of the first prisoners to draw my attention was a young fellow in the bed diagonally across from me. A case of beriberi had rendered his legs useless, so he never left his bed, relying on his neighbors' help for everything from meals to toilet. What amazed me most about him was the way he smiled all the time.

Whether asking someone to get his meal tray or bed pan or responding to the doctor on his rounds, his face would invariably light up with a silly-looking smile. In part, of course, the smile expressed his gratitude, but it also seemed to contain a curious cross of self-deprecation and presumption that ultimately suggested he might be taking everyone for fools.

He ate his meals lying down, with his tray on his chest, and he always took his time about it. This meant his neighbors had to go to extra trouble for him at cleanup. But since he claimed he could not remain in a sitting position long enough to get through a meal, there was nothing anyone could do. It generally required very little provocation for men in the army to accuse one another of slacking, and many must have suspected that this fellow was in fact perfectly capable of taking his meals sitting up, but for some reason no one challenged him.

Finally one day, the nisei interpreter who accompanied the doctor on his rounds barked at the man to sit up. The doctor, preparing as usual to examine the patient lying down, turned to look at the interpreter in puzzle-ment. I could not see the interpreter's expression from where I lay, but the grim look on the patient's face as he slowly raised himself up gave me a fairly good idea. The next moment, that trademark smile spread across his face.

"Cut the charade," the interpreter said. After that the young man ate sitting up.

I never learned the man's rank, and I know nothing about his career except that he was from the Sixteenth Division defending Leyte at the time of the American landing. I had no desire to find out anything more about him.

What surprises me most in retrospect is that I never experienced any feelings of contempt for this con artist. It was not that my POW's daze had made me incapable of such feelings, for I seethed with contempt for "the Japanese staff" from the moment I first observed their ruddy complexions. Rather, something had changed inside me to suppress my usual curiosity and permit the little cheat to pass without drawing either my interest or my disdain.

This man showed the same glassy-eyed daze as everyone else, and I could easily speculate here about the social station and personality and talents that lay beneath that exterior. I believe I could do so without engaging in fiction. Yet any truths I arrived at through such an effort would pale before my utter indifference toward him. Even remembering the man today, I still feel nothing for him—I really cannot say why.

I spent the days conversing with my immediate neighbor. He was a man of few words, but something within me egged me nervously on and refused to let me remain silent even for a moment.

He answered exactly what I asked and nothing more. His questions of me never went beyond routine inquiries about my military career; once that ground had been covered, he apparently had no further interest. Since it is not in my nature to talk on and on about myself, I decided to continue plying him with as many questions as I could think of.

He came from a farm in Aomori Prefecture, so once I had learned all about his family, I proceeded to ask about the geography and flora and fauna of the northern Tsugaru region, about the Edo-period rebel Sōma Daisaku, and about anything else I associated with that part of the country. For example, when he mentioned a river flowing near his village, I asked about its pools and its shallows, whether it had a rocky or muddy bottom, what kind of plants grew along its shores, and what its bridges were like. He revealed that salmon came up the river. Great! Now I could pass another thirty minutes asking whether they said saké or shaké for salmon in the local dialect, how and when they harvested the salmon, and what methods they used to prepare it. What started out as a few casual questions would soon turn into a full-blown interrogation. He showed no particular objection to the barrage, and he answered each of my queries carefully and politely. After three days, however, I completely ran out of things to ask.

I learned from those three days that hollow-hearted efforts at communion with others are fruitless and that communion between people does not necessarily come from conversation at all. To be sure, I did develop a strong affection for this my first POW neighbor, for his modest and artless character; but the only way I could find to express this affection was through a one-sided curiosity that sprang solely from the desire to fill the hollowness in my own heart. It was a measure of his magnanimity that he responded so amiably to my unremitting inquisitiveness.

That we were in neighboring beds in a POW hospital should have been sufficient foundation for our mutual love. Thus it was that he brought me water, shared the tobacco he gleaned, and shaved my face for me. All that I offered in return, however, was an interest in his past, and I egotistically resented his failure to reciprocate the interest, when in fact I was only getting my just deserts for never having approached another person except to gratify my own swollen-headed curiosity.

Among all the people I have ever known, my neighbor in that hospital stands out as a man of rare virtue. I regard it a stroke of genuine good fortune that my first acquaintance after I returned from the dead was a man like him.

What impressed me most was that he displayed no trace of the arrogance or cunning so typical of Japanese NCOs. Initially I attributed it to our shame making us equal, but as time passed and I became acquainted with a great many more prisoners, I learned that most of those accustomed to the prerogatives of advanced rank continued to behave self-importantly toward men of lesser rank even in prison camp. This farmer from northeastern Japan, I concluded, must have been blessed with a natural gift that allowed him to avoid being poisoned by the special privileges that accompanied advancement in the military.

The authorities had appropriated his family's apple orchard and plowed it up to be cultivated for other crops during the war. I could discern no tone of resentment in his voice as he told me this, even though it reduced the income of their already small holdings and forced his mother and younger sister, who were looking after the farm in his absence, to turn management of the farm over to relatives and become their dependents. So far as he was concerned, it seems, none of their misfortunes, including his own conscription, exceeded the bounds of endurance, and in this sense none of them held any special significance.

Yet, I would not characterize him as an enervated peon. He embodied not only humility but strength. For example, when he later borrowed a cardboard *shōgi* set from the Japanese staff and challenged me to a match, his moves showed an aggressiveness that seemed out of keeping with his usual mild manner, and he easily overpowered me in spite of my familiarity with many of the standard openings and tactics. No one else in the beds nearby could match him, either, and he soon found himself waving the *shōgi* board around without any comers.

He simply did not know how to exert the strength he held within him.

He left the hospital about ten days after my arrival, not yet entirely free of his limp. He effused excitedly about going to a camp where they served meals of rice and gave the inmates work to do. I called on him two months later when I moved to the same camp, but I discovered to my chagrin that we still had nothing to talk about. I did not stay long. By then his leg had grown strong enough for him to do heavy lifting and hauling. The speed with which wounded soldiers recovered from their injuries never ceased to amaze me. Much later, when a sumo tournament took place, I watched him enter the five-in-a-row challenge. He lost to his third opponent when he went down on his knee. Not surprisingly, it was the knee of his injured leg.

———

When our conversations broke off, I gazed out the gate of the compound. A constant flow of GIs and barefooted locals plied the road sloping gently along the base of the green hillside. I was never bored. Viewing the outside world from within the confines of a prison was a new experience, and the scene stretching before me had a certain freshness I never tired of.

At the left end of the hills that defined my field of vision, a tall spur jutted forth like a cape into the sea, and at a lookout post on its summit a small tent, appearing so forlorn that it was hard to imagine anyone could really be inside, stood misty in the rain. The road that wound along the foot of the hills came into view directly below this tent, sloping gently down from there toward our gate. The white building that served as the Americans' surgical hospital filled the scene to the right and directly ahead, burying one of its wings in the side of the hill. Behind the building the line of hills fell some distance back, delineating a saddle-shaped curve that ultimately thrust forward again beyond the right end of the building. This austere backdrop of green and gray remains imprinted in my mind's eye as clearly as a photograph.

A bulldozer came to widen the road, plowing back and forth in the rain. The operator turned his head and moved the control levers with jerky, robotlike motions. Rocks caught under the tracks crumbled resoundingly to bits. I watched in fascination, my heart sometimes with the rolling tracks, sometimes with the disintegrating rocks. At one point the bulldozer swung its blade around and came rolling and rolling all the way to our gate, filling in the huge puddles that mired the approach to the compound.

I decided to attempt a journey to the latrine. My legs were still weak, so I borrowed the broken wooden tent-pole my neighbor had scavenged for use as a crutch. Hanging onto the five-foot-long staff with both hands, I made my way forward as if poling a boat.

I discovered that the tent's center aisle had the same wavy bumps and indentations as the dirt-floored workrooms in old farmhouses back home. The natural result of human feet trampling moist earth was the same in the Philippines as in Japan.

To get to the latrines at the back of the compound, I had to pass through several other tents. I had heard excruciating groans coming from these tents, so I should have been prepared to encounter something quite different from my own tent, where the patients had relatively minor illnesses. But what I saw far exceeded anything I could have imagined.

In the tent for the most severely injured, bodies encased in all manner of grotesquely shaped casts lay in beds on both sides of the aisle. The sour smell of blood and medicine suffused the air.

My pen balks at attempting to detail the state of the mutilated bodies in that tent. For one thing, I must admit, I deliberately avoided looking at them too closely; but I also have no intention of writing about those twisted forms that happened to fall, willy-nilly, within my field of vision. Beginning with Jean Henri Dunant's *Un Souvenir de Solférino,* we possess innumerable records of such sufferings. Yet governments persist in making war, and no nation's coffers spill over with sufficient abundance to fully and adequately compensate disabled veterans for the rest of their lives. To persist in depicting their tragic figures under these circumstances would only compound the insult.

Only with the eyes of a doctor or a philanthropist can one confront suffering of this kind. But even the doctors were able to do no more than exchange a quick death for a slow one—or for a long life of wretched disability.

I could scarcely endure the stench of blood. Eventually I learned to take a deep breath before entering the tent and to pass through in a single burst as though swimming the length of the tent under water. Even then, I could not always make it through without breathing. Someone would call to me, and I would have to stop. It would be one of the patients with a lesser injury, relatively speaking, and he would ask me to empty his urine jar or bedpan for him. Wary of the gratuitous cruelties the Japanese orderlies made a habit of inflicting on them in their helplessness, these patients were reduced to begging assistance from a chance passerby, even one who was clinging with both hands to a wooden staff.

Grasping the handle of the urine jar together with my staff, I made my way through the rain across the boards bridging the mud between the tent and the latrines. Lined up in two even rows were eight wooden boxes with holes cut in their tops like Western-style toilets. These had been placed at seat height over deep pits dug in the ground. A swatch of tent canvas made a simple roof overhead to keep off the rain. All four sides were exposed to the world, but of course, I had discarded my usual feelings of modesty upon becoming a prisoner.

This spot where the latrines were gave the most commanding view of the fence that surrounded us. Foot-thick palm logs cut into ten-foot pillars were planted twelve feet apart in a row, and horizontal strands of barbed wire stretched between them at intervals of about eight inches. Back at my bed the other tents blocked my view, making it impossible to see more than a thirty- to thirty-five-foot section right by the gate, and in fact, my main impression of the fence there was that I was glad it allowed me a clear view of the outside. Here at the latrines, however, with nothing else around, I had an unobstructed view of the fence surrounding the back of the compound. Beyond the fence, the marshland, with its patches of wet earth poking out among scattered clumps of swamp grass, stretched across to the hills rising on the far side of the valley.

In light of the atrocities committed by our troops against the local citizenry, I realized that the fence served more to protect us than to prevent our escape, but it was nevertheless a fence. Though in my own case illness was a greater constraint than the barbed wire, there could be no doubt that the vague melancholy I felt came from the presence of that fence. I wondered if it would always remain only a feeling of melancholy.

At the right, the fence turned a corner toward the rear of the power station on the neighboring lot, and the hills bordering the front of the marshland came circling out beyond. Islanders' homes, a jumble of nipa houses and shabby little painted wood structures, extended in a haphazard line along the base of the hills. Protruding above the top of one of the hills, like something out of an otherworldly dream, stood a building with a Renaissance-style dome. Beneath the faded green of the rounded roof, a series of white columns punctuated an equally faded pink wall. I guessed it to be a church.

I liked the churches I had seen in the Philippines. The sight of their friable chalkstone structures, faded from exposure to the tropical rains and sun, soiled and crumbling, had given me great comfort as I drifted from one day to the next, tormented by premonitions of defeat and death.

The Romanesque facades and bell towers we passed in the towns along the road from Manila to Batangas had a certain somber yet splendid beauty of a kind I had not seen in the much plainer, imitation-Gothic facades of Catholic churches in Japan. When viewed from the sea, the dome of the church in Batangas that rose high over the surrounding town joined the cone of the isolated volcano towering above the highlands far beyond to bring a kind of desolate beauty to a scene that otherwise presented a lush tropical paradise.

To judge solely from the upper portion I could see protruding above the hills, the church in Tacloban was not a comparably spectacular structure. The curve of the dome and the bulk of the columns beneath it both looked like cheap efforts to affect the dignity characteristic of capitol buildings far and wide. If its reds and greens had not been faded, the effect would no doubt have struck me as quite hideous. Nevertheless, this dome was the sole vestige of "culture" that found its way into my life at the POW hospital. My somewhat unnecessarily frequent trips to the latrine were in large part to contemplate the fence and gaze at this dome.

After emptying the contents of the urine jar and rinsing it out, I would set it on the drying rack and pick up a dry jar to take back in its stead. Holding my breath, I dropped the jar off at the patient's bed and hurried on through the stench of blood as swiftly as I could. Back at my own bed, I flopped down exhausted, my heart pounding furiously.

———

It rained day in and day out. Mindoro had been dry, but on Leyte the wet season was in full swing. As with the rainy season in Japan, water fell from the sky almost without cease, sometimes accompanied by gusting winds that drove it in upon my pillow, sometimes crashing down in torrents, occasionally easing to a soft drizzle. If by chance the downpour took a short break in the evening, I could sometimes see, between an opening in the tents, a tiny red sunset like the embers of a fire lingering beneath the low dark clouds. Gradually its colors would dim and fade away as though absorbed by the clouds. Then the deluge would resume.

At night I lay alone within my own little mosquito net, but I seldom found myself bored with this nocturnal solitude. Since being called up for service, I had spent countless hours in forced idleness, after lights out or when standing watch, and I had grown quite accustomed to passing such solitary hours in contemplation and thought. In all my life, I had never been so contemplative as in the military.

Now I found myself returning repeatedly to the question of what had really kept me from shooting that young GI in the mountain meadow. No matter how many times I replayed the scene in my head, I could not determine whether my actions through the entire encounter remained consistent with my decision beforehand to refrain from shooting. In fact, in spite of the consensus that will is the most basic element of human consciousness, each new effort at introspection seemed only to obscure further the shades of my intentions. Set against the inner quickening I had experienced when I decided to die without shooting my opponent, it was deeply vexing to be forced to accept this gap in my understanding of the event.

It was then that I was visited by a most eccentric idea: Perhaps it was the voice of God that had prompted me to hold my fire, and perhaps Divine Providence had been responsible for the shots that rang out and turned the GI's steps away at the very moment I might have ceased to heed that voice.

Concepts such as "the voice of God" and "Divine Providence" had been familiar to me since my youth. While attending a Christian missionary school in Tokyo at the age of thirteen, I was moved by the teachings of the Bible and became a believer (that is to say, I believed that I believed). My faith was quite feeble, however, collapsing strengthlessly when I discovered the nature of human egotism, so copiously delineated in modern literature, and witnessed the hypocrisy of the church elders. I had wondered ever since whether having been drawn to God in my formative years had permanently altered the fundamental inclinations of my heart; and even as my beliefs continued to turn yet farther away from God, it troubled me that my adolescent infatuation with Him might have left me with a lasting weakness.

The ideas that came to me in my hospital bed were therefore no more developed than the naive notions of God and Providence that had taken shape in my head as a young boy, and they could hardly stand the test of close examination against the actual events of the encounter. Still, it did not seem impossible that some kind of link existed between those inclinations of my heart that had drawn me to God early in my life's journey and those that made me decide not to fire on my enemy in the Philippine mountains.

When the American army chaplain visited our compound one day, he had with him several copies of the Bible. I asked for one and began rereading the first two gospels, wondering what my impression of them would be now.

Not surprisingly, my response to rereading the life of Jesus was utterly different from my response twenty years earlier. Even in the words of disciples so innocent as to present accounts of miraculous cures that were patently absurd I could sense the strength and remarkable gifts of the personality that came so vividly alive in the gospels and that had inspired their writing. The strength and gifts were indeed most worthy of one called the Son of God. At the same time, it astonished me to discover that Jesus' teachings were penetrated through and through with the primitive belief that the end of the world was imminent. What could I have thought of this barbarism at the age of thirteen? I had not the slightest recollection. I could but assume I had been moved instead by Jesus' teachings of love. Now, however, those teachings impressed me only for their supreme rhetorical genius. My heart had donned a heavy coat of armor.

I was struck, too, by the ubiquity of paradox in the Sermon on the Mount and Jesus' other inspirational teachings. "Love your enemies," he taught, but he failed to indicate the nature of those enemies. To my mind, paradox has always been the philosophy of the weak. In one sense or another it embodies a submission to the accepted truths against which it purports to rebel. "Render unto Caesar the things that are Caesar's" is Jesus' sole teaching with direct practical implications, but unless the "Kingdom of God" of which he spoke is indeed immediately at hand, one could scarcely take a more abject stance. No wonder Caesar ultimately adopted Jesus' teachings and flourished all the more.

I realized dolefully that I had fallen in thrall to paradox at the age of thirteen. Though Christianity had to be credited with awakening my mind as a youth, it had also instilled in me an affinity for paradox. That I subsequently developed a habit of contrarian thinking, always rebelling inwardly against one thing or another, is surely no unrelated accident. Yet if my rebellion never went beyond inner defiance, then it meant I had been nothing but a coward.

Ultimately, I had to conclude thus: Though my adolescent attraction to the God of Jesus might indeed have played a role in giving me certain humanistic propensities, the supposition that those propensities had suddenly put in an appearance at a crucial moment after having been repudiated for twenty long years simply did not hold up. A habit of mind gained from the twentieth-century vogue for bringing to light the underlying continuities in a person's biography led me to hypothesize such a turn, but when I examined my actual feelings and beliefs, I could find no valid evidence to support it. There is no reason boyhood fancies cannot pass with boyhood; regardless of how much the ideas that came to me in the hospital resembled beliefs I held as a boy, it did not necessarily follow that what I experienced at the time of the actual encounter was a sudden resurgence of my boyhood humanism, or of any other naive notions I might once have held.

Still, there can be no denying that as I lay contemplating the encounter in my sickbed, the idea of deliverance by God took powerful hold of my heart and mind: If God looked favorably on the decision I had made with the humblest of intentions, He surely would have watched over me from heaven to make certain that I carried through my resolve. And when He saw me yielding to my primal instincts and began to doubt whether I would stay the course, there was nothing to prevent Almighty God from causing shots to ring out in another quarter, thereby removing temptation from before me.

I could apply the same reasoning to the abruptness with which I had abandoned my long-held presumption that I would kill any enemy I might encounter. This little miracle could most easily be explained by supposing that God had sent a message to me with his soundless voice saying, "Don't shoot." And why had God blessed me with such favor? Because He loved me.

Needless to say, I could not possibly subscribe to such a self-serving view today. At the time, however, as a bedridden prisoner groping for understanding from within my POW's daze, this God-as-my-deliverance theology brought a welcome measure of comfort. I even came perilously close to believing again—had not the utter egocentricity of that theology stood in the way. To be sure, it might conveniently explain how my own rifle had remained silent in the encounter with the young GI, but it failed to address in any way what was even then being repeated on countless other battlefields of the war.

This is why I chose not to introduce the self-styled theology I developed in the hospital when I wrote of the encounter in chapter 1. Though the temptation was there, I did not wish at that point to tarnish my account of the event—an event that proved truly fateful for me—with the absurd ideas I had silently nurtured at a later time on my sickbed. After repatriation, I came across the following highly apt passage in *Tannishō*, written by a disciple of the Buddhist priest Shinran:

> His Eminence said, "It is not from goodness of heart that you do not kill. A man of different karma might kill a hundred or a thousand quite in spite of wishing not to kill." We think that if we have good hearts it is good for our salvation, and if we have evil hearts it is bad for our salvation, but we forget that none but the mysterious power of Amida's original vow can save us. That is what His Eminence was saying.

These words seemed to apply so well to my situation that I used it as an epigraph for chapter 1.

My present thinking about the encounter goes roughly like this: Japan's industrialists sought to solve their economic crisis through expansion on the continent, and the Japanese Imperial Army recklessly embraced their cause. This ultimately led to my arrival in the Philippines armed with a Model 38 rifle and a single hand grenade. Meanwhile, Franklin Delano Roosevelt determined to save the world for democracy by means of military force, and this brought that innocent young man into the meadow before me with an automatic rifle in hand. Thus were we placed in the position of having to kill each other, even though neither of us had any personal reason for wishing the other dead. Government policies had ordained our encounter on the battlefield—though we had not necessarily had any voice in choosing those government policies.

At that moment, on that battlefield, the will to reject the use of my weapon unexpectedly asserted itself within my psyche. This was possible because I had been left all alone by my hastily retreating brethren and could now make my own decisions about what I would or would not do. Love of humanity, primal instincts, and even God may indeed have played a role in determining my psyche at the time, but they were no more relevant to determining my actions than they would be at the moment a soldier kills his enemy.

Ultimately, all I can establish with certainty is the existence of a moment in which I did indeed forsake the opportunity to shoot my state-designated "enemy." I believe the most crucial determinant lay in the fact that he was not an enemy of my own choosing—which is to say, in effect, that my action had been predetermined before I ever departed for the battlefield.

The man I faced at that moment was not my enemy. The enemy existed, and still exists, in another quarter.

Understandably, my Bible drew the Americans' interest. Was I a Christian? they wanted to know. Where had I learned English? And so forth. It pleased them immensely when I told them I had studied at a missionary school run by one of the American denominations. A note of special friendship seemed to soften their eyes. I could never have imagined such an odd turn of events—that the middle school I had chosen entirely by chance should reap benefits for me when I became a POW so many years later.

The senior doctor gave me his particular attention and often stayed to chat after completing his rounds. A gentleman in the British mold, he stood quite tall, with a relatively small head. His age was thirty-seven, effectively my own age. He sought out my political views, and I openly expressed my hatred for our military government. He brought me a copy of Ambassador Joseph C. Grew's *Ten Years in Japan,* along with a wide variety of other books and magazines. I learned what had actually happened in the Battle of the Philippine Sea, and I also read about the fall of Manila.

The doctor pressed me to relay this information to the other prisoners. Though I did not doubt that he meant well—he wanted all of the Japanese prisoners to have access to the truth—I was loath to undertake the task. In their present circumstances, what could it profit them to learn that the Battle of the Philippine Sea had brought defeat for Japan rather than victory? Compelling them now to face the inevitability of defeat could serve no purpose but to exacerbate their misery. Most of the prisoners obviously still clung to the hope of a Japanese victory, even though they knew it would make life after repatriation intolerable for anyone who had been a POW. I decided merely to tell my closest neighbor what I had read and leave it at that. If he chose to pass the word on to his neighbor, that was his concern.

The doctor turned to the nisei interpreter standing beside him and said, "It's men like this who must lead the Japan of tomorrow."

I felt insulted. Though I had nothing but contempt for our recent politicians, I also believed that politics was a complex art requiring abilities and energies far beyond my own. It irked me that they would take so light a view of contemporary Japan as to think a person like me could be a leader. It was not until I saw the broad-ranging democratic reforms initiated by the Americans after my repatriation that I realized my notion of politics had been a considerable distance removed from theirs. The doctor was merely saying that I had the qualifications to stand for election as a town councilman.

This doctor, who was from Chicago, impressed me as a man of quality more than any other American I met while a prisoner. That I pictured him as a descendant of the original *Mayflower* Puritans was no doubt an excess of imagination; but he knew how to articulate his moderate and well-reasoned views effectively (he believed our emperor should be permitted to retain his position), and in his bedside manner he demonstrated a warmth and solicitude quite different from the professional stoicism so typical of other doctors. I learned it had been entirely through his efforts that conditions in the POW hospital had become as good as they were. In the way he walked, the way he wore his hat, the way he gestured—in all he did, he affected an offhandedness that reminded me of characters I had seen in American movies; these mannerisms seemed to stand in odd contrast to his solemn personality.

The bespectacled chaplain also visited me from time to time. He brought me copies of a prayer book and a Bible-reading schedule that had been prepared for American servicemen, and he inquired about my faith. I contemplated asking for his thoughts on my encounter with the GI and why I had held my fire, but my long-standing aversion to men who make religion their profession won out. Knowing he and the other Americans would most likely rejoice in my story also made it harder to speak up. In the end I simply explained that I had developed a curiosity about God because my illness had weakened me so. He assured me that curiosity, too, was a way of seeking.

While at that hospital I spoke at length with one other American—an MP who stood guard at the gate. Because the water in the Lister bag (a large bag holding drinking water, which was made of rubberized canvas and had several stopcocks at the bottom) was constantly turbid due to the neglect of the Japanese staff, I often went instead to fetch water from a tank outside the gate. The MPs discovered that I could speak English when I asked permission to go out the gate (there was no barrier, just an opening), and they would sometimes stop me on my way back.

One night the young MP on duty seemed particularly intent on talking to me.

"My sergeant'll be coming by pretty soon, so you have to go inside for now, but come back out here and talk to me when he's gone," he said.

I gathered that the guards were forbidden to speak with prisoners. When I went back later, he offered me a cigarette and started showering me with questions about Japan. This fellow did not merely ask about "Fujiyama" or "geesha girls."

He was from New York City, and though only twenty, he was already out of college and married. He described the bustle of the city and its skyscrapers. I have never been especially impressed by the American penchant for boasting of the world's best-most-greatest this or that, but as I listened to his description of the skyscrapers turning five different colors in the setting sun, I could well imagine the beauty of the scene in which human artifacts mimicked nature.

"In America, relatives take care of your family when you go to war," he said. "Is it the same in Japan?"

I was taken aback. "Japanese culture has always emphasized the importance of family," I replied, "but we hear that family ties in America are weaker because of your emphasis on individualism. Isn't it backwards for an American to be asking how strong Japanese family ties are?"

At that point we heard footsteps on the road. He squinted into the darkness and whispered, "Get inside!"

The hour had grown late, so I lowered my mosquito net and lay down. Some time later, the MP came and thrust his hand under my net: He wanted to shake hands. He asked my name and told me his.

"I'll be on duty here again at ten tomorrow night, so come on out and we'll talk some more," he said as he left.

I could not suppress a smile. Why this young man had taken such an interest in me remained a puzzle, but I smiled because I could well imagine the satisfaction he found in shaking hands and exchanging names with a prisoner. Not one American soldier I encountered during my captivity treated me with anything but the greatest courtesy, but this was the sole instance that anyone offered me his hand.

Unfortunately, he failed to appear at the promised time the next night. I lay awake and watched for the changes of guard at midnight and 2:00 A.M. but to no avail. Nor did he appear the following night or the night after that, and though I continued to keep an eye out for him, I never saw him standing guard at our gate again. I can only surmise that he was assigned to new duties. At any rate, I lost forever the chance to discuss with this fine young man the differences between Japanese and American families.

Sometime later, I read an article about a GI on Saipan who was trying to get a group of Japanese civilians in a cave to surrender; a lone Japanese soldier hiding among them threw a hand grenade and killed him. For some reason the story reminded me of this young MP guard. Americans are quick to throw caution to the wind. I can still picture the guard's face, shaded by his steel helmet in the dim light by the gate, his rounded cheeks and ski-jump nose just barely visible. I remember only that his given name was Jack.

———

The rains persisted. My temperature dropped back to normal in a week but still left me drained of strength, so it was a while longer before I could walk without leaning on a staff. As soon as I was on my own feet again, I abandoned the clipped, marching gait they had drilled into us in the army and returned to my former open stride. I noticed how the Americans thrust their legs forward in broad, rhythmic steps, and I imitated them. It gave me a kind of dark pleasure to sweep away the vestiges of my slave days by adopting the manner of the enemy in this way.

I was also beginning to feel once again the joy of life. For one thing,

I had the books the doctor gave me to read. I had read almost nothing since being called into active service in March of the year before. What a wondrous thing the written word is!—even if it records a foreign tongue only half understood.

I had not had any significant contact with the English language since college, but because it shared many of its words with French, I found I could follow the gist of what the author was saying. (I had been amazed to discover, when captured and suddenly surrounded by Americans, that I could still speak English. Necessity is the mother of all things.) Having no dictionary forced me to rely on context to determine meanings for many of the words, but that proved to be a perfect way to kill time. Since I had more magazines than books, I read every ad, referring to the pictures to help me guess the meanings. The way language establishes a word (or several words) to correspond to an object is an extraordinarily beautiful thing. In the case of a foreign language, the attraction is further enhanced by novelty.

I spent my days perusing magazines and detective novels the doctor had brought me. As I began reading again after having passed a more elemental, animal-like existence for a year, I was struck by how heavy-handed American journalists could be in their efforts to captivate their readers, but I confess that I yielded willingly and with delight. Over the next six months, I gamboled about in the world of this vulgar literature ten hours a day, even as I regarded it with scorn in my heart. I do not doubt that it has left its mark on my consciousness in one way or another. The bulk of this record of my life as a POW essentially reports those events that periodically managed to startle me from the cloud of desultory reading that so absorbed me.

One day, about ten days after my arrival at the hospital, I recognized a man from my unit on Mindoro among a group of newcomers gathered in front of the medics' tent. He had been with the detachment originally stationed at Bulalacao, but because he had contracted malaria, he had remained with us in our mountain encampment instead of going with his platoon to the ridge overlooking San Jose. On the morning of January 24, he had departed with the column of ambulatory ill and civilians who evacuated just before the American attack.

I felt again the surge of shame I had experienced when I arrived at the hospital and faced my compatriots as a prisoner for the first time. This time the sensation might even have been described as approaching terror. The appearance of this unexpected intruder from the world I had left behind felt as eerie as encountering an actual ghost from the past. I had seen and heard enough at the time of the American attack to conclude that the evacuees had all gone to their deaths. Curiously, in spite of my own safe deliverance as a prisoner, it had never occurred to me that others from my unit might have survived.

Lest I mistake someone else for him, I took a closer look at his emaciated face, now scraggly with a beard. There could be no doubt. Still, I could not immediately bring myself to go out to greet him; instead, I shrank back to observe him from where I lay. He stood gazing shiftily into the prison tents with a moronic grin on his face. The smile reflected such innocent jubilation that no one could have wished to awaken him from it.

His family owned a farm west of Tokyo, but he had taken up bamboo craft and was apparently making a very good living at it when he received his induction notice. He was thirty-four. Though quite tall and athletic in build, he had a dull manner and possessed none of the tactfulness necessary to win favor with his superiors in the military. Lacking distinction in any way, he applied himself mutely to his tasks, contracted malaria like everyone else, and went with the majority when they evacuated. He now represented my first source of news about those evacuees.

Failing to notice me and still with that same grin on his scraggly face, he disappeared into one of the farthest tents. His right arm was bandaged and in a sling, but he apparently had no other injuries; his steps seemed strong and firm. As he moved away, his broad jostling back seemed to emit an unashamed cry of joy: "I'm saved!"

I could not go on maintaining my distance indefinitely. In particular, I needed to inquire what had happened to my sergeant and squad mates who had evacuated with him. After allowing a reasonable interval for him to get settled, I asked one of the Japanese orderlies where he had been placed and paid him a visit.

I found him on his back in the tent used by the Japanese staff, at the rear of the compound. As I approached his bed, he lifted his head and greeted me with a "Hey!" as if it were the most natural thing in the world—though his smile did seem a trifle awkward. He had taken a bullet through his right hand. He gave the following account of the evacuation party's fate:

The column included ten signal corpsmen besides the approximately fifty civilians and ambulatory ill from my unit, which brought the total to around sixty. Our company commander had given them a pep talk as they were preparing to move out.

"The rest of us will make our stand against the Americans here while you withdraw to Ridge 517 to assist the platoon there in carrying on observation of enemy activities. If there are any among you who wish to die with me here, now is the time to step forward." About five of the younger men stepped out, but my informant did not.

As the evacuees marched up the side of a mountain about two kilometers out, machine-gun fire suddenly swept their ranks. The carabao bearing their communications gear fell crashing into the valley, and the men scattered in every direction, taking cover in twos and threes in the underbrush. About fifty of them reassembled after dark and commenced trekking northward, hoping ultimately to cross over to Luzon. My squad sergeant was now in command. Their number dwindled further as roughly five more men dropped from the column during each night's march. Then one day, when they stopped on a riverbank to cook their tiny ration of rice, guerrillas attacked. Without pausing even to grab their rifles, most of the men plunged into the water and fled across the river. My informant, however, was immobilized (as he put it) by a bullet to the hand and fell prisoner. His captors took him to a village along the coast, then transported him by boat to the field hospital in San Jose. After receiving treatment for his wound there, he had been airlifted to the Leyte hospital, just like myself.

No one else was wounded in the attack. Needless to say, he could not tell me what had subsequently happened to those who escaped across the river. When I asked him about S, the one I was most concerned about, he said he turned up missing after their first night's march.

The bullet had entered from the back of his hand and had torn a large exit hole in his palm. Severed nerves had paralyzed two of his fingers.

"No more bamboo craft," he said, but he did not seem especially upset about it.

He had already become acquainted with the prisoner in the bed next to him, who had helped him get settled. As a matter of courtesy, I asked if I could do anything for him, told him where he could find me, and then took my leave.

As with my neighbor, this man and I really had nothing to talk about. Being from different platoons, we had never been on particularly familiar terms, but even so I was disappointed that I failed to experience the dramatic joy of reunion I had seen described in novels. I knew why I could not feel such joy, but I did not know why he did not.

After that, I looked in on him from time to time when returning from the latrine, and he made special trips to visit me at my bed on two or three occasions, but the visits never went beyond the bounds of courtesy calls.

Though we continued to live together within the same prison fences during the ten months from then until our repatriation, we remained the most indifferent of acquaintances. In fact, his indifference did not apply only to me, for he paid little attention to any of the twenty-odd men from our company who ultimately came to the same POW camp. He did not smoke, but instead of sharing his ration of cigarettes with men from his outfit, he traded with the prisoners around him for candy and soap. He ate the candy immediately but stockpiled the soap.

The news about S saddened me immeasurably. S had been my best friend and the one who had helped me believe we could escape from the Philippines after the Americans forced us from our refuge. Knowing that he suffered from malaria at the time of the attack, though, I could not imagine that he had had the strength to survive by himself in the mountains once he had fallen from the column. He had believed categorically in his safe return and had spoken of it with such confidence that he made me truly believe no bullet could strike him down. But of course, it had been nothing but delusion.

———

Still the rains continued. The bulldozer started laboring in the marshland behind the compound, and before long a new swatch of land had been filled in. Gigantic crates the size of small sheds were stacked in rows, and gyroplanes began landing and taking off from a short airstrip on the other side.

An air-raid siren occasionally sounded at night and all of our lights would be blacked out. The sky overhead remained undisturbed by the characteristic putter of Japanese warplanes, however, and the alert would soon be canceled. One time, after such a warning in the night, the light of dawn revealed a tower of black smoke rising far away beyond a hill—from a burning fuel tank, we guessed. It continued for two or three days. Many of the prisoners stood endlessly in the rain along the fence by the latrines, watching the smoke climb into the sky.

The power generator next door broke down and fell silent for twenty-four hours. Taking advantage of the quiet, a tent in which most of the patients had only minor wounds organized a talent show: A man with a limp, a man without an arm, a man who had lost part of his shoulder, and so forth, giving their off-key renditions of old folk songs from home. Talent shows were an army tradition that I found even more distasteful than duty assignments, and this particular talent show of cripples, held in the dim light of a POW hospital tent, proved more than I could stomach. Our temporary reprieve from the accustomed roar brought me no pleasure; it only magnified my misery. I hurried back to my bed.

4

Sunny Palo

The Americans announced a relocation of the hospital. The new site would be on the far edge of Palo, two kilometers to the south. Unlike our present compound, the hospital there would be surrounded by forest, they said, and the facilities would be better. In anticipation of the move, each prisoner received a new issue of pajamas, U.S. Army fatigues, and a towel. All of our current doctors and medics were scheduled to be replaced.

I do not remember the exact date, but the move took place around the middle of February. Fortunately the rains gave us a break that day, and we even had the sun peeking through openings in the clouds from time to time. The patients in casts left first by ambulance; those of us with lesser afflictions followed by truck. Amidst the bedlam before departure, I fetched some water for one of my neighbors who was nursing a leg injury and then lent him my shoulder as he made his way to the truck. Immediately afterward, I noticed my heart pounding at an furious rate. It seemed to be rattling away all by itself, quite without connection to the rest of my body—a very odd sensation indeed. I climbed into the truck with a feeling of mounting disquiet.

The senior doctor brought me a new stack of books and stood by the gate to see us off. Several of the prisoners paused to salute him on their way to the truck.

"Sank-yoo," they said in heavily accented English.

I discovered then that this doctor's kindness had touched other prisoners besides myself.

A gyroplane broke through the clouds and came in for a landing.

"Oh, no," the doctor joked. "Now you've all seen our secret weapon." He laughed.

The truck started up. It circled around the base of Lookout Hill and continued on up the winding gravel road, which led us from the valley into town and ended at a large highway. Vehicles of all kinds raced in both directions at uniform speed, one after another, as if carried on conveyor belts. Soon our truck, too, found a place in the procession.

Local residents came rushing out of their houses along the highway and shouted something at us, slicing their hands horizontally across their throats as they yelled. I suppose they meant we were going to get our heads chopped off. It was a new experience for me but obviously not for them; they seemed to be doing it as an automatic reflex, from force of habit rather than from any deep-seated feelings of enmity. We put our hands to our throats and made the same gesture. It seemed to catch them by surprise for a moment, but then they raced after us with renewed shouts and brandished fists.

The road proceeded through the flatlands, crossed a muddy river, and entered a dense jungle zone. We came upon a row of barracks. Nurses in high heels and GIs wearing dark red hospital gowns walked about this way and that. An octagonal gazebo stood in what appeared to be a recreational area. This was apparently the new American hospital.

We stopped at an office of some kind for roll call and then started up again. After threading our way among towering palms and other trees for a while longer, we finally arrived at a compound surrounded by a tall barbed-wire fence.

Besides having a higher fence than our former hospital and a gate with a secure barrier, the facilities inside were also far superior. Two rows of five rectangular "hospital tents," all the same size, stood in the middle of the compound with ample space between them and the fence. The tents even had wooden floors. At the back were a serving station, showers, and latrines, but a single tap also delivered running water directly to each of the tents. One row of tents was the surgical section; the other, internal medicine. In the center of each tent was a medic station with American personnel always on duty.

The compound had obviously been carved right out of the jungle, which came all the way up to the fence. Beneath the deep-green canopy of trees towering overhead was a dense tangle of underbrush and smaller trees in paler shades; birds I could not identify flew out of the underbrush and darted back and forth along the fence. The air was deliciously clear, and except for explosions from nearby roadwork that shook the tents from time to time, the surroundings were completely quiet. Having grown accustomed to the constant roar of generator motors, it was almost too tranquil.

We received tent assignments, but then we were free to choose our own beds. It took until evening to unfold cots, distribute blankets, and install wires for hanging our mosquito nets. When food arrived for our evening meal, the portions were small—less than half the size we had received before.

The food came from a central mess, measured out according to the patient census. The servings struck me as roughly equivalent to what I had received at the field hospital on Mindoro. For men trying to recover not only from wounds but from long-term nutritional deprivation as well, I doubt any amount of food would have seemed adequate. The serving sizes, which remained unchanged for quite some time, became the single most acutely felt hardship among the POW patients after we moved to the new hospital.

Under these circumstances, the Japanese orderlies' and food servers' egregious abuse of their positions rose to new levels. On grounds that they provided vital services for everyone in the hospital, they claimed the right to eat their fill by skimming from the others' rations. Then they turned around and railed at the starving patients who fought over the trays with the largest portions, and they pounced viciously on anyone caught scavenging in the bin of scrapings afterward.

Infuriated by the servers' hoarding of food, the American medics spread the word that anyone who did not get enough to eat should speak up, but of course, no one dared. We knew what to expect from the servers if we complained.

Because of my age and because I had long had a sensitive stomach, I suffered less than most. I did well enough, in fact, that I could sometimes share part of my meager ration with my new neighbor, a beriberi patient, whose manifest suffering I found painful to behold. In exchange, he took care of a variety of small tasks and scrounged extra cigarettes for me. Even after I moved to the regular POW camp later on, I always had someone like this who acted as my servant in exchange for food—until rations finally increased to more adequate proportions. Though hierarchy had mostly given way to egalitarian, democratic principles among the prisoners, I gained a measure of ascendancy, in effect, through a kind of natural selection.

I must confess, however, that I did not gain this new status entirely without cost. The need for less sustenance was only half the reason for my generosity; I was also putting on airs, after a fashion. My constant reading had already tagged me as a "different sort" among the prisoners. Most of those wounded on Leyte had been career soldiers, and almost none of them knew English. They regarded me with much the same suspicion as anyone reading a Western-language publication on the train was viewed back home at the beginning of the war. Surrounded by such eyes, I self-consciously retreated into my own bookish isolation. For better or for worse, this act of pride was the first thing to rise out of my POW's daze. And when I endured my own hunger in order to give food to someone else, that, too, was an act of pride.

The new hospital did not permit the lights inside the tents to be extinguished at night, and bright lights mounted atop the fence shone in from outside as well, so I could read however late I chose. Only when my eyelids started to droop did I pull the blanket up over my head and go to sleep.

And what sort of things did I read? I read detective novels in which five people would be murdered in the space of a hundred pages, or pulp magazine fiction about naive young maidens beguiling their way to fulfillment of their most cherished desires in a mere ten pages. My secret goal was to master English and build a foundation for reading Shakespeare in the original after my return to Japan, but in fact all I really mastered was the ability to kill time by skimming my way through vulgar novels in the Armed Services Editions series and the like. Worse, I was letting it go to my head.

The elevated heartbeat I experienced at the time of the move continued to weigh on my mind. When I tested myself by walking from one end of the tent to the other and back, I discovered that my pulse rose abnormally even after such ordinary activity. Similarly, just two or three sit-ups in bed were enough to set my heart pounding.

When the doctor came on his rounds, I described my symptoms. He listened with his stethoscope more carefully than usual.

"You have a murmur, and I think your heart is enlarged," he said after finishing his examination.

Two or three days later another doctor came. He was introduced to me as a heart specialist, and he soon confirmed the first doctor's diagnosis.

"The blood flows backwards," he explained. "It's because of an abnormality in one of the valves. The condition is congenital, just like the features on your face, and your malaria has merely aggravated it."

A little later, a medic came to run an electrocardiogram. Although my newest blood test showed that I was completely healed of malaria, this newly discovered heart condition postponed my release from the hospital.

The abnormality was declared untreatable, but this actually became something of a badge of honor for me, since I had been feeling rather awkward going about among men who had lost their arms or legs while I myself suffered neither from injury nor from any particular pain. And more than anything else, I was grateful for the delay in being transferred to the regular POW camp where I would have to take up work responsibilities. In the meantime I could go on enjoying my reading in the peace and quiet of the hospital.

A heart condition, however, takes a grinding toll on one's nerves. I tested myself again to discover exactly how much activity brought on the elevated heartbeat, and I learned that I could walk the distance of five beds or do three sit-ups. I reduced my trips to the shower and latrine and made every effort to keep my other activities within these limits. Unfortunately, it was not long before I was forced to give up this self-imposed regimen.

————

One evening, about ten days after we moved to the new hospital, I got back from the latrine to find four or five new patients getting settled in their assigned beds. Among them was the emaciated and unspeakably forlorn figure of my former squad leader.

"Sergeant," I called, as I started toward him.

"So you're here, too, Ōoka," he said. "Man, they confiscated everything."

As the first words to emerge from a soldier's mouth upon arrival at a POW hospital, this struck me as a rather odd thing for him to say.

"What do you mean by 'everything'?" I asked.

"The briefcase and the watch and everything," he said.

I only barely managed to stifle a guffaw. To explain why, I must backtrack a little.

This sergeant was a veteran of the fighting on the continent in the late 1930s who had been called up for a second tour and was assigned to our squad at the time we were organized into transport parties for deployment to the front in June 1944. He was only thirty, but he treated us with kindness and he was an excellent drillmaster. We rejoiced among ourselves at our good fortune in having him as a leader. When we arrived in Manila, our transport unit was kept intact and sent directly to Mindoro, so we continued to enjoy his leadership. Because he was easygoing in his style of command and allowed relatively relaxed discipline, he became the most popular NCO in the company. Then, one time when our platoon was on a pacification mission and the bivouac site came under attack by guerrillas in the middle of the night, the sergeant was the only man to charge outside with our company CO to meet the attack. After that he rose to near-hero status in our minds.

Still later, however, when the Americans landed at San Jose and our unit sought refuge in the mountains, the sergeant's behavior took a decidedly strange turn. He went along on the first reconnaissance patrol to the San Jose area as second in command, but when one of the men fell ill, he eagerly volunteered to escort him back to camp. En route, the sergeant displayed no regard at all for the sick man's condition, marching him and the four others with them at nearly double time the entire distance. The sick man took to bed immediately and died five days later.

After that it was whispered about that the sergeant had cunningly

taken advantage of the man's illness to remove himself from the danger
zone. Soon, as malaria began to spread among the troops, it grew increasingly clear that the sergeant who had so bravely distinguished himself in
battling the guerrillas had now become extraordinarily protective of his own
life. He always kept his distance from any sick troops, refusing to sleep next
to anyone with a fever, and he even declined to attend wakes for the men
in his own squad who had succumbed to the disease. These precautions
were silly, conflicting as they did with our knowledge that malaria is carried
by mosquitoes—one of the most basic elements in our modern understanding of disease. His inordinate dread of sickness seemed to put the super-
stitions of an old country granny to shame. (He was, in fact, a farmer from
Saitama Prefecture.)

The sergeant's hypochondria also manifested itself in an extreme ob-
session with medical supplies. While serving a stint at the coastal outpost
where our boats landed when we were stationed at San Jose, he had bought
a large black leather briefcase from an islander, and he zealously guarded
it at all times. (He later admitted that the money for this purchase had come
from official funds, which he had embezzled with the help of a fellow sergeant, the paymaster from the Bulalacao platoon, who stopped by the outpost en route to San Jose on business of some kind. This was the briefcase
he told me had been confiscated.) Our medic angrily revealed to us that the
briefcase was crammed full of gauze bandages and other medical supplies.
Though regulations clearly prohibited anyone from hoarding such supplies,
on the march from San Jose the medic had found himself with too much
to carry, and he made the mistake of asking the sergeant for help. When
he later realized that some of his supplies were missing, he repeatedly asked
for their return, but the sergeant adamantly refused. Worse, he tried to keep
his stash of remedies secret from us, the members of his squad, and withheld them even when we were most in need. For example, he turned me
down flatly when I asked for some creosote pills to control the diarrhea that
accompanied my fever.

"Those are for pain, not for diarrhea," he insisted.

Thus, the man who had been a dream sergeant became a fiendish
nightmare for anyone who fell ill after our retreat into the mountains. Since
we all eventually came down with malaria, this made him the worst possible
squad leader to have.

The personal effects of those who died also went into the sergeant's
precious briefcase, including the watch he said had been confiscated. It was
an unusual watch, with a number showing the date changing each time the
hands went twice around—just the sort of newfangled gadgetry he would
take a liking to.

By claiming to have come down with malaria himself, the sergeant avoided being assigned to patrols or other duties that would take him away from camp, and at the end he joined the evacuation party for the ambulatory ill. (I could present ample evidence that his illness was feigned, but I will not try my readers' patience with the details.) When the evacuees moved out, he made one of his ailing privates shoulder the heavy briefcase, while he himself carried only a light haversack.

In essence, so long as we were stationed in San Jose, this NCO had served his superiors well and shown an unusually generous spirit toward the men under him. But the moment we went into retreat, he transformed himself abruptly into a sheer egotist who cared only for his own survival. He obviously intended to take home as his own both the briefcase purchased with public funds and the personal effects gathered from the men under him who had died.

He gave an uneventful account of his experiences after fleeing across the river and being separated from the soldier shot through the hand. He and the others with him wandered aimlessly about the mountains for about a month, growing weaker and weaker. Eventually, a persistent case of diarrhea robbed him of the strength to move, and the group was discovered and captured by guerrillas. He alone had been sent here to the hospital because of his diarrhea.

In the hospital, this mysophobe who had shunned all contact with the sick in the mountains quickly proved himself an impossibly demanding patient.

"I'll die if I don't have someone to take care of me," he whined. "You'll look after me, won't you, Ōoka?"

I had my own health to think of, however, and could not assent. I explained my heart condition to him and reassured him that his ailment was a common one from which he would recover in no time at all. He gazed back at me looking quite forlorn, but he did not press the matter right away.

When one of the Japanese orderlies came by a little bit later, though, he asked to move his bed next to mine. Fortunately, this request met with summary rejection. Just this once, I was grateful for the orderlies' callousness. I let the sergeant know that the orderlies would take care of his bedpan during the night, fixed his blanket, and hung his mosquito net. Then I returned to my bed.

I pondered the situation. The sergeant's bed was a considerable distance from mine, and going back and forth to take care of him would violate the regimen I had established to limit my exertions. But the fact that the man in question had been my immediate superior officer remained a sticking point. Of course, I ought not overestimate the debt I owed him for the kind of routine favors he granted me as my superior in the army, and I had ample reason to hold it against him that he had treated me so shoddily when

I was laid up with malaria. Even so, given his present condition, I could not very well ignore him altogether. The following day, I decided after some deliberation, I would bathe him, give him a shave, and help him get completely settled; after that I would turn him over to the care of others.

The sergeant, however, began demanding my attention that very night. As I started to doze off, I was awakened by a voice calling, "Ōoka! Ōoka!" I felt my gorge rising. Had I not explained that my condition prevented me from walking about? I ignored his calls.

I heard the footsteps of the orderly on duty, then voices:

"What's the matter?"

"There's a guy over there called Ōoka. Wake him up for me, will you?"

"What do you need? If you only need to go to the bathroom, I can take care of it."

"Just go wake him up."

The orderly came to summon me. Willy-nilly, I had to drag myself out of bed to go and see what the sergeant wanted. Sure enough, all he wanted was a urine jar.

"I'll get it," the orderly said and walked away.

I explained again. "Sir, if I were in good health, I would attend to your every need, but you must understand that my condition forbids me to engage in any more activity than absolutely necessary. I can't walk more than five beds without suffering from chest pains, so please don't ask me to do things for you."

"But I'll die if you don't look after me."

"You'll be fine. Everyone feels that way at first."

The orderly brought the jar. The sergeant rolled his body the other way to urinate but kept his head twisted toward me—I suppose to make sure I did not leave. I paid no attention.

"You'll be fine," I repeated curtly, and returned to my bed.

I called the orderly. "He'll probably tell you to wake me up again," I said. "But it's bound to be the same thing, so you can take care of it yourself. He was my sergeant, so I'd appreciate it if you could look after him in my stead. I can't blame him for feeling the way he does, but given my condition . . ."

"Don't worry," he said. "I won't disturb you again."

The next time I woke up, I could hear the sergeant arguing with the orderly. The orderly set a bedpan down forcefully enough to make a hard, metallic clang and walked away. Taking a rather cruel pleasure in the thought of the sergeant straddled uncomfortably across the pan, I drifted back to sleep.

The next morning I unhitched his mosquito net and folded his blanket. We ate breakfast together, sitting face-to-face on his bed. I traded his meat for my vegetables. I thought it too soon to try to take him to the showers, so I fetched some water and sponged his face and arms and legs. Quite in spite of myself, I felt my heart going out to him as I gently scrubbed at the grime encrusted on his skeletal feet—like the tenderness one feels when cuddling a small animal. These pangs of pity came from the physical warmth I could feel in his feet, shriveled as a chicken's, as I bathed them. I was touched by my own act—washing the feet of the man who had forced me, in my illness, to make my own way to the latrine on hands and knees. No other patient in the POW hospital received such attentive care, and I felt quite certain that the sergeant knew it.

"Thanks for all your trouble," he said, deliberately avoiding any mention of last night.

"Not at all. I'm only doing what I would do for any passerby in need," I said with a note of sarcasm. "And since I am also ill, this will be the end of my service for the day. Tomorrow I'll get those clothes washed for you."

He had not yet received his fatigues, so all he had besides his pajamas were a sullied shirt and pair of shorts the guerrillas had given him. He knew he would get the fatigues eventually, but he also knew army ways too well to be willing to give up any extra clothes he had in his possession. I had decided that I would offer to wash them for him.

"Then day after tomorrow I'll help you to the showers," I continued. "And that'll be all I can do for you. From there on out, you're on your own. That's the way it was for me and for everyone else here."

He seemed on the verge of tears, but I had not yet forgiven him for his cruelty in the mountains. He had proved himself an absolute egotist, and I determined not to be overly moved by his misery of the moment.

I will refrain from describing at length how relentlessly the sergeant demanded my attention after this. We were a fine pair: the former squad leader who thought diarrhea would kill him and his former grunt who trembled in fear over a heart condition. Try as I might, I could not get it into the sergeant's head that I had my own health problem to attend to. In the end, a PFC got to feeling so sorry for me that he burst out in rage at the sergeant. He was from the Sixteenth Division, so he spoke in Kyoto dialect (the Sixteenth was made up mostly of men from the Kyoto area).

"Give the guy a break," he yelled. "You can't work him like that just because he's a buck private. You'll kill him. You may have been his commander before, but you're a prisoner now, and that makes you equals. A lowly noncom like you has no business lording it over his men so high-and-mighty anyway."

After this, the sergeant finally started folding his own blanket and going to the latrine without leaning on my shoulder. The gratitude I felt toward the PFC for his outburst brought with it a few pangs of guilt, but if I had known then what my platoon's medic later told me—he had been with the sergeant at the time of his capture—I could have been spared any such burden of conscience.

"He was a real bastard," the medic said (this man was a native of Osaka). "First he flies down the path at this unbelievable pace, not caring a whit whether anyone can keep up. Then when he comes down with diarrhea, it's 'Carry my rifle,' 'Take my pack' all the time—suddenly expecting us to wait on him hand and foot. He always ate more than his fair share of rations. And when we finally got caught, it was all because he had diarrhea and couldn't move anymore. The bastard still had his hand grenade, but he wouldn't use it."

An ambiguous look crossed his face as he said this. Obviously, the medic himself owed his life to the fact that the sergeant had, for better or for worse, refused to throw his hand grenade at that juncture.

"And things didn't get any better after we got caught," he continued. "When we were being taken from Pinamalayan to San Jose on an American cutter, I woke up with a start in the night, and lo and behold, he's getting ready to hang himself right there in our cabin—trying to string himself up with a rope he'd made by tearing up a towel. 'Sergeant, you're a disgrace!' I said. 'I can't let you do that.' "

Another prisoner listening nearby spoke up at this point. "He probably wanted to kill himself because he was ashamed of being taken alive. What's so disgraceful about that?" The man's tone suggested he had taken considerable offense at the medic's words.

"Sure, fine, if that were really his reason, but actually he had just gotten sick and tired of the diarrhea. 'Don't be an embarrassment, Sergeant,' I said. 'If you want to kill yourself, that's your choice, but wait until we get there and you're healthy again and you can do it right. Think of all the trouble it'll make for me if you do something like that here."

The medic's logic started to sound a little shaky at this point, but this much was clear: In the eyes of the startled Osakan, the figure of the sergeant preparing to string himself up had been devoid of any qualities that could be called tragic. On the contrary, he had appeared merely ridiculous.

In our normal view, diarrhea represents an exceedingly weak motivation for suicide, but I suppose it was not entirely out of the question if the sergeant possessed some special sensitivity to his own physical condition. Given his inordinate fear of illness and death—which is to say, his extreme attachment to his body—I can understand how the ultimate expression of his physical suffering might take the form of an attempt to destroy his corporeal self. At any rate, his failure to make use of his hand grenade showed that this attempt at suicide could not have come from the shame of capture.

What hit me hardest in the medic's description was his account of the sergeant "flying" down the path without the least concern for whether anyone could keep up. It meant he had quite forsaken my friend S. Though I cannot criticize military men in general for behaving egotistically, when their lives are on the line, I have every right to despise the man who so heartlessly turned his back on my beloved friend.

One day the sergeant said to me, "When we get back home, let's you and me visit the families of the men who died in the mountains."

"And what're you going to tell them?" I retorted sarcastically. "Are you going to introduce yourself as the man who abandoned their sons beside the mountain path?"

As I have said before, however, in San Jose this incarnation of pure egotism had been the most loved and respected of all the squad leaders, and he had held the confidence of our company CO more than any other noncom. Our tour at San Jose was supposed to be a continuation of our basic training, and the instructional plan the sergeant submitted to the lieutenant was deemed virtually flawless. He had also shown courage in battle. Though I have already referred in passing to our pacification campaigns, perhaps a fuller account of his valor during these campaigns will at least in some small measure help to redeem this man's honor.

During the first ten days of October 1944, a detachment of three squads was sent out to bring the Sablayan area on the western shore of the island under our control. This was guerrilla territory, and we had observed clear indications that the insurgents were being supplied by American submarines. But the troops in the pacification force did not take the guerrillas seriously, regarding their mission as little more than a recreational junket for them to eat their fill of rice and pig; an earlier mission on the eastern coast had turned into just that when the guerrillas had pulled back to avoid confrontation. This time the men took along a great cooking pot, remembering how inconvenient it had been without one the time before, but in retrospect, perhaps this was carrying things a little too far. Their lack of alertness resulted in one man dead and three wounded. (Since I was code clerk, I did not participate in any of the pacification missions.)

The expedition found no guerrillas in the town of Sablayan, and the troops promptly slaughtered a pig, helped themselves to some local brew, and enjoyed a great banquet. They bivouacked that night at the town school, lighting a torch at the top of the front steps and placing a guard there to stand watch. At about 3:00 A.M., the kitchen detail got up to start a fire under the great pot, which had been installed next to the wing of the schoolhouse, about twenty yards to one side of the main entrance. Just as the flames leapt to life, a barrage of gunfire poured into the space between the kitchen fire and the watchman's torch.

Jarred awake by the thunderous racket of guns, the troops sleeping on the floor inside saw the air above them light up like fireworks as dozens of tracer bullets smashed into the ceiling. One man was hit in the side, another in the shoulder, and yet two more took bullets in their legs. One lucky fellow later claimed to have felt a bullet skim through his hair. (The man wounded in the side died after three days in the hospital at Batangas.)

The men hugged the floor as they scrambled to retrieve their rifles and helmets and other equipment, but no one was about to risk getting shot by venturing outside. All of a sudden, our squad leader leapt valiantly through the window and dropped to the ground outside. (I can envision exactly how he must have lain: The sergeant had a way of flattening himself on the ground like no other NCO I knew.) The shots were coming from the stand of trees about a hundred meters directly ahead. Each time they fell silent, a high-pitched whistle would sound, followed quickly by another volley.

By the light of the torch the guard had neglected to extinguish, the men inside the building saw that the lieutenant had preceded the sergeant outside and was pacing slowly from right to left across the school yard between them and the enemy. (The guard had simply abandoned the torch and run inside for cover; his sergeant later received a severe reprimand for this from the lieutenant.)

The sergeant began returning fire almost as soon as he hit the ground. "But it was tough with the lieutenant wandering back and forth in the way," he groused afterward. His solitary fire represented only the meagerest of responses, but it may well have saved the detachment from suffering heavier casualties. Almost as if his first shot were the signal, a long blast of the whistle pierced the air and the enemy volleys ceased. Guerrillas always do their utmost to avoid casualties. To them, the sergeant's shot represented the beginning of a Japanese counterattack.

The other men now emerged through the windows and began shooting, but they drew no return fire. Knowing it would be too dangerous to pursue the enemy in the dark, they dug foxholes under the school building, just deep enough to lie in, and remained on alert. Before long, rain began to fall, quickly collecting in the foxholes and miring everyone in mud. At daybreak no trace of the enemy could be found. The men dispatched to root them out came up empty-handed and transformed themselves into frustrated plunderers. The casualties were evacuated to the hospital in Batangas, the town's mayor and one of his clerks were taken prisoner on suspicion of having called in the guerrillas, and the detachment returned dispiritedly to San Jose.

"That must have taken real guts—to leap outside at a time like that!" I exclaimed in admiration.

The sergeant laughed. "If I'd stayed inside and they'd stormed the building, we would have all been killed anyway."

"But couldn't you have gone out the back window?"

"Whether I went out the front or the back, it was dangerous either way. And just think what it would have done to my reputation if I'd gone out the back." He laughed again.

To me at the time, he was a shining hero. So when he shrugged off my admiration by saying that they "would have all been killed anyway," I assumed he was merely being humble. I thought I saw in him something I did not have.

When I consider this incident against his conduct in the mountains later on, however, it becomes obvious that his words in no way reflected humility; rather, they accurately expressed his motive for leaping out that window. The other NCOs hesitating inside were also seasoned veterans of war on the continent, and they presumably had about as much experience at judging such situations as the sergeant. The difference was simply that their self-preservation instincts were not as strong. This exact same difference revealed itself again in the mountains when these other NCOs found themselves unable to turn a cold shoulder to their men the way the sergeant did with his.

That the sergeant did what the other NCOs could not bring themselves to do does suggest a quicker wit. For example, before he leapt out in the face of the bullets, he had managed to gauge the precise rhythms of the enemy's firing so that he knew when there would be a pause. In his ability to do this, we see another of his gifts, complementing his wisdom as an instructor and his easiness as a leader (these, too, reflect a kind of social wit). As a farmer from outside Tokyo, he presumably had acquired and nurtured this ability entirely during the war. However, this ability was not what pushed him out that window at the moment he judged to be safe. Sad to say, both for him and for everyone else, what pushed him out that window was pure survival instinct; it had nothing to do with love of country.

This union between egotism and courage is perhaps the most curious of the many abnormal compounds that make up the creature known as the professional soldier. Because that compound exists in a volatile state, it must be seasoned through experience in live combat.

(In recounting this episode, I have coincidentally described another example of courage—namely, that of the lieutenant, who wandered back and forth across the schoolyard in the direct line of guerrilla fire. For reasons I have detailed before, I regard his behavior as essentially manifesting a death wish, but I also believe his display of courage reflected a similar vanity. During Japan's expansion on the continent, a great many of our officers died meaningless deaths or suffered unnecessary wounds out of this kind of vanity. Ultimately, such vanity is merely a cheap counterfeit of real courage, and neither for the individual nor for his country do the resulting actions represent truly noble motives.)

The sergeant had not put himself up for promotion to the rank of NCO entirely of his own volition; the shortage of replacements when he was fighting on the continent had more or less compelled him to do so. As is widely known, however, the life of a noncom in the Japanese military offered far greater creature comforts than that of a small family farmer back home. For this sergeant in particular, it was certainly more attractive than returning to the farm to slave away submissively under an aging father who stubbornly clung to his position as head of the household. He chose instead to leave the farmwork to his younger brother while he waited comfortably in central China for his father's death. Conveniently for him, his father died in 1941, the year of his discharge, so he succeeded to the headship of the family and took a wife. He had not figured, however, on being called up again near the end of the Pacific War to take charge of a unit of green reservists. That was why he could so abruptly begin shirking his obligations to us as our sergeant.

As the sergeant's health improved, his attitude toward me chilled. From his perspective, I suppose he thought me contemptible for having forgotten the debt I owed him as my superior officer. But for my part, I had had quite enough of him. We gradually had less and less to do with each other, especially after being transferred to the regular POW camp and placed in different units. Like the man who had been shot through the hand, the sergeant spent his time alone, not associating with the men from his outfit. (As a rule, men of farm stock associated more with their new neighbors bunked near them than with their old comrades who had been assigned to different tents. To them it was a simple matter of necessity and convenience. The practice of making long excursions to distant tents in order to visit old comrades belonged to reservists who had been called up from salaried jobs.)

Among his new neighbors, the sergeant was regarded as a good natured, likable fellow. When he ran into anyone from his former outfit, though, he avoided their eyes. Perhaps in the starkly contrasting relationships he had with these two groups, we can see the true nature of this man who possessed such an inordinate fear of illness; perhaps the relaxed leadership he showed as squad leader and the courage he showed in battle were nothing more than costumes draped over his shoulders by his environment. I do not doubt that he is once again making out very nicely in the postwar environment as well, having installed a bread oven or some such and turned himself into a shrewd country black-marketeer.

I began my portrayal of the sergeant meaning to use him as a prototypical example of Japan's professional soldier, but the man I have described seems to have emerged as a unique character all his own—in essence a one-of-a-kind rural eccentric. Before moving on, I would like to record his physical traits. He was about five feet four inches in height, dark-skinned, not of an especially stocky build, but with a comparatively large, elongated head. He had slightly kinky hair, a broad forehead, bushy eyebrows over deep-set eyes, a slender nose, prominent cheekbones, and an undistinguished mouth. Though his face was tall and lean, his broad forehead made his eyes and nose and mouth seem a little too small, so he could not be described as good looking. On the whole, he gave the impression of being a gentle person. For our twice-daily roll calls in San Jose, he led us in singing the popular martial tune, "Across the Sea," instead of reciting from the Imperial Rescript to Soldiers and Sailors, but he had a weak voice and could not carry a tune.

―――――

Not long after the sergeant, another man who had evacuated with him arrived at the hospital—a member of the weather unit that had been stationed with us at San Jose. He came from a farm family in Ōita Prefecture and had been drafted directly into active duty in 1944. A quiet, light-skinned youth with European features, he was indisputably the most handsome man in our midst. Rumor had it that the sergeant of the weather unit was fond of young men and tried repeatedly to seduce him, even after we had retreated into the mountains.

The meteorologist still had a bullet lodged in his left ribs, but at a glance he appeared quite hardy, and he described the circumstances of his capture at considerable length. Constrained by their sense of shame, most of the POWs found it difficult to speak in any detail about how they had come to be captured. In light of this, it would be remiss of me not to record this soldier's rare account here.

When the man from the Bulalacao platoon got shot in the hand, the meteorologist was among those who fled across the river, but he and the sergeant who was in love with him and one other soldier got separated from the group that escaped with my former sergeant. After straggling through the mountains for four or five more days, the three of them were suddenly ambushed from behind on a path in the jungle. The two others, walking ahead of him, took off running, but my informant tripped and fell on an exposed tree root. Now he heard more gunshots from the direction the two others had gone. To his right was forest, to his left a meadow. Beyond the meadow, perhaps three hundred paces across, stood more forest. He said he did not know why he chose to run across the meadow instead of diving into the underbrush at this point. (If I were to hazard a guess, I'd say he knew from the gunshots he had heard in both directions that he would likely encounter more of the enemy in the forest, whereas a single glance told him there was no one at all in the meadow.)

As he ran he heard bullets zip by his ears, and though he thought some of them might actually be coming from in front of him rather than behind, he could not very well stop in the middle of the meadow. Racing full tilt into the forest on the other side, he began pushing his way through the underbrush. He came upon a pond, circled around it, and started to proceed in the same direction, but then heard voices approaching from that way as well and threw himself to the ground in a patch of tall grass.

Now the voices seemed to approach from every side. They were apparently all Filipinos. One of them was whistling. The meteorologist no longer had a rifle, so when the footsteps came closer, he leapt to his feet and made a mad dash for the pond, which seemed to offer the only refuge. He dove head-first for the water; a powerful jolt stung his chest as he flew through the air. His face skidded into mud, and when he shook his head to extract it from the mire, he broke the surface right away: The pond turned out to have been no deeper than his forearm. He struggled to stand but felt like a huge weight pinned him down across the chest. Feet sloshed through the water as he flailed back and forth, and the next thing he knew his captors had grabbed hold of him by both arms.

Filipinos in sundry states of dress surrounded him. They hurled curses at him and slapped him in the face, but they stopped when they noticed his wound and carried him to dry ground on their shoulders. The meteorologist now realized that he had to kill himself, and he thrashed about as much as he could, hoping to aggravate his injury. His captors tied him to a tree and then talked amongst themselves for a while; he of course had no way of knowing what they were saying. Before long, someone came back with a stretcher, to which they moved him and bound him securely. As they carried him thus on their shoulders, he made himself breathe as deeply as possible—since his bindings prevented him from moving his body in any other way. He thought he could feel a new spurt of blood flowing out each time he took a breath, and this gave him a measure of solace.

His captors carried him into a hut and lowered the stretcher to the floor. They opened his shirt and administered first aid.

"Kill me, kill me," he cried, but the voice he heard sounded weak and far away. He wondered if he had gone partially deaf.

A middle-aged man came in and looked him in the eye. "Settle down!" he said firmly in surprisingly smooth Japanese.

"Kill me," the meteorologist repeated.

"We're not going to kill you," the man said with a smile. "We're going to turn you over to the Americans. The Americans will treat your wound for you."

"I don't want my wound treated. Kill me. I'm Japanese."

Tears suddenly spilled from the man's eyes. It came as such a surprise that the meteorologist's agitation began to subside. Repeatedly wiping the tears from his eyes, the Japanese-speaking Filipino squatted down next to him.

"I understand how you feel," he said. "But think about your mother and your father. How will your father feel if he finds out you insisted on killing yourself when you could have been saved? Come on, now. Struggling like that isn't good for your wound. Lie quietly and rest."

By this time the meteorologist was weeping as well. The man's mention of his mother had choked him with grief. During his days of wandering through the mountains, all he had been able to think about was his mother.

Now as the tears flowed, he resigned himself to accepting whatever happened. The man took out a bright patterned handkerchief and wiped away his tears for him.

"That's better," he said, smiling again.

The man accompanied the meteorologist as he was taken to a U.S. Army outpost on the coast. En route he spoke about his background. He had lived in Japan for two years as a young man, working in a Chinese-owned shop in Yokohama, and he had taken a Japanese wife while there. They had one son, now eighteen. When the Americans landed on Mindoro and the islanders began openly cooperating with them, the boy suddenly declared that he was Japanese and intended to cross over to Luzon and join the Imperial Army. The man and his wife had done everything they could to dissuade him, but the boy simply would not listen. When they refused to give their permission, he ran away from home in the middle of the night. Someone in the next town to the north had seen him walking northward with a duffel over his shoulder the following morning, and that was the last they knew of him.

"I don't know why he decided he was Japanese," the man said glumly. "I told him that since I was a Filipino and he was my son, he was a Filipino, too, but he wouldn't accept that. I guess maybe he'd grown fond of the Japanese troops stationed here earlier in the war because they were so nice to him. I wonder all the time where he could be now. He may well be dead."

I asked the meteorologist if he had met the Japanese wife.

"I'm not sure," he said. "A woman brought me some food at one point, but I just thought she was a Filipino."

After that I visited the meteorologist each morning without fail, but I had nothing to talk about with him any more than with the others. Once I had seen how he was, I excused myself quickly, saying it would be bad for his wound if he talked too much. One morning four or five days after his arrival, he lay with a damp towel across his face. The man in the bed next to him said his condition had taken a turn for the worse. The following day I was reading a detective story or something and did not visit in the morning.

When I went in the afternoon, his bed was empty. He had died in the night, and they had already removed his body. With his tent so far away from mine, I had remained unaware of anything amiss.

For a while I sat stunned on the edge of his empty bed. The area had been cleaned thoroughly, both above and below his bed, and no trace of him remained. He had utterly vanished in the space of a single night.

Once again, someone who had finally started to rekindle a feeling of human warmth in my heart had been abruptly snatched away from me. I was not responsible for his death, but it had been foolish of me not to have imagined its possibility when I saw him with the towel across his face the day before. I had never even asked his name!

I consoled myself that I really had no cause to be upset. We had in fact had nothing to talk about—just like the soldier from northern Tsugaru whom I had been drawn to before. In neither case were we very likely to have truly opened our hearts to each other or to genuinely rejoice in each other's joys. In neither case had our friendship been based on anything more than sentimentality.

Remembering my heart condition, I rose to my feet and walked slowly back to my tent.

"The young meteorologist died, sir," I reported to my former sergeant as tears overflowed my eyes.

———

The rainy season finally took its leave, and bright, clear days followed one upon the other. The canvas overhead roasted in the sun and relayed the scorching heat to the patients lying below. For the first time, I had cause to curse that product of civilization known as a tent.

The patients talked on and on about food. When they were not talking about food, they played Twenty Questions, the game in which you guess the answer to a riddle by asking only yes-or-no questions. I had no patience for their unimaginative riddles and clumsy questions, which lacked any of the wit shown by true masters of the game, so I immersed myself in my reading. I could not escape the incessant clamor of their boisterous voices, however, even by covering my ears. Communal living can truly grate on one's nerves when a communal purpose is lacking.

We heard about an American landing on Taiwan, then learned that it had actually been Iwo Jima. Some prisoners advocated a pitched battle to defend the homeland at all costs, while others argued that the government should move the Japanese capital to Changchun in Manchuria and let the Americans have the home islands. The debates were at least an improvement on the incessant talk of food.

My heart condition showed gradual improvement. The doctor had stressed that I needed to build up my strength, so I gave myself the task of sweeping and sprinkling water on the deck around my bed once in the morning and once in the evening.

As time passed, the food servers decided to organize the prisoners, after a fashion, by designating an officer for each tent. It was typical of the Japanese military mentality to always want to establish a clear locus of authority, but when they passed over several NCOs in our midst to select me, simply because I was the oldest, I wondered if even the food servers were beginning to adopt the more liberal-minded posture I had observed among the other prisoners. In any event, I thereby entered the ranks of privilege within the POW hospital.

Every second or third day, the tent officers met at the serving station in what we called a "planning session," but being officers in name only without specific duties to fulfill, we did not actually have anything to plan. The meetings essentially became an occasion for the servers to regale us with choice items they had skimmed from the others' rations—a blatant attempt to turn the tent officers into an auxiliary organ serving their own interests. I made myself exceedingly popular among my tent mates by taking most of the goodies back to share with them. It did not take long, however, for the servers to ban this practice.

"We wouldn't want the patients to start raising eyebrows," they said.

From my perspective as an officer, even if in name only, the prisoners behaved like good-for-nothing sloths. My tent was the internal medicine ward for patients with the most minor afflictions, such as beriberi due to malnutrition or diarrhea caused by something they should not have eaten in the mountains. Yet in spite of being in relatively good shape, these patients were all too lazy to follow the doctor's orders to get ten minutes of sun and take two showers daily. They preferred to lie around inside the sweltering tent and talk about food from morning to night.

By comparison, the patients in the surgical wards showed an active desire to recover. They did not play invalid the way the internal medicine patients did. Even those who would be permanently disabled had already begun the process of adapting themselves to their new condition. It would seem that external injuries poison the spirit less than internal illnesses.

For some of the patients, it was the spirit itself that had been wounded. One of these was a young man of about twenty-five who performed a special ritual before each meal. Kneeling formally in front of his tray, he would meditate for a time and then bow his head in a deep kowtow. Only after that would he pick up his spoon to eat. He had no doubt suffered from starvation in the jungle.

This man was the one and only patient to challenge the food servers for their skimming, boldly demanding that he receive his full ration. Even the usually unmoved servers apparently could not stand up to this simple-minded madman. He would walk back along the tent's center aisle holding his tray high in both hands as reverently as if he were carrying the Imperial Rescript.

Another such man was a seaman in his forties. He suffered only from diarrhea when he first came to my tent, but soon he began to manifest classic symptoms of prison psychosis. Without any provocation, he would leap up from his bed and race outside shouting "Open fire!" He had been a gunner on a light cruiser sunk while on a solo mission near Leyte.

The orderlies tried tying him to his bed, but then he befouled himself. Cleaning him up was considerably more trouble than dealing with his outbursts, so after that they left him unrestrained, and fortunately he stopped having fits so often. Next he started saying he needed to go to the bathroom all the time, refusing to use a bedpan and insisting that he be taken to the latrine. Perhaps this, too, was a symptom of his particular psychosis. The night orderlies refused to help him, so it fell to the unlucky man in the next bed and to myself to respond to his calls in shifts each night.

After waiting ten minutes or more while he sat on the throne without results, we would finally persuade him to return to bed. However, almost as soon as we got him into bed and lay back down ourselves, he would roll out onto his hands and knees on the floor and start trying to get up again. If you asked him what was the matter, he would say he needed to go to the latrine. It takes a good deal of patience to look after a patient of this kind, but it was hard to get angry with him when you considered that his compulsive desire to go to the latrine probably came from not wanting to repeat the indignity of incontinence. Oh, the piteous compulsions of a middle-aged man!

One night as usual I accompanied him to the latrine. He sat motionless on the throne with his eyes closed. Suddenly I had an idea: Perhaps it would be better to let him stay there as long he wished—twenty minutes, a half hour, whatever it took. If I first let him grow tired of sitting there and then escorted him back to his bed, he might fall right asleep and not ask to go again.

Since I would likely have a long wait, I decided to return to my bunk for a cigarette. As I sat there rolling a cigarette, I sensed something moving across the brightness of the floodlights beaming down from atop the fence. Stepping outside, I saw the stooped figure of a man running swiftly along the fence. I would hardly have believed he had that kind of strength in him, but the pointed profile of his head was unmistakable.

I could not fathom his intentions, but running near the fence in the middle of the night was a suicidal act.

"Don't shoot! Don't shoot!" I shouted as I unsteadily started after him, very conscious of the strain on my heart. Reaching the gate, he shook the barrier with both hands, then turned to the fence on one side and grabbed hold of the barbed wire to climb. It was then that I finally caught up to him. I knew it was dangerous for me to be there, and I continued shouting "Don't shoot! Don't shoot!" as I looked for the sentry outside the gate.

The guard approached. "What's going on?"

"It's a madman, sir."

"Hurry up and get back to your tent."

He was more than I could handle by myself, however. Even after he had let me pull his bloodied hand off the barbed wire, he kept his feet planted firmly in place as he continued to stare at the ground straight ahead of him through the fence. Displaying greater reserves of strength than anyone could have guessed his emaciated body possessed, he resisted all my efforts to drag him away. I could not budge him an inch.

A Japanese orderly came and slapped him across the face—once, twice, three times. With each slap, the madman's head rolled first one way, then the other as though tumbling in the wind, but his eyes remained fixed on the ground straight ahead.

When the orderly slapped him a fourth time, I forced my way between them. "Knock it off!" I yelled. "Beating him isn't going to make him better!"

"Oh yeah?" the orderly yelled back, curling into a fighting stance as if preparing to throw a punch at me next. He seemed to think better of it, however, and ran off to find another orderly.

I took the madman's arm again, to lead him back to the tent, but he continued to resist. I could not imagine what had made him decide to plant himself in one spot and refuse to budge that way. I felt like belting him a good one myself.

All of a sudden he shook himself free and strode away. Entering the nearest tent, he walked straight up the central aisle, out the other side, and into our tent. When he got back to his bed, he lifted his mosquito net and flopped himself down with a thud.

"Open fire," he murmured.

After this incident, he stopped asking to go to the latrine all the time. The psychology of a madman is indeed beyond our comprehension. Ten days later his diarrhea stopped. Except for his absolute refusal to speak, he now became indistinguishable from any of the other patients in our ward of relatively minor afflictions.

My heart continued to grow stronger. I could now participate without adverse effect in the calisthenics led by an American medic every morning and evening, and sweeping the area around my bed no longer tired me out.

As I regained my vitality, however, a new concern, or perhaps I should call it a fear, took possession of me: namely, the fear that I would be declared fully recovered and dispatched forthwith to the regular POW camp.

I had learned that the camp was largely self-governed, administered on a day-to-day basis by a Japanese commandant, and that the inmates spent their days weaving nipa to build and maintain camp facilities. Needless to say, I did not relish the thought of having to relinquish the freedom that had allowed me to spend most of my time reading—especially when it meant exchanging it for such mindless labor. What I dreaded most, however, was coming under the governance of my fellow countrymen once again. Of course, I had experienced the high-handedness of the Japanese staff at the hospital, too, but here they were always under the watchful eyes of the Americans, and our need to rest and recuperate made for a generally relaxed atmosphere. If the camp was under Japanese self-government, with the leaders given free rein, it would most likely mean having to submit once again to military-style authoritarianism and prejudices—a distasteful prospect indeed. A far more agreeable course would be to remain in the hospital until the war ended, even if that meant having to wait somewhat longer to go home by hospital ship.

Unfortunately, my only avenue for remaining there was to apply to become an interpreter's aide, and two other men already acting in that capacity were jealously guarding their territory. They had in fact perceived my knowledge of English as a threat from quite early on. For example, the main medic station at the new hospital was equipped with a Japanese-English and English-Japanese dictionary, but these two men claimed an exclusive right to it and refused to let me borrow it. This avenue was therefore closed to me.

The inevitable day finally arrived. After examining me carefully, the doctor turned to the interpreter who was making notes on my chart and said, "Discharge."

"The camp has a sick ward, too," the interpreter told me, trying to ease my fears. "They won't put you to work right away."

The following day I washed my pajamas and towel and turned them in, then donned the U.S. Army fatigues I had been issued when we moved. I could think of no one I had met in the hospital whom I would particularly miss, so saying good-bye was easy. My former sergeant showed his obvious pleasure at being selected to succeed me as tent officer. I do not remember the exact date of my discharge, but it was around the middle of March; I had spent almost two months in the hospital.

That afternoon I climbed into a U.S. Army ambulance with several other patients being discharged that day, and soon we were on our way to the camp. Since the back of the ambulance was enclosed, we experienced no heckling from islanders along the way this time. Briefly we drove back the way we had come on our move from Tacloban; then we turned several corners to emerge on a dusty road we had not traveled before. The ambulance rattled on and on along this road.

Eventually we came to a stop at the entrance to another barbed-wire compound, considerably larger than the hospital, laid out on a flat, treeless swatch of land. Besides a double fence surrounding the entire compound, a single fence separated the main section from the receiving area just inside the gate, where the American camp office was located. The guards showed us to a nipa shelter facing this camp office—open across the front with a number of grimy cots lined up in an unkempt row inside. New arrivals apparently stayed in this shelter while waiting to be interrogated and processed for admission to the camp. Since it was near evening and the interrogating officers had departed for the day, we would have to spend the night here.

Our evening meal arrived—a gruel of corned beef and rice cooked by the Japanese kitchen detail and served up in old food cans. No one could complain about the quantity, which was more than we could eat, but the taste was far inferior to the meals prepared in the Americans' central mess at the hospital. In a kerosene tin was some unsweetened black tea to wash it down with. We were supposed to dip our mess cans in it after we finished our gruel.

The cots were covered with dust, the blankets were soiled, and the mosquito nets had holes. A bucket in the corner had to suffice for the calls of nature. Though the place served only as a temporary "waiting room" for one group of newcomers after another, everything was filthy and disarrayed and reeked of the Imperial Army.

From the nipa barracks lined up inside the main enclosure came the sound of boisterous singing late into the night. We did not see any lights.

The next morning we were interrogated one by one in small huts built for that purpose in the receiving area. A stern-looking nisei in a large steel helmet asked me the names of the officers who had been in charge of my training unit back in Japan. Fortunately I had forgotten them all. My interrogator gave me a cigarette when he was through questioning me.

It took until afternoon for everyone to be questioned. As we lay on our cots with nothing to do, a swarm of Japanese men dressed only in loincloths came pouring out of the main compound, some carrying bolos, the others shouldering long sections of green bamboo. Not even seeming to notice us, they set to work with their bolos, cutting the bamboo into shorter lengths, splitting those sections into one-inch-wide slats, and sharpening one end of each slat to a point—all accompanied by a great deal of shouting and laughing amongst themselves. Then they pounded these bamboo pickets into place one after another in a solid line across the front of the shelter, creating a barrier that filled the space between the hut's main posts to about waist height. Only as they were finishing up did we realize they had erected a new front wall for the shelter.

The men were darkly tanned and remarkably robust. Their loincloths had been made from U.S. Army fatigues, flour sacks, and any other shred of cloth they had been able to get their hands on. None of them wore anything else.

Continuing their constant clamor, they completed the barrier in a matter of perhaps twenty minutes. "Mission accomplished," one of them shouted, and they commenced gathering up the scraps, swept the area clean, and streamed back into the main part of the compound on the other side of the fence.

I could not stop smiling for quite some time after this hale and hearty troupe of my compatriots had gone. It was hard to believe that these naked creatures chattering and clamoring about like monkeys were the same men who had waged a valiant defensive battle along the Leyte coast only a brief time before. Now, in the gravest hour of the war, with our homeland on the brink of annihilation as U.S. forces, already in possession of Iwo Jima, prepared to drive northward by way of the Ogasawaras in the east and Taiwan and Okinawa in the west, this was how those men spent their time. Lying back on my filthy bed I smiled on and on to myself, little imagining that I, too, would become one of their kind in the space of a few short months.

↜ 5 ↝

Living as POWs

. . . Which with unerring memory I shall hereby portray.
—Dante (*The Inferno*, Canto 2)

The typical image of POWs is of captured soldiers who have nothing to do but wait for repatriation to their homeland. In my own experience, however, POWs are neither "soldiers" nor "waiting." They have lost their ability to take part in combat, so they are no longer soldiers. And the conditions of life in a POW camp hardly permit them to simply wait. They must *live*.

As the term *prisoner of war* clearly denotes, these men have not been imprisoned for any crime of their own. They are being confined solely due to membership in their country's armed services—a status that makes them potentially harmful to the enemy. Furthermore, many of them did not become soldiers by their own volition.

In return for relinquishing, or forcibly being relieved of, their freedom as soldiers (that is to say, the freedom to make war), they have gained freedom as individuals (that is to say, the freedom to live). Unfortunately, for reasons that go beyond the individual, they have also been placed in confinement.

A POW's sole consolation is the knowledge that he will one day be released from that confinement. Yet, because his sentence is of indefinite duration, he has no clear objective on which to focus his waiting. And in any case, to merely wait would not be to *live*.

In speaking of POWs here, I do not refer to the soldiers who cast down their arms after the emperor proclaimed an end to the war. Such men were only detainees. The men I speak of are those taken captive while the war was still in progress, either through voluntary surrender or through loss of their ability to fight.

When I entered the POW camp on Leyte in mid-March 1945, it held about seven hundred officers and common soldiers of the Imperial Japanese Army and Navy captured on Leyte and the surrounding islands, including as far north as the southern end of Luzon. Four hundred of these men were among the last survivors from a total of 135,000 troops originally deployed to defend Leyte.

The camp was located in Tanauan, six kilometers south of Tacloban on the island's eastern coast. It was a roughly two-acre compound surrounded by barbed wire and set back twenty yards or so on the western, or inland, side of the coastal highway. The main gate, a large wooden frame with barbed wire stretched across it, faced out onto the road at the far left of the compound when viewed from the highway. Inside this gate was a receiving area of perhaps 120 to 130 square yards separated by an internal fence from the camp proper, which extended to the right.

Immediately inside the receiving area, on the left, stood a small nipa hut with an officer and three NCOs working at desks. This was the camp office, and the officer was the camp commandant. Across the driveway, on the right, was the long, narrow nipa hut that served as a waiting room for new arrivals. Next to the office, filling the remaining space on the left side of the driveway, three more nipa structures barely two yards square stood in a row. Entry to these cozy little huts was from the back, and the three sides visible from the driveway had no windows. Inside each were a table and two chairs. Nisei interrogators summoned the new arrivals into these huts one by one to question them. Since new prisoners usually arrived in groups, the questioning alone could take half a day.

When their interrogations were finished, the new arrivals emerged into the light outside for pictures—like police mug shots, one facing the camera and one in profile. They also had fingerprints taken of all ten fingers.

Only after the entire group had completed this process were they permitted to join their predecessors in the camp. Next to the waiting room was an opening in the internal fence separating the receiving area from the main compound. From there, a road about twenty feet wide extended straight ahead, with five crudely built nipa huts lined up on each side. The huts were roughly twenty-five feet wide and forty feet front-to-back.

First on the left came the cookshack. The structure was mainly just a roof under which the mess crew labored around a large cauldron made from a thirty-six-gallon U.S. Army water tank, turning the canned rations provided by the Americans into all manner of goulash. A long window extended the full width of the front wall—the wall actually being nothing more than the counter where the food was distributed in buckets made from kerosene tins to the kitchen details sent by each hut. The other three sides of the cookshack were enclosed only with a chain-link fence—to prevent starving prisoners from raiding the pantry.

On the road in front of the cookshack was a small nipa structure—just a roof, really, like over a well—under which a Lister bag holding chemically purified water always hung.

Across the central drive from the cookshack, fifteen feet or so back from the road, was a well reserved solely for kitchen use. Next to it stood a gasoline stove topped with a pot identical to the one in the cookshack—this one for boiling dishwater. The prisoners were supposed to sterilize their dishes here after each meal, but with only a single pot and with the water quickly turning cloudy, this rule went largely unenforced. The cooks lived in a nipa hut at the back of this lot.

The hut next to the cookshack was our Headquarters. This building housed the official representative of the POWs—he liked to style himself "Japanese Camp Commandant," though of course this meant only "commandant of the Japanese in the camp," not "commandant of the camp interning Japanese"—along with his staff and the hut adjutants from each of the other buildings. A partition about six feet from the entrance created a small front office where the officer of the day and a runner remained constantly on duty.

The following hut was popularly dubbed the NCO Club. Since there were not enough leadership posts to go around, the noncoms who got left out were bunked together in this building. This preferential treatment eventually came to an end when a reorganization of the prisoners into U.S. Army–style companies increased the number of leadership posts sufficiently to absorb most of these men.

Across from the NCO Club was the infirmary. A wall about one-third of the way back divided this building into two main sections, with the front section further partitioned in half down the middle. One of these front chambers was the doctor's examination room, the other a surgery clinic for treatment of injuries. The rear two-thirds of the building was called the "intensive care ward" and housed patients who were not so bad off that they needed to be sent to the hospital but who required regular nursing care. This is where I was placed when I first arrived.

The next building on the same side of the road was the infirmary annex, or regular sick ward. This building housed patients who had mostly overcome their illnesses but remained weak. A Japanese staff of two medics and two orderlies looked after their needs.

The remaining four huts, which is to say the last two huts on the Headquarters side of the road and the huts before the infirmary and after the infirmary annex on the other side, were ordinary POW barracks. Each held about sixty prisoners in three tightly packed rows of cots spanning the room from front to back.

In sum, then, starting just inside the gate, the buildings to the left of the central drive were the cookshack, followed by Headquarters, the NCO Club, and two common barracks; to the right were the well and cooks' quarters, followed by a common barracks, the infirmary, the infirmary annex, and another common barracks. A smaller nipa hut at the end of the right-hand row of buildings housed the latrines.

These buildings did not comprise the entire camp, however. Another barbed-wire fence cut across the compound at the end of the two rows of buildings, with an opening in the middle as wide as the central drive allowing free passage into the next sector. This second sector was about the same size as the first but had no buildings. The fence between the sectors was a vestige of the camp's gradual expansion from a much smaller facility to its present size. At one time, tents had been pitched in the now open sector to accommodate the swelling numbers of prisoners. When even this overflow sector filled up, the prisoners were moved to a new area still farther on.

One might assume that they could simply have continued to expand the camp at will onto immediately adjacent land as the population grew. As it happened, however, the next patch of land was already occupied. Another fence open in the middle crossed the compound at the far end of the second sector, and on the other side of this was the Taiwanese sector of the camp. Taiwanese laborers impressed into service by the Japanese military were interned there in some ten small tents holding about a dozen men each. The Americans had built them a separate passageway for entering and exiting the camp so they would not have to come in contact with the Japanese, and because of this their sector could not be moved farther on.

Though the Japanese prisoners were for the most part forbidden to enter the Taiwanese sector, they could not avoid it entirely, for beyond yet another fence at the far end of this sector was the new expansion accommodating the entire population of Japanese prisoners that had outgrown the first overflow sector. Communications between Headquarters and the new overflow sector perforce required going through the Taiwanese quarter, and in fact that was precisely why the several fences crossing the compound had been left open in the middle. Persons traveling on official business were therefore permitted to pass through the quarter. However, it proved difficult to limit the license to such individuals, for it was impossible to strictly monitor everyone's comings and goings. Bored prisoners frequently passed through on their way to visit friends in the other Japanese sector.

The Taiwanese wanted nothing to do with the Japanese and deliberately avoided the eyes of anyone passing through. Though they gave no sign of gloating over their liberation from Japanese control, I could sense a buoyant mood of relief and optimism among them. Most of the Japanese believed the Taiwanese were receiving better provisions than we were.

The men from Taiwan showed a great fondness for music. Someone had improvised a Chinese fiddle by stretching wires across a sound box patched together from some scraps of wood, and with that for accompaniment they raised their voices in song. They were good cooks as well, making delectable fried buns. Some Japanese prisoners went secretly at night to trade cigarettes for these buns.

Beyond the Taiwanese sector, the newest Japanese quarter sprawled expansively, with an open square in the middle and tents like those in the Taiwanese sector pitched all around. The camp ended there.

The prisoners housed in the nipa huts near the main entrance were called Group A, while the prisoners in the last sector were called Group B. Group B had its own Headquarters and cookshack, but it lacked an infirmary.

The "commandant" of Group A continued to be regarded as the supreme representative for the Japanese prisoners as a whole, but he took great umbrage when the American commandant ordered the appointment of a separate leader for Group B. Since he controlled the initial division of food supplies between Group A and Group B, he retaliated by making sure that Group A always received an ampler share. He justified this on the grounds that the old-timers in Group A needed more energy for the labor they were expected to do now that they had recovered their health, whereas most of the newer arrivals in Group B remained too weak to work. In truth, of course, the prisoners trying to recover their strength in Group B needed the extra nourishment far more than the already robust men in Group A. This preferential treatment of Group A extended not only to food but to medical and recreational supplies and anything else that required dividing up. The staff at Group B Headquarters gritted their teeth, while the men in their charge continued to go hungry.

Before elaborating further on such intrigues, I would like to complete my account of the physical layout of the camp and surroundings.

Gazing up "Central Avenue" with our backs to the entrance, we could see the North Star shining directly ahead. That is to say, the compound stretched out along a precise north-south axis, and the main gate was situated at its southeast corner. The highway paralleled the eastern fence of the compound with a space of some twenty yards separating the road and the fence. Low-standing tents were pitched in a row all along this strip of land, and American GIs returned to sleep in them each night. They read or sang songs late into the evening. Filipino women came to visit them from time to time.

A second gate faced out onto the road at the dividing line between Group A's sector and the now empty second sector. It dwarfed the gate at the southeast corner, with two large panels swinging open to either side, and next to it stood a tall, wooden, guard tower. At the foot of the tower was a nipa storehouse where food supplies, clothing, work equipment, and the like were kept. When POW labor details went outside the compound to work, they exited and entered from here. The mazelike corridor built for the Taiwanese to be able to come and go without entering Japanese territory connected to this gate. The guard tower was equipped with a machine gun, but we could not see it from below.

A stand of palm trees began on the other side of the storehouse. The trees looked stunted, with poor color, and failed to present an impression of beauty. I imagine the soil in which they grew lacked the proper nutrients to support more vigorous growth.

This unsightly stand of palms wrapped around the compound past the northeast corner, overlooked by a second guard tower, and across the entire north end to the northwest corner, where yet another guard tower stood. Moving southward again from there, the terrain rose briefly to form a grassy knoll, and then the remaining strip immediately west of the compound was marshland. Murky water peeked from between large mats of floating moss and scattered clusters of water lilies. Islanders often used wetlands like this for planting rice, but here they had not.

The marsh was only about twenty yards across, with jungle rising on the other side. The dense green foliage of low-lying nipa palms reminded me of the tropical landscape paintings of Henri Rousseau.

Not far past the southwest corner of the compound, the strip of marsh apparently connected at right angles with a stream flowing down from the mountains to the West, but American tents pitched in the area obscured our view of the confluence. The stream continued on past the southern end of the compound at a distance of approximately twenty yards, flowed under a parapetless wooden bridge elevating the road, and meandered on toward the sea about a kilometer away. At the foot of the bridge on the far side, diagonally across from the camp's main gate, stood a U.S. Army motor pool with a hodgepodge of vehicles cluttering the open lot out front and a tin fence running along the side facing the stream. The flowing water paused in a pool directly beneath this fence, reflecting the tin's dull glow in the morning twilight.

On the highway, trucks, trailers, jeeps, and other vehicles rushed back and forth in a typically American hurry. Occasionally a truck drove by carrying what appeared to be a Filipino work party. As they passed, they turned as one to jeer at us and make mocking gestures, persisting in this as long as they could see the camp—which is to say, until they moved beyond the north end of Group A's sector.

The fence around the perimeter of the camp was a double fence, with the two layers erected about two feet apart. The second layer had gone up only about a month before my arrival, following the breakout of four pilots.

The men in the main compound were all NCOs and privates. Fifteen or so officers were housed in small tents on the small corner tract directly west of the receiving area, separated from the cookshack by the first of the barbed-wire fences cutting east to west across the compound. As a rule, the officers were not permitted to have contact with the men in the main sector. The Americans apparently feared they might attempt to rekindle the prisoners' martial spirit and organize a resistance, but it was a needless worry given the vengeful glee with which the common POWs regarded the straits to which their former overlords had been reduced.

Deprived of the personal orderlies who had waited on them in the military, these former officers stumbled clumsily through their daily lives. Laundry hung in complete disarray on their tent ropes. Lacking their own latrine, they had to share the ones at the far end of Group A. When the former privates made a point of ignoring him, one young former officer, obviously a product of the officer candidate's course, gave a contemptuous smirk and swaggered by with all the more leisurely steps.

The American commandant soon took note of the antipathy, and after that, whenever the common prisoners failed to toe the line to his satisfaction, he threatened to bring in their former officers to straighten them out.

Imamoto, the man ensconced as commandant at Group A Headquarters, had belonged to the Sixteenth Army Division. He had actually been only a PFC but fraudulently claimed the rank of sergeant major. Since his entire company had been decimated except for himself, there was no one in camp to contradict his claim—at least initially. Later, whenever someone arrived who might know his true rank, Imamoto would immediately call him aside.

"You may have met a PFC in such-and-such company who looked just like me. That was my younger brother."

He fooled no one with this story, of course, but he had amassed such great power within the camp that no one challenged him to his face—only behind his back.

Not very tall but of stocky build, Imamoto appeared to be in his mid-thirties. Creases and wrinkles crossed his square, weather-beaten face in unexpected places, and he had buckteeth. His short legs bowed markedly.

In civilian life he had been in the trucking business, and he maintained his authority over the POWs essentially by treating them the way he would have treated his laborers. He seemed to believe that leadership consisted of railing at his subjects at every opportunity and otherwise making them feel his watchful and ill-humored presence at all times.

As one of the first prisoners taken on Leyte, in the early period when the Americans lacked sufficient rations for their prisoners, Imamoto had led them to his old regiment's food depot, thereby gaining sustenance for himself and his comrades. Actions like this had earned him the confidence of his captors, and that was how he had won his post.

His position as autocratic boss was not necessarily one in which he could rest easy, however. The other personnel at Headquarters included a deputy, a clerk, and the hut adjutants. Of these men, all but the clerk had been petty officers in the navy.

American forces first landed on Leyte and established control over Tacloban and vicinity on October 20, 1944. Then, on October 25, three major naval battles were fought in the straits to the north and south of Leyte and on the sea northeast of Luzon, resulting in the annihilation of the Imperial Navy. A majority of the men in this POW camp were survivors of the task force of destroyers and battleships, including the *Yamashiro* and the *Fusō*, that had come through the Surigao Strait south of Leyte. They had been picked up by American patrol boats after drifting in Leyte Gulf for a day and a night, and their arrival at the camp had generally preceded the arrival of men from the Sixteenth Division, who typically managed to hide out in the mountains for quite some time before being captured by guerrillas.

As a result, the initial construction of the camp had been largely carried out by navy men, and most of the leadership posts got filled early on from among their number. Surrounded and outnumbered by these navy men, Imamoto had managed to retain his position only because the Americans regarded it as too much trouble to change already established responsibilities, and the navy men had tacitly accepted the status quo.

Thus, as is true of all sovereigns, Imamoto's legitimacy and longevity derived in large part from essentially accidental developments at the time his dominion originated. Added to this was his rather simpleminded nature, which ideally suited him to being manipulated as a puppet. Most importantly, he did not understand English.

Imamoto's deputy was a former chief petty officer named Oda. Before entering the navy he had worked for a spring manufacturer in Osaka as director of the company's Employee Welfare Section. He evinced both the dignity of a military man and the deferential demeanor of a salaried civilian employee, but it was the latter quality that he exercised to greatest effect in the POW camp.

At thirty-two, he was a well-favored man with a small mustache. He was in effect Imamoto's aide-de-camp, and in that capacity he served as a kind of buffer between Imamoto and the hut adjutants, all of whom were navy men. He probably could have supplanted Imamoto without a great deal of difficulty. That he chose not to owed, I suspect, to an awareness of just how delicate the position of Japanese commandant was, and to his feeling more comfortable, as so many organization men do, serving in the lower-profile role of an executive assistant. He always treated others with the greatest of courtesy, addressing them crisply and respectfully, and he believed that this was precisely why he enjoyed the smooth cooperation of the hut adjutants.

Oda understood a little English, and consequently no separate interpreter was posted to Headquarters. When written translations were needed, or when the necessary interpreting exceeded his abilities, he relied on the help of a college graduate who had served the army as a civilian adjunct. Though there were a few men who understood English even among the regular-army men who made up the majority of those captured on Leyte, Oda deliberately chose the civilian candidate because of an unwritten rule that said civilians could not become part of the leadership. In other words, he was ensuring that his special position as the English speaker at Headquarters would not be eclipsed.

Imamoto and Oda's duties were on the one hand to relay orders from the American commandant and make sure the prisoners complied in full, and on the other hand to act as the prisoners' spokesmen in the event of any grievances or requests they might have. The latter role, however, remained almost completely unexercised, for the prisoners were so stunned not only at having their lives spared but at being provided with food and clothing to boot that they voiced virtually no complaints. Besides, they knew that even if they did raise a complaint, Imamoto would be sure to quash it anyway.

The POW clerk was a former staff sergeant named Nakagawa from a field artillery unit of the Sixteenth Division. He was a self-seeking sycophant, pure and simple, and as the reader will no doubt have guessed by now, Imamoto had a weakness for sycophancy. Nakagawa endured Imamoto's every whim, and a twitch of Imamoto's jaw was all it took to send him scurrying to the four corners of the camp. The hut adjutants openly derided him, and in return he invented nasty tales about them and whispered them to Imamoto on a daily basis. Every so often he would hatch a plot against one or another of the adjutants, but never with notable success.

Nakagawa knew a little English and assisted the Americans in maintaining the camp roster. He claimed that the supposedly top-secret roster indicated for each prisoner whether he had surrendered voluntarily or been captured (except he pronounced the English words "sullended" and "capted"). Since the Americans had no reason to distinguish between those who had surrendered and those who were captured, he had obviously made this story up as a means of intimidating the prisoners. To my mind, this false claim merely betrayed that he had himself been among those who voluntarily surrendered. He also said he had eaten human flesh in the jungle. It was a ludicrous sort of boast to make, and I do not doubt it was another lie.

In short, he was nothing more than a common scoundrel, a breed found in every nook and cranny of civilized society. I regarded him with contempt and never inquired about his career history.

As my description has made clear, the group of men who headed up our little POW autocracy were utterly typical of men found in such positions everywhere. It would seem that all governing organs sculpt the men who run them into essentially similar shapes.

As already noted, Imamoto's supremacy was sustained largely by inertia on the part of the Americans, who had no desire to change the status quo. A secondary factor, however, was the apathy of the prisoners themselves, who figured that so long as they had to have someone in that position it made little difference who it might be. And like any government standing on the shoulders of an apathetic populace, this one, too, functioned quite arbitrarily. Interestingly, however, the arbitrariness never turned particularly reckless; the autocrat's demands seemed to settle quite naturally within the bounds of reason.

A notch above Nakagawa but under Oda were the seven hut adjutants, all former petty officers. Their duties were to supervise and maintain order in the particular huts for which they were responsible, but they in fact spent very little time there. They bunked at Headquarters, waited upon by young prisoners who served as their orderlies and enjoying meals prepared separately from the fare the rest of the camp received. Apart from putting in an occasional appearance at their assigned huts to throw their weight around, they mostly passed their days at Headquarters gloating amongst themselves over their special privileges.

In substantial part, the camp leaders owed their power to their rank in the Japanese military and to their native instincts and intelligence. But most of all, they owed it to being among the first to be taken prisoner—a most curious sort of qualification for becoming a leader.

———

After spending a night in the waiting room and undergoing our interrogations, my companions from the hospital and I found ourselves ranked shoulder-to-shoulder in front of Headquarters. Imamoto eyed me up and down from head to toe and shouted "Intensive care!" I had already been issued a set of dark green U.S. Army fatigues at the hospital, so I received nothing new here.

As directed, I headed diagonally across Central Avenue to the ward at the back of the infirmary. The basic structure of the building was the same as the other nipa huts: Thick, palm-log posts, a little over six feet high and spaced about twelve feet apart, supported a gabled roof of bamboo rafters thatched with dried nipa fronds. The four sides were enclosed with a chest-high wall made of split bamboo pickets packed tightly together in a row.

It was getting on in the afternoon by this time, and the day's sick call had already ended, leaving the two infirmary rooms at the front deserted. Beyond the bamboo partition separating the infirmary and the ward stretched three rows of cots. As I came in from the sun, the air beneath the high roof felt pleasantly cool.

Against one wall stood a rather precarious-looking wooden table, no doubt the handiwork of one of the inmates. A young prisoner got up from the table to show me to my bunk. I soon learned that the men in the ward called him Chief. He was the one in charge of the actual day-to-day operations of the ward.

I already knew one of the men there—my hungry neighbor from the hospital who had put himself at my service in a variety of ways out of gratitude for the portions of food I shared with him. He had been discharged from the hospital to the camp the previous week. A native of Kawachi in Osaka, he was about my age and like me had been called into active duty from the reserves. Perhaps because he was a produce distributor and accustomed to having all the food he could eat, he possessed an inordinately hearty appetite for a man our age. He would down the meager American-style meals served at the hospital in little more than a gulp and would then be left staring forlornly at his empty plate.

This man had secretly come out to greet me in the waiting room the night before (contact between inmates and new arrivals was officially forbidden until after the interrogations were through) and had already made me a mess kit for my meals. This mess kit was in fact nothing more than a set of empty tin cans, but not just any cans would do. The main course can, side dish can, and beverage can each had to be of a certain regulation size. Prisoners retrieved tin cans that the cooks had rudely pried open with bolos, carefully trimmed the sharp, jagged edges using the can openers attached to American field rations, and pounded the trimmed edges flat with a stick to make sure they did not cut their lips. The task required a good deal of elbow grease, but my friend had already taken care of it for me. He had also whittled me a pair of chopsticks out of bamboo.

He got up and moved his bunk next to mine as soon as I arrived, and he gave me a complete rundown of the intensive care ward. I also learned that he continued to go hungry.

Of the three rows of beds, two were for patients and one was for the Japanese medics and orderlies who took care of them.

The bunk closest to the doctor's office against the far wall belonged to the aforementioned Chief. He was twenty-four or twenty-five, a former sergeant in the Sixteenth Division Medical Corps, and the son of an old tea merchant in Kyoto. He had the light complexion and easy grace so typical of pampered Kyoto youths.

He went by the name of Dateno Chūji. The first name he gave when captured had been Kunisada Chūji, but when the nisei interpreter told him not to play games he changed it to Dateno Chūji, because in Kyoto parlance *date no* means "false." Even the nisei who knew that Kunisada Chūji was a famous gambling boss from the nineteenth century failed to recognize the joke in "Dateno" and let it pass. Many of the men used assumed names, but such witty ones were rare. Dateno believed the Japanese would soon take back the Philippines and liberate the camp.

In the next bunk slept the chief's deputy, a former PFC, likewise from the Sixteenth Division Medical Corps, likewise from Kyoto, and likewise in his mid-twenties. He was relatively heavy-set, with a well-rounded face. He had been an assistant director at a film studio prior to his induction, but the quiet manner in which he undertook this or that task seemed quite removed from the image generally associated with those engaged in film-making. It made better sense when I later learned that, under the division of labor demanded in the making of talking pictures, he had merely had charge of a single, well-defined assignment. He harbored a violent hatred for the military, and the assumed name he chose to go by was that of his superior officer, Hirano.

Sleeping in the next bed was the ward interpreter. An American doctor and an American medic were assigned to the infirmary and commuted here each morning from their quarters elsewhere. The interpreter filled a crucial role in relaying patient complaints to the doctor on rounds and in working with the medic to dispense prescribed medications.

The twenty-year-old interpreter's name was Sakurai. Besides being a preparatory student at a private university in urban Tokyo, he had spent his early childhood in Pittsburgh, so he spoke very good English. He cut a far from dashing figure, however. Dark in complexion and not very tall, he leaned over backward as he walked, with his arms dangling awkwardly behind him. He had an unruly stubble of a beard that stuck out every which way—like Takeda Shingen in pictures of samurai warlords.

Sakurai seemed to look down his nose at us. I do not think it was from conceit about his linguistic skills; he simply had no patience for the way grown men got so flustered in front of the Americans. All told, he struck me as still a child, but I liked it that he displayed no sign of the fawning attitude so typical of POW interpreters.

Orderlies had the next three bunks. One was a middle-aged reservist; the other two, regular-army men in their twenties. All had been deployed to Leyte as reinforcements, landing on the western shore in November 1944 and later.

These three men swept and cleaned the ward inside and out and brought us our meals. The job of dishing up the food fell to the head orderly, the middle-aged reservist named Aoki, and it proved to be a very tricky business indeed. The kerosene tins of food brought in from the cookshack contained not only the patients' portions but the orderlies' and medics' portions as well. Following the same principle by which Imamoto divvied up more food to the "working" Group A and less to the "idle" Group B, in our ward Aoki had to make sure that the medics' and orderlies' portions were larger and the patients' portions smaller. At the same time, he had to avoid any appearance of excessive imbalance: At the infirmary annex next door, the patients had banded together and protested the imbalance to Imamoto, and this had led to a shake-up of the annex staff, including the hut adjutant and the orderlies.

Aoki obviously did not relish the task of making the necessary discrimination, especially when, by whatever whim, the kerosene tins from the cookshack contained less food than usual. He agonized endlessly, adjusting over and over the portions in the fifteen or so mess cans placed before him, often requiring more than twenty minutes before he could be satisfied that he had got it right.

Back home this man lived and worked as a tinsmith in the shadow of a brothel district on the outskirts of Nagoya. A widower with two children, seven and nine years old, he had a shallow forehead and wide mouth and went around with a partly smoked cigarette behind his ear. He could be described as an ordinary townsman, a "man of well-balanced character," so to speak, who seemed to hold great pity in his heart for any man who lived in the face of adversity, including himself. He was also quite taciturn, growing visibly flustered when he found himself face-to-face with someone and could think of nothing to say. Quite possibly, he never finished grade school: I once passed by his bunk when he was sitting on his bed practicing the recitation for the silent film *Kantarō of Akagi*, and I noticed that his notes were written entirely in katakana.[1]

The other two orderlies are a little harder to describe. Physically, one had large eyes and a square face, while the other had slit eyes and a round face; the first was muscular, with shoulders as broad and square as a portable shoji screen, while the other was chubby with sloping shoulders. In character and mannerisms, however, they were as alike as Dubchinski and

---

1 One of the two forty-six-character sets that can be used for writing Japanese phonetically. Normally, for all but the minimally literate, these simplified phonetic characters are mixed with the far more complex kanji characters, of which there are thousands.

Bubchinski in *The Public Prosecutor*. Though they both strove diligently and with the best of intentions to fulfill their duties and gain the pleasure of the hut adjutant and Chief, they nevertheless always seemed to come up short. The food tins they washed and took back to the cookshack were often rated unacceptable by the cooks, and only rarely did they sweep out the infirmary offices without leaving behind scraps of gauze or wads of cotton. They also constantly bad-mouthed the prisoners who had preceded them to the camp, as well as all the other members of the medical staff.

They had volunteered to work as orderlies, and on the whole they treated the patients in the ward with solicitude, but for some reason the round-faced one had it in for my starving neighbor. At mealtimes he always found something to rail at him about, whether it was that he came to pick up his food too soon or that his mess can was the wrong size. It seems that men quite naturally turn ugly when forced to live under conditions in which their appetites must be held in check.

"What's the big deal?" my neighbor would mutter scornfully. In pursuit of satisfaction for his appetite, he was no more inclined to consider the other point of view than anyone else.

I observed all these things about the orderlies from my very first meal at the camp. That meal consisted of rice gruel mixed with pieces of canned meat. This gruel filled my regulation size mess can (about 2½ inches in diameter and 4 inches tall—the regulation sizes were actually specified according to what the can had originally contained) about two-thirds full. We also got a chunk of corned beef on the side: It came in those familiar, tapered-at-the-bottom rectangular cans imported to Japan before the war, each of which was divided into three portions. The rice was a glutinous, long-grained Australian rice.

Rations had been reduced following a recent breakout, I learned, but even so the quantity of food was twice what I had been accustomed to getting at the hospital. It proved too much for my shrunken stomach. My neighbor happily wolfed down what I could not eat. An unwritten rule required those who received leftovers to wash dishes for their benefactors, so my neighbor gathered up my cans with his and went out the back door.

A strip of land ten or twelve feet wide ran between the rear wall of the barracks and the fence, and four wells had been dug there, each at about the demarcation line between the two huts it served. Probably because of the stream that flowed past the southern end of the compound, the camp stood on sandy soil, and digging down just six or seven feet yielded relatively good water. We drew this water using a large powdered-food tin attached to the end of a pole. Flanking each of the wells were two drain boards fashioned from split bamboo. On one side the drain board was just two or three inches off the ground, on the other at waist height—each spanning the entire width of a hut. The low drain board was for bathing, while the raised one was for washing our mess cans.

Three months after my arrival, we were all moved to a new camp outfitted with showers and heated water tanks for washing dishes and many of the same amenities the American soldiers' barracks had. This camp, however, had been built by the prisoners themselves, piece by piece, beginning in early December when the battle for Leyte was still raging, so we had to make do with a variety of primitive arrangements the inmates had improvised. Except for the boots and single set of fatigues issued to each prisoner, we had to improvise even for clothing.

For example, my resourceful neighbor made me a loincloth using the fabric from a flour bag and stitching it together with thread he had unraveled from the same bag. To straighten the thread, he soaked it in some surplus hot water obtained from the cookshack, and then he sewed the loincloth with it using a section of wire he had ground to a point on a piece of metal. I was truly amazed when I saw how he had flattened the tail end of this needle with a rock and had somehow managed to open a hole for the thread to pass through.

A sewing kit was available at Headquarters, but due to high demand it was almost always checked out, leading the men to improvise in this manner. Old safety-razor blades were used for cutting fabric, and since these blades had many other uses as well, most of the men managed to get hold of one and hang on to it. This was the only "lethal weapon" any of us possessed at the time.

Evening rations were at four o'clock, and roll call was at five. The officer of the day on duty in the front office at Headquarters (squad leaders from the barracks served in rotation) shouted out the order, and prisoners came streaming from the barracks to fall into five ranks along Central Avenue. Roll was then taken by an officer or noncom from the MPs who guarded the gate (they apparently belonged to a different chain of command from the commandant).

This was the time when you could see the camp's inmates gathered in a single place. Most of the day the men went about wearing only their loin cloths, but uniforms were required for roll call. Dragging their feet in cavernous size-eleven boots and wearing oversized fatigues marked "PW," with sleeves and pants cuffs rolled up to make them fit, the men slouched grimly into their assigned ranks. The sight brought no other comparisons to mind; it was plainly and simply an assembly of POWs.

Though most of these men had been taken prisoner and placed in confinement against their will, they had by now spent over three months in captivity and had grown quite comfortable in their lives as POWs. They had grown fat on the plentiful rations supplied by the Americans, settled securely into their new lives of collective idleness, and devised ways of passing the time enjoyably. Each roll call, however, served as a rude reminder of their true circumstance.

When the master of roll call came through the gateway accompanied by Imamoto, Oda barked, "Attention!" As the master counted off the first group, the other hut adjutants ordered their men at ease. Then when the master approached their group, they would bring their men back to attention again.

The prisoners stood erect and motionless. As many of my readers will know, this was the stance that regulations said must "inwardly swell with the warrior's spirit, outwardly manifest solemnity and uprightness." In the military, which is to say when these men were still warriors, the sight of massive ranks of neatly uniformed figures standing crisply at attention evoked a kind of beauty, but now the ranks were of POWs wrapped in ill-fitting clothing that each man had to adjust in his own way. There was a certain disconsonance between the men's appearance and the way they snapped to that "solemn and upright" stance.

For a small minority of the men, staunchly maintaining this and other military disciplines was a point of honor—a way of showing the Americans the strength of the Japanese military spirit. These men folded and stacked their clothing neatly beside their pillows in the military manner and always kept their beds and surroundings in inspection-ready order. Some of them ardently believed that friendly forces would return, and they buried food under their cots in anticipation of that day.

The vast majority, however, snapped to motionless attention as a mere reflex. In this case, one could say the scene of the men standing at attention was in fact a tableau of docile submission. And whether the men were aware of it or not, it accurately reflected the true nature of their position as prisoners.

Imamoto attended the roll call master, comparing his count against the number of men currently belonging to each group as reported by the hut adjutants. When the totals at the end matched the official count already determined by the Americans, the roll call would be over: "Fall out!"

The master counted using the eraser end of a pencil. Even with the men lined up in five neat rows to facilitate easier counting, he often made mistakes, especially when he was a noncom. Perhaps it was because he counted each row and added up instead of simply using multiplication. The errors became the brunt of repeated jokes among the prisoners, who were used to the Japanese military's efficient system of counting men ranked in four rows. The conquered are quick to take glee in the conqueror's failings.

The patients in the two sick wards had only to sit up in bed for roll call, and the weakest were permitted to remain lying down. When the roll master came through the doctor's office and appeared in the doorway, the ward chief yelled "Attention!" and everyone stuck out his chest. The master counted from where he stood in the doorway and then turned to go.

These head counts were repeated at 7:00 A.M., 5:00 P.M., and at 2:00 in the middle of the night. The last of these was added after the recent breakout.

The breakout had left its mark in a variety of ways: The second fence was erected; rations were reduced as a punitive measure on suspicion that other prisoners had aided the escapees—or at least had failed to stop them; and the distribution of cigarettes was suspended. In the ten months between the battle for Leyte and the end of the war, only this single breakout occurred, but since the incident had such a significant impact on our lives, I cannot pass over it without recording a few words about it.

The breakout took place toward the end of February, and the men involved were a former petty officer named Azuma, twenty-four years old, and three others, all naval fliers. Friends not included in the plans speculated that the four men had purposely chosen to keep their group small in order to increase their chances of success.

Their aim was to sneak onto the airfield at Tacloban and steal a plane to fly to Cebu. At the time, it was widely held among the prisoners that American forces had not yet landed on Cebu and that the occasional air-raid warnings issued in camp were due to Japanese planes flying up from an air base there.

Azuma, the mastermind, had been good friends with Dateno, who had in his possession the only flashlight in camp—for attending to medical emergencies in the middle of the night. On the eve of the breakout, Azuma came to borrow the flashlight saying that he needed to look for a needle he had dropped under his bed. Before leaving, he asked Dateno to tell him his home address and memorized it.

Azuma failed to return the flashlight either that evening or the next morning. When the orderlies invited Dateno to join a game of cards that afternoon, he looked distinctly blue in the face and his eyes were bloodshot. He had guessed what was going on and had chosen not to demand the flashlight's immediate return.

That night, the men broke out at the northwest corner of the compound. The northwest corner still lacked a lookout tower at the time, and the floodlights mounted atop the tower at the northeast corner did not reach that far. During the day, the plotters had woven together a screen of nipa fronds (left over from thatching roofs) and had placed it there to shield them from view. Since the fence consisted of horizontal strands of barbed wire nine or ten inches apart, it was probably fairly easy to spread them wide enough to crawl through.

They began their escape quite early, around 9:00 or 10:00 P.M., presumably in order to have that much more time to make way under cover of darkness before daybreak.

The escape came to light when a note was found on one escapee's empty bunk the next morning: "A lone wolf, testing his mettle," he had scrawled in pencil. The incident was reported immediately to Imamoto, but he decided to let the Americans discover it at morning roll call. The roll master gave Imamoto and his staff a severe dressing down and ordered that every one of the prisoners be checked carefully against the mug shots taken when he was processed for admission to the camp.

Afterward, Imamoto assembled the prisoners. "I pray for their success," he said. "But until we can confirm how far they got, let me warn the rest of you to refrain from undertaking anything rash."

That night, roll was called every two hours starting at 8:00 P.M. Two or three days later this was reduced to just 10:00 P.M. and 2:00 A.M., and then eventually it became just 2:00 A.M. The commander of the MPs guarding the gate was replaced, and all fliers in the camp were transferred to Australia. A watchtower went up at the northwest corner of the compound, and a great many more lights were mounted atop the fences to brighten the perimeter through the night. Two massive new floodlights were also mounted at either end of Group A's Central Avenue, expressly for use during the 2:00 A.M. roll call. A reduction in rations turned meals into thin rice gruel, and the weekly allotment of twenty cigarettes per person was suspended.

When I came to the camp in mid-March, the majority of the prisoners believed that the fugitives had successfully reached the airfield and flown to Cebu. A few declared confidently that two had been caught but Azuma and one other made good their getaway.

One former pilot had a different view. "Even supposing that they managed to elude American patrols and got to the airfield, and even supposing that there happened to be a plane all fueled up and ready to go, I doubt they could have gotten an unfamiliar American plane off the ground. Every plane has its own idiosyncrasies about how its controls work."

This pilot admitted that Azuma had indirectly offered him a chance to join the escape, but he had deliberately ignored the overture.

"I can understand why they might have felt they couldn't just sit around here in this camp," he said. "But I don't think most of the people here feel that way. I certainly don't."

He did not state any more clearly exactly how he did feel. Everyone in camp shied away from talking about such things, and I myself had no desire to pursue the question at the time, so all I can do here is record his words as I remember them. Being a POW carries with it many ambiguities.

This pilot, a man in his mid-thirties, had long held a flight instructor's post at an air base near Tokyo, but the beginning of the Leyte showdown in October found him in Taiwan. He flew to Leyte Gulf in a torpedo bomber as part of the first kamikaze-style attack and had just released his torpedo at the hull of an American cruiser on the sea east of the island when he took a hit and blacked out as his plane crashed into the water. Some kind of mix-up prevented the Americans from ever discovering that he was a pilot, so he remained with us until the end of the war.

We eventually learned that the escapees had not gotten even as far as this pilot had hypothetically granted. Not only had they failed to make it to the airfield, but they had failed even to make it out of the forest on the other side of the marshlands skirting the camp's western edge. They were discovered one after another—one shot to death, two captured with injuries, and the last giving himself up (rumor had it that this last was Azuma). Instead of being returned to our camp, they were sent to Manila. Most of the prisoners believed the fugitives were executed there; one man even wrote a song telling of their tragic end, but the song did not catch on. As for myself, I never believed that they were executed.

Following the evening roll call came free time. Of course, with the construction of camp facilities essentially finished, even during the day we had very little work to do apart from minor daily chores like cleaning the latrines and disposing of the garbage. But the time after evening roll call had customarily been free time even in the military, so that was when these former soldiers felt they could really relax.

Darkness fell by around six o'clock, and we were not provided with lights, so the prisoners rushed to enjoy themselves in all manner of recreation during the time between roll call and darkness. Central Avenue resounded with sumo, jump rope, and men playing catch using hand-sewn "balls" of cloth filled with sand, while games of cards and mah-jongg—again, using handmade tiles meticulously carved from bamboo—took place indoors. Since no one had anything of value to wager, those bent on gambling staked portions of their next morning's breakfast.

As a nightly feature of this hour of escalating clamor, the cooking staff came pouring out of the cookshack after finishing their work. These men were the only ones in camp who always put in a full day's work, and their faces shone not only with the satisfaction of a job well done but with the conviction that they had provided a vital service to others. Their position permitted them to eat their fill of whatever they wanted, so they were both the stoutest and the most energetic men in camp.

In the normal order of things they first gathered raucously in their own quarters, then a short time later emerged to visit friends awaiting them in the barracks. They were of course welcome guests wherever they went.

Being friends with a cook meant you could receive gifts of additional food from time to time. Even Imamoto could be spied humoring the cooks in an attempt to get them to devise special menus for him.

The infirmary wards remained quiet. By Imamoto's order, the sick were forbidden any kind of recreation. Since none of us were sick enough to be sent to the hospital, we would have liked, at least, to play some cards. However, Imamoto justified his order on the grounds that it would otherwise be unfair to the working prisoners.

When I arrived at the camp, there were six men in the intensive care ward counting myself. Next to me was the starving Osakan, and beyond him was a young infantryman with a mild case of pulmonary tuberculosis. While in the jungle, he had attempted to kill himself using the sword he carried as a side arm, and the scar arced across his throat like the crescent-moon collar of a Japanese bear. Besides looking quite sickly in the face, he was a gloomy and taciturn fellow, but his crescent collar somehow endeared him to me. He and the Osakan and myself had beds against the opposite wall from the staff.

In the middle row, directly in front of me, was a forty-year-old civilian, the owner of an inn in Tacloban. He had fled into the mountains with Japanese troops and had gotten shot in the ankle. Originally from Aichi Prefecture, after the Manchurian Incident he had moved to Manchuria to get his start working as a clerk at a small inn in Changchun, and from there he had worked his way up to his present station. He had a sallow complexion, with small eyes and a broad mouth. The disproportionately well-developed lower half of his face made him look a little like a hippopotamus. The only thing he ever talked about was how much money he had blown all at once on this or that occasion in the past.

At forty, he was only four years my senior, so we could quite reasonably be regarded as belonging to the same generation, but I found it hard to think of him as my contemporary. Rather, he struck me as taking more after the fortyish men my generation had known when we were children. I suppose he had spent his life trying to emulate the successful forty-year-olds he had known as a youngster, and he had succeeded in the emulation but nothing more.

He complained about how Imperial Army officers had drunk his establishment into the ground. "Japanese troops are nothing but thieves," he said. "The army teaches its men to be crooks."

As one of the implicated troops, I decided one day that he needed a little warning. "Your business could be considered a kind of thievery, too," I said. "Everyone here feels responsible for failing to protect your property, ill-gotten though it was, so we take your bad-mouthing without offering any retort. But I suggest you be careful, because there's no telling how long our restraint will last."

Taken aback, he muttered something under his breath as he turned nervously from one prisoner to another in our circle, but he could hardly have expected to find a sympathetic countenance among them. My challenge, of course, had not come from any confidence in my own physical prowess. I had counted instead on the acclamation of my comrades and on their supportive strength. This mode of operation was a bad habit I had had since my youth, and I cannot say that using it now left a very good taste in my mouth.

The young patient next to the innkeeper cast me a look of gratitude. This man had been shot sideways through the windpipe and had lost his voice. The medics and orderlies could figure out what he wanted by reading his lips or hand gestures, but he communicated with newcomers like myself in writing.

He was the son of a farmer in Wakayama Prefecture, and he had joined a group of gangsters in Wakayama City at a very young age. My own parents had been born and raised in that city, and the man's creased forehead and round eyes reminded me of a woman from there who had visited my home when I was a child. He told me his family lived along the middle reaches of the Ki River. Though I had been born in Tokyo and had seldom traveled to my ancestral home, I held a particular fondness for the view of this great land-dividing sash of water separating the Kii Peninsula from the rest of our main island. That he had come from a place within the gorge formed by that river made me feel a special affinity for him.

After a time, he asked me to teach him English. Since he would never speak again, I saw little point in his learning a foreign language, especially when his station in life otherwise gave him no need to know English, and I told him so.

"I'm bored just lying around doing nothing," he replied in writing. "It can't do me any harm to study a little English."

Since he wanted to learn not merely to read but to actually express himself in English, I began instructing him in English composition. With so little time to do it in, I do not imagine I succeeded in imparting a true grasp of English grammatical structure to a man who had never gone beyond grade school, but for a time, giving lessons to this mute student became the most enjoyable part of my day. I, too, had grown quite sick of idleness.

In the bed next to my English student was a thirty-two-year-old shipping engineer who prior to entering the service had worked as a salaried employee at a firm in Tokyo. Reassigned from his firm to a munitions factory, he seduced one of the young women in the office into going with him to a hot spring, then later married another. The first young lady appeared at the night watchman's room one night when he was on duty; she took a massive dose of Calmotin but survived. Oh, what a relief it was, the man said, when he received his notice the following day.

His slender, tallish nose gave him the good looks of a late-twenties movie star. I enjoyed listening to him recount his conquests because I could sense, even in his own descriptions of how he had won them over, just how much contempt the women had for him.

As evening fell, the others in my ward lay quietly abed with their dark green U.S. Army fatigues buttoned against the gathering chill. Now and then one of them said something to his neighbor in a low voice, as if suddenly remembering he was not alone. As a pleasant darkness took over the nipa hut, an efflorescent white powder from the split-bamboo roofbeams high overhead filtered soundlessly down through the air. A blanket of white speckles invariably covered our clothes and beds by day's end.

The cacophonous din that filled the air all around was interrupted from time to time by the roar and quake of a heavy truck passing by on the road outside the compound. From the water stations behind the huts came an endless succession of splashes as inmates bathed themselves in the evening chill.

The cacophony rose still further after nightfall and gradually gave way to song. The prisoners sang every imaginable kind of tune, from military marches to sentimental pop songs to the kind of regional recitatives that you hear in talent shows everywhere. For the most part, the voices in each hut formed a single chorus, whose song rang out to mingle with the others over Central Avenue.

Only Headquarters received candles, but the bright floodlights mounted every thirty feet or so atop the fence came on and lit up the rear third of the huts all night long. The other floodlights, the ones mounted at each end of Central Avenue, went out at eight o'clock. Someone at Headquarters shouted "Lights out!" at that time, but since there were no other lights to be extinguished in the huts, it was really just a signal for everyone to go to sleep. Still, the singing failed to die down for quite some time.

In the intensive care ward, the four medics and orderlies from the regular ward next door would join our own medics and orderlies around Chief's table for a bedtime snack of food set aside during the day. They, too, joined their voices in song.

For one who had spent the previous months in a hospital where lights out was accompanied by complete silence, the unabated din was quite a surprise on my first night in camp. I bristled a bit at the behavior of the medical staff, whose first consideration should have been for their patients' rest, but as a newcomer I did not have the courage to protest. As the days passed, however, I became quite accustomed to the singing, and the more my condition improved, the more I grew to enjoy the clamor. When it comes to how we respond to the society around us, it seems the old French politician was right in saying that one should never trust one's first reaction because it is always false.

As I lay in darkness letting my mind wander, I had to inwardly "raise my voice" in order to keep my thoughts from being drowned out by the singing. Before long, I drifted off to sleep.

———

I awakened to the shout of "Ro-o-oll ca-a-all!" The voice repeated the command several times, each time stretching the words out as one does when shouting out over the ocean. Clicking tongues and low grumblings were soon joined by the sound of boots scraping the ground, and the dim figures of inmates began to appear all along Central Avenue. Suddenly the figures lit up as the floodlights at both ends of the avenue came on.

"Attention!" brought silence. The men stood motionless, with the bright floodlights illuminating their noses on both sides. The roll call master glided past the ranks.

Those in the sick wards merely had to lift their mosquito nets and stick out their heads. The American officer went by counting the men as if they were so many heads of squash.

"Attention!"

"At ease!"

The commands came again each time the officer finished one group and moved on to another, and then after a brief delay, a distant shout came from Imamoto: "Fall out!" The ranks dissolved in silence and the men scattered in their several directions, bumping and jostling as they went. Men wishing to stop at the latrines while they were up formed a separate current in the throng. Before the flow of this current came to an end, the floodlights at either end of the avenue went out and the roadway returned to shadows.

I will take a moment here to write about a scene that left a singular impression on me. The stage on which it took place was at the opposite end of Central Avenue from the gate, in the area just past the two rows of nipa barracks flanking either side of the street. Floodlights on the watchtower standing to the right cast their dazzling brightness down upon this stage.

A lone prisoner, bearing the rays of light on his back, trudged slowly across the compass of the stage from right to left and disappeared, his head bowed as if to elude the onrushing light.

I cannot recall at exactly what time of night or what point in my internment I observed this scene, nor can I recall exactly where I stood or what I was doing at the time—though, clearly, I had to have been standing somewhere on Central Avenue.

I do not know why this seemingly unremarkable scene has remained etched so clearly in my memory, but I cannot help feeling there must have been a reason. To have figurative expressions like "bearing the rays of light" and "the onrushing light" emerge quite spontaneously from my pen, as they did a few moments ago, would seem to show that the scene held special significance to me at the time. Perhaps something had deeply moved me. Though my mind is now a blank as to what that something might have been, a certain vague sentiment I feel rising within me as I replay the scene in my memory seems to confirm that I had indeed been deeply moved. Whatever this vague sentiment actually represents, it seems clear that it not only affected my state of mind during my entire internment but also lingers in my subconscious even today.

Now, the reason I chose to introduce the scene at this particular juncture is that it could legitimately have been treated as following seamlessly upon the 2:00 A.M. roll call I described from my first night in camp. To do so would not have substantially violated the truth, for the scene has to have taken place after one of our nighttime roll calls.

If I wished to shape the scene as in a novel, I could have presented it as follows:

> The floodlights at either end of the avenue went out, returning the roadway to shadows. The footsteps of prisoners padding back from the latrines to their barracks gradually grew softer and fewer, and before long all fell silent again. Spurred by something restless within me that would not let me lie still, I rose to go outside. As I emerged onto the roadway, I saw . . .

Then, after describing what I beheld, I could have written, "This symbolic scene that I witnessed on the first night I spent at the camp has remained etched in my memory ever since." By introducing novelistic elements into my account in this way, I could have provided an explanation of why I remember the scene so vividly.

The truth, however, presents an obstacle to such a narrative—to wit, the truth about where I was standing in that roadway.

According to the images preserved in my memory, a sharp contrast between the prisoner's brightly illuminated back and deeply shaded chest persists throughout his journey across the stage, and the contrast is still present when the man disappears behind the last hut on the left. If I had viewed the scene from immediately in front of the infirmary, on the right-hand side of the road, or from somewhere between there and the middle of the road, I should have been able to see only his shining back at the end. Since this is not as I remember it, I must ultimately conclude that I observed the scene from the left-hand side of the road.

In that case, what might I have been doing there? Neither then nor for a long time after did I have any friends in the barracks on the left-hand side of the road, so I can think of only one reason why I might have crossed the road: to obtain a drink of water from the Lister bag hanging in front of the cookshack. Perhaps I had gone to the bag and drawn some water into my beverage can, then stood back up and turned around—either to drink it on the spot or to take it back to my bed—and it was then that I witnessed the scene. This view, though hypothetical, is certainly consistent with how I remember the perspective from which I viewed the scene; it also stands in the way of the novelistic "explanation" I hypothetically presented above.

The question remains, then, of why the scene should have left such a powerful impression on me, but I am wary of making my account more novelistic in an effort to force an answer. The life of a POW is filled with meaningless actions. Attempting to claim a special significance for every action would, I fear, undermine the authenticity of my account.

So perhaps I should never have brought up an event whose circumstances have become so obscure in my memory. Still, it was not necessarily a waste for me to reflect on this scene. For example, in contemplating where I stood in the roadway, I have recalled going to the Lister bag, and a host of sensations associated with the many occasions when I squatted down before it in the middle of the night.

The bag, which was filled each morning by the cooks, would by then have grown nearly empty, its canvas skin wrinkled and limp, and I would have had to push the bottom of the hanging bag away from me to make the water collect around one of the taps. The water was always bitter from the chemical used to purify it. With an attention to detail characteristic of Japanese sensibilities, on the ground directly beneath the bag lay a split-bamboo frame, roughly a foot square, holding a neatly arranged bed of stones retrieved from the nearby stream.

Thirst was not my only reason for going to get a drink from the Lister bag in the middle of the night. Sometimes I went merely for something to do.

I usually took only a single sip of the bitter water and splashed the remainder on the ground. The darkened sand immediately absorbed the water, leaving scarcely a trace. Sand holds a dominant place in my impressions of this camp. It was a dark, ferruginous sand, blistering in the sun but cool in the shade, with a pleasantly soft touch under bare feet.

I also recall a certain sound. When I think of squatting down before the Lister bag to draw water, my ears seem to hear again a steady, high-pitched whine somewhere in the distance. It is a sound I have heard at other times in my life as well—the sound, I would guess, of an electrical substation, which became audible only at night after all the clamor had died down.

The North Star shone low over the palm trees at the far end of the road, Orion stood high overhead, and behind me spread the black southern sky. The stars familiar from home but now in different celestial positions reminded me of the vast curve of the globe lying between my homeland and the island of Leyte at ten degrees north latitude.

I experienced no longing for home. In the sense that any means of reaching home was utterly beyond our imagining, Japan had become like the moon to us. Our brothers and sisters might be perishing beneath falling bombs, they might be fleeing in panic from their burning houses, but such possibilities could not generate concern when we knew we could do absolutely nothing about them.

Life in camp began and ended with minutiae like getting a drink of water, splashing what was left on the ground, walking barefoot in the sand, or getting in and out of bed. Actions that in normal life do not even enter one's consciousness became etched with significance in my memory under the influence of a sentiment that, likewise, does not normally enter one's consciousness. Perhaps it could be called the prisoner's melancholy.

———

Each day began at 5:30 A.M. with a wake-up call from Headquarters. The sun did not begin to appear until six, so the prisoners sprang to action in darkness, removing their mosquito nets, folding their blankets, heading for the well to splash some water on their faces. Then they waited for the meal call, which came thirty minutes later: "Chow!"

Two men from each meal group (the division of each barracks into four squads was primarily for the purpose of meal service) emerged from the barracks and ran to the cookshack, where they picked up kerosene tins of food at the front window. Each group also got a second tin containing unsweetened black tea. Full daylight arrived by about this time.

For a brief duration the camp resounded with the clatter of tin-can mess kits, the meaningless grunts of the servers as they divided up the food, and the chatter of the prisoners waiting in line, speculating on the nature of the food being served. Then the commotion yielded to silence: The men were eating.

With no other means of satisfying physical appetites, food becomes the greatest of pleasures for men in captivity. I arrived at a time when rations had been reduced, and the men never stopped complaining of hunger, but I believe the calorie count remained quite adequate. At any rate, the men continued to put on weight.

In part, I suppose, the hunger pangs came from our country's customary diet of rice, which has the effect of expanding one's stomach, but they also owed to the prisoners having nothing else besides food to occupy their minds. Cravings increase in proportion to the amount of attention paid.

After breakfast the servers washed the two kerosene tins and sterilized them in the pot of boiling water by the well across from the cookshack before turning them back in at the window. Roll call, already described, followed at seven o'clock, and then the day's work began—except that there was actually very little work to do.

Perhaps out of reluctance to deprive the locals of work, the Americans had not yet developed a plan for utilizing POW manpower. Labor details were therefore limited to constructing facilities within the camp, and when they did go outside, it was only to cut bamboo or haul lumber needed for internal projects. Furthermore, with all of the essential facilities already in place by this time, there was virtually no internal construction left to be done apart from minor improvements proposed now and then for lack of anything better to do.

Even so, there were a number of routine chores that needed to be taken care of on a daily basis. By turns, each barracks group cleaned the latrines by scrubbing them down with water, sweeping the ground all around, and sprinkling kerosene into each hole. Garbage disposal also rotated through the barracks groups. Each morning a great mound of empty food cans and other kitchen waste had to be hauled from the cookshack to the incineration spot behind the compound, where the Americans doused it with gasoline and set it ablaze. Blazing like a small house on fire, the flames leapt as high as the nearby palm trees.

Another daily chore was tool retrieval. Shovels, pickaxes, bolos, and any other tools that could potentially serve as weapons had to be checked out each morning from the storehouse outside the gate on the east side of the compound. All tools checked out for the day were brought to Headquarters, where they were distributed according to requests submitted the day before by each barracks. Keeping a record of the tools checked out and making sure they all got collected and returned to the storehouse in the evening was the most important responsibility of the head of the barracks group in charge for the day.

The occupants of each barracks used these tools for making repairs both inside and outside their building and for clearing their drainage ditches; even when nothing new was being constructed, routine maintenance did demand some attention. The bolos in particular had a great many uses around huts made mainly of bamboo and nipa, so the prisoners would often try to conceal them somewhere instead of returning them in the evening. Then the head of the tool detail had to conduct a top to bottom search of all the barracks.

Once the group chores had been taken care of, next came laundry. We Japanese seem to have a special fondness for doing our wash. I have heard that in jungles all across the Pacific, our troops' laundry, hung out to dry among the trees, served as targets for enemy bombers. Group A's clotheslines behind the cooks' quarters and at the end of the left row of huts, across the way from the latrines, were invariably full by 9:00 A.M. We were given a virtually unlimited supply of laundry soap.

The inmates had not yet been issued underwear, so the laundry consisted mainly of fatigue shirts and pants. Though these were seldom worn during the day except at roll call, they became soiled with perspiration from serving as pajamas at night. Some of the prisoners also advocated frequent laundering for a purpose quite removed from the pleasure of sleeping with freshly laundered pajamas next to their skin: They wished to diminish the prominence of the "PW" labels printed on those shirts and pants.

"PW" was supposed to be stamped in large letters on the back of the shirt and the seat of the pants, and in smaller letters on the front of the sleeves and two inches above both knees—a total of six places. These letters were stenciled on in either black or white paint, using a template kept at Headquarters. Though many tried their best to avoid having it done, Imamoto would eventually catch them and make them get the stamps. Then they would set to laundering their fatigues vigorously in an effort to make the letters fade.

Soap had little effect on the paint, however. In the case of white paint, the letters only seemed to stand out more as the fabric around them faded.

Blankets also appeared on the clotheslines. These were fine woolen blankets from Australia, luxuriously soft compared to the Japanese-made cotton blankets we had been accustomed to. One young fellow declared that they had the soft touch of a woman's skin, but this was perhaps going a bit far.

While I am on the subject of blankets, I should note that the camp remained completely free of lice. Upon arrival, each man was stripped of every last thread he wore, bathed, and given all new clothes. The old clothes were incinerated, so there was no way for a louse to find its way into camp. Furthermore, the beds were canvas cots, and the ground around them was regularly sprinkled with kerosene, so fleas and bedbugs could not survive either. This was one of the greatest blessings of American POW camps when compared to Soviet camps. It is amazing what money can do.

One final order of business each morning was sick call. The afflictions for which the men sought treatment ranged from combat wounds, to tropical sores and other ailments contracted while in the mountains, to new injuries sustained while engaged in one of the camp's work details. Dermatological complaints made up the greatest number. The Japanese army had always been famous for ringworm, and scabies was very common among the newer prisoners in Group B. I do not know why such skin diseases flourished so in the mountains, but I recall one of the sufferers observing that the parasites seemed to gain force in direct proportion to the carrier's loss of vigor from malnutrition.

The numbers of dermatology patients were so great that the Americans had difficulty keeping the infirmary supplied with sufficient ointment. So, quite apart from the regular hours, whenever a new supply arrived, the medics immediately set up shop at Group B and sent out a call for the affected patients to gather. Two lines of men stretched out more than sixty feet as they waited their turn to have the ointment applied.

The regular sick call began at 8:00 A.M. in the rooms at the front of the infirmary. Several thick palm logs cut to a comfortable sitting height and placed on end served as stools for the patients to use while being examined or having their wounds dressed.

The infirmary's hut adjutant was a medical NCO from the navy. Though he bunked at Headquarters, he came to the infirmary to help with treatment during clinic hours. All the other Japanese medics gathered as well, including the two from the infirmary annex next door. These men took their medical duties very seriously, carrying them out with the greatest of deliberation. Along with the mess crew, they were the most hard-working men in camp. In the army, the cooks and the medics had enjoyed a certain privileged status, and in the turmoil of retreat they had been known to egregiously abuse their special positions. Now, however, among POWs shorn of their fighting power and seeking only to satisfy each man's personal needs, they were the ones with the most to offer. Within the rigid institutional environment of the army, out of natural psychological needs, they had let themselves glory in their power, and this stood as a black mark against them. But as inmates of the POW camp, where everything had been reduced to purely biological needs, they proved themselves not only useful but generous.

The line of patients waiting for treatment in front of the infirmary snaked around into the alley between the barracks and all the way to the back of the building. As they waited, the men leaned on the walls of the intensive care ward and gazed inside. Since I lay with my pillow to the wall, I found myself looking straight up into their faces.

The relationship between fellow POWs is a curious thing. We were of course all strangers who had not previously met or known one another, but we held two things in common: We had once fought for the same objectives in the Imperial Army, and we were now POWs. On some level that should have endowed us with feelings of affinity, but curiously enough, far from making us feel closer, it somehow made us more reticent with one another. The faces I observed as I looked up from my bed seemed caught between wanting to reach out and wanting to maintain their guard; they were timid and wary and profoundly befuddled. I had never seen my compatriots wearing such expressions before, and I doubt I will ever again.

That is to say, the situation those Japanese men found themselves in, enjoying in shame the privileges accorded to POWs by a civilized nation, are unlikely ever to be repeated. Now that Japanese troops have tasted what life as a POW can be like, they will henceforth throw down their arms without hesitation as soon as the battle appears lost. Men who once blindly laid down their lives without reflecting on what it truly meant allowed themselves to become intoxicated with the sweetness of POW life, utterly oblivious to what the ultimate implications might be. They will be disinclined to pick enemies in the future. I would not recommend the hiring of Japanese men as soldiers of fortune.

A Japanese army surgeon from among the POWs arrived shortly after the line of patients formed. He was an unprepossessing man in his midforties, with a salt-and-pepper beard framing his face. He had come into the service as a conscript. The stethoscope around his neck carried a note of authority and stood out in elegant contrast against his humble POW uniform.

His job was to make a preliminary diagnosis and determine who needed to be seen by the American doctor. He pronounced my heart murmur trivial. Being an inpatient, however, I could ask to be reexamined by the American doctor when he appeared by and by.

The American doctor was a first lieutenant, a Jewish man named Silverman. With an American medic and the POW interpreter Sakurai in tow, he made the rounds of the two wards. When Sakurai asked each patient how he was doing, if the patient said "Better," the doctor went right on by; if he said "Not so good," the doctor stopped to examine him. Dr. Silverman affirmed the other doctor's evaluation of my heart condition, but he diagnosed me with jaundice and forbade me to eat meat. Since the food prepared in the cookshack was usually a gruel of corned beef and rice, he made special arrangements for me to receive American field ration hardtack.

The medic was an American of Italian descent named Melchior. I have never known how far to believe the stories about Italians' legendary ebullience and vitality, but there can be no question that this man was the liveliest of all the foreigners I met. He had reddish brown hair and a ruddy complexion, with small brown eyes that never stopped moving. A relatively short man, he walked with something of a swagger, his toes pointing outward and his shoulders shifting broadly back and forth. He was always making jokes, via Sakurai, flattering us with remarks like "Japanese soldiers are the bravest in the world. They just don't have anything to eat." When he saw me reading, he brought me a copy of *Moby Dick*. He had been a sailor before joining the army.

Though Melchior treated us prisoners kindly, he was always getting into altercations with his own colleagues. Outside the camp fence, on the other side of the receiving area by the entrance, was an infirmary for the

Americans, and Melchior would often go there to obtain medicines or on some other errand—except sometimes it seemed like he actually went there just to pick fights. I would see him ranting and carrying on like a spoiled child having a tantrum, and I could never quite tell whether he was being serious or just playing some kind of game. A tall, blond Swede and a dark-haired Pole would stand on either side of him, both looking much distressed and trying desperately to calm him down; I found it amusing to watch their expressions.

Even speaking entirely without prejudice, when compared to the doctors with the rank of major and captain I had met at the hospital, our camp's Dr. Silverman seemed to be of a somewhat lower class directly proportionate to his lower rank. Or perhaps it was that he had grown accustomed to the relaxed atmosphere of the camp and had set aside the professional mask that doctors are wont to wear, so that his more down-to-earth qualities were exposed for all to see. He was a Viennese who had fled from Hitler, and he liked to sing.

By the time the doctor completed his rounds at about ten o'clock, the outpatients were usually done as well. He and Melchior were apparently obligated to remain in the infirmary office until noon, however, so they passed the time surrounded by the idle Japanese medics singing songs. The doctor was particularly fond of Schubert and often asked the medics to give him a chorus of "Serenade." He himself sang a difficult piece from "Die Winterreise" in a remarkably polished baritone.

One time as he listened to the chorus of "Serenade," he turned to Melchior and said, "It's hard to believe a bunch of fellows with this kind of harmony could do all those terrible things."

"They didn't have anything to eat," Melchior retorted.

Our interpreter repeated the exchange in Japanese, and the singers threw themselves even more cheerfully into their singing.

———

I went outside. On the bulletin board in front of Headquarters, the recently revised camp regulations were posted in both English and Japanese. In my boredom I eventually memorized the entire English text of the regulations, but only a few fragments come back to me today.

"All petitions must be submitted through the official spokesman."

"Spokesman" meant Imamoto. The Japanese translation posted next to the English faithfully rendered this as *daibensha*, the Japanese equivalent of "spokesman," but this had been crossed out and replaced with the equivalent of "Japanese Camp Commandant"—I suspect at Imamoto's own bidding.

"No food is to be kept in the barracks."

As a rule, we did not receive sufficient quantities of food to set anything aside, but I have already noted how some of the men buried cans of food under their bunks in the belief that friendly forces would return.

"Walking within three paces of the fence is prohibited."

The guards were especially sticky about this when an air raid warning had been sounded. Carelessness had resulted in a number of injuries when the rule was first established.

"Anyone attempting to escape over or through the fence will receive two warnings to 'Halt!' If he still fails to heed the warning, he will be shot."

Besides the airmen who had broken out, there had been only one other incident in which a deranged man climbed two or three levels up the barbed-wire fence. He was dragged back down with lacerations on his arms and legs and was sent to the hospital.

Even supposing that someone had been able to get away from the camp, Leyte was surrounded by ocean. Most of the POWs had spent time fleeing through the mountains and were well aware how difficult it would be to find their way to the sea, let alone cross it. In truth, the fences did more to protect us from the local population than to guard against our escape. Even without the Americans' guns and bayonets, outside the fence lurked nothing but danger and privation, whereas inside the fence we enjoyed safety and an endless supply of corned beef.

All of the daily chores and maintenance work were completed by late morning, and the entire camp relaxed as we waited for lunch. Some of the prisoners played games on Central Avenue, while others returned to their barracks to rest. In contrast to the infirmary wards, the sixty-man common barracks had three rows of cots lined up practically one on top of another, and the prisoners sat or lay about wearing nothing but loincloths. The naked bodies, sandy soil, and sunlight filtering through the none-too-thickly thatched nipa roofs overhead reminded me of the reed-screen huts set up as changing rooms on public beaches back home—especially the way the men lounged about in languid idleness.

Some played regular cards; others, flower cards.[2] Some sang songs; others learned the songs. Some just sat and talked with their neighbors, the invariable topic being food—or, more particularly, prognosticating what was on the menu for lunch. Others lay on their beds and literally did nothing. Readers may wonder how one could stand to pass the time doing absolutely nothing, but POWs in fact grow quite accustomed to it. As Dostoyevsky suggested, a cardinal trait of the human animal is that he can adapt to anything.

At such times when we had nothing to do, the more vigorous among us

---

2 A gambling game played with a deck of forty-eight cards in twelve suits based on trees, shrubs, and flowers, each associated with a particular month of the year.

played outside in the street: sumo wrestling, pole pushing,[3] and games of catch. It was quite a peculiar sight—this scene of former Japanese troops with their close-cropped heads frolicking gleefully under the hot tropical sun.

I suppose what impressed me more than anything else was the effect of so many well-endowed, all-but-naked male bodies milling about in a single pulsating mass. In our normal lives, we often have occasion to observe the male anatomy exposed to varying degrees. We see, for example, the corpulent flesh of gigantic sumo wrestlers, the steel-like muscles of boxers, and the finely tuned bodies of track and field athletes, as well as the virile physiques of young men at the beach. For myself, the owner of a feeble, middle-aged body, such occasions had brought certain feelings of intimidation on an animalistic level. I had felt no particular alarm, however, for as a member of the species that is master of all creation, I considered it abnormal to be well-developed in body only.

The mass of bodies I now observed in the camp had none of the unsightliness of such excessive physical development. According to the plan devised by the army brass as a means of compensating for the shortage of ordnance, these bodies had been trained primarily for endurance, and inasmuch as the resulting physiques had a practical purpose, they were not the least bit abnormal. In the end they may have failed to accomplish the intended purpose, affecting the outcome of the war only in increasing by a small margin the enemy's expenditure of troops, but in defeat those same bodies had served admirably to preserve the lives of individual soldiers. One of the men captured on Leyte had escaped death by retreating a full kilometer on his stomach.

The sight of those uniformly well-honed bodies ranked in full dress had been magnificent, and in the bedlam of the army baths they had been beautiful, too. The moment they were liberated from battle, however, those bodies had become devoid of purpose, and in turn, as abnormal and gratuitous as the athletes' bodies.

On top of that, thanks to the canned foods supplied by the Americans, they had started to add some unnatural girth.

A prisoner who dabbled in traditional poetry had composed a short tanka poem:

How magnificent
The generous benevolence
Of the United States:
Not once in all our lives
Have we ever been so fat.

---

3 A contest of strength between two men grasping opposite ends of a pole.

One could see new layers of fat forming especially on the prisoners' cheeks and bellies. Small lumps of excess flesh bulged at the corners of their mouths, making them look like thick-witted imbeciles, worried and scared.

The military spirit drummed into them back home had been rendered useless when they lost their ability to fight and were confined within a fenced compound. Now even their military-hardened flesh was being transformed into the appearance of useless imbeciles.

The men were particularly fond of sumo. I suppose this sport whose very lifeblood is in the unity of physical prowess with fighting spirit titillated whatever remained of their martial consciousness. Burly titans confident of their superiority in sheer physical strength stepped into the ring with arrogant glee. Smaller men adept at the various trips and throws smirked back, uncowed. Men of average build eyed their foes with tense concentration as they calculated their opening move. A clown who played the role of dauntless doormat, always coming back for more even though he could never win, became the perennial crowd-pleaser. Some others entered the ring to lose merely because they wanted to be part of the general excitement.

Covered in perspiration and sand, they wrestled under the tropical sun. The same sun shone over the unfettered landscape beyond the camp's fence, over every remaining battlefield in the western Pacific, over the homeland even now being ravaged by bombs, and over the ten thousand Japanese troops said still to be hiding in the northwestern jungles of Leyte.

The camp commandant appeared, a tall first lieutenant in his midtwenties. His face wore a look of naive detachment, as if he were a grownup version of the villainous rich man's kid in an American children's movie. His voice, however, resonated deeply. His management style could be summed up as rational and legalistic, permitting anything the regulations specifically allowed but never anything more. His ancestors were from Romania.

The camp commandant avoided unnecessary contact with the prisoners and preferred not to be bothered by matters of courtesy. The fortyyear-old innkeeper in the intensive care ward was once reprimanded for smiling at him on Central Avenue. The commandant summoned Oda and demanded to know what the innkeeper had had in mind. He had merely smiled to be sociable, out of professional habit, but because of the effect his buckteeth had on the shape of his smile, the commandant had taken it as a sneer. Oda painstakingly explained the benevolent motives of the smiling man. Even so, the commandant thereafter prohibited the prisoners from smiling at him.

When he entered the compound, he usually brought with him his head clerk, a brown-haired, bespectacled sergeant of about thirty. This man had a heavily creased face, with a paper shuffler's smugness pulling at the corners of his mouth. He, like the commandant, was quite tall.

The two men made their way slowly among the groups of prisoners playing in the street. The commandant walked with his chest thrust forward and his shoulders and arms swinging gently, rhythmically back and forth. The head clerk walked with his lips set and his gaze always trained straight ahead. At least once each day they came into the compound to walk casually among us like this, conducting, in effect, a tour of inspection.

The prisoners lowered their eyes and stepped aside long enough for the two men to pass, then resumed their play. The two men moved on.

These men ruled and watched, and the prisoners lived. But can prisoners really *live*? Are they truly *human*?

6

Brothers in Arms

Several men from my unit on Mindoro were already interned at the POW camp when I arrived. Though these men had all been captured considerably later than myself, they had preceded me to the camp while I recuperated in the hospital.

After routing my company from our Rutay Ridge base near Bulalacao on January 24, the Americans proceeded to occupy Ridge 517 overlooking San Jose by the following evening. The platoon camping there had already vacated the position, however, having foreseen the danger as a result of patrols sent to scout the Rutay Ridge area the previous day. Numbering about fifty, this platoon made its way northward, intending ultimately to cross over to Luzon. About ten days later, they crossed paths with a group of twenty or so men who had fled Rutay Ridge. Then on February 8, when they were resting at an islander's home, a large-scale guerrilla ambush sent them scattering. I had heard while still at the hospital that the platoon commander and six others had been captured and sent to the camp.

The first of the men I met after my arrival was Second Lieutenant Yamada, the platoon commander. I found him in line with a load of dishes at the sterilization pot across from the cookhouse, taking a turn on kitchen detail for the officers.

Yamada had served his first tour in the army as a Taishō era volunteer (that is to say, as a secondary school graduate who paid ¥200 in order to gain a shorter tour of duty and rapid advancement) and had subsequently become the proprietor of a haberdashery in Tokyo's old downtown area. His thick beard gave him an imposing appearance befitting his position as commander, and in the mountains he made a great outward show of boldness, but we had all seen through his facade and perceived his secret terror. The men who had been with him to the end castigated him for the way he treated the stragglers who faltered as they fled to the north, ending their misery with a blade instead of with his pistol, purportedly to conserve ammunition, only to surrender without using any of that precious ammunition when guerrillas finally had them surrounded.

I suggested that perhaps rust had rendered his pistol useless.

"At least he could still have bluffed," retorted one of the men. "But all he did was run around in a blithering panic, desperate to live. Talk about stabbing you in the back!"

Still, I have no desire to level charges at Lieutenant Yamada. The human animal has many weaknesses. At the time he killed the debilitated stragglers, he may have had every intention of using his side arm in battle. He could not help it if the man who stabbed the faltering stragglers to conserve bullets and the man who surrendered without a shot were two entirely different people.

He had heard through the grapevine that I was in the hospital and smiled weakly when he saw me. Somewhat stuffily, he inquired about the attack and my capture. He told me he had tried to pass as a sergeant, but contradictory testimony from one of the men captured with him had exposed him.

"Him and his big mouth," he groused, but of course the soldier had no obligation to cover for the commander, whether for his vanity or for his attempt to evade responsibility. I should add, however, that after his repatriation, Lieutenant Yamada conscientiously visited the families of the fallen men in his command, thus fulfilling his duty as the only officer from our unit to return home alive. He himself succumbed to a sudden illness two years after arriving home.

More bitter than anyone else toward the lieutenant was a man named Yoshida, the one who spat out the remark about back-stabbing. He bore a particular grudge because of the way the lieutenant had railed at him when he had been nearly crippled by an infection in his ankle. This experience led him to express increasingly vituperative opinions of the Imperial Army, and once back in Japan he began traveling far and wide to make those views known. In my own humble opinion, however, it is not only facile but utterly misguided to censure an entire institution out of bitterness arising from a narrow personal experience: facile because anyone can denounce the institution's faults while ignoring his own complicity; misguided because it focuses solely on conditions encountered in the institution while ignoring that institution's raison d'être. The Imperial Japanese Army and its many feudalistic abuses are not to be denounced merely because they wrought such great suffering on the rank-and-file soldier; they are to be denounced because it is in those very abuses that we can find the cause of the army's defeat.

Yoshida was a thirty-four-year-old reservist, formerly the proprietor of a mah-jongg parlor in Tokyo's Shitaya district. During the war, the authorities closed down his business and assigned him to work in a factory. Endless grousing about the factory became a staple of his conversations on Mindoro. He thought the infection on his ankle was a tropical sore, and so did everyone else, but the camp's American doctor diagnosed it as a symptom of venereal disease. After that, Yoshida started receiving regular injections for it, and he rejoiced gloriously that he was getting the problem taken care of for free while a POW.

A younger soldier named Kagura had also been captured with Lieutenant Yamada. The younger men in our unit were for the most part conscientious and hard-working—certainly more likely to have their performance rated "very satisfactory" than the lazy over-thirty crowd. But some chose to apply their youthful vigor to sloth and guile instead, and in those cases they made far greater nuisances of themselves than their older counterparts.

Upon finishing school, Kagura had taken a desk job with a munitions manufacturer. There he had observed the behavior of his seniors under the wartime policy of full-employment and had incorporated it into his own "philosophy of life," as it were. Whenever one of the middle-aged reservists took him to task for shirking, he had a ready retort: "You're a fine one to talk after spending the last ten years inventing ways to sit at a desk and look busy at doing nothing."

Kagura approached military life by toadying up to his superiors and ignoring his peers. The middle-aged reservists had no scruples about toadying up to their superiors either, but the rough and tumble of life had made them too weak-kneed to bluntly shove aside their peers.

When we ran into each other at the camp, he did not seem particularly pleased to see me. We proceeded through the obligatory exchange of capture stories, but he obviously found it tedious, saying as little as possible on his part and scarcely listening to my account. He kept turning his head one way and another as we talked, apparently more interested in what was going on around us.

Suddenly he let out a whoop and took off at a gallop. He had spied some of the old-timers in his barracks group gathering for some sumo in the street. Going through some silly antics, he cut in for a bout and immediately took a tumble. His highest priority now was to toady up to his seniors in camp.

Eight men had fled with Lieutenant Yamada at the time of the ambush on February 8; of that group, only Yoshida and Kagura remained. All told, the column of stragglers numbered sixty-seven before the guerrilla attack. The night before, they had stayed in a village overlooking a river about six kilometers inland from Bongabong on the east coast of the island, and they spent the day waiting out some heavy rain. As they prepared food for supper, a barrage of gunshots erupted from the jungle behind the village. Everyone ran for the river, some heading upstream, others downstream, and still others taking to the mountain rising up on the other side. The lieutenant's group was the last.

Four men who fled downstream also preceded me to the camp. One was the office manager of a letterpress print shop in Shibaura named Miyata, and another was the eldest son of a machine shop owner in Ogu named Kanai. Both of them being of reserved temperament, they had become inseparable buddies while garrisoned in Bulalacao. They fled the ambush together and were ultimately captured together.

Because of the way the guerrillas were treating them, Miyata and Kanai became convinced they were to be killed, so rather than suffer unspeakable cruelties, they decided to take matters into their own hands. Lying one on top of the other so as to keep their arms free, they tried to strangle each other with the drawstrings of their trousers. Miyata, who lay on his back on the ground, explained how he began to feel faint and feared he might black out before Kanai died. Lest he fail his friend, he tried desperately to pull harder, but he could not tell whether he was succeeding. When he came to, Kanai's head was hanging limply by his ear, but he was drawing deep breaths.

"You still alive?" Miyata asked.

"Uh-huh," came Kanai's surprisingly strong answer.

They realized that method would not work, and because they were being held in a bare detention cell in the town jail, they could find no other means for accomplishing the deed. That experience had cemented their friendship with an even stronger emotional bond.

Though Miyata had a salaried job, it was solely for appearances: Not only did he own property in Tokyo, but he was the son-in-law and adopted heir of a large landholder in Gunma Prefecture. His womanish, pigeon-toed gait seemed quite out of keeping with his tall, robust build. When the camp was eventually reorganized into U.S. Army–style companies, he and I wound up working together as overhead staff for the same company, and I found his cravenness and paranoia exceedingly hard to stomach. After the war was over, as our time for repatriation neared, he painstakingly fabricated a diary showing that he had surrendered only after the emperor had proclaimed the war's end instead of being captured during the war.

Kanai had earned the favor of his superiors as an industrious worker on Mindoro, and this did not change in the least after he became a POW; he continued to apply himself to his assigned tasks with quiet diligence. Both he and Miyata suffered from severe nearsightedness, but whereas Miyata had lost his glasses to the guerrillas and now went about looking as though he had lost his bearings, Kanai had by some miracle retained his glasses, and they now gave him a look of confident assurance. Today he owns and operates a food processing plant.

The third of the men captured after escaping downstream was an acupuncturist and masseur named Iketani. On Mindoro, he liked to invite himself into local homes to be entertained—a practice that not only earned him the islanders' hatred but also alienated his compatriots. Separated from his platoon mates after the ambush, he wandered through the jungle alone for a time and twice attempted to hang himself from a tree branch only to have the cord break (so he claimed, at any rate—we did not really believe him) before he fell into the hands of guerrillas. He boasted of the special treatment he had received after offering the guerrilla officer a massage.

"As they say, 'Learn a trade, for the time may come when you will need it.' And to think I became a masseur because I wanted to ease my sick mother's suffering. It just goes to show you: A good deed is never lost."

This was what he said to me, but I also overheard him telling one of his barracks mates, a stranger, that he was a manager in a fertilizer company. He was of relatively slight build, with dark skin and thick hair. Nothing seemed to faze him, and when he spoke, his words emerged slowly from between his lips as though he were deliberating on them one by one. I suppose you could call him a kind of confidence man.

As I write about these men, I am forced to conclude, regrettably, that the middle-aged officers and reservists sent to Mindoro not only left a great deal to be desired as soldiers but were not very likable as people, either. The unnatural environment of the battlefield brought out the ugliest sides of these worldly-wise middle-agers, and if this owed essentially to their lack of a will to fight, then their deployment to the front was a grievous error both for the men themselves and for the nation that sent them there.

Obviously, the far better course would have been to send machines, but lacking the necessary ordnance, our country substituted men in whom a fighting spirit had been inculcated through training. A fighting spirit that has merely been taught, however, will crumble to nothing in the face of battlefield realities, and it makes little difference whether the fighter is a reservist or regular army.

The last of the men who escaped downstream was a career army man named Masuda. Corporal Masuda had served two tours of duty on the continent, and he was without question the most seasoned NCO in Lieutenant Yamada's platoon. When the platoon on Ridge 517 heard the artillery pounding Rutay Ridge on January 24, it was Corporal Masuda who persuaded the vacillating lieutenant to dispatch a squad of reinforcements, and it was he who went to scout the American positions the next morning.

Fearing imminent attack, the remainder of the platoon fled northward without waiting for his return, but because they followed the route he had suggested beforehand, he was able to rejoin them without difficulty.

However, the man who displayed such composure and courage on that occasion chose a most unmilitary course of escape after the guerrilla ambush. The river that skirted the village flowed directly toward the town of Bongabong on the coast, so the most obvious escape route was back the way they had come, into the mountains upstream. Yet, even though the great majority of the men did in fact take this route, the corporal chose instead to go downstream on his own, and he was then discovered and taken prisoner by guerrillas while walking along a road. In retrospect, however, the description he gave of his capture sounds somewhat suspicious.

Of course, no Japanese prisoner in the camp would admit to having surrendered voluntarily; their sense of honor forbade it. After repatriation, however, once they saw that civilian attitudes toward POWs had changed, some confessed the truth. If one compares these true confessions with the stories those same men concocted in camp, one often discovers that their fabrications contained certain telling truths.

For example, a man taken prisoner on Leyte gave the following account while interned: "I decided I'd just take my chances, and I went out onto the highway and started walking. Then some guerrillas came along in a horse cart and captured me."

The truth, which he revealed after returning home, was as follows: "I had been planning to surrender for quite some time. I purposely dropped back from the column and hid myself in the jungle near a highway. When I saw an American jeep carrying some noncombat troops, I stepped out in front of it with my hands up."

The common element in these two accounts is the highway. The highway system in the Philippines had been built by the Americans to promote automobile transportation. For a fleeing Japanese soldier to show himself on one of these main thoroughfares was most surely to be discovered by the enemy, and it could hardly be a matter of "taking one's chances." The disingenuousness of such a characterization would have been immediately apparent had the audience been anything other than a group of befogged POWs.

I suspect Corporal Masuda's "downstream" was, like the Leyte soldier's "highway," a telling truth mixed in among his fabrications. Obviously, a seasoned warrior like the corporal knew perfectly well that going downstream meant going into Filipino or American-controlled territory. In fact, even the soldiers with far less battle experience knew this and chose to flee upstream instead.

For the sake of his honor, however, I hasten to emphasize that this speaks only to the probability of his surrender; the actual facts of the case may be entirely different. Surrender is a particular, individual act. On the verge of starvation in the jungles of the Pacific, a great many soldiers must have contemplated surrender, yet very few found the courage to actually turn themselves over to the enemy. At the same time, it would not have been the least bit implausible for a man who had never dreamed of surrendering to suddenly find his hands in the air when confronted with the incontrovertible superiority of his foe.

Many of those writing today about their experiences as POWs discuss the psychology of surrender in elevated terms, speaking of "rediscovered humanity" or "a passion to live." In my view, however, there exists no need to find profound psychological causes for impulsive actions of this kind.

One Leyte POW spoke of advancing forward to attack the enemy at close quarters and, upon seeing an American tank as big as a house, being suddenly overcome by the desire to go home, even if it meant falling prisoner. Until that moment he had never once contemplated surrender or thought of home. Training is the acquisition of appropriate habits for dealing with predictable circumstances, so when faced with an altogether unanticipated circumstance it can break down in an flash. Such psychological fault lines essentially have no anchorage in time.

Nothing requires us to conclude that the courageous Corporal Masuda of January 24 had secretly decided to surrender as his platoon marched through the mountains sometime before February 8. When he dropped down to the river bank, he may have found the terrain on the downstream side more open and some inexplicable intuition told him that this was the way to survival. The same inexplicable intuition may have continued to guide his meanderings over the next few days, ultimately leading him before the guerrillas with his hands up. No one can say decisively that that is what happened, but neither is there a single shred of evidence to the contrary.

From the human perspective, a battlefield is made up of individual actions and facts and nothing more. The rest boils down to intentions— and the tales told.

So far as the facts of the battlefield are concerned, Corporal Masuda was an unregenerate liar. In civilian life, he made his living as a broker, which is to say, an occupation that requires constant dissembling, but I have to wonder whether any broker could close many successful deals if he pitched his products the way the corporal spoke of the "facts" he had purportedly witnessed.

When discussing "facts" no one else could know about, he was forever claiming firsthand knowledge as a participant or witness.

I had a friend named Watari in Masuda's squad. Though he came from Tokyo, he was related to one of my colleagues at the Kobe shipyard where I was working when I received my notice. We had not previously met, but the accident of being drafted into the same unit at the same time led us to become friends. Though once we were on Mindoro our platoons were stationed apart, en route on the transport ship Watari and I found time to swap stories about acquaintances we had in common; after reaching our stations, too, we occasionally exchanged brief letters by way of messengers going back and forth between our platoons.

According to Corporal Masuda, Watari had to be dead. He was sitting right next to Watari, he said, when the guerrillas attacked. As the jungle erupted with gunfire and a bullet whizzed between them, Masuda leapt behind some lumber piled beside him, and from there rolled on down the steep embankment to the river. Since Watari's side got hit by a massive barrage, he could not possibly have escaped alive.

A month after the corporal told me this, however, the supposedly dead Watari showed up at our camp with seven others from his platoon. Not only was he alive, but when I asked Watari about the ambush, he said he had not been sitting beside the corporal at all.

Meanwhile, the corporal had led Watari to believe that *I* was dead. When the corporal returned from scouting the vicinity of Rutay Ridge the day after the Americans attacked my platoon, he told Watari he had seen my dead body. When we met in camp, Watari and I clasped hands and rejoiced together over the other's survival, and I must credit the corporal's lies for redoubling the joy of our reunion.

The group of eight men including Watari represented all that was left of the more than twenty men who escaped upriver from the ambush. After picking their way northward for another month and a half, they were captured in the mountains behind Calapan on March 26. They arrived at the camp on April 8, the last of the survivors from our company.

———

Watari's group comprised three NCOs and five privates. One NCO and one private were shipping engineers marooned on Mindoro and rescued by our company. The other two NCOs and four privates had belonged to our company from the beginning. These two NCOs were in fact both from my own platoon—which is to say, they had been among those who escaped safely from Rutay Ridge on the day of the attack.

When I trotted up to greet them, Sergeant Kurokawa turned his head away and said, "You know, Ōoka, we've lost this war." His tone of voice seemed to imply all was hopeless now that even he had been captured.

The other, Corporal Satō, said, "Is it true you've got a commissary here?"

Three of my superior officers had been taken prisoner, and in all three cases the first words out of their mouths when we were reunited as POWs made me bristle. When my own squad leader arrived at the hospital, his first words had been, "Man, they confiscated everything." As I have already explained, "everything" referred to his precious black briefcase in which he kept pilfered medical supplies and the watches and other personal effects of deceased squad members.

The experience of Watari's group between February 8 and March 26 was like that of other retreating troops all across the Pacific: They scraped along eating berries and wild roots, making periodic forays down to the coastal zones in search of food only to be chased back into the mountains by the locals. About the time they came into the highlands above Calapan (though with neither map nor compass in their possession, they had no idea where they were), Sergeant Kurokawa suggested that they should kill and eat the next Filipino they saw. Watari said at first he thought it was a joke and paid no attention, but when the sergeant kept repeating it, he took a closer look at the sergeant's eyes. The mad glint he saw there sent a chill up and down his spine.

They followed a tiny stream out of the mountains and came to a fenced cornfield in the coastal lowlands. An islander wearing a broad-rimmed sun hat was walking along the far edge of the field. Only one of the group still had his rifle, and it is not clear what role Sergeant Kurokawa's suggestion may have played in provoking him to shoot at the man and thereby risk disclosing the group's position. The gunman himself claimed he just felt like he was at the end of his tether and thought "I'll show him!" In any case, without saying a word to anyone else, he fired. The shot missed, and the man took off running, screaming something at the top of his lungs. The group turned and fled back into the mountains; the gunman himself threw down his weapon as he ran after the others. The din of kerosene tins being beaten in alarm arose all around, and within a very short while the eight stragglers found themselves trapped in a narrow canyon, surrounded by thirty or so well-armed Filipinos.

The guerrillas bound them with ropes, spinning each of them around like a wooden doll as the others looked on. Then they took them by wagon to Calapan and turned them over to the Americans. A week later a patrol boat brought them to Leyte.

Sergeant Kurokawa was the company's paymaster, and since I was the code clerk, we had shared adjoining desks in our San Jose headquarters even though I was not directly under his command. He had seen action in over seventy battles on the Chinese front, and a shoulder injury he incurred there prevented him from raising his right arm above shoulder level. This disability presumably explained why he had been appointed paymaster, but in his first stint at a desk job he was so terrified of making errors that he adhered strictly to the book. He won the ire of all the other NCOs in the company for refusing to doctor his reports in ways that would enrich our payroll. On the whole, my sentiments toward him at the time could be described as sympathetic.

When I learned that he had advocated cannibalism, however, the very sight of him became repulsive to me. Since the creation of humankind, there have been many examples of cannibalism, ranging from primitive tribes who believed they partook of vital human energy when they consumed the flesh (even in twentieth-century Japan, there are rural areas lacking proper crematoria where corpses are burned in graveyard bonfires built by the villagers, and afterward pieces of flesh left unconsumed by the fire are eaten as a universal remedy for whatever may ail) to castaways at sea who turned to cannibalism as their last hope of survival—and other such examples about which the well-fed majority has no right to say a word. The disgust I felt at Sergeant Kurokawa, however, came from the fact that he alone had proposed cannibalism at a time when conditions were still sufficiently tolerable that the others in the group automatically assumed he spoke in jest.

The tragic events aboard the raft of the *Medusa* cannot draw our censure, but the Japanese officers who dined on the flesh of prisoners they had taken must be condemned—not only because their act violated international conventions regarding the treatment of POWs, but because the consumption of human flesh purely as an epicurean indulgence is so unspeakably inhuman. It was a lunatic deed made possible by a dark and cruel hatred for the enemy and an institutional culture that sanctioned all manner of excess on the part of its officers. Similarly, the fact that Sergeant Kurokawa was the first to think of cannibalizing local islanders even though everyone suffered the same pangs of hunger owed to the institutional culture he had assimilated from other officers while fighting in China: namely, the "anything goes" mentality that had allowed soldiers to run amok there, together with the oppressor's propensity to dehumanize the population of the occupied territory. Once this battlefront culture had swollen within him to the point of obliterating his innate humanity, he had become a monster.

I avoided speaking to the sergeant after that, even when chance conspired to throw us together. At first he seemed somewhat bewildered by my attitude, so inexplicably altered, but I suppose he eventually must have dismissed me as just another of the ungrateful subordinates, of which there were a good many in the camp, who had forgotten the debt they owed their superiors. Before long, he, too, began avoiding eye contact with me. Much later, after he had used his former rank to push his way up to a position of power among the camp leaders, he called me aside one evening and demanded to know why I refused to greet him properly. That I escaped the punishment of his iron fist I owe solely to the fluency of my tongue; at any rate, I did not divulge the truth. Somehow I felt it would be too cruel to tell him the real reasons to his face.

Indeed, there was something about Sergeant Kurokawa that made me feel genuinely sorry for him. The immediate cause of his ineptitude as paymaster was his temperamental indecisiveness: He could never make up his mind about anything. He had found a young private skilled on the abacus to serve as his assistant, and it was quite something to watch this twenty-two-year-old youngster working the beads on his abacus and steering his boss toward this or that decision as he vacillated endlessly over what supplies to order for the next shipment.

I might note in passing here that this young soldier represented yet another type of character created by Japan's wartime conditions. He had completed only grade school, but observing that the war had generated an increased demand for accounting clerks, he decided to make his living with the abacus and earned his license to teach it when he was only eighteen. His approach to civilian life had been to obey his superiors to their face but thumb his nose at them behind their backs, and this seemed to work nicely for him in the military as well. He managed to manipulate Sergeant Kurokawa and the handling of purchases in such a way that the locals had to pay him a kickback on their sales, and as if that were not bad enough, he schemed with one of the cooks to steal food supplies from the pantry and sell them off. He was a small-framed fellow with intelligent good looks who constantly informed on his peers. The sergeant, I scarcely need say, never caught on to his shenanigans.

Sergeant Kurokawa's inability to make up his mind displayed itself even as the stragglers retreated through the mountains. For example, whenever they came to a fork in the path, the sergeant invariably called for a rest, which commenced at least a quarter-hour of dithering and temporizing about which path to take. On one occasion, some of the men lost patience with him and decided to go their own way, only to discover that the paths converged again farther along.

Besides this most unmilitary lack of resolution, the sergeant had a very hot temper and often raised his fist against his subordinates. Large eyes, a tall nose, and a prominent Adam's apple gave his features something of a sculpted appearance. He was from Hokkaido but for some reason refused to reveal the name of his hometown.

I also recall that he showed more presence of mind than our company CO when we withdrew from San Jose under bombardment by U.S. warships. The bombardment went on for some thirty minutes with the shells falling just short of the school building we used as our barracks, four kilometers inland. When the shelling stopped, I saw him calmly eating breakfast all by himself. The rest of the men had left their food behind and taken to their heels. He remained in the barracks even after the others had departed, taking time to make sure everything vital had been cleared out, and he caught up with the rest of the company along the way.

I had contracted malaria by then and was battling a fever, so I turned the code books over to another soldier whom I had trained with just such a contingency in mind. Then I joined the party of ailing men who followed the main column at a slower pace.

The next morning, the meteorologists on whom we had been relying for communications with battalion headquarters at Batangas decided to incinerate their radio equipment. They had concluded that transporting the equipment through the rugged mountains would be more trouble than it was worth. Our company CO made a final report for the battalion detailing our plan of action, and as the official code clerk, I wanted to prepare this last message for transmission myself.

"Morale is exceedingly high; all vow complete annihilation of enemy."

Ignoring my fever, I began dictating to my assistant the code numbers for a message to this effect, but a rising tide of foolish tears overwhelmed me.

Sergeant Kurokawa happened by. "What're you crying for, you blithering idiot? If you applied yourself to your duties properly, you'd have no time for tears!"

His implication of negligence on my part was cruel. I had not distinguished myself at drill, but as the only code clerk for an independent garrison stationed in an isolated outpost, I had devoted myself unstintingly to the task of coding and deciphering the radio messages that made up our sole line of communication with other Japanese units. I deeply regretted that I had taken ill at such a critical time, but the reason I had turned the code books over to someone else was that I feared my illness might make me lag behind and that I might then fall into the hands of guerrillas. My paramount concern in stepping aside was to ensure the security of my unit's only means of communication.

Be that as it may, there was an element of psychological truth in the sergeant's assessment of my tears. Had I retained the code books in my possession, had I been able to act with the vigor of a soldier and not with the listlessness of a sick man, and had my part in the coding of that last message not been motivated by sentimentality, then surely I would not have wept.

Having previously observed the sergeant's endless hemming and hawing, I was taken quite off guard by his penetrating assessment on this occasion. I imagine he was merely parroting a cliché he had heard repeated frequently in the military, a nugget of wisdom he did not even know he possessed. Yet, even if it was something he had picked up from others, it is not a bad thing for a person to be in possession of such an insight. In this I am forced to acknowledge that, despite its numerous failings, the old Imperial Army did have positive things to teach—like any other human organization.

Having come to regard him with a measure of respect after that incident, it was quite a shock to learn that he had advocated cannibalism. However, inasmuch as he had absorbed this insight subconsciously from the organization to which he belonged, his monstrous excess, too, should probably be considered a product of the evil culture that had permeated the Imperial Army's conduct of Japan's war with China. To carry this line of reasoning to its logical conclusion is to recognize that one cannot judge as an individual anyone who is caught up in the machinery of war. We have only the "facts" of what happened, and that is all. Yet, while at the POW camp, I found myself unable to take such a magnanimous view. I loathed the sergeant remorselessly and to an extent even took pride in my loathing.

A full discussion of the psychology of cannibalism should probably proceed at this point to the private who shot at the Filipino under the power of Sergeant Kurokawa's suggestion. I am inclined, however, in the same manner as I argued with regard to the psychology of surrender, to avoid assigning deep psychological causes to acts of impulse. Apart from that incident, the soldier had always been the most mild-mannered and modest of men. He was a farmer from west of Tokyo.

If I wished to pursue the psychological angle still further, I could expand my portrayal of Watari, who said he thought the sergeant spoke in jest: "He's just joking, Watari thought. But at the same moment he felt a strange stirring within him, as though the sergeant's words had awakened something deep in his subconscious."

I could certainly fabricate some such heavy-handed description of this incident if I chose. However, I will leave it to the psychological novelists to explore those inner movements of the human psyche that fail to culminate in external action.

———

Let me proceed by writing about the other NCO from my platoon.

Corporal Satō was a machine-tool operator for a machine shop in Tokyo's Fukagawa district. He was a small, thin man with piercing eyes. The way he held his chin, always thrust slightly forward, gave him a combative look reminiscent of an old-time neighborhood rowdy. In fact, he may well have been exactly that. His downtown Tokyo dialect carried a sharp edge.

As I mentioned before, this man's first words to me upon arriving at the camp were, "Is it true you've got a commissary here?" I suppose he had been told during his week of detention in Calapan how well-equipped the camp on Leyte would be. He was sorely disappointed when I informed him that we had been given no real work to do and, consequently, neither received any wages nor had a commissary to spend them in.

Since I had been happy just to have a clean bed in which to sleep and plenty of food to eat, I was taken aback by the corporal's words. I know his interest in such practical rewards was an entirely understandable response from a man whose government had initiated a war without regard for the harm it would bring upon ordinary citizens like himself. Yet, at a time when our homeland was collapsing, it saddened me a little to see a military man whose foremost interest, scarcely a week after being taken prisoner, was whether the camp had a commissary.

The corporal had been the leader of one of the other squads in the San Jose garrison, so although I had not been directly under his command, he had been one of my superiors. I had learned my lesson, however, from the way my own former squad leader had mercilessly taken advantage of me at the hospital, so on this occasion I determined to plainly demonstrate my independence by treating both Corporal Satō and Sergeant Kurokawa coldly. Fortunately, they and their fellow arrivals were all assigned to the same tent, whereas I was still in the sick ward; my illness shielded me from being forced to have contact with them.

Except for suffering from malnutrition, the men in the group had nothing wrong with them, and they quickly recovered their strength. Corporal Satō, in particular, was soon absorbed in gambling at cards. He came to borrow cigarettes to pay off his debts, but I turned him away.

When the doctors declared me fit a month later, my command of English won me a place among the leadership. One day I saw the corporal waiting in line in front of the infirmary, looking exceedingly haggard and pale. I offered him some candy I had with me as one of the perks of my new position and asked him what was wrong. He complained of a persistent pain in his side and worried that it might be something serious. The Japanese doctor said he could find nothing wrong, however, and refused to admit him to the sick ward.

I forgot about him for two or three days but then remembered and went to check on him. He lay on his bed holding a cold compress to his side, obviously in considerable pain. I urged him to go to sick call again, but he shook his head. "Nah, it won't do any good. The bums're all too lazy to give me a proper workup." Accustomed as he was to the ways of the Imperial Army, resignation came easily.

He told me he had been unable to eat the gruel of meat and rice that was our standard fare, so I got him some bread and milk at the cookhouse.

"This's really good of you," he said, looking up at me from his bed. "I never did anything for you, so I suppose you're sharing your own food with me just because I used to be your superior officer."

I flushed. I would never have deprived myself in order to help him. I was merely being generous with a portion of the ill-gotten gains of my new position.

I recalled that I did indeed have cause to feel grateful to Corporal Satō. During the time we were in San Jose, I had suffered more than anyone else from tropical sores, but some of the NCOs had made a point of ignoring this when handing out work assignments because they considered me something of an upstart in my position of code clerk. When Corporal Satō was in charge, however, he took one look at my legs and immediately sent me to weed the vegetable patch—one of the easiest jobs. I still remembered the way he had looked at my legs, not with the eyes of a superior officer or of a military man, but with eyes of simple human sympathy. For a first-year grunt, it was a rare moment, not easily forgotten.

I told him about this.

"Really? I sure don't remember anything like that," he said, looking very much affected. A moment later he added, "You know, it's not until you get sick that you really begin to appreciate what people do for you."

I did not invent this sentimental cliché for him—about appreciating what people do for you. Those were his actual words. Corporal Satō had a knack for coming out with glib pronouncements of one kind and another on almost any occasion. When we were searching for an escape route shortly after the attack in the mountains began, he was the one who had said, "Let's try that way. If that doesn't work either, then, hey, we'll just have to dig in at the gun emplacement and fight to the finish."

On one of our trips into Bulalacao, we came upon the badly decomposed bodies of the men from the seaplane base who had been ambushed by guerrillas ten days before. A large axe had been thrown down right beside the head of one of the corpses.

As we returned to our mountain encampment, Corporal Satō said, "Hey, we'd better watch our tails, huh? It'd be a real bitch to wind up like those guys, with our heads all bashed in."

What he said actually had very little to do with the gruesome scene we had observed. That scene had contained real corpses, while the corporal's remark was nothing but a hollow wisecrack. Clearly, those words were his way of dropping a veil not only over the savage realities of the war but over his own inner feelings as well.

"I suppose this pain is what I get for leaving so many men behind in the mountains," he said. I experienced no indignation on behalf of the men he claimed to have abandoned, however, for I knew he was really just mouthing a commonplace formula of moral retribution; I knew he was not the sort to willfully cast anyone off.

In retrospect, even the expression I saw in his eyes when he looked at the tropical sores festering on my legs must have reflected a "formulaic" sort of sympathy. That, no doubt, was how I immediately recognized it.

This does not rule out the possibility that he also experienced genuine sympathy at that moment. As a creature of urban culture, he lived a dual existence.

For Corporal Satō, I suspect life in the military was merely an extension of his life as a neighborhood rowdy back home. He brought the same bravado, the same glib facade to both. For the very reason he could be so quick with his last-ditch, do-or-die gallantry, he was quick to accept the transformation to POW and eagerly began anticipating a commissary.

I asked one of the Japanese medics I knew to give Corporal Satō another examination. The next day he was admitted to the sick ward and three days later was transferred to the hospital. He made a good impression on the leadership at the hospital and was tapped to join the Japanese staff in charge of distributing meals to the patients; he remained there until repatriation. I would like to believe he did not abuse the special privileges he would have enjoyed in that position, but I have to admit that it seems rather unlikely.

I spent many hours talking with Watari. He was in the weakest condition of anyone in the group he arrived with, and he soon joined me in the sick ward, taking the bed next to mine. Though we had been friends since the transport ship, we never actually had a chance to talk at length until we became POWs. The majority of inmates at the Leyte camp were regular-army men, and the two of us belonged to a very small minority of intellectuals.

At thirty-three, Watari was three years my junior, but no matter what happened he always seemed to keep more of his wits about him than I did. After one of the ships in our convoy was sunk in the Bashi Channel, I wound up having to sleep on deck, and I envied the cool, almost mocking, composure with which he held onto his place in the crowded rooms below.

Being drafted was to him like going through some kind of natural disaster, and his only concern was to somehow weather it and make his way home alive. Wasting no energy in useless struggle, he coolly braced himself to ride out all adversity while keeping himself as unsullied as possible.

He was the son of a well-to-do government official, now retired. After graduating from the economics department of a large private university in Tokyo, he had become secretary to the president of a well-known brewery. The passage of years had made him a father of five, but his well-proportioned, refined features kept him looking quite youthful.

As we lay next to each other in our prison beds, whiling away the hours in idle talk, I finally discovered the secret of his unflappable calm. He believed in the trigrams of the *Yi Jing—The Book of Changes*.

His father was something of a China scholar and had studied the *Yi Jing*.

"Don't worry. You'll come home alive," he had told Watari as he departed for the battlefront. "Japan will lose the war, and you'll have to endure some tremendous hardships, but just remember that it'll be nothing compared to what the emperor will have to suffer."

The elder Watari's divinations had often hit the mark. He sometimes read the trigrams for friends, and he even got calls from stockbrokers in the middle of the night. Watari had grown up watching his father's prophecies come true. Although his advanced education had wholly discredited the possibility of divining the future by such means, Watari clearly could not bring himself to abandon the faith he placed in his father's trigrams. He showed obvious displeasure when I scoffed.

A book so attached to the present life that it perceives death as the sole great tragedy of existence betrays its own superficiality. Yet, for men on the battlefield, this "superficial" view is the only one possible. The lowly tragedy of death simply looms too close.

In my squad was a Buddhist monk of the Nichiren sect who read palms. He examined the palms of everyone in the platoon and declared that we were safe because he saw indications only of great distress, not of death.

When I laughed in scorn, he turned indignant. "Your palm's the only one that shows the face of death," he said.

Naturally, I placed no stock in his fortune-telling, but after that, the words "face of death" began insinuating themselves disconcertingly into my daily thoughts. To the degree that I was actually bothered by a prophecy I did not believe, I can hardly fault Watari for believing in his father's trigrams and drawing comfort from them.

Watari had spent his time in college learning about Marxism, leading student strikes, and going to movies. Now and then an interested young prisoner would come by with some question like "What's this Red ideology all about, anyway?" and Watari would launch into a practiced explanation of the theory of surplus value. To me, however, his words came across as no more than the hollow shell of ideology. He could toss off all manner of pithy phrases like "Patriotism is merely another form of egotism," but he obviously had expended very little energy contemplating how his many pronouncements might relate to one another philosophically. I believe his faith in the glorious future of communism was of the same order as his faith in his father's trigrams.

Watari taught some of us a fancy card game he knew. In marked contrast to his usual self-deprecating manner, he became overweening in the extreme when playing this game. Simply to enjoy the successes of his card handling never satisfied him. He always had to explain how logical and brilliant his play had been.

I will describe the two other men from my company only in brief. One was a motion picture projectionist. Immediately prior to being called into active duty he had been working as a cook in the labor corps dormitory of a munitions factory. Shortly after his arrival, he joined the mess crew and became intolerably arrogant. The last man was a civil servant employed by the Imperial Household Ministry and today continues to work as a guard at the Sakashita Gate of the Imperial Palace in Tokyo. His benign personality made a favorable impression on the leadership, who soon appointed him the head of a fifteen-member barracks group. Almost all of the reservists from my unit on Mindoro came up in the world as POWs.

The original company deployed to patrol the southern half of Mindoro had been composed of 180 men, of whom seventeen ultimately came to the camp on Leyte. We were an "over-the-hill" unit of mostly middle-agers, sent to the front after completing barely three months of basic training in early 1944, and we could hardly be called soldiers. When Mindoro became the Americans' next target after Leyte, we experienced great hardship and suffering, but again, not from anything that could really be called combat. Thus, we emerged from our experiences on the island with our civilian identities intact. We never became true "brothers in arms."

We may never have been proper soldiers, but we did become bona fide prisoners of war. In fact, we were first-class POWs who enjoyed clean quarters and clothing, a ration of 2,700 calories a day, and ultimately even distributions of PX goods. Some of the men still refer to the camp as "paradise" and speak of the time they spent there as the best year of their lives.

We encountered nothing particularly new on the battlefield, but we did in the POW camp. Most notably, there was the fence that encircled us. Though we brought nothing back from the battlefield, something has unquestionably stayed with us from our lives as POWs—something that occasionally whispers in my ear, "You're still a prisoner, you know."

～ 7 ～

Seasons

A simpleminded taxonomy would classify POWs according to their former rank in the military. When considered against the realities of the prisoners' daily lives, however, such a method proves inappropriate—at least for prisoners of the kind that populated our Leyte camp, who were captured after the tide of war had clearly turned against our homeland.

Earlier in the war, until about the time of the grudge match over the Solomon Islands, the handful of Japanese soldiers taken prisoner apparently remained supremely self-assured, wearing their patriotism on their sleeves and maintaining the same order and discipline in captivity as they had in arms. In a camp like ours, however, made up entirely of captives from an army in headlong retreat, such patriotic fervor could no longer exist. The POW leadership had themselves experienced firsthand the chaotic scramble for survival after defeat, and they knew instinctively that any attempt to incite such fervor was doomed to fail. Though vestiges of the old army hierarchy continued to be preserved as a kind of courtesy, the prisoners' faces seemed to assert a new order: "As prisoners, we are all equal."

To achieve a more accurate picture of POW life, the better course is to classify the prisoners according to their new stations in camp. In the most general terms, they may be divided into two large categories: those who had official responsibilities and those who did not.

The former category included the self-styled "Japanese Camp Commandant" and his staff, the hut adjutants, the medical staff, and the cooks. Of these various subgroups, the last two required special skills, and the men had been appointed accordingly; but all other positions had been filled by former NCOs. You could say, in essence, that a skeleton of the old Imperial Army survived among us.

This did not mean, however, that every former NCO belonged to the camp leadership. Gaining appointment to such posts depended on many different factors, including an early capture date, native abilities and intelligence, personal qualities such as how much of a busybody one was or how much one pitched in when needed, one's skill at currying favor, and other purely accidental considerations. The NCOs who did not become part of the leadership blended in indistinguishably among the other prisoners in most respects. In this we have one of the key reasons why any useful classification of the camp's inmates must focus on their present rather than on their past.

The category of common prisoners may be divided into several subcategories as follows:

First, the ill—the men housed in the infirmary and infirmary annex. Those who actually required regular attention were in the so-called intensive care ward at the back of the infirmary, whereas the annex was for men suffering from beriberi, malnutrition, or other lesser ailments that merely made them too weak to transport their own meals. Whether one could transport meals was crucial because of the way meals were distributed at the cookshack in large kerosene tins holding enough food for about fifteen men. Whoever was on kitchen duty for the day had to have strength enough to haul the heavy tins back to the barracks.

Second, the weak—those who had recovered sufficient strength to carry the aforementioned kerosene tins but not for exerting themselves at anything more strenuous. These men lived with the healthy prisoners in the regular barracks, but because they could not join in the various labor details, they felt a certain constraint in the company of their barracks mates. They were on permanent kitchen duty.

Being part of this subcategory essentially meant your days as a prisoner were still young. Except on the rare occasion when a place happened to open up in Group A, newcomers went to Group B, so most of the weak belonged to the latter group. With Imamoto favoring group A when dividing up the daily rations, the weak in Group B had difficulty getting the nourishment they needed to recover from their long deprivation. Some of the starving newcomers secretly visited Group A to trade cigarettes for other prisoners' leftovers.

With their hunched backs, sunken chests, dull eyes, and emaciated limbs, the new arrivals manifested typical signs of malnutrition. The sight of these men dragging ridiculously oversized army boots on the ends of their bony legs, twisting their faces with effort as they lugged heavy kerosene tins loaded with food—a scene repeated each mealtime—was among the most painful sights in camp to witness.

I could generally tell merely by looking at an inmate's physical appearance how many months had passed since his capture.

The third subcategory of common prisoners comprised those who had fully regained their strength. Once the men had put on a certain amount of weight, they all began to look pretty much alike, and it became impossible to distinguish the old-timers from the more recent arrivals. After that, differences of personality and occupation became the distinguishing features rather than physical appearance. As I have already mentioned, there were no salient differences between former NCOs and rank-and-file soldiers. Some minor distinctions could be discerned between regular army and the reserves, but with many of the reservists serving extended tours since fighting first began in China, they had become virtually indistinguishable from career soldiers. In fact, what few differences remained on this count could as easily be attributed to differences in the occupational backgrounds from which the men had originally come, for most of those from farm families were regular-army men, whereas the salaried workers were by and large reservists.

There were also laborers, small merchants and tradesmen, civil servants, a few clerics, and some gamblers, but by far the greatest majority were of farm stock. Most of those taken prisoner on Leyte itself had been regular army.

I liked the young regular-army men. The ranks of my company had been filled in substantial part by older reservists like myself, and I had become thoroughly fed up with their petit bourgeois egotism during the ten months I had spent in close quarters with them. I knew well enough why they did not like the war. The war had torn them from the placidity of their comfortable lives and dragged them off to face untold hardships and the constant threat of death. It was careless of them never to have considered what the tranquil lives they enjoyed might someday levy upon them. At the front, they exercised the craftiness they had honed in their daily routines back home and thought only of getting themselves as "routinely" as possible through each day's quota of calamities. On the field of war where the violence of nations collide, nothing could have been more nugatory.

By comparison, the young regular-army men I met—both those I had gone through training with back in Japan and those I met for the first time in the camp on Leyte—though uneducated and ignorant, understood quite clearly that they had certain obligations as citizens and that they were even then fulfilling those obligations as part of a disciplined fighting machine. Accordingly, most of them were cheerful and free of cares, and save in the performance of their assigned jobs, exceptionally easygoing. Regrettably, they had in fact been hoodwinked by corrupt militarists, but so long as they remained unaware of that fact, it had no effect on either their spirits or their demeanor.

Among the regular-army men, I also met a few old-timers who had turned mean-spirited in the wake of promotions denied, or due to other causes, but they were the exceptions. To exaggerate the harm brought about by such deviant misfits and imagine that all troops in the old Imperial Army were scoundrels would no more accurately reflect the truth than to point to the atrocities committed by a tiny fraction on the front lines and conclude that all Japanese troops were inhuman brutes.

My fondness was limited to the rank and file, however, and did not extend to the NCOs. As soon as NCOs experienced the comforts of their position in the military, they became zealous defenders of the institution for the sake of their own personal gain. Men who succumb to the temptations of special privilege inevitably slide into corruption. (Even among the ordinary soldiers, the leading privates and lance corporals must be lumped together with the NCOs on this score. In my experience, the majority of these model soldiers who had risen to the top of the rank and file showed themselves to be barefaced flatterers.)

The fact that these NCOs, once they had become POWs, displayed the same cheerful and easygoing manner as the young, regular-army rank and file would seem to show that the turpitude of the NCOs within the military was a factor of their rank and position rather than of their innate character.

The once-hardened bodies of the young regular-army men recovered speedily from injury and prostration. With virtually no work to occupy them in camp, they lacked an outlet for their pent-up energies, so they sought out recreations that required the exertion of strength. They were the ones who drew sumo rings and wrestled under the hot tropical sun.

The merchants and salaried workers liked to talk, but the best of the talkers, no doubt owing to the nature of their occupation, were the handful of clerics among us. They almost always had a circle of listeners gathered about them. Others preferred to keep to themselves and lay quietly on their beds. The fact that such men seemed to come from all walks of life suggested that their fondness for silence derived not from present circumstance but from congenital temperament. No doubt the reason they stood out so conspicuously at the camp was that our social life as POWs consisted almost solely of conversation.

The more recent arrivals gradually moved up into this third group of common prisoners. As the war advanced toward its conclusion and the front moved away from the Philippines, the number of newcomers dwindled, and at that point, except for those who had sustained permanent disabilities, all prisoners apart from those with official responsibilities came to belong to this group. They were, in effect, the "populace," the "average Joes" of the camp.

When I arrived at the camp in the middle of March, I belonged to the first of these categories—namely, the ill. In May, I moved into the second category and began hauling meals. Then in June, before I had fully recovered my strength and without ever moving into the third category of the common prisoner class, I became a member of the leadership. My knowledge of English had won me a position as interpreter.

Until that time, there had been just two interpreters among the prisoners—one assigned to Headquarters and the other to the infirmary. None other was needed. This changed, however, when the camp's inmates were reorganized into U.S. Army–style companies, and an American NCO was assigned to each unit as a liaison. The need for interpreters suddenly multiplied, and a number of newcomers like myself were recruited to fill the openings. Our erstwhile Headquarters now became equivalent to a battalion headquarters.

The purpose of the reorganization was apparently twofold: to cope with the increased number of inmates and to prepare the way for labor details. As more prisoners recovered their strength, the Americans began planning, in accordance with international conventions, to put the POWs to work for eight hours per day, with due compensation.

The camp's census of seven hundred at the time I arrived had swollen to more than a thousand by June due to a large influx of newcomers from Mindanao. The reorganization plan called for the men to be divided into five companies of about two hundred each.

The same plan was responsible for removing me from the sick list. In mid-April, the camp's usual American doctor and an additional doctor brought in from outside conducted thorough medical evaluations of the roughly forty patients in the intensive care and regular sick wards. Some of the patients remained on the disabled list, but many were reclassified as either fit to work or nearly so. I had already been moved to the regular sick ward by this time, but now my heart condition was dismissed as no longer a concern. My name was listed among patients who would soon be able to work.

In conjunction with these events, the infirmary annex was closed down, and the nipa hut that just thirty of us had occupied with plenty of elbow room was converted to a barracks for sixty regular prisoners. Those of us who had been living there were moved to a newly pitched tent in the open area adjacent to Group A's sector, and we now had to haul our own meals. Compared to the nipa huts with their high, cool ceilings, the oppressive heat from the scorched, low-drooping, canvas roof was nearly unbearable.

I was not at all pleased with the changes the Americans were making.

Besides suffering from the stifling heat in our new quarters, I especially took exception to the judgment that my heart condition need no longer prevent me from working.

The doctor at the hospital had diagnosed my valvular abnormality as congenital and cautioned me never to engage in strenuous activities. He had been a major, whereas the doctor at the camp was only a first lieutenant, and my faith in the former surpassed my faith in the latter by about as much as the difference in their ranks.

In the end, the lieutenant's evaluation may well have been the correct one. When I had a physical examination a year after my repatriation, my heart remained enlarged, but all traces of the murmur had disappeared. Today even its size has returned more or less to normal. My doctor here at home now tells me I was in all probability experiencing a coronary dysfunction brought on by malaria.

At the time, however, I still had difficulty walking any distance, and even light exercise sent my pulse climbing. A disorder of the heart can also weigh heavily on the nerves; just thinking about it is sometimes enough to make one's pulse shoot up.

Having been lucky enough to escape certain death on the battlefield, my only desire now was to make it through my internment without incident and return home with my precious life intact. If I could escape some of the demands of my unwelcome condition on grounds of illness and spend my days in idleness, all the better. The lieutenant's diagnosis dragged me rudely away from that hoped-for life of ease.

I exaggeratedly imagined dying of a heart attack while on labor detail. If such dire imaginings had come from anything other than plain laziness, the simple desire to avoid having to work, I would no doubt have protested in earnest.

In any event, a prisoner's personal displeasure seldom holds any great weight, especially in cases like our own where we were in fact treated very well and had a great deal to be thankful for. In my idleness, I rehearsed my anxieties endlessly but pointlessly: Such is the inevitable lot of the POW. On the other hand, I could not very well spend all my time tied up in knots of anxiety. There were other matters that filled my time: Such is the inevitable condition of being human.

Each day brought with it interminable boredom. At the hospital I had become friends with the doctors and medics, who had provided me with a constant supply of books and magazines. By contrast, very few Americans ever came into the camp compound, and even those who did seemed to be on their guard against requests from the POWs—perhaps because, given the large number of inmates, they feared setting a precedent with one prisoner that they could not honor for all. I quickly finished the books I had brought from the hospital and ran out of things to read—except for the Bible, which still had a great many unread pages. Having developed a taste for pulp detective fiction while in the hospital, I no longer had the patience for such heavy-going reading as the Bible.

As a means of filling the void, I decided to try some writing.

I do not generally think of writing as an altogether natural activity for human beings. Though language itself may have evolved naturally enough, to facilitate mutual communication of thoughts among us, the impulse to set that language down in written symbols must have come from the desire to invest the speaker's thoughts with greater longevity and to communicate them to numerous others who are temporally or spatially beyond the compass of the speaker's voice. To get from that desire to the point where an individual in the throes of ennui first conceived of writing as a potential pastime required an accumulation of many cultural advances, but the most important of these advances was for the writer to apprehend himself as the reader. Writers came to anticipate a later day when they would themselves read back over their record of the thoughts and feelings they had had or events they had witnessed or heard about at an earlier time. This, indeed, is the basis for the popularity of diaries in contemporary society. The impulse has now been turned into a widespread social custom by grade schools that foster it in composition classes and by publishers who produce and sell a wide variety of daybooks for the convenience of diarists.

One of the things that surprised me most during our occupation of Mindoro was the fondness my platoon mates had for keeping journals. In the brief span of free time following the regular evening roll call, a good many of the men faithfully recorded their thoughts on the day's events in the dim light of coconut oil lamps. Meager as the offerings were at our garrison exchange, they always included pocket notebooks and pencils.

I made my living as a salaried office worker, but having been a literary enthusiast in my youth, I viewed this kind of narcissistic behavior with contempt. To my mind, both life as an office worker and life in the military were exactly the sort of thing that should be allowed to recede into the past and fade from memory. They did not deserve to be recorded in writing and reexperienced at a later date.

Instead, during the vacant days we spent prior to the American landing, I fancied writing a good old-fashioned novel. The work would be titled after the name of a certain chemical element produced by a manufacturing company I had worked for as a civilian, and the plot would center on the political and social pressures brought upon that company by the war, along with the friction those pressures generated among its employees. Stealing moments when my superiors were not present, I took up my notebook and pencil and began writing. Such moments were few, however, and in any case, I was not really in the right frame of mind for crafting sentences. I abandoned the effort after writing about ten pages in which I sketched the city in western Japan where the action of the novel was to have taken place.

Starting a regimen of writing did, however, give rise to the idea of reflecting on my past. Since I faced imminent death, I had good reason to explore just who I had been in my life. I pondered this question each night after lights out and then briefly set down those reflections in my notebook the next day. Moment by moment, I examined my life from early youth until being called into active service, and I ultimately arrived at the conclusion that I was, in essence, nobody—I could die a meaningless death on an unknown island in the southern sea and not be missed one whit. With that, I lost my fear of death. Following Stendhal, I chose an epitaph for myself and wrote it on the last page of my notebook: "A solitary, forlorn man."

When I saw that my great novel had been reduced to an epitaph, I finally understood what motivated all the diarists who surrounded me. No more than I could they hold any hope of rereading their diaries at a later date. They simply carried on a habit, acquired as civilians, of reflecting on their lives each day as a means of consoling themselves. Life in contemporary civilian society had been filled with suffering, much like life on the battlefield.

I kept my notebook with me for a time even after the Americans landed and my unit retreated into the mountains. Then, when word came that they were advancing on our position, I tore it up and, since I was flat on my back with malaria, asked one of my platoon mates to burn it in the cooking fire. Though written in characters no one in the Philippine mountains would likely be able to decipher, I felt vaguely uneasy about having something I had written outlive me there.

In the ennui of the prison camp, I still had no desire to keep a journal. The idea of keeping a record of what took place in the camp so I could turn it into a piece of reportage after my repatriation did not enter my mind. I never dreamed I would later find myself reconstructing my POW experiences as I am doing now.

The idea that did occur to me was to resume writing my great novel. I was still affected by what I have called POW's daze, however, and found myself facing the same difficulty I had experienced on Mindoro with regard to shaping my words and ideas into a flow of narrative. Then an extraordinary thought occurred to me: I could write the story as a screenplay. Instead of having to weave my ideas together in a continuous flow, I could simply string together a series of images.

This inspiration may be traced to the arrival of my friend Watari in camp. Watari had been a great cinema buff since his college days, helping to edit a coterie journal for a time, and he was intimately familiar with the history and the various schools of the medium. When he became my neighbor in the infirmary annex, I soon began acquiring an intricate knowledge of the cinema from him.

As we talked, it surprised me to realize just how much the cinema had insinuated itself into my life. I had never possessed particularly high regard for this artistic medium. Because of the way motion pictures are produced, they necessarily must adhere to lowest-common-denominator themes; to make things worse, they force the viewer into an inordinately passive position. I therefore considered the cinema to be a distinctly anti-intellectual art form. Yet even as I harbored intellectual reservations about the form, there could be no denying that in the darkness of the theater I invariably found myself enthralled by the images so true to life flickering before me on the screen.

Mine is the first generation of city dwellers to acquire the custom of attending motion pictures in our formative years. The air of frivolity that separates us from those who are seven years our seniors probably can be attributed to a slothfulness fostered, at least in part, by the passivity of cinema viewing. In watching American films, even though we may not subscribe to the same values, our feelings and our behavior have somewhere along the line begun to mimic American ways. For example, when I walk outside after taking in a Gary Cooper film, I realize that I have unwittingly adopted his gait. Of course I am neither as tall nor as handsome as he is, so I cannot actually reproduce the full effect. But because of certain sensibilities I have absorbed from the images on the screen, that is definitely how I feel inside. Ultimately, the deluge of films affecting our feelings and our behavior in this way is bound to have changed our ways of thinking as well. The generation before us grew up without our viewing habits, and it is because their thoughts are not distracted by the gratuitous profusion of images that they are so much more serious-minded than we are.

There can be little wonder that governments take such a great interest in the influence motion pictures exert upon their citizens.

Based on what I learned from Watari, I decided to turn my great novel into a screenplay. In this literary form, one had only to rough out the scenes while leaving the complex task of producing the images to the actual makers of the film, so it was an ideal medium for the dazed mind of a POW. If I could envision a scene, I could write it.

I had become friends with one of the medics in the infirmary by teaching him English, so I asked him to get me some ledger paper, made a cover with cardboard from an empty medicine box, and bound them together with a length of gauze bandage. I then took up my pencil and began writing. For my first effort, I chose to adapt a spy thriller by E. Phillips Oppenheim that I had read in the hospital, turning it into a melodrama of suspense and opulence in the manner of American films. Next I tried a short story called "Quiet Snow, Secret Snow" (the author's name escapes me), which I had read in the Penguin Books *Anthology of Modern American Short Stories*— a story dealing with the abnormal psychology of a young boy. I followed this with a musical based on the film about Chopin called *A Song to Remember;* an adaptation of a Kigi Takatarō detective novel; and so forth. Once I had gotten started, I completely lost sight of my original intent and immersed myself in the pleasure of manipulating my characters like puppets to create facile sentiment and cheap suspense.

Never in my life had I been so prolific. I turned out some of my titles in as little as a night or two, one after the other, and in the end I really did manage to produce a screenplay of my great novel. Altogether I created eleven screenplays by the time of my repatriation in December.

And to my delight, the screenplays found a broad readership. They were at that time the only books in camp written in Japanese, so inmates starved for something to read fought over who would get to borrow them next. I charged one cigarette apiece. Before long I discovered that others were copying the books and starting up their own rental businesses. I immediately accused them of copyright infringement and wrote "Copying Prohibited" in one corner of the cover, thereby establishing myself as a professional writer within the camp.

I recount these things here not to boast of my talents, but rather to offer my story as an example of how one relatively well-educated man slid into decadence. The screenplays remain in my possession today, but they are unreadable trash. They testify to just how meager and threadbare our imaginations become when we yield ourselves up to the flood of motion picture images. In the final analysis, the sole merit of these creative activities was in allowing me to eliminate from my system the part of me that had become permeated with the influence of film.

My literary debasement reached new lows when I later responded to requests for pornography. That was much later, however, after the war was over. I will write of it at the appropriate time.

————

Whatever I may think of their merits now, the screenplays bear notations that amount to my only contemporaneous record of life in the POW camp. Though the contents themselves have no connection with camp life, each book bears on its cover a record of the dates when I started and finished writing it. By recalling the locations where I wrote each particular screenplay, I can today reconstruct an approximate chronology of my movements within the camp.

The spy story with which I made my writing debut is dated May 2 through May 10, 1945. This tells me it was shortly before this that the infirmary annex was shut down and I started living in the tent. In one of my works I compiled a record of my experiences between the American landing and my capture in the form of a documentary film called "A POW's Tale," and I remember finishing this manuscript in the nipa hut to which all the leadership personnel for the newly formed companies had been assigned. Since the notation on the cover indicates that it was written from June 3 to June 6, I must have taken up my new duties as interpreter sometime between those dates.

Watari was appointed interpreter at the same time. So few of the regular-army men taken prisoner on Leyte could understand English that two of the five interpreters for the newly formed companies had to come from the tiny contingent of reservists who had been stationed on Mindoro.

More specifically, however, we owed our selection to the recommendation of the former flight instructor shot down during the Battle of Leyte Gulf, who had been our hut adjutant in the infirmary annex and continued in that role when we moved to the tent. His warm and generous temperament did not mesh well with the avarice of the big shots at headquarters, and he had often come to vent his spleen with Watari and me. He took advantage of the reorganization to withdraw from the leadership after recommending us as interpreters.

In the following months, he continued to refuse any position of responsibility and participated only in regular labor assignments as a rank-and-file POW. By contrast, Watari and I gradually raised our stock, so to speak, and improved our positions. Though we went to visit our benefactor among the regular prisoners from time to time, little by little a certain awkwardness began to creep into the relationship. Inasmuch as he had chosen his "commoner" status of his own volition, he had every reason to be pleased with himself, and that was how we expected to find him. But as time passed we saw the light go out of his eyes and detected a note of cravenness creep into his attitude toward us. The effects of privileged position were the same among the POWs as in any other social group. For our part, as well, I can but imagine that we were guilty of inadvertent insensitivities that he found hurtful.

The newly formed companies were organized as follows:

Leader	1
Overhead staff	20
Four platoons	53 members each, including platoon leader
Total	233

The platoons were in turn divided into four detachments of thirteen men each.

The company staff included the following positions:

Clerk	1
CQs (charge of quarters)	3
Cooks (including one mess sergeant)	8
Medics	2
Sanitation officers	2
Barbers	2
Stewards	2
Total	20

Group A became Companies 1 and 2, and Group B became Companies 3, 4, and 5. The reorganization was completed by the end of May, and all business was handled under the new structure beginning in June. Since Group A's nipa huts each housed sixty men, detachments from more than one platoon had to be mixed under the same roof. The company and platoon leaders, in most cases former hut adjutants, continued to bunk at Headquarters, separated from the men under them. The full overhead staffs of both companies moved into the so-called NCO Club, which had formerly housed the NCOs who lacked leadership positions—except for the medics, who remained in the sick wards.

We soon learned, however, that this scattered quartering was only temporary. We would presently be moving to a new camp being constructed in Palo, the same town as the POW hospital, and each company would then have its own unified sector. An American NCO would also be assigned to each unit at that time.

Labor details had begun already in May. The commandant specified how many men were needed for the day, and each company provided its quota of able-bodied men, who departed a little before eight o'clock in the morning and returned around half past four. Tired of sitting around in the camp with nothing to do, inmates volunteered enthusiastically for the work, but unfortunately the American labor sites provided work for only about a quarter of the men on any given day. The work included such basic tasks as restacking boxes at supply depots and leveling the ground for new building sites.

In conjunction with the reorganization of the camp and the beginning of outside work (we simply called it "outwork," in contrast to the work of building and maintaining the facilities inside the camp, which we called "inwork"; I will use these expressions here as well), we also received new issues of clothing. Like the Americans themselves, over the course of time we acquired two sets of fatigues, four T-shirts, four pairs each of undershorts and socks, a pair of boots, a hat, a mess kit, and a cup. We also received safety razors and toothbrushes, but it struck me as rather odd from the standpoint of priorities that the razors came first. Apparently the inspecting officers objected to prisoners growing beards.

Inspections were stepped up. Besides the regular weekly tour by the commandant, who was a first lieutenant, field-grade officers from outside appeared about twice a week on no particular schedule. These inspectors presumably came from the Intendance Department for the purpose of verifying that all the items released from army stores had indeed been properly issued to the prisoners. We were required to lay everything out at the foot of our beds during each inspection.

Our rations also increased. Today the U.S. Army prides itself on having provided the same rations for POWs as for its own soldiers. For us small-framed Japanese, however, the full ration of 2,700 calories was actually somewhat excessive. Most of the men probably would have left food in their mess cans if the officers and cooks had not been skimming off choice items for their own consumption.

The illicit skimming and lavish feasting indulged in by the Japanese leadership in POW camps far and wide have already been well reported by others, so I will not write about them here. In essence, we had all grown so accustomed to these abuses in the army that we took them for granted and simply looked the other way. Just as we never dreamed of protesting the panoply of injustices we witnessed in the army, we were little inclined to raise our voices against the improprieties of the leadership in the POW camp.

Of course, I myself had no need to raise my voice, for I had now entered the privileged class as one of its lesser members. The positions of company clerk and CQ were not actually on the same level as those of company or platoon leader; in fact, even the battalion clerk effectively ranked below the platoon leaders. Still, having charge of personnel matters or of distributing clothing brought with it certain benefits, quite apart from not having to participate in work parties.

The post of CQ, in particular, was widely perceived as a sinecure. Though practices varied from one company to another, the men tapped for CQ tended to be old-timers who had been passed over in the selection of platoon leaders rather than men who possessed the appropriate clerical skills. In the case of Company 1, a surfeit of such candidates triggered a lengthy dispute that ultimately prevented even an interpreter from being included, and this had dire consequences later on.

The reader may readily imagine what the CQ appointment meant to me, anxious as I was about my heart condition. I thought of my good fortune as a heaven-bestowed means of self-preservation, and I experienced a sense of great joy at having escaped the danger of physical collapse. In retrospect, however, I am inclined to think it was more the joy of a lazy man unaccustomed to physical labor rejoicing at being exempted from any real work.

As I have already mentioned, with the exception of the medics, the staffs of Companies 1 and 2 were quartered all together in the same building. By nature of their jobs, the clerks and CQs received desks and set up shop near the front entrance. In the weeks before each company moved into its own unified sector at the new camp, however, business remained exceedingly slow. The clerks compiled company rosters and then had nothing else to do. The interpreters remained idle because the American NCOs for whom they were to interpret had yet to arrive. Each company's three CQs shared the task of distributing the various new items of clothing issued from time to time, and each evening they compiled and delivered to the battalion clerk a romanized roster of the men who would participate in outwork the next day.

As we put these lists of outworkers together by candlelight each evening, we must have looked deceptively industrious. Inmates who saw us working as they passed by outside sometimes called to us through the window: "Thanks for all your tireless work."

Inwardly, we cringed. The prisoners had so little to do that even a simple task like that looked like hard work.

My company's clerk was Miyata—one of the pair who had tried to kill themselves with the drawstrings of their trousers. He had won his new post by offering to help with clerical tasks at Headquarters when the reorganization first got under way. Of my fellow CQs, a fellow named Fujimoto, came from a family that owned a leather-goods warehouse in Osaka. A former shipping engineer, he was placed in charge of distributing clothing because he had handled the same task while in the military. The other CQ, named Morozumi, was a salesman for a neon sign company in Tokyo. He was another middle-aged reservist called into active duty in 1944. I do not recall hearing how he came to be selected as CQ.

Ours was the only company whose clerical staff consisted entirely of former office workers. Every one of the others had at least one man on its staff who had gained his position by influence rather than by the nature of his prior work experience. In fact, in the majority of cases, the company clerk was the only person capable of compiling the romanized outworkers' roster. In Company 1, even the clerk's skills were pretty shaky, and he often came to us seeking help.

The leader of our company was a man named Hiwatashi, the owner of an electrical appliance store in Yokosuka who had been chief petty officer on a destroyer that went down in the Battle of Leyte Gulf. A shrewd man, he had made it a special point to assemble a clerical staff with prior office experience. He did not get along very well with Imamoto and was on particularly bad terms with Nakagawa, the battalion clerk. I suspect the secret motive behind his choice of staff was to put the heat on Nakagawa.

As a clerical staff made up entirely of middle-aged reservists, we maintained firm solidarity in our dealings with the outside, but a certain amount of friction did occur among us. For example, since the clerk's position was regarded as supervisory to the CQs, Hiwatashi always relayed his instructions to us through Miyata. This irked us CQs, so on trivial matters we often ignored Miyata's instructions and did things our own way, then watched him squirm when Hiwatashi asked him something he could not answer.

To begin with, Miyata was the sort of fellow who made an easy mark. To the same degree that he was deliberate and precise in his clerical tasks, he displayed a temperamental timidity in everything else. Furthermore, he had a large appetite—a characteristic regarded with considerable disdain in a camp where food always loomed as such a large concern.

Once the outworkers had departed for the day, we mostly played cards—a simple game called "Two-Ten-Jack" in which spades count against you and you can generally throw them on whomever you choose. Miyata always ended up with a lot of spades. Since we wagered cigarettes on the games, it meant he suffered material losses as well.

Miyata had been in my platoon on Mindoro, so I should perhaps have stood up for him more, but I could not bring myself to do it. One of my long-standing faults is that I am easily annoyed by men like him.

It did not take long for us all to acquire nicknames. Miyata's given name was Kamekichi, written with the character for "turtle," so we called him "Turtle"—not exactly a flattering appellation. Fujimoto, something of a dandy, befitting his former rank, had sewn a white F on the front of his hat, and that had earned him the moniker "Mr. F." Morozumi was the youngest and least serious among us. One night he was walking along with a cigarette dangling from his lips when someone called out to him: "Hey, buddy, give me a light, will ya?" After that we all called him "Buddy."

I was dubbed "Jin"—short for "Jinroku." When I happened to mention in the course of some conversation or other that I was the eldest son in my family, I got a chorus of surprise: "How could a goof-off like you be the firstborn?" After that I became Jinroku of "first in birth but last in wit" fame.

Thus, with each of us bearing a humorous nickname, we passed carefree days content in our posts. By swapping our old clothes for new whenever another issue came through, we kept ourselves in ever-crisp outfits. Most of the undershirts and shorts came dyed in standard army green, but when we discovered occasional whites mixed in among the others we made them our own. Pangs of conscience prevented us from wearing them out of doors in broad daylight, but if we never wore them at all it would be pointless to have claimed them for ourselves in the first place, so we donned them for strolls outside after dark. Being white, they stood out even in the dark, however, and we often got ribbed: "Hey, there, Mr. CQ. Nice duds you got on!"

Our boisterous merriment over cards during the day attracted attention. "Listen here, CQs!" Imamoto yelled at us. "You may have to work in the evening, but you should still show some restraint during the day."

Another of the benefits of our position was that we were in the same hut as the cooks. The justification institutional cooks will give for treating themselves to special fare is always the same: By the time they have prepared such huge quantities of a dish, they have no appetite for it, so they have to make something different for themselves even if it is not as good. You will get the same line every time. Obviously, though, the cooks would never make anything for themselves that did not taste at least as good as what they have prepared for everyone else. As a rule, when they made gruel for everyone else, they baked bread with lots of butter and sugar for themselves, and when they made bread for everyone else, they steamed rice and opened some special canned meats for themselves.

The cooks occupied the rear end of our hut, and the shelves against the back wall always held kerosene tins filled with things like coffee and cocoa. As occupants of the same building, we were permitted to dip into these stores at will, and on occasion the cooks shared their own special fare with us. They also treated us to wine they had made by fermenting raisins with bread yeast.

Reflecting on how I had viewed the privileged class when I first entered the camp, I experienced twinges of guilt over my altered frame of mind, but these tugs of conscience did not lead me to any new standards of behavior. Something to unite my conscience and my conduct was missing. Nowhere in my life as a POW could I find grounds to refrain from swapping green skivvies for white.

Perhaps this was because I had never found grounds for denying myself any such perquisites in my civilian life either. Within human society, each of us constantly seeks to place others beneath himself. To truly mend ourselves of these ways would require us to become saints or revolutionaries; the reason we find it so difficult to do this is that we learn to enjoy privilege from the time we are tiny children.

My only defense against the claims of the regular prisoners was to simply push them from my mind. I suspect members of all classes instinctively adopt this same measure, enjoying the perquisites of their class while closing their eyes to the question of where those perquisites came from.

It was true, too, however, that the rank-and-file prisoners had one pleasure that we did not. On outwork assignments at American food dumps, they pilfered sundry items to smuggle back into camp. Often they found choice canned goods or brands of cigarettes never included in the camp's rations. It need be no surprise that they did not share such booty with us.

One exception was a PFC from the First Army Division named Odaka.

He regularly brought part of his stolen goods to the cooks. Once they had accepted his largesse, however, there was no turning back. To repay him, they had to assent to his endless demands for food. He was a big, burly man and had an appetite to match his girth, which the standard rations could not satisfy. Even before this, he had been the one rank-and-filer bold enough to openly ask for extra food at the cookshack.

Since I expect this eccentric fellow to appear again in this record, I will go ahead and present a somewhat more detailed portrait of him here.

At the time of his induction, Odaka was a forty-two-year-old reservist working in Tokyo's Asakusa district as a tinsmith, but he had gone through a variety of occupations over the years. In his youth he had worked at a coal mine in Hokkaido, and for a long period after that he hopped about from one place to another in Tokyo and vicinity as a construction worker. Age had now begun to take its toll on his body, but even so he was shaped like a cobra from his chest up, evidence that he still retained a formidable physical strength. In the army he had frequently found himself in the lockup for throwing punches at his superior officers. Even as a POW, his violent behavior continued unabated at first, but the Americans' disciplinary measures finally taught him to exercise more restraint.

Like unruly men of his kind everywhere, he was quite aware of the fear his physical prowess instilled in others, and he knew he could get his way with anything and anyone. The cooks, being sturdy youngsters themselves, could probably have ganged up on him and prevailed, but every time they appeared on the verge of doing just that, Odaka knew how to defuse the whole matter into a joke and laugh it off. Partly due to the difference in their ages, the young cooks were simply no match for him—on any score.

He had a pointed head with large eyes and mouth, and his thick neck looked like it had been wedged down into the top of his barrel-chested torso. Because his behavior was so erratic and brash, even the top brass put on a show of deference—which in turn made him grow even more insolent.

He loved to talk about his career as an outlaw. His favorite tale was of how he had run away from the mine in Hokkaido and traveled by foot from Aomori to Tokyo, committing burglaries all along the way. In the mountains near Shirakawa he had raped a woman right in front of her husband, the details of which made up the high point of his story. He also recounted with particular relish the episode in which he made his way to a dairy farm run by a man and his daughter in the highlands of Nasu, lived for a year as the daughter's common-law husband, and then made off with all the money in the house.

Seeing the sour looks on our faces as we listened, he snorted derisively. "Hah, you guys look disgusted, but I know you love it," he said, and walked away.

I was quite taken aback to learn that bandits of the old school like this still existed, for I had been of the impression that outlaws today had to be more subtle. Still, in looking at Odaka I could not help but feel that there were probably any number of scoundrels ten times worse than him among the less demonstrative prisoners in the camp.

———

Scuttlebutt said not only that the beginning of outwork would also mean the beginning of wages but also that a commissary would be opened where we could spend our wages on beer or cigarettes or whatever else we chose. It seemed a little too good to be true, but given the Americans' track record of exceeding our expectations every time they did something to improve conditions at the camp, no one dismissed the possibility out of hand. Animated talk about the yet-to-be-won prize blossomed all over camp, and even one of my former superior officers whom I almost never spoke to anymore came to ask about the rumors.

We presently learned that we would indeed be paid in mid-June for the work done in May but not in the form of wages we could spend freely at our own commissary. Instead, the payment would come in kind, with three dollars' worth of preselected items from the American PX. All talk immediately shifted to what those items might be.

At long last the merchandise arrived. Late one night the Americans suddenly called for a work detail to be organized, and in a very short time a massive pile of cardboard boxes had been hauled in. Never before had such a huge quantity of supplies flowed into the camp all at once.

Battalion Clerk Nakagawa struggled all night long to take inventory and divide up the goods, but the labels on the boxes and the manner in which quantities were indicated exceeded his command of English. The task remained unfinished in the morning.

Nakagawa clung to his post solely on the strength of his toadying up to Imamoto. To those of us who had to deal with him in the course of our clerical duties, his interminable and pointless obfuscation and secretiveness had been nothing short of exasperating, and we were not about to let pass a chance like this to show him a few things. The clerks and CQs from all the companies descended on Headquarters together, took an inventory of the boxes, and advised him how the supplies needed to be divided. He decided to turn the task entirely over to us.

Each prisoner received ten packs of cigarettes at ten cents apiece for a dollar, and five candy bars and five bars of soap at ten cents each for another dollar. The final dollar included five-cent packs of chewing gum, some hard candy, replacement blades for our safety razors, and toothpaste. None of the boxes contained any beer.

Together with the men detailed for the distribution, we broke open the boxes on the street in front of Headquarters and divided up the contents into separate piles for each company. The entire camp gathered around to watch us work.

"Come on, men. Everyone not on this detail, back to your barracks," Imamoto shouted. "You can wait for the distribution there. Standing around to watch won't get you the goods any sooner."

The prisoners silently moved away, but they halted their steps and turned to watch again when they thought they had gone far enough, or they pressed together along the near wall of their barracks where they could still observe what was going on.

We clerks and CQs worked up quite a sweat along with the other workers. Besides wanting to make sure we got our full share of the merchandise, our ulterior motive was to claim some of the empty cardboard boxes to use as storage chests. These were the sturdy, gray cardboard boxes with a green and black stripe and a black star in one corner that everyone in postwar Japan has grown to recognize. The boxes were far and away the sharpest looking possession any of the prisoners had, and those of us who worked in the company offices assumed it was our natural right to claim them. It took until afternoon to complete the distribution to everyone in camp.

The prisoners sat on their beds with their merchandise spread out before them, quietly puffing on cigarettes or eating candy. In each face shone the innocent joy of a child who has just received a new toy. For the first time since being captured, they had become owners and consumers.

Most welcome of all were the cigarettes. The ration had until then been one pack of twenty cigarettes per week—not nearly enough. Furthermore, we had never had more than one pack in our possession at any given time. It was immensely satisfying now to see ten packs of attractively packaged Lucky Strikes and Camels stacked in two rows of five each, one on top of the other.

The soap was a toilet soap called Lux. This, too, was welcome, for we previously had only laundry soap with which to wash whatever needed washing, including our faces. Many of the men, however, chose to go on using the laundry soap so that they could save their five bars of Lux and take them home to Japan. A few soap freaks even traded their other goods to obtain more. They wanted to use their soap but also save some for taking home.

The candy proved to be more than anyone really cared to have all at once, so the men were quick to share it. The clever ones ate other people's candy at first and then started trading their own candy for cigarettes at advantageous rates about the time most of the candy in camp had disappeared.

These items from the American PX did not actually come free of charge. They had been provided for us in accordance with international conventions, and our own national treasury would ultimately have to pay for them. That is to say, the costs would revert to us in the end. Essentially the same principle was at work here as with the commissary merchandise in the Japanese military, which had all seemed like such a bargain. At any rate, both in the military and in the POW camp, the apparent giveaways brought us immense satisfaction, and we were grateful.

The lack of beer among these provisions disappointed us to no end, but in anticipation of this day the cookshack crew had prepared an especially large batch of their raisin wine and distributed it to all of the men after evening roll call. Each man received about a cup and a half. Because of the crude fermentation techniques, the wine proved to be extremely potent, and the entire camp was soon in its cups.

The boisterous singing and general clamor surged to heights unknown since the inception of the camp. Here, there, and everywhere the men gathered in circles and joined their voices in song. Drunken figures stumbled and bumped into one another as they roamed through the darkness.

Two incidents of violence occurred that night.

First, a squad leader named Shinoda from Company 2 got beat up by one of the platoon leaders from Company 1. Until recently, Shinoda had been a member of the food service staff at the POW hospital, but some kind of internal dispute among the personnel there had ended in his transfer to the camp along with two or three others. Tall, quiet, and still quite young, he claimed the rank of PFC, but some contended that he was actually an officer. He and the two or three others who came with him had been among the more considerate of the food servers at the hospital.

Though he had been in a position of power at the hospital, at the camp he was a rank newcomer. He apparently resented it that men for whom he had done many favors now lorded it over him merely because they had arrived at the camp first. That night, in a state of intoxication, he found his way to the bunk of one such ingrate in Company 1, and discovering him laid out in a drunken stupor inside his mosquito net, yanked on his leg. Instead of the man he had come for, however, it turned out to be the man's platoon leader. This platoon leader, a former petty officer, already had a low opinion of Shinoda for being so full of hot air every time he visited the barracks, and so a fight ensued.

I witnessed only what happened after Shinoda was dragged in front of Headquarters, where he took a one-sided beating. The platoon leader was pummeling him with a wooden clog, and a large red bump newly formed on Shinoda's forehead shone in the candlelight. The platoon leader had worked himself into a drunken frenzy. "I haven't been eating army rice for fifteen years for nothing!" he screamed.

Sobered by the scene before him, Imamoto sat without a word in his chair, his eyes averted. The camp was no different from the army in leaving the ranking officer powerless to mediate in incidents of this kind. As the platoon leader's rantings deteriorated into endless repetition, Imamoto told Shinoda to go back to his barracks.

Shinoda had to step down as squad leader, and after that he could no longer look anybody in the eye. A crescent-shaped scar remained etched into his scalp at the hairline.

In the second incident, a squad leader named Nakazawa from Company 1, along with one other man, received a drubbing from a platoon leader in Group B. That night, Group B Headquarters had organized a talent show. They brought a table outside for a platform, and the drunken prisoners took turns crooning their favorite pop tunes and intoning old narrative ballads. Nakazawa and his companion went to see what fun they could have at the performers' expense.

Before becoming a corporal in the First Division, Nakazawa had been a city ward official in Tokyo. He was fond of jazz, played the guitar, and knew a good deal about music. Emboldened by his state of considerable inebriation, he proceeded to offer loud commentary on each performance. He and his friend were eventually dragged aside by the aforementioned platoon leader, who administered a navy-style punishment with a pep stick.

No mere fist fight, the beating bore camp-wide implications—as is most clearly indicated by the fact that a member of the Group B leadership rendered punishment to men from Group A without first notifying their leaders. This reflected the ongoing antagonism Group B leaders felt toward their Group A counterparts, and the members of the Group A brass who received word of the incident and went to escort the men home were quite cognizant of it. At the same time, they sensed there could be no benefit in blowing the incident up into something bigger when it was clear that Nakazawa and his buddy had been at fault. Imamoto gave the two men a dressing down of his own, and that appeared to be the end of it. Two weeks later, however, the Group B platoon leader who had administered the punishment found himself being transferred by the Americans to another camp in Manila. Imamoto was, after all, the supreme power.

Around midnight, after the carousing came to an end and everyone was in bed, a new prisoner from Group B got caught trying to break into the Group A cookshack. The June arrivals had not received any of the PX merchandise, and for this man, having to sit by and watch all the reveling around him had finally gotten to him. The fierce punishment administered upon his emaciated body quite obviously included an element of repayment for the treatment Nakazawa had received.

A Group B officer came to retrieve him. "If you're gonna break in somewhere, you should break into our own cookshack, you dumb fool," he said sleepily, as he gave the man a slap and led him away.

And so the memorable day came to a close.

————

Why are the tropics so hot? I suspect few people have so much time on their hands as to pose such a question to themselves, but I would wager, too, that if they did, they would find it difficult to arrive at a clear answer. The same was true for me. However, the answer that emerged from having actually spent a year and a half in the Philippines is quite simple: The tropics have two summers—that is, two hot seasons each year.

Japan, of course, has only a single summer, occurring when the sun lies over the Tropic of Cancer, which runs through Taiwan at 23.5 degrees north latitude. South of that line, however, the sun comes directly overhead twice on its annual circuit between the Tropics of Cancer and Capricorn. For Mindoro and Leyte, which stand at approximately 10 degrees north latitude, these two occasions come at the end of April and at the end of August. The worst of the heat lasts between one and two months from these times.

The Philippine islands and their environs also experience a rainy season for one third of each year, however, and since this usually corresponds to one of the hot seasons, the Philippines in fact experience only a single really hot summer. But the story does not end there, for the timing of the rainy season differs dramatically from one place to another within the islands. For example, when I was captured near the end of January, the island of Mindoro was dry, but when I arrived on the island of Leyte a few days later I found it to be in the very midst of its rainy season.

During my stay on the island, I had no means of discovering why this might be so, but I have since gained a general idea. Situated southwest of Luzon and facing westward onto the South China Sea, Mindoro bears the brunt of summer winds blowing in from the southwest where they pick up moisture over the seas of the southern hemisphere. This gives that island a rainy season that runs from summer into early fall. By contrast, Leyte, which faces eastward onto the Pacific Ocean, is exposed to winter winds blowing in from the northeast, which bring with them a season of rains from winter into early spring. In each case, the hottest time of year comes in the dry season when the sun passes directly overhead and the parched earth below reflects its scorching heat most intensely. On Mindoro this was in October, whereas on Leyte it was in June. Since I spent October of 1944 on Mindoro and June of 1945 on Leyte, I did in fact experience two summers in considerably less than a year.

Ordinarily in the tropics, even when it is hot in the sun, you feel immediately cooler upon entering the shade. At the height of summer, however, we dripped with perspiration even inside our nipa huts. The scorched sand outside reflected the sun's blinding glare, sending its relentless heat deep into the shaded interiors. Even the most vigorous of the prisoners no longer went outside for recreation. Some outworkers suffered heat prostration.

The heat still hung heavily in the air after sundown. In close ranks for the evening roll call, the warmth radiating from our neighbors' bodies added to the oppressiveness. Often the heat of the day lingered well into the night, preventing sound sleep.

On Mindoro during the summer of October 1944, I hauled dirt with a yoke and baskets, building earthworks. For that kind of hard physical labor, I had found the burning heat and blinding light to be quite congenial companions. Now, however, in the camp on Leyte, I was spending all my time inside a nipa hut, puffing on cigarettes and holding down a desk, and the heat proved to be utterly unwelcome company.

In my present recollection, the prodigious heat lasted roughly until the end of June. After that, either I had grown accustomed to it or the season had passed. Whichever the case may be, the insufferable heat fades from my memory.

With the changes of season came changes in camp conditions and POW morale. In March we had lounged about in nothing but loincloths; now we wore brand new T-shirts and boxer shorts, and we had cigarettes to smoke and gum to chew. Not only were we being fed all the calories we needed, we were in fact enjoying a general quality of life far superior to that of civilians in wartime Japan. We grew more and more at ease in our station.

During this same period, the war situation continued to deteriorate for Japan. In April, U.S. forces landed on Okinawa. A rumor sprang up from somewhere that Japanese suicide attack planes had fallen en masse upon an American task force and decimated it. The weekly bulletin issued by the U.S. Army, however, reported that Japanese heavy bombers with German-designed rockets strapped to their bellies had been shot down before releasing "the idiots," and the only damage was a small fire aboard one of the aircraft carriers. On May 5, Germany declared its unconditional surrender, but this evinced no reaction from the prisoners. The POWs took pride in the continuing resistance on Okinawa.

The nisei GIs assigned to the camp were all transferred to Okinawa, so we stopped seeing men of our own blood wearing enemy uniforms. Though each of them had treated us a little differently, they had all been kind to us on the whole. They pitied us for having been led astray by our rulers but were reluctant to show it. For our part, we refrained from asking them about their ancestral homes. As a rule, we did not talk about Japan.

The MPs standing guard at the gate were thereafter Filipinos. One of the prisoners claimed it was because the Americans had suffered a huge defeat on Okinawa and needed reinforcements, but most now recognized that our homeland had entered the final stages of defeat. When they persisted in talking tough, it came merely from lack of anything else to say.

At about this time, a German prisoner came to the camp. He was quartered by himself in one of the interrogation huts in the entrance sector, and he received rations directly from the American mess. Since our latrines were the only toilet facilities available, however, he frequently visited our part of the compound.

He was a tall, blue-eyed man of twenty-seven or twenty-eight. He was apparently recovering from a broken leg, as he walked slowly, always holding one leg perfectly straight. His hair was cropped right down to the scalp, but I do not know whether this was the custom of the German navy or if the Americans had ordered it.

In time we learned that he spoke English, and those of us who knew English started conversing with him. I recall only his first name: Fritz. He thought he was probably the only German POW in the entire Pacific. His submarine had surfaced near Palau to recharge its batteries when it was attacked and sunk by an American destroyer.

Fritz was a laborer from Cologne. I happened to have a copy of *Life* magazine containing a picture of a cathedral in Cologne that had survived the allied bombings, and I showed it to him. He contemplated it gravely without displaying any sign of joy. I thought I had shown him a picture of a cathedral that remained unscathed, but to him it was a picture of a city in ruins.

It pleased him enormously to learn that I understood a smattering of German. Since I had grown tired of writing screenplays by this time, I decided I might as well take advantage of the opportunity to practice my German while I was a POW. I got special permission from the American commandant and started going to Fritz's hut for an hour each day.

Unfortunately, I had difficulty getting him to teach me what I really wanted. For example, he knew the words to "Lorelai" but not "Erlkönig." Instead he taught me popular ballads by Schiller—no doubt pieces he had memorized in grade school. He wrote in Gothic script, which I found almost impossible to read after twenty years away from the language.

To answer the ballads he so proudly offered, I translated a poem by Nakahara Chūya into German and took it to him, telling him it was the work of Japan's greatest living poet. From Nakahara's *Goat Song*, I chose the poem "Evening Glow," beginning "With their hands to their breast, the hills draw away." The poem had remarkably fluid phrasings for a work by Nakahara, and it had remained in my memory for that reason. Back on Mindoro, when I stood on sentry duty in the evening, I had gazed at the mountains glowing in the sunset and intoned in my own unpracticed way:

Even at a time like this, I do exist.
The flesh of a shellfish
Trampled by a child.

Yea, at a time like this, the courageous
With right and worthy resignation
Fold arms and walk away.

These verses aptly expressed the state of my mind during those empty days of waiting for the enemy to land.

Fritz admired the poem for the most part but said he could not understand my German for "the flesh of a shellfish." The problem was that I had not known the proper term to use; I drew a picture to show him what I meant and asked him what it should be called. Since Nakahara's poetry will probably never be translated into German, this might be a good opportunity to present the translation rendered jointly by a Japanese and German POW, but I cannot recall the term he gave me for "shellfish flesh" so I will let it pass.

One day our mess sergeant, a former petty officer, asked me to go with him to see Fritz. He said he had something he wanted to talk to Fritz about and needed an interpreter. I had no reason to refuse and assented willingly.

He took along some raisin wine as a gift. Fritz sipped it and said "It's good"—though I am skeptical whether the native of a famous wine district at the northern edge of Europe's venerable viticulture zone could truly have approved of the home-brew Japanese POWs had made from raisins.

The cook had already had quite a bit to drink. He wanted me to inquire if Fritz really believed that Germany had been defeated. I thought it an absurd thing to ask but reluctantly relayed the question exactly as the cook had posed it.

"Yes," Fritz answered, looking a bit puzzled.

"You really think so? But you can't. Germany hasn't been defeated. You have to believe that Germany hasn't lost. Tell him that," the cook said.

This time I interpreted a bit more loosely.

"He says he wants you not to believe that Germany has lost, even if it has. As a citizen of a fellow Axis country he's trying to offer you some words of comfort."

Fritz looked at the head cook again and said, "Thank you." Then he turned back to me. "You fellows can say things like that because Japan hasn't actually been defeated yet. You don't know what it means to be without a country."

He was right.

"Did you fight for Hitler because you believed in his principles?" I asked.

"Not really. I just went along because everyone else did. I know now that it wasn't the right thing to do."

I visited him frequently, and the time I spent in conversation with him became my most enjoyable hours. One morning, however, he was gone. He had mentioned before that he expected to go home by way of the United States. When I inquired, I was told a space had suddenly opened up on a midnight flight.

The time for our move came. Men returning from outwork at the new camp in Palo informed us that the site had been leveled and foundations put in place. The compound was quite large, they said, with lots of palm trees and much cleaner air.

As with other events, I can roughly determine the date of our move by looking at the dates on one of my screenplays—this time the adaptation of my great novel. It took place sometime between June 15 and July 17, most likely right about the middle of that period.

8

Labor

The new camp at Palo, four kilometers south of Tacloban, was a patch of land two hundred meters square surrounded by barbed wire. The main gate stood on the north, and from there a road four meters wide bisected the compound. Inside the entrance, a second barbed-wire fence stretched along the left-hand side of the road for about two-thirds of its length, then turned at right angles and continued to the eastern fence. The Taiwanese prisoners were to live in this segregated sector fenced off within the larger compound, and the remaining L-shaped area was for us Japanese. All told, the site offered more than enough room for the camp population at the time—approximately twelve hundred Japanese and five hundred Taiwanese—and the back part of the Japanese sector remained an open field covered with weeds. In the far corner behind the Taiwanese territory yet another barbed-wire fence enclosed a separate sector for some fifty former Japanese officers.

Though this new site had been completely leveled, most of the necessary buildings had yet to be erected. For the first month, we lived in tents pitched on the leveled red clay while constructing the nipa barracks and other buildings that would become our permanent camp facilities.

Each of the five companies was assigned to its own rectangular tract of land spanning from the bisecting road to the western fence. Battalion headquarters, an infirmary, a barbershop, and a trash incineration site had been laid out on that side of the road near the main gate.

As a professional writer I would normally rely on words to convey an image of the object under description, and I feel somewhat embarrassed stooping to diagrams. However, since progressive trends in education have made contemporary readers more reliant on visual aids, and since I imagine my readers will attempt to convert my verbal descriptions into mental dia-

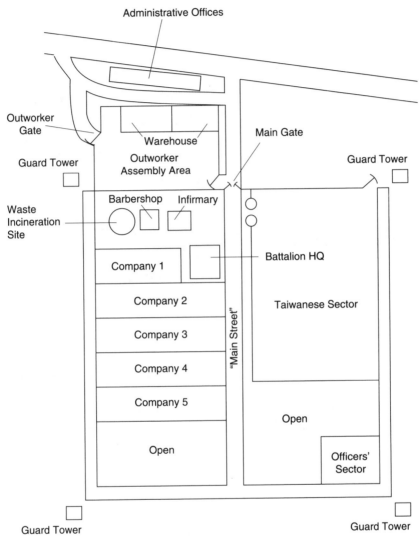

Diagram 1: Camp Layout

grams in any case, I believe it will make things easier for everyone if I simply provide the diagrams to begin with. Diagram 1 delineates the overall layout of our new camp.

I should note that in using solid lines to denote the boundaries between one tract and the next, I am merely following the standard conventions of our day for diagrams of this kind and do not mean to suggest that there were barriers separating the tracts. The American support facilities

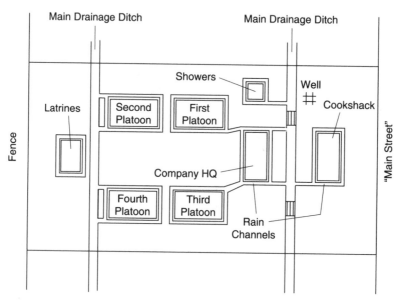

Diagram 2: Company Buildings

outside the compound should be self-explanatory from the labels on the diagram. Similarly, the functions of the infirmary and other common facilities were exactly as their names suggest; I need not elaborate further until I present the men who staffed each of these facilities, along with the nature of their work. The facilities within each company tract were the ones most intimately affecting the daily lives of the prisoners, so I will begin here by detailing them.

We constructed buildings on the company tracts as shown in Diagram 2. The tracts were thirty meters wide and one hundred meters long. In the case of Company 1, battalion headquarters occupied the first fifteen meters in from Main Street, but for the rest of the companies this part of the tract remained open, forming a kind of front yard. Each company's own facilities then began with its cookshack and extended across an inner courtyard to the latrines at the far end. In between were the company HQ, the showers, and the four platoon barracks as indicated on the diagram.

At the time we moved, the cookshacks had been completed and roofs had been raised for the headquarters buildings on tracts 1 and 2 only. Each company pitched tents on the spot that eventually became the inner courtyard and lived there while constructing their nipa barracks.

One of the prisoners composed a tanka poem about the barracks:

With nipa fronds
All dried and brown,
We thatch the roofs;
That must be the reason why
They're known as nipa huts.

Nipa is a variety of palm that grows without a trunk and whose pliable leaves are commonly bound together into two- to three-foot bunches for use as roofing thatch. The bunches of thatch are not actually made of dried leaves as such, but even those leaves that begin as a verdant green soon dry out and turn brown. Of course, there can be no doubt that the structures are called nipa huts because of what their roofs are made of.

The Americans apparently intended us to live in tents at first, but because the war dragged on with no end in sight, they decided to have us build our own semipermanent facilities in the form of nipa huts—with the exception of the latrines.

The huts were all in the gabled style. As I am sure many of my readers are aware, a gable-roofed building is relatively easy to construct because it has only two flat surfaces sloping down to either side. The Americans had not ordered any particular design, so an experienced carpenter among us had suggested we build in this style. (I might note that most native Filipino nipa huts I saw had roofs sloping in all four directions.)

First we cut palm logs into posts of about ten feet and planted them at twelve-foot intervals in two straight rows. Next, we spanned each opposing pair of pillars with a gently sloped isosceles triangle made of bamboo, linked the vertices of the triangles with ridgepoles and the lower corners with purlins, also of bamboo, and lay bamboo rafters all along the two slopes from one end of the building to the other. With that, the basic skeleton was finished. Finally, we thatched the roof and filled in the two gables with nipa, put up an awning, placed two pillars under the base of each triangle for additional support, and erected a waist-high barrier of split bamboo on all four sides for walls. The space between the two support pillars under each triangle became a central corridor running between entrances at each end of the building.

This was the basic structure of the buildings for each company's head-quarters and platoon barracks, but the cookshacks were a little different. There, we skipped the extra pillars supporting the triangles, and left only a single entrance at the back; in front, the waist-high barrier continued all the way across and became the front face of a counter for serving food.

The Americans hauled in the necessary construction materials, and the inmates enthusiastically took to the task of building. Many of those in Companies 1 and 2 had already built nipa huts at the old camp and knew the process well. The nimbler ones climbed up onto the roof to wire the bamboo together and attach the nipa thatch, singing cheerfully as they worked. It soon became a contest to see which company and which platoon could finish their buildings first. Companies 3, 4, and 5, made up of relative newcomers who were weaker and less experienced, took longer than the others, but even so all of the facilities were completed within a month. Outwork details for the U.S. Army were suspended during that time.

The satisfaction that comes from building something for oneself with one's own hands gave birth to an ever more democratic dynamic among these former members of the Imperial Japanese Army. The platoons refused to provide workers to help build their company's headquarters or cookshack on the grounds that their barracks construction demanded the labor of every last man available, so the overhead staff had no choice but to do their own work. For Companies 1 and 2, this only meant raising the dirt floor inside headquarters with fill and constructing the waist-high wall around the outside, but for the remaining three companies, the overhead staff had to construct their buildings from scratch—which proved a severe blow to longtime members of the leadership who had grown accustomed to their privileged status.

The most pathetic case was battalion headquarters. At the old camp, Imamoto had monopolized all contact with the Americans and had enjoyed virtually absolute authority. At the new camp, with American liaison officers assigned to each unit, his power was divided and curtailed. As the battalion-level leader, he became a mere symbol.

At the old camp, Headquarters had housed all of the company and platoon leaders as well, but now its occupants had shrunk to only Imamoto and the battalion staff: his deputy Oda, the clerk Nakagawa, the interpreter Sakurai, and two orderlies. Since it was in fact impossible to construct a nipa barracks with so few men, they settled for erecting a waist-high bamboo barrier around the four sides of their tent. The scene of Imamoto testily bossing the two orderlies as they pounded split-bamboo pickets into the ground represented the first manifestation of his reduced authority.

The American sergeants responsible for his fall arrived about the time we finished building our barracks. They spent each day on duty at their assigned company HQs, relaying the commandant's orders and making sure that camp regulations were being observed. They also conducted the morning and evening roll calls, company by company. This, too, deprived Imamoto of a key role that had helped legitimize his authority before: accompanying the American roll call master in his duties several times each day.

The sergeant assigned to my unit, Company 2, was a man of German descent named Walsdorf. Blond-haired, blue-eyed, and sporting a mustache, he was a relatively short man. He slouched forward and pointed his toes outward like a duck when he walked. To me he looked more French than German, and I decided he must have descended from a farm family in southern Germany (I knew that the "dorf" in Walsdorf meant "village"). When I asked him if it did not feel strange for a German to be fighting against Germany, he said his family had come to America a long time ago.

At twenty-seven, Wally (which is how we referred to Sergeant Walsdorf among ourselves) remained a bachelor. He had had a desk job at an automobile factory in Detroit until being drafted three years before. The Americans I met all seemed rather unsoldierly in their manner compared to what I had grown used to in the Japanese military, but Wally struck me as particularly so. He was a congenial supervisor, always smiling and almost never losing his temper. On those few occasions when he showed up in a foul mood, we usually found out as the day wore on that another buddy of his who had done about the same amount of time had received his discharge papers the day before. Having fought on Kiska and the Marshall Islands as an antiaircraft gunner, the sergeant had already earned all the points he needed and was merely marking time until discharge in this quieter assignment of overseeing POWs. In spite of his somewhat austere nature, I believe he exemplified the character of the average American more typically than anyone else I met.

Wally immediately sensed how we felt about the battalion brass and took great pleasure in helping us circumvent Imamoto. For example, though Imamoto had formerly controlled the distribution of tools from the American warehouse each morning and their return each evening, this responsibility now fell to the sergeants. Tools were handed out at the warehouse based on lists our sergeants gave us, and since each of the sergeants compiled his list thinking solely of his own unit's needs, the supply of tools quickly ran out. The battalion brass, lacking an American liaison of their own, fell to a considerable disadvantage.

Finally one day, a hysterical Imamoto stormed a group of prisoners passing by battalion HQ on their way back from the warehouse and sent their tools scattering all over Main Street. In the aftermath of this incident, he complained to the commandant, and a directive came down informing the sergeants that thenceforth Imamoto would be in charge of checking the tools out of the warehouse and distributing them among the companies. Imamoto saw this as his chance to start throwing his weight around again, but we did not intend to stand idly by. We persuaded Wally to write up a requisition for more tools and demanded that Imamoto provide them. When Imamoto refused to budge, claiming his hands were tied by the officer in charge of the warehouse, Wally went to negotiate directly with that officer and pestered him until he got every last tool on the list. The relationship between the warehouse officer and the sergeant may well have been something like that between Imamoto and us.

This little gambit vented a good deal of our pent-up resentment against Imamoto. Imamoto, for his part, persisted in fighting back for quite some time, but eventually he gave up and started addressing us more respectfully as *antagata* instead of the patronizing *omaera* he had used before. Oda, molded by a corporate environment prior to entering the military, had always displayed a more deferent demeanor; he addressed us even more politely as *anatagata*.

Imamoto still had charge of dividing up food supplies, but in this he became more evenhanded now that he no longer had reason to favor Companies 1 and 2 with their large contingents of old-timers. Thus, at least at the top, the Japanese-style big-boss authoritarianism that had prevailed at the old camp was mitigated by the placement of American sergeants as liaisons to the five companies.

The same could not be said, however, regarding the state of affairs within the individual units. The company and platoon leaders and the mess sergeant continued to act as bosses. Even so, their power could not compare to the power Imamoto had wielded at the old camp by invoking the name of the exalted American commandant sitting high above the clouds, for the constant presence of the sergeants, issuing orders and exercising direct supervision over each company, held them in check. The Japanese leaders' power became primarily a matter of maintaining their popularity among the men by pandering to their sloth, devising crafty ways of turning the sergeants' directives to the prisoners' advantage. One consequence of this was that the interpreters who served as the sergeants' mouthpieces now bore the brunt of any prisoner dissatisfaction.

––––––

We need not make too much of the technical facility so often attributed to navy men, but former Petty Officer Hiwatashi, the leader of my unit, was certainly a man of many talents. From rough-and-ready work like leveling ground and digging ditches, to carpentry and woodwork, to sewing—he proved himself to be a jack-of-all-trades. GIs would bring him scraps of duralumin used in aircraft construction to craft into buckles for watchbands, one of his specialties. He took payment in cigarettes, storing them away neatly.

In front of our company HQ, Hiwatashi landscaped a small ornamental garden about six feet square, burying some pipe he had picked up at an American outwork site to create a fountain. The water came from a tank made of kerosene tins installed behind the garden, raised several feet off the ground and masked by a bulletin board. The company stewards were responsible for refilling the tank when the fountain ran dry.

Wally heartily approved of the fountain and was fond of showing it off

to inspecting officers on tour as well as to the other liaisons. No one else
shared his enthusiasm, however. The prevailing view seemed to be that it
was well and good to encourage neatness in the construction and maintenance of prison barracks, but adding such purely aesthetic appurtenances
was out of keeping with our station as POWs.

In being chosen as one of five company leaders from among the many
former hut adjutants, Hiwatashi was helped not only by the length of time
he had been a prisoner but by having demonstrated a resourcefulness of
this kind in a variety of camp projects. Back when the old camp was first
being built and the prisoners still slept on the ground in tents, he had distinguished himself for his efforts to improve the facilities. He had taken the
initiative and pulled others along with him.

He was a man of medium height. His head stuck out a little more than
usual at the back, and he had heavy eyebrows, deep-set eyes, a slender nose,
and a large mouth (though with thin lips). In the wide space beneath his
nose he wore a small, square mustache. All in all, one might say he resembled a crow-billed goblin.

Though he was unmarried, it was a point of pride to him that he
faithfully returned to the same woman at each of his liberty ports so long
as she did not take up with another man. A woman in Yokosuka had remained faithful to him for seven years.

Hiwatashi was as sharp in mind as he was dexterous in his motor skills.
The role of a company leader was to serve as a kind of buffer between
American orders and POW desires, and Hiwatashi's mental acuity manifested itself most saliently in his manipulation of the platoon leaders who
reported directly to him as representatives of the rank and file. His strategy
for dealing with his intermediary position was, by the quickness of his wit
and sheer force of his personality, to parry and sidestep the various requests
the platoon leaders brought forth.

I have my doubts about how committed this man of many talents was
to giving his life for his country. The warship on which he served emptied
all its magazines in battle, then set its course directly for shore, only to be
sunk before grounding. I suspect, however, that Hiwatashi operated strictly
by rote during those events. Later, when we learned of Japan's surrender,
he was among those who seemed the least affected by it.

The platoon leaders, former petty officers all, lacked Hiwatashi's wit
and in fact displayed instead a denseness that suited them perfectly to being
manipulated by him. Of course, just because this was so provides no reason
for me to imagine that they had been any more selflessly dedicated to their
mission as soldiers.

Petty Officer Yoshioka, leader of our first platoon, was a farmer from
Mito. About two years older than Hiwatashi, he was a tall man with a large,

ruddy face and deep voice. He took a personal interest in each of the men under him, being especially fond of the younger ones. His platoon consisted mostly of working class men who maintained very good discipline.

Yoshioka had been on a cruiser that sailed through the Surigao Strait between Leyte and Mindanao as part of the same task force as Hiwatashi. Their military careers had apparently followed much the same course, and Hiwatashi made a show of deferring to him.

The men in our second platoon came from the barracks for which Hiwatashi had been hut adjutant, and their new leader, Petty Officer Okada, had been promoted by seniority from among the hut's former squad leaders (now detachment leaders). As a result, he never managed to establish his authority, and the detachment leaders maintained independent control of their men, standing largely in opposition to him. Hiwatashi could perhaps have corrected the situation by stepping in to make it clear that Okada stood in the direct line of command, but he chose not to take this responsibility upon himself.

Okada was a small man with a poor complexion. A farmer from the mountains of Shikoku, he came across as the very embodiment of the disgruntled but fainthearted peasant. He joined in grousing about American orders, but in his case he seemed to do it mainly from fear of being attacked by his platoon's detachment leaders. Always grumbling about one thing or another, he was the most colorless of all the platoon leaders.

The leader of our third platoon, a cheerful and loquacious man named Hirota, could at least in some ways be called the most colorful of the platoon leaders. Given the underlying anxieties inherent in our captive condition, I wondered at first if his relentless good cheer was in fact a kind of stiff-upper-lip mask he put on to hide his true feelings, but I ultimately had to conclude I had gotten this idea from watching too much kabuki. The truth seemed to be that he was exactly the person he appeared to be. He approached every job in camp with a happy-go-lucky manner, and I can only imagine this was a direct reflection of how he had always done things in his civilian life back home. Because his erratic, undependable behavior resulted in genuine inconvenience for others, Hiwatashi shunned him and the men in his platoon scorned him.

Hirota was only twenty-seven or twenty-eight, but because of the mustache he wore, few would have thought him under thirty. Hailing from Kumamoto, he had a round face with chubby cheeks that made him appear utterly guileless. He walked with an offhandedness that carried a note of affectation, dangling his arms limply at his side. He never entered a place where others were gathered without offering some loud comment or opinion as he arrived.

He, too, was from one of the Surigao cruisers, but before that he had been on a cruiser that collided and sank at Midway. The lot of a seaman transferred to a second ship after his first has sunk is apparently not a happy one; he grumbled constantly about the scorn heaped on him for having been on the crew of a "sinker." In the final stages of the Battle of Midway, the American base on the island had just entered the range of his ship's batteries when an order to reverse course came down. According to Hirota, that had been the crucial mistake that cost Japan the battle.

Hirota belonged to a right-wing organization of some kind, and from time to time he made fun of what he called my "liberalism."

"There're a hundred thousand people across Japan who would give their lives for me just like that," he claimed, and I could tell that he sincerely believed it to be true.

"Where does the money come from to support an organization of such amazing solidarity?" I asked.

"We raise it in the overseas territories," he said.

He told me that he had once been spirited away by the gods as a child and had possessed clairvoyant and prophetic powers for a time afterward. When a murder occurred in Kumamoto and the authorities' inability to find the murder weapon prevented resolution of the case, the prosecutor's office decided to try calling in the young Hirota who had created such a sensation with his marvelous powers. In the end, however, the weapon did not turn up at the bottom of the river where the clairvoyant seven-year-old claimed he could see it. The prosecutor subsequently became an essayist and wrote retrospectively about the incident, concluding that Hirota was "nothing more than a kid who told accomplished lies." Hirota took even this as something to brag about—which is to say, he was not really very bright.

Our fourth platoon's leader, former Petty Officer Kamimura, had been on the crew of a destroyer in the *Yamato-Musashi* First Striking Force that threaded its way through the San Bernardino Strait on October 24, 1944, making way for Leyte Gulf via the Philippine Sea. His ship was sunk near Mindoro on October 26 as it returned from battle on the Philippine Sea, and he swam to Ilin—a small island just off of San Jose, where I was then stationed. Some islanders promised to put him in touch with Japanese forces and brought him across to Mindoro, but the Filipino home they led him to concealed American troops instead of Japanese. Kamimura was the sole survivor from his ship.

He was twenty-seven or so and of medium height, with a sturdy, angular build like a wrestler's. His broad, jowly face was every bit as square as his shoulders. Owing to a physical disorder, his head tilted slightly to the left. Most of the time he skillfully hid the disfigurement, but it had a tendency to show up when he exerted himself, such as when he joined in sumo wrestling.

This man's most salient personal quality was his great conceit. He laid ostentatious claim to all of the common virtues—courage, patriotism, generosity, self-control, and so forth. He boasted, too, about the effect his good looks and virility had on women.

Kamimura's selection as platoon leader from among the old squad leaders owed to precisely this kind of charlatanism. He fawned on his superiors and made a show of being a benevolent master to the men in his unit, but he could not live up to his own billing and soon earned the contempt of the former and the hatred of the latter.

The Americans had ordered platoon leaders to stay in the barracks with their men, but none of ours obeyed this order. To bunk at our company HQ and share in the special meals prepared for Hiwatashi by the company cooks were, to their minds, inalienable prerogatives of their status as bosses.

Out of their general ignorance of office work, the rank and file treated the company clerk and CQs with a measure of respect, but as testified to by the fact that we received no special meals, our actual status fell somewhere below that of the platoon leaders. The clerk handled official paperwork and personnel matters for the unit, while the three CQs included one interpreter, one uniform officer, and one man to take care of other incidental matters. With our white-collar backgrounds, we had been strictly on the bottom rung as soldiers, but as prisoners we had done very well for ourselves, so to speak. Since I have already described my unit's clerk and CQs, I will not repeat myself here.

Nakamura, the mess sergeant, ranked a notch above the office staff. He, too, had been a petty officer in the navy, the galley chief on one of the older battleships that went down in the Surigao Strait. He may be described as an amiable and easygoing fellow, always wearing a smile on the diminutive, light-skinned face that rested atop his diminutive frame. He peppered his orders to the seven cooks under him with puns and jokes and spared no flattery on the company and platoon leaders. He had a fine voice for singing pop tunes and intoning old narrative ballads.

In his social skills, he displayed much the same acumen as Hiwatashi. However, he had served on a battleship bearing a massive crew, whereas Hiwatashi had come from an intrepid destroyer with a smaller, more tight-knit crew, and this seemed to have led to certain differences of approach. Nakamura made himself agreeable to one and all, like the beauty queen who is everybody's friend; Hiwatashi's interactions with others showed individually defined objectives.

Only once did I hear Nakamura raise his voice. One of his cooks got involved in an argument with Hirota, the right-wing, swollen-headed leader of our third platoon. Nakamura was on his bunk, reading, when Hirota appeared, two bolos in hand, and challenged him to a duel.

Nakamura leapt to his feet. "So you wanna fight?" he bellowed military-style, his voice exceedingly sharp-edged. I saw then that he was, after
all, a military man, but his face was like a mask, and his movements seemed
exaggerated for effect. Theatrics had been evident in the dim-witted Hirota's
challenge as well, however, and the two duly allowed themselves to be restrained by the others in the room. They then got drunk together on bootleg
wine and ended up becoming better friends than before—like the ground
that becomes firmer after a rainstorm.

I need not describe the seven cooks individually. They were all young
and bursting with energy, sharing the satisfaction that comes from hard
work well done, proud of the respect they earned for their role in the all-
important business of providing sustenance to the prisoners. They spent
their days in the cookshack, singing cheerfully as they prepared the meals
and responding with good grace to the men who tried to curry favor with
them. One does not encounter such people except in POW camps or in the
military. Of course government bureaucracy throughout the ages has been
full of men who find their sense of power in taking what is handed down
from above and dispensing it as they see fit below, but whereas bureaucrats
are wily and treacherous, our cooks were full of good cheer. The difference
no doubt came from knowing that what they dispensed was food, the first
and foremost requirement of human survival, and that the general populace
could not go on living without them.

The barbers took turns cutting hair in the hut next to the infirmary,
with barbers from two companies on duty at any given time. At first all of
the prisoners had short-cropped hair, but when the war ended, more and
more began letting it grow out in anticipation of being sent home. The
American sergeants made frequent use of the barbershop, too, apparently
finding it convenient to take care of their personal grooming during work
hours; they also seemed much intrigued to see Japanese men getting American-style haircuts.

So far as possible, the barbering positions were filled by veterans of
the trade in civilian life, but the shortfall had to be made up by tapping
other prisoners who had proved themselves clever with their hands. In Company 2, one was a veteran, the other a novice.

The veteran was an army reservist in his thirties named Suda. Called
into active duty early in the war on the continent, he had been among the
troops who occupied Nanjing. He spoke willingly of the atrocities he had
perpetrated not only in Nanjing but also later, while stationed in the interior. His lighthearted, matter-of-fact tone suggested he had absolutely no
awareness of having done anything reprehensible.

"They take us on this incredible forced march, telling us, whatever it
takes, we have to make it in time for the triumphal entry into the city, and

then when we get there, they break out the sake, so of course everyone's going to run wild!" he exclaimed.

Suda was a native of Hirosaki, short and thin, with the light skin and dense beard so often seen on Northeasterners. He had a generous heart and loved to talk. I simply could not see in this genial man the image of a soldier run amok in Nanjing.

Our prevailing standards of monogamy seem to have inculcated in us an acceptance of rape and other sexual acts perpetrated against women. Anyone who doubts this need only ask a prostitute. Suda claimed the Chinese wives and daughters put up no resistance.

My unit's other barber, a former staff sergeant named Sagara, had also fought on the Sino-Japanese front, and Suda's stories led him to recount his own experiences. His tales, however, were of scenes he had witnessed rather than of any personal deeds.

He described the scene on a levy outside Nanjing. A half-naked woman with her clothes in tatters sat against the trunk of a willow tree in a traumatic daze, her legs thrown out in front of her. I will refrain from presenting the lurid details here, but what jolted me even more than those details was the utterly impassive tone in which Sagara gave his account.

A silversmith from Akabane in Tokyo, Sagara was a mild-mannered man who always treated others with the utmost of respect, and he had refused to join in the brutalities himself. Yet he could describe the victims of his comrades' violence without the slightest hint of agitation in his voice.

Clearly, this kind of dispassion comes from the inuring effect of repeated exposure to such behavior. Ultimately, however, one cannot become inured to the point of indifference without there also being some kind of external sanction for the behavior. For example, even on the field of war, a man does not become inured to murder.

I hasten to add: In saying this, I do not mean to condone the raping that took place in China; I merely wish to point out that too much can be made of it. Rape has been a constant in wars for thousands of years. This is not to say that the conjunction between the two is inevitable, but the quickest way to eradicate the raping that accompanies war is to put an end to war itself. Libertines routinely rape prostitutes, and husbands sometimes rape their wives. While advocates call for greater respect for women's rights and the abolition of prostitution, prostitutes continue to ply their trade and wives continue to submit to their husbands. The quickest way to attain the advocates' goals would no doubt be to abolish the conditions of ownership that are the ultimate cause of prostitution and marriage as we know it.

The sanitation officers collected kitchen waste and other trash and burned it at the incineration site behind the barbershop. They also sanitized the latrines and the drainage ditches that serviced the barracks area by sprinkling them with kerosene. These were the least attractive of the staff positions, and the men who filled them were commensurately, you could say, the least distinguished of the men on my company's staff. One was a longtime reservist from Aichi Prefecture, the other a more recently drafted fisherman from Kagoshima. Both in their forties, they stoically went about their duties without comment. Some prisoners responded to POW life utterly impassively like this.

One of the company stewards was seventeen, the other fifteen. These boys were responsible for cleaning our headquarters building and its immediate surroundings, waiting on the company and platoon leaders at mealtimes, and other miscellaneous tasks. Since none of these responsibilities amounted to a great deal of work, they served more than anything else as playthings for the rest of the staff. When two persons fill such a role, it generally transpires that one becomes more popular than the other. Typically, the younger wins out.

The fifteen-year-old was an impressed sailor named Tamiya who had been a steward aboard ship as well. His family had a farm near Kanazawa, but he had been working on seagoing vessels since the age of twelve, so everyone assumed there must have been some kind of special circumstances in his background. Hirota guessed the boy was probably a geisha's son who had been put up for adoption.

Tamiya's ship had been attacked by Filipinos in mid-May along the northern coast of Mindanao. The islanders massacred the rest of the crew but left him untouched because of his youth. He spoke so matter-of-factly about the incident that I had to conclude he was a bit feebleminded. Even if he had never finished grade school, it seemed telling that he could multiply only single-digit numbers.

The boy slept with someone different every night. I have no idea what the grown men might have been teaching him, but I saw no indication that he was being sodomized. No fights broke out among the men, but the boy did become spoiled from being loved by so many. Hiwatashi attempted to reeducate him in his spare time with the help of some of the other men, but it proved fruitless. Tamiya's nighttime excursions gradually extended beyond the company, and eventually it seemed he could not be happy without knowing that he had won the affection of every man in camp. My indifference must have particularly nettled him: One evening as I stood by the entrance to our hut, he sidled up to me and took my hand.

The seventeen-year-old Yoshida was a melancholy fellow who had joined the navy as a volunteer. He willingly chose to place himself in a lower position than Tamiya, often taking on all of their chores himself so that Tamiya could have more time to amuse himself with the men. No doubt he, too, loved Tamiya. Born into a farm family in Nagano Prefecture, he had apparently endured a great deal of hardship after being orphaned as a small child. His favorite dictum was "Take your meals with the same strangers for three years, and you're no longer taking meals with strangers."

Finally, by custom established at the old camp, our two medics belonged more to the infirmary than to the company. They spent their days entirely at the infirmary, holding sick call for outpatients and looking after the needs of the inpatients, and they returned to our hut only at night. As a result, their places in our building usually sat empty. Even what little time they spent with us apparently made them feel ill at ease, however, and they eventually moved their bunks to the far end of our second platoon's barracks on the improbable grounds that it was closer to the infirmary.

They had both been medics in the army, and at the old camp they had congregated with the other medics in the sick wards, which were a kind of world apart for them where they could continue to exercise the privileged power they had enjoyed in the military. At the new camp with its company-based order, however, the medics had been broken up and assigned to separate units. Not only were they responsible for attending to all of their unit's medical needs, but now they had to answer directly to the company hierarchy. These changes had softened them up considerably. Even so, they remained aloof from the other members of the unit, preferring to spend their evenings relaxing with their colleagues at the infirmary.

This concludes my résumé of the men who made up our company staff. If some of my readers have grown weary of the detail and fear I might attempt to write about every member of the company in this same manner, let me set them at ease. The dream of improving on the camp roster has repeatedly flickered through my mind since I commenced this record, but I continue to shrink before the immense weariness an exhaustive enumeration would hold.

I look back with a great deal of fondness for the men who brought spice to my ennui in camp. I would like nothing better than to describe each and every one of them exactly as they came into contact with the boundaries of my consciousness and sentiments. My pen is stayed, however, for I know how pointless it would be to bore both myself and my readers with an exhaustive list.

Critics may say I should simply describe the typical prisoner. I do not believe that such a figure exists. Prisoners lack the kind of willful actions that allow people in the world at large to be typed.

If this were a work of fiction, I could bring life to the numerous characters I describe by injecting a variety of dramatic incidents into my account. However, in the absence of willful actions, no such incidents of any real significance can occur among prisoners, either. The incidents described in typical POW novels invariably represent wholesale fabrication or wild exaggeration.

In this record I wish merely to recount, without artifice and in simple chronological order, the plain, uneventful days we passed behind barbed wire as we waited for our repatriation.

————

The platoons were divided into four detachments, each with its own leader. With just twelve men in their charge, the detachment leaders need not be described as bosses. Following the custom in the Japanese army, they continued to be addressed as superiors, but in the more egalitarian society of prisoners, detachment members thought of their leader merely as the easiest person to complain to rather than as a commander whose orders must be obeyed.

The responsibility of the rank and file was labor—their assignments being divided between outwork and inwork. Battalion divided up outwork assignments evenly among the companies in response to requests submitted to the American commandant by the various outside labor sites. At first, labor details took only about half of each unit's men, but later on orders came down (reportedly from MacArthur himself) saying all prisoners must work eight hours a day, six days a week. After that, a tally of the men able to work the following day went out to the labor sites each morning, and the sites were expected to provide work for everyone. When the outwork sites could not find enough work to go around, company leaders had to find inwork for the men to do.

Among these laboring prisoners, I could distinguish only two kinds: workers and shirkers. Other individual traits, such as how bright they were, simply did not reveal themselves in the context of physical labor.

The workers were those who had a biological need to burn off their physical energies, or who understood that the shelter, food, and clothing we currently received from the Americans levied certain obligations on us in return. The shirkers were exactly the opposite in their needs and understanding. For some of the men, the shirking could be traced to their physical condition, such as obesity or physical frailty; for others, it was a matter of mental attitude—they had long ago learned to expend the least amount of effort possible in fulfilling any given social obligation. I suspect these differences among the men would remain even in a utopian society where no one could eat unless everyone worked.

For example, the differences could also be observed quite apart from labor details. At a rate of about one man in fifty, our number included men who had lost an arm or had some other permanently disabling injury, and I observed workers and shirkers even among these men who had been deprived of the capacity to work. The shirkers rejoiced in their inability to work and lay on their bunks all day. The workers voluntarily engaged in the only labor they were capable of: helping keep our living areas clean from day to day.

A member of our third platoon who had a shattered shoulder blade used his good arm to sweep not only in and around his own barracks but also a substantial portion of the inner courtyard each morning and evening. He told me he could not stand being idle when all the others worked.

This example suggests that whether a person loves or hates to work has more to do with mental attitude than with physical condition.

The laborers sent out from camp worked eight hours and earned eight cents each day. These wages, distinct from the three-dollar stipend each man received on a monthly basis, accumulated in an account to be paid out at the time of our repatriation.

By the same token, company staff were credited ten cents a day. As our work was unquestionably easier than that of the outworkers, the pay scale could be considered unfair, but apparently every population needs a bureaucracy.

A small circle of elites arose from among the eight-cent workers: the carpenters and the artists. Carpentry skills had been much in demand at our military posts, and soldiers who had worked as home builders prior to joining the army enjoyed special treatment from their superior officers. As POWs, too, the carpenters proved themselves invaluable when we built our camp facilities, and they even got pressed into service by the Americans for building or repairing their barracks outside the fence. Japanese carpenters had apparently gained a name throughout the world for their fine workmanship. Of course, one of the reasons the Americans called on our carpenters so incessantly was that they provided cheap labor, but I doubt they would have been sought out to the extent they were if they had not also possessed superior skills. We had about one carpenter per company. They were permitted to go in and out of camp freely, quite apart from the other outworkers, and they had all the cigarettes and candy bars they could possibly want pressed upon them.

The camp had no true artists, but my company had one man who had studied Japanese-style painting recreationally for a couple of months and another who acquitted himself quite respectably with watercolors. The first man painted traditional-style pictures of dragons, of the wedded rocks at Futamigaura, and of young geisha apprentices; the second, pictures of Mount Fuji and of peonies. Though they painted exactly the same pictures over and over, never varying the composition, they had no shortage of takers among the souvenir-loving GIs, who paid one pack of cigarettes apiece for them. With an ample supply of paints and brushes provided by the Americans, these "artists" painted all day long at their bunks. By special dispensation, they were excused from labor detail.

These, however, were the only special talents the Americans had any use for. A *geta*[1] craftsman and a tailor among our number helped make the lives of the company bosses more comfortable, but otherwise their skills went begging.

The outworkers assembled at 7:00 A.M. They lined up in each company's inner courtyard wearing their dark green U.S. Army fatigues and caps—with "PW" stamped on them in white paint—and with their pant-legs tucked into tall, lace-up boots. At their leader's signal, they moved out. The separate files of men emerging from each tract crowded together on Main Street and advanced toward the front gate like a massive flock of sheep. Forming ranks again in front of the warehouses outside the gate, they divided up and boarded trucks dispatched from the various labor sites; the trucks departed in time to reach their respective destinations by 8:00 A.M.

The men worked mainly at supply depots along the coast at Tacloban—unloading cargo, restacking crates, and other such simple tasks. Many of the tasks had the appearance of work made up solely to give the POWs something to do.

Bored by this gratuitous work, the men understandably sought ways to amuse themselves while working. The principal amusement they hit upon was what the former navy men among us called bluebottling—otherwise known as pilfering.

When the guards were not looking, the POWs broke open boxes of canned goods, candy bars, cigarettes, and such; or they lifted pictorial magazines from desks through open office windows. When the Americans finally wised up to the POWs' sticky fingers, they tightened the search procedures at the end of the day, but the men still found ingenious ways to hide their stolen merchandise—such as in secret pockets sewn into their pant-legs below the knees or into their loincloths. When on occasion they still got caught, they usually went to the American guardhouse for a day. There they received only hardtack and water for nourishment and had to sleep on the bare concrete floor without any bedding, but this constituted tame punishment for men who had wandered through the mountains day after day without food or shelter.

"I don't care what they do to me," one of the habitual offenders declared. "It's the only fun I get, so I'm not about to give it up."

The variety of items stolen expanded over time and came to include sweaters, gloves, shoes, and even cosmetics. Without knowing what it was, one man brought back a menstrual belt intended for American WACs.

The bluebottlers dug holes under their cots to hide any items that were

---

1 wooden clogs

not part of the standard issue. One man actually buried an entire oil drum to protect his treasures, winning the admiration even of the GI who discovered it.

The men stole beer as well, but usually consumed it on the spot. One work party ordered to restack piles of beer cases conspired to leave a hole down the middle of the new pile. They then took turns lowering themselves into the holes, ripping open the cases of beer around them, and drinking their fill. They had built three such piles before the Americans discovered the scheme because one of the men got too drunk to climb back out. Those responsible were ordered to stay up all night if necessary to get the cases of beer restacked properly.

As time went by, new kinds of outwork appeared, such as stonecutting and road construction, but regardless of the nature of the work, all the Americans really seemed to care about was that the labor details spent the required number of hours at the site. Some of the men were happy just to be able to get out of camp for a while, but the shirkers grumbled over having to go someplace and be tied down there for a prescribed length of time.

Once the outworkers left for the day, those remaining behind turned to inwork. This work was aimed mainly at upgrading the camp facilities, and since the camp was so new, there were many things that still needed to be done. To begin with, the Americans required us not only to build our own facilities, but also to maintain them according to the sanitation standards they applied to themselves. Their standards were considerably higher than our own, so it was a good thing.

The salutary effect of those standards could be seen, for example, in the design of the latrines. The latrines were nothing more than pits dug in the ground and capped with large boxes in which multiple European-style toilet seats had been cut, but a crucial specification required that the pits be a full eight feet deep. Eight feet was apparently the highest altitude young flies could attain, so the idea was that, with a dose of kerosene sprinkled into the pits every day, even those few larvae that managed to grow into flies would be killed before they could make it out of the pit. The same set of specifications stipulated one toilet seat for every twelve men. Each unit of 233 men got eighteen seats (one box of ten and one box of eight), so even for enemy POWs, the Americans had relaxed their standards only by about one man per seat.

As it turned out, the latrines had fewer flies than anyplace else in camp. A far greater number of flies were attracted to the cookshacks, which operated more according to our own standards of cleanliness.

Drainage for the camp had also been planned carefully. As shown in Diagram 2, two large drainage ditches stretched from north to south through the barracks area, one behind the cookshack and the other in front of the latrines. Each of these was a full meter wide, and in order to carry the runoff to the marshlands behind the camp, the bottom of the ditch was set at an incline, starting at only about one foot deep for Company 1 and reaching a depth of nearly six feet for Company 5. Smaller gutters were dug around each building to collect the rain dripping from the eaves and feed it into the main ditches. So as to divide the runoff evenly between the two main ditches, these gutters sloped downward from the center of each company tract, with the watershed running in a north-south line between the first and second platoons.

It was a highly rational plan but failed to work as intended for Company 2 because our tract naturally dipped down instead of rising at the center. With the intended watershed line actually lying lower than the main ditches, if we sloped the gutters up from the main ditches, they would disappear before reaching the watershed, whereas if we sloped them down from the watershed they would wind up being too deep by the time they reached the main ditches, and drainage from the main ditches would then back up into our gutters.

The only solution was to dig the main ditches deeper, but then the water they carried would no longer drain into the marsh at the edge of the camp. In the final analysis, the natural conditions of the land on which the camp had been constructed thwarted the Americans' best-laid plans, and whenever it rained the water that collected in the gutters in the middle of our tract went nowhere. All we could do was wait for it to dry up by evaporation.

A conflict between human design and the conditions of nature created another inconvenience later on, when we built a mess hall next to the cookshack. The oblong building was as wide as the cookshack and about fifty feet long. Inside, T-shaped supports hung upside down from four long beams, with tin-covered countertops laid on the cross of the T's for the men to eat at standing up.

The Americans apparently wanted these mess halls built in a great rush because some general had announced an inspection. Instead of having us thatch the roofs with nipa, they provided us with metal sheeting, and they sent in prefabricated countertops and supports as well.

Construction took only one week. In supervising the work, Wally stretched string across the crosspieces of the T-supports and used a level to make sure the counters would come out perfectly level. This ultimately did more harm than good, however, for much the same reason the drainage gutters had not worked as intended. The ground underfoot sloped lower and lower the farther you got from the cookshack, so the counter, already a bit high for Japanese physiques at the cookshack end, rose to nearly chin level at the far end.

"We'll be laying concrete, so we can level the floor when we do that," Wally said, but when the cement arrived there was only enough for Company 1, and once the general's inspection had passed, all incentive to do anything about the problem disappeared.

A new directive required us to eat only in the mess hall, but with usable counter space limited to half the intended amount, the result was a serious case of overcrowding, and many of the men used this as a convenient excuse to take their food back to the barracks as they had done before. After all, secretly supplementing their meals with stolen food had become one of their paramount pleasures. Wally threw a fit and established a system for eating in two shifts, but the men found ways of circumventing this, too, and the custom of eating in the barracks persisted.

In an effort to bring an end to the inconvenience caused by the unusable counters, Hiwatashi made an unconventional suggestion that came from a typically Japanese approach to engineering. Namely, he proposed that the counters be sloped parallel to the ground—or as close to it as possible without causing the soup to spill. Unfortunately, the suggestion offended the Americans' sense of geometric order too much for them to assent to the idea. Those who are so inclined may find in this the grist for countless observations about the differences between the Japanese and Western minds.

Let me add a further example that may profit those seeking to make such comparisons. At the same time as we built the mess halls, we were also ordered to build wash stations. Up to this point, the cooks had been washing their cauldrons and large food tins right out onto the floor of the cookshack, which meant that food residue got carried into the drainage ditch along with the water—in violation of U.S. Army sanitation practices. To correct this situation, we were to build a special wash station where the gray water could be processed through a kind of filtration system before being released into the drainage ditch.

The filtration system consisted of four old fuel drums lined up next to the wash station, linked together with water pipes. When the gray water flowed into the first drum at the top, some food particles floated while others sank to the bottom, leaving cleaner water to flow out through the pipe attached to the middle of the drum. This pipe carried the water to the top of the next drum, repeating the process, so that by the time the water came out of the fourth drum and drained into the ditch it had become relatively clean. Each morning the sanitation officers skimmed off the food and grease floating on top with a net and burned it with the rest of the kitchen waste. Wooden lids covered the drums at all other times.

This ingenious device, however, had the disadvantage of requiring that the floor of the wash station be raised to the height of a fuel drum. It was no easy feat to climb up to that level carrying large tins laden with leftovers. Furthermore, this hastily added wash station had no running water, which meant another old fuel drum had to be installed as a water tank and kept filled by hand. Having to use this water station immediately became the cooks' single greatest grievance.

To my mind, the proper way to install a wash station of this kind would have been to bury the filtration device so that the drainboard could be at ground level. I cannot help wondering if the real reason it was installed above ground had something to do with the desire to show it off to visitors. Our camp, now officially designated Leyte POW Camp 1, had more advanced facilities than any of the newer camps going up around us, and when generals from other islands came to Leyte, ours was the camp they visited before returning to their stations.

"They say this place is the best in the whole Pacific," Wally told us.

The difference between Japanese and American approaches to engineering became apparent as we prepared to build the elevated wash station. The platform was to be two meters square. The basic steps for construction were as follows: Establish the perimeter of the base with sandbags, fill that base to the brim with sand, build a wooden frame for the top, and pour concrete into that frame to complete the wash station floor.

Wally's instructions for accomplishing all this were to split up the tasks, so that with, say, twenty workers in the detail, five would fill and stack the sandbags, five would haul the sand to fill in the base, two would build the wooden frame, and three would mix the concrete. All the steps were to be carried out simultaneously, and the job could be completed in a day.

Hiwatashi argued, however, that all twenty men should work together, first filling the sandbags, then stacking them to the specified dimensions, then filling in the base with sand, then building a wooden frame to fit the actual size of the completed base, and finally pouring the concrete. This way, too, the job could be completed in just one day.

"Even if you start out stacking the sandbags exactly according to measurement at the bottom, there's no telling how far off you'll be by the time you get to the top," he reasoned. "If you have to keep measuring and adjusting to make sure the dimensions stay the same, it could take forever."

As interpreter, I was caught between them and did not quite know what to do. Being Japanese, I thought Hiwatashi's method was more realistic, at least for us. But I also recognized that by American engineering principles, Wally's method made complete sense. First make all the parts according to specification, then put them together—that was their way of thinking. They were a race capable of stacking the sandbags precisely, without departing from the specified dimensions.

The usually accommodating Wally showed a rare firmness on this occasion. His orders from the commandant had included the exact steps to follow in the construction process, he said. I urged Hiwatashi to accept it as a supreme order and try it the way that required precision sandbagging, but he, too, refused to bend. He ordered all of his workers to come with him and they began filling sandbags.

"I'm the boss here!" Wally shouted, his face changing color.

I tensed up, expecting an absolute order to follow, but to my surprise Wally proposed a compromise instead.

"Your CO has a point," he acknowledged. "But it's my responsibility to make sure that the top isn't so far off that the officers notice. So here's my suggestion. Pull three of those men working on the sandbags and have them build the wooden frame. Then use the frame to check the sandbags as you stack them."

Adding my own commentary to emphasize Wally's conciliatory tone, I relayed the suggestion to Hiwatashi. He agreed. Displaying his usual handiness, he made the frame all by himself in next to no time at all.

Layer by layer, Hiwatashi lowered the frame over the sandbags and turned to Wally with a smile: "OK?"

So by a method that combined the American and Japanese approaches, the work proceeded without further ado, and the wash station was completed as scheduled in a single day.

It took two days for the concrete to dry. The builders installed some broad, sturdy steps to make it easier to haul heavy tins up to the wash station. Even so, the cooks avoided using the wash station any more than they had to, and the drums took a long time to fill. When it seemed like it would take forever for the water to reach the last drum, Wally ordered that all the drums be filled immediately with clean water.

"It's for camouflage," he said with a wink.

Of the relatively few Americans I came into contact with as a POW, I liked Sergeant Walsdorf the best. I found him to be a most affable and understanding man. Though unmarried, he never talked about women. Once, when he was showing me some pictures from home that he kept in his wallet, he pointed to the woman standing next to him in one of the pictures and said, "She's a friend," then hastily added, "Not a girlfriend, just a friend." What did it matter whether a POW in his charge thought she was a friend or a girlfriend? I somehow got the impression that he did not like women.

––––––

Before 9:00 P.M. each evening, company interpreters were required to submit two documents by way of battalion HQ to the American camp office: (1) a tally of the men available for work on the second day following, and

(2) a summary of the next day's work assignments. As best I can recall, the content of the first of these was as follows (the numbers are hypothetical):

Men Available for the Date of _____ (*day after tomorrow*)	
Company strength	233
Staff (including company leader)	21
Invalids	19
Sick	20
Day off	29
Improvement (i.e., inwork)	10
Subtotal	99
Men available	134

Though at a glance it appears very systematic and precise, I am sure my readers can readily guess that every figure except the one for "Staff" was open to manipulation.

"Invalids" referred to those unable to work because of permanent war disabilities, but there was so much gray area in determining the extent of an individual's disability that the number could be increased almost at will simply by having the men come forward with a subjective complaint of pain. Then if some of the nominally invalid joined the labor detail for the day, an equal number of able-bodied men could take the day off. We deliberately inflated this figure in the early days, before the Americans began monitoring disabilities more carefully.

The sick included those who were already laid up as well as those who had signed up for sick call that day. There could be no question about the former, since the infirmary had confirmed their illnesses, but the latter was a self-selected group, so even healthy men could sign up. Their diagnoses might be negative, but in the meantime they got the day off. We encouraged this kind of self-selection.

After subtracting the staff and invalids from total company strength, one-seventh of the remainder were permitted to take the day off, giving them one day off per week. By this calculation, even the sick got an official holiday. In time, the Americans saw through the ploy and ordered that the one-seventh figure be calculated based on the number of men actually available for work.

Inwork was generally finished by noon on any given day—which is to say, the men got a half day off. Initially we put down whatever we thought we could get away with and let the men have some time off, but the Americans later set a limit of five (except when they had ordered the improvements themselves) and eventually reduced this to none at all. We were told instead to make use of the day's self-selected "sick" who had been pronounced fit at the infirmary and any other floating labor capacity our units might have.

"We believe we are being quite generous with you. Why are you so bent on loafing?" the American commandant asked with a note of exasperation in his voice. It is generally true, however, that men who lack a guiding purpose for their lives, as this group of POWs did, do not act according to moral imperatives. In order to put an end to the loafing, the commandant had only to start paying outwork wages on a monthly basis, just like the stipend. With the prospect of improving their present lives, the men would have fought to get more outwork.

For my own part, too, if I had had a guiding purpose to my life, I would not have aided and abetted the men's indolence by manipulating the figures. My tricks were in essence adapted from subterfuges I had learned while working in the front office of an industrial firm during the war—circumventing regulations by falsifying our reports of stocks on hand, production capacity, and the like.

Upon receiving the documents submitted by the five companies, the battalion staff compiled the totals for each category and added an overall summary before passing them on to the American camp office.

The next day the camp office considered the requests it received from the various labor sites for the following day, decided how many of the available workers would go to which site, and informed our battalion headquarters in the evening. Battalion in turn divvied up the assignments among the various companies. After evening roll call at seven o'clock, the interpreters stopped by the battalion office to copy down the figures for their companies. Finally, each unit's office staff was responsible for dividing up the assignments among the platoons.

The platoons were all the same size, but since the number of invalids and sick varied from one platoon to the next, the distribution of work assignments could not be determined mechanically. As representatives of the men under them, the platoon leaders strove to reduce the number required to go from their platoons. Early on, when the American requests remained relatively light, the entire matter could be decided by mutual consent between Hiwatashi and the platoon leaders, but this proved impossible when it became necessary for all of the available men to work six days a week.

Complicating the process were last-minute cancellations or reductions in the day's work requests that occurred at the time of departure in the morning. The men thus sent back naturally thought of the day as theirs to do with as they pleased, and it was nigh impossible to corral them for any kind of work. By regulation, they were supposed to stop in at their company office on their way back to the barracks, but no one adhered to this rule. The worst offenders proceeded directly to other companies' barracks and enjoyed themselves for the day, then nonchalantly returned to their own quarters at about the time the outworkers got back. Since everyone carried his own lunch, no one went hungry.

One way and another, company staff remained in the dark about the men excused from work that day, but the platoon leaders usually knew exactly what had happened. As a result, frequent arguments broke out among them in the evening.

"I know a lot of your men didn't have to work today, so you have to send more tomorrow."

"Forget it! Not as many came back as you think!"

At Hiwatashi's bidding, it became my job to walk through the barracks and make note of all the men who had been excused, but that still left us with the knotty problem of just how to deal with the constantly shifting numbers when dividing up work assignments.

Ultimately, I hit upon the idea of monitoring the assignments by statistical means. I knew a little bit about statistics from my civilian job, and I had seen how the general manager of my firm's sales division used his numbers primarily to pull the wool over the eyes of our directors. I decided I would try doing the same with the platoon leaders.

Lest it unnecessarily burden this narrative, I will refrain from detailing my particular methods. The array of sums and weights and percentages I presented so bewildered the career military men unfamiliar with such business tools that they were forced to accept my verdicts. Hiwatashi expressed his gratitude.

After the platoons submitted work rosters in accordance with their assigned numbers, I romanized the names and attached them to the "Summary of Work Assignments for Tomorrow," the second document I had to submit each evening. Then my work was through. I need not present the full form of this summary here; it merely took the previous day's tally of men available for work on the second day following and added a breakdown of where the men would be going, bringing the bottom line to zero.

———

Once the outworkers had departed at 7:00 A.M., a hush came over the camp. Those who had the day off swept their barracks clean, then flopped down on their bunks to contemplate the monotony of the hours ahead. Those going to sick call gathered in the sunny inner court, and the medics led them off to the infirmary. The cookshack was quiet except for the sound of splashing water as the cooks finished cleaning up from breakfast.

Soon Wally would summon me to accompany him on a complete tour of the company facilities. He needed to make sure everything was in order for the commandant's daily inspection.

He paid particular attention to the following:

1. Interior neatness: He expected to see clean-swept aisles, orderly bunks, and proper attire and grooming (the importance he placed on clean-shavenness presumably reflected the codes of his more heavily bearded race).

2. Well-washed mess kits, free of rust: The Americans were considerably more sensitive about potential outbreaks of disease than the Japanese military. Our food was of course monitored very strictly, but Wally also kept a vigilant watch for soiled mess kits that might give flies a chance to spread germs, or rusty ones that could cause lockjaw.

In the Japanese army, any such concern would have come strictly from fear of potential manpower losses, but the sensitivity shown by the Americans seemed to come from a genuine desire to ensure the comfort of the individual men who had been drafted into the nation's service.

3. No cigarette butts on the ground: From the perspective of life in a collective society, the custom of burning the leaves of a plant to inhale its smoke has the serious drawback of requiring the use of fire. All of the Americans, including Wally, made a habit of separating the paper from the tobacco when throwing away their cigarette butts. Early on, this had been a source of considerable lament among the prisoners, most of whom craved tobacco and would like to have smoked the Americans' leftovers. Some of the men accused the Americans of deliberately tearing the cigarette butts apart so that we could not pick them up, but in truth it was done in the interest of fire prevention and to avoid leaving behind an unsightly profusion of cigarette butts on the ground: When the unsmoked portion of a cigarette is pulled apart, the fire generally goes out, and it is the paper that creates the unsightly appearance when the butts are discarded whole.

For some reason, however, the POWs seemed incapable of performing this simple act. By this time the PX goods issued against our monthly three-dollar stipend included twenty packs of twenty cigarettes each. Since some of the men did not smoke at all, this meant the camp had essentially reached the saturation point for cigarettes, and butts could be found everywhere. At Wally's direction, I admonished the men repeatedly and in every way I could think of, but it was a losing battle. They could never seem to grasp why they should not throw down their cigarette butts anywhere they pleased.

We were ordered to install ash trays beside every fourth bunk in the barracks, but the men made little use of them. To my mind, this kind of behavior could not be attributed merely to the apathy that comes from being a POW; rather, it revealed a kind of habit we had acquired as a nation. These men had lived so long under the thumb of authoritarianism that, once the threat of punishment was removed, they had immediately succumbed to the indolence of leaving everything to whim.

A reward was offered for the company with the neatest facilities. They were to be judged on the cleanliness of their sectors, and the winning unit would receive a Ping-Pong table and equipment. Wally wanted badly to win. Out of friendship, I decided I would do what I could to make him proud. Since I knew I could not expect the men to cooperate, I simply took it upon myself to pick up all of their cigarette butts.

It proved a lonely task. None of my fellows could understand why I should want to spend my time as a POW diligently picking up cigarette butts. And I doubt Wally knew, either, why I chose to work so hard on his behalf—especially when the work was essentially that of a ragpicker. To put it most simply, I did it because I wanted some real work to do. My job as interpreter called only for the idle application of my linguistic knowledge and required no physical effort.

As I made my way around the sector gathering cigarette butts, I also picked up other paper litter, as well as any pieces of food I found in the drainage gutters (from the men who still ate at their bunks). Lacking the kind of tongs ragpickers use to pick things up off the ground, I simply used my hands. Once the outworkers had gone, Wally would take a cigarette break, and that would be my chance. When I got back, he was ready for his daily tour.

"Well, shall we take a look, then?"

Hiwatashi complimented me for my efforts in a rather sarcastic tone.

"Actually, it's for my own benefit," I told him. "It saves me the hassle of having to make excuses to the sergeant in English."

This was not entirely untrue. The strain and tedium of my half-year stint as a POW interpreter genuinely wore me down in the end. When foreigners ask me directions on the street today, I pretend not to understand English. I rarely go to American movies because I dislike hearing the English soundtrack.

A month later, our unit won the contest. I experienced a surge of pride, and the men in my company could now play Ping-Pong. Between this distinction and Hiwatashi's skill at maintaining discipline among the men, we came to be viewed as the model company in camp.

The Japanese custom of always having a hand towel at the ready also drew the disapproval of the Americans. We were in the tropics, so of course we perspired a good deal, but the heat was not such that we constantly had to be wiping ourselves off even when we lay quietly on our bunks inside the barracks. Nevertheless, the men's typically Japanese sensibilities for personal hygiene seemed to require that they keep a moistened hand towel laid across their bare shoulders, or across their chest (when they had nothing to do, the men spent most of their time just lying on their bunks), or twisted around their head as a sweatband. Some settled for keeping their towels hung nearby on one of the wires that stretched the length of the building to hold up mosquito nets. Each man seemed to associate a different color with cleanliness, and the towels that hung at random here and there created quite a colorful array. But this, it turned out, offended the Americans' sense of neatness—especially that of the inspecting officers. The command "Remove all hanging items!" was always the first warning of an officer's impending visit.

This Japanese fondness for anything that helps a person feel fresh and cool is certainly not a bad thing. As prisoners in a position of utter subservience, however, the men's inability to alter old habits so as to better accord with their captor's wishes, even if only for the sake of appearances, made them look to me like useless simpletons. Had they paused to ponder the true nature of the violent political forces responsible for their current condition, they would simultaneously have discovered the best strategy for coping with that condition. Merely continuing with their old habits without any considered strategy showed that they had never pondered that question—again, a manifestation of the indolence that comes from living under authoritarian rule for too long.

The high marks my unit received in the competition spurred the other sergeants into action. For example, the sergeant from Company 3 appeared at our headquarters with his interpreter and ordered that the members of his unit should thenceforth emulate ours. It was a gross insult to both the interpreter and his company leader.

This sergeant was a man of Hispanic descent. Dark-skinned, with black hair, he wore the typical Spanish mustache, but in contrast to the dissipated horse-face look we so often see in the movies, he had a square, nondescript face. The essence of his management technique was simply to avoid being bested by the other companies. He toured each of the others' facilities and demanded that his unit imitate any features he deemed desirable.

Once, when his own barracks and nearby facilities experienced an interruption in water service, he ranted that it was wrong for POWs to have the benefit of showers when he and his fellows did not.

"You guys made a sneak attack on Pearl Harbor," he said. "And yet now we spend our taxes to feed you. Are you grateful?"

"Yes, I'm grateful."

"Good, but it still doesn't make any sense that you can take showers when I can't."

When we had this conversation two days in a row, I griped to Wally. "Everyone knows we bear an immense debt to your country. But I don't think it's fair for him to always be pointing it out."

"He's not very bright," Wally said sympathetically. "He's a Long Island racketeer. He doesn't have many friends among us, either."

Hearing our cooks singing as they cleaned up, the Hispanic sergeant whispered to Wally, "You shouldn't let them sing."

"What's the problem?" Wally replied. "It means everyone's happy."

The sergeants had been ordered to exercise special care not to offend us. For example, they always said "the emperor" instead of "Hirohito."[2]

Another American sergeant who visited us was a man named Evans, from the signal corps. He had no duties connected with the camp, but he had initially come to have Hiwatashi make a buckle for his watchband, and after that he returned periodically with similar orders from his friends.

He was a tall and skinny youth, his slender face a mass of freckles. Since he always brought a young Airedale with him, we referred to him as "the dog sergeant" among ourselves. Hiwatashi also built him a doghouse.

He looked a little sheepish when he came in, always humming a tune, "La la, la-lan lan lan." He preferred to talk with Hiwatashi rather than with me. Lacking a common language, the two carried on conversations in gestures and signs, and it made quite an odd spectacle to watch.

"You should become a politician," he once told me.

I was taken aback. "Do you like politics?" I asked.

"No, I don't," he said. In other words, I had to conclude, he did not like me very much, either.

"You know," he said another time, "war is really no good. You have a family, and I have a family, and we're both living happily in our own countries, far apart, without the slightest connection. But then we get sent to the front at a place like this, and 'Click' (he pretended to pull a trigger), as easy as that, one of us dies and his unfortunate family is plunged into grief. It's completely senseless."

I could understand why he did not like politics.

He took a picture from his wallet to show me. It was a half-length shot of a schoolmarmish woman with her head tilted a bit to one side, smiling.

"This's my wife," he said.

"How old is she?" I found myself asking, forgetting my manners.

"Thirty-four. She's really nice."

"And how old are you?"

"Twenty-nine. We got married because we were so much in love."

This fellow who seemed to have such a pure and innocent heart, however, used the same foul language as the other GIs without batting an eye. He poked fun at us when we were working so hard to get the mess hall and wash station built: "Fuck it, man. Fuck it! You know the only one who's going to get any credit for this is the commandant." Another time he declared, "WACs're just appendages for the officers." When he talked like this, he seemed no different from any other GI.

I suspect that Sergeant Evans was something of a loner in his outfit.

---

2 It is considered disrespectful to refer to the emperor by his personal name.

Some Filipinos eventually killed his dog. He suddenly stopped coming to see us after remarking one day that people were saying nasty things about him because of his frequent visits.

He worried a great deal about soon being sent to Japan, where he would have to face combat again. "They're training us to fight in mountainous terrain," he said. "Is it cold in Japan?"

"Some parts are cold and some are warm. Even the coldest parts aren't like the American North, though. And I doubt you'll have to fight in the mountains. The war'll be decided on the flatlands, where the big cities are."

At the time, I was imagining an American landing on the Pacific beaches of Kujūkuri, east of Tokyo. What the sergeant said about training for mountainous terrain made more sense when I later learned that the Americans intended to land first in southern Kyushu.

———

After our daily inspection of company facilities, Wally and I had little else to do. Sitting in the section of our headquarters building that had been partitioned off as an office, Wally lost himself in the detective novel he had brought along. I took a few minutes to enter the day's outwork-assignment information on my statistical charts, and then I, too, was free—though being sociable when Wally tired of his book and wanted to talk was also part of my job.

Wally lent me a wide variety of reading material. At the old camp, where I had only fleeting contacts with American personnel, I had been unable to obtain anything to read. Now I could once again immerse myself in an endless supply of detective novels and magazines like *Time*, *Collier's*, and *Life*. Wally also brought along a copy of the *Stars and Stripes* every day.

By way of the magazines, the sumptuous affluence of American life entered my consciousness once again. Clever, full-color advertisements presented a bounty of mouth-watering foods, an airplane soaring through the sky like a flying horse, an old-fashioned gentleman and lady wrapped in passionate embrace (a perfume ad), and so forth. I gawked like a fool at the beauteous images.

The deft prose of the American journalists likewise held me spellbound. Blended with a moderate dose of wit, their style represented a kind of perfection, capable of making the most mundane of events fascinating and the deepest of tragedies more endurable—which is to say, capable of making any topic a fit subject for office chatter. This kind of harmony between ends and means must owe, I concluded, to a competitive market in which only the best could survive, and to the availability of devices that simplified the labor of writing no less than the process for reproducing vivid color photographs.

I could not help but wonder, however, whether the Americans who lived under the influence of this polished journalism were truly happy. Would not the poor in America look upon the magnificent roast beef with the same deep but unfulfilled craving I experienced as a POW? American readers presumably accepted more or less blindly the version of the truth expounded upon by their seasoned journalists, but was this not in fact quite similar to the ignorance of POWs who were completely cut off from the outside world?

I tried asking Wally about the roast beef. "The way I figure it, not just anybody can eat a mouthwatering roast like that even in America."

"Why not?" he replied. "Just bring your money, and you can buy one any time you please."

I knew, however, from a work I had read in an anthology of contemporary American short stories he had lent me, that Americans, too, could be destitute. The story had been about unemployed workers in the 1930s. When I mentioned this to him, he had an easy answer. "It's fiction," he said.

This was in fact one of his favorite lines. Every time I read a story in a magazine and asked him about something in it, he dismissed it as fiction. Once when the topic of Japanese atrocities came up, I protested. "The Japanese don't have a monopoly on atrocity, you know. The heinous deeds of your country's mobsters are famous all over the world."

"Those things only happened because of our stupid prohibition laws. Now that the laws are gone, the mobsters are gone, too."

I knew this to be a spurious argument. I pointed out the illustration of a wartime black market crook that accompanied a magazine short story I had read, only to get his usual facile retort: "It's fiction."

I had been surprised that so many of the stories from America, the celebrated land of individual freedom, told of troubles in the home. When I asked Wally about it, this, too, was simply "fiction."

The stories at which Wally turned up his nose were all masterfully written. Drawing on the British tradition of narrative realism and mixing in an appropriate dose of suspense, their skill at lending plausibility to the extraordinary and interest to the commonplace rivaled the journalists' polished explications of current events. That was precisely why Wally so enjoyed reading novels and short stories, yet his verdict never changed: "It's fiction." What he really meant, I suppose, was that it had nothing to do with *him*.

At the same time, Wally refused to read editorials on current events. "I can't stand politics," he said.

Between my own random reading of American magazines and my conversations with this man of typical American sensibilities, the impression I gained was of an apathetic populace living under the umbrella of a massive and useless befuddlement machine. The expensive machine did nothing to connect the gentlemen on Wall Street or in the White House with the general population. It merely provided people with a security blanket that allowed them to remain indifferent to journalism.

I came across a photo essay entitled "Pathological Curiosity." The photographs were of curiosity seekers—for example, a shot of faces pressed against the window of a car carrying an accused murderer, taken from inside the car. The article asserted that the interest such people showed in extraordinary incidents having nothing to do with them was a manifestation of a "repressed dissatisfaction with society."

It made me laugh. The typical American magazine flaunted the easy and sumptuous life, and Wally was quite satisfied that he could buy anything he wanted so long as he brought along his money. That this does not necessarily allow us to conjure a united populace of eminently contented individuals should be obvious, even when not viewed from the jaundiced perspective of a POW. However, neither can anyone conclude that every spontaneous activity those individuals engage in each day derives from repression—at least there is no basis for such a conclusion in the activities themselves.

"Repression" and "sublimation" are favorite terms of Freudian psychology, but invoking such ill-conceived analogs to explain social phenomena teaches us nothing about their true causes. It merely reveals the authors' own "dissatisfaction with society." These intellectual snobs who reap their profits by insinuating themselves between the rulers and the people are, in essence, lamenting their eternal exclusion from the bourgeois society of which they so yearn to be a part.

Just once I came across a photograph reflecting true dissatisfaction with society. Tucked away among items of lesser interest in the magazine, a blurry picture showed a crowd of black people gathered to demand restoration of their voting rights. A row of women sat on a bench in the foreground, their heads tilted up as though listening to a speaker. These rather unattractive faces that displayed the sorrow and resignation of hopes betrayed were, of all the glamorous and grievous photographs I saw in all the magazines I read, the only ones I felt telling me the genuine truth.

A second picture showed one of their popular religious bosses. The massive black man was dressed to the teeth in white man's finery, and the mad rush to sumptuousness captured by the camera, in tandem with the florid prose of the accompanying caption, graphically exposed the pathetic charlatanism of this clown.

Elsewhere, I read a biographical article about a talented young black boy that contained all the pathos and candor of *David Copperfield*.

Before the war, I had read a history of Black Africa written by a black man. According to this historian, blacks were responsible for the birth of all the great civilizations of the world. "Egyptian civilization was built by the black race," he declared emphatically. "Cleopatra and Othello (a rather incongruous pairing, to my mind) were both black. Pushkin was part black. Arabian civilization derived from black culture. The rise of modern, Western European industrialism was made possible by the superior labor of blacks." And so on and so forth.

On the racial superiority of blacks, I cannot readily agree with this fanatical author, but belonging as I do to a race that the world regards as second class, I applaud his frontal attack on racial prejudice. No doubt it was because of the damage my own racial self-esteem had suffered that I was so drawn to pictures of blacks in the magazines I read.

I asked Wally what he thought of black people.

"Niggers are cowards in combat," he replied. "You just can't count on 'em on the front lines. And I'm betting we'll have all kinds of trouble with 'em once this war is over because we buttered them up so much in the services."

He went on to tell me about a black man who had only recently been sentenced to hang for raping a white nurse at the American hospital near the POW camp.

I had not seen many blacks myself. At the hospital, there had been two or three who came to do the foundation work for the latrines. It may be that they were not full-fledged soldiers, but whatever their status, the manner in which they went mutely about their work with their eyes to the ground contrasted sharply with the free and easy manner of the white men I had seen. In essence, they still acted like slaves.

————

At half past eleven, when the signal for lunch sounded, Wally left to eat at the American mess. Dawdling as long as possible afterward, he would typically return around two. I took advantage of his absence to catch up on some sleep. Since all the bustle around me usually kept me awake until midnight or so, taking a nap had become an indispensable part of my day. Sometimes I was still asleep when he got back, but he did not wake me up unless he needed me.

If there was little to do in the morning, there was even less to do in the afternoon. I passed the time by reading detective stories. I enjoyed an occasional mystery as much as anyone, but churning through them at the rate of one every couple of days quickly grew old. They were all of a piece— the tricks they used, the way they insulted your intelligence. Given the immense quantities of such works being produced, perhaps America really did harbor "dissatisfaction with society." In peacetime, crime is the sole outlet for our violent instincts.

Although I sincerely admired the strides English and American detective fiction had taken during the war, I lamented the intellectual energy that had been wasted on them by both authors and readers. What a shame it was to see talented authors directing their considerable literary skills and understanding of human nature toward dressing fiction in a mask of truth for no purpose other than to hoodwink their readers. If the readers of these stories were fools, the authors were even greater fools.

The camp sprang to life again around half past four, as dust-covered outworkers began streaming back through the gate. They did not look particularly weary as they came up Main Street, laughing cheerfully and gradually dispersing into their respective barracks areas. Most of them carried their fatigue shirts draped over their shoulders, partly because of the heat, partly to conceal stolen goods they were smuggling in from their labor sites.

As the other men welcomed them back, the returning outworkers groused about their hard day for a spell. "Whew, what a day! The Yanks were impossible today. Always pushing us, 'Let's go! Let's go!' and no breaks at all."

Then all at once the showers would be jammed. At about this time, Wally would head back to his barracks for supper.

Supper was served at half past five. The men lined up in front of the cookshack with their tin-plated U.S. Army mess kits and cups and then proceeded to the counters in the mess hall next door. Or, with half of the mess hall rendered useless by the sloping floor, they went back to their bunks where they could garnish their meals with something they had pilfered at an outwork site.

Breakfast usually consisted of what were known as C rations—a package containing coffee and biscuits and a small can of meat or poultry. Lunch was some kind of meat on bread baked by the Japanese cooks. Supper was Australian rice, again with meat. On top of this, many of the men would open a can of stolen food, so it was hardly surprising that they got too full to finish everything. Table scraps from a unit of 233 men filled two large oil drums every day—an appalling state of affairs indeed at a time when the people back home were starving.

After eating, we washed our mess kits in two large cans set up next to the showers. One contained warm soapy water, the other, boiling-hot rinse water. Two or three swipes with the brush in the first can washed away the grease, then a quick dip in the rinse water, and your cleanup was finished. The men did not like waiting in line for this, however, and many of them took their mess kits back to the barracks and washed them with the plain water they kept at their bunks.

Roll call followed at seven. Once more donning their uniforms and pulling on their boots, the camp's nearly twelve hundred men lined up by company in ranks stretching up and down Main Street—quite a magnificent sight. The Taiwanese formed ranks at the same time, facing us on the other side of the fence.

It surprised me at first that their features were completely Chinese. Of course, when I stopped to think about it, it only made sense, since Taiwan had originally belonged to China, but in my life back home, I had grown so accustomed to ignoring this fact of history and thinking of Taiwan as Japanese that their Chinese features took me by surprise. I can well understand why they proudly posted a sign saying "Chinese" on their battalion headquarters as soon as Japan surrendered.

"You Japanese work hard on outwork and goof off for inwork," Wally said, "but the Taiwanese are the opposite. They don't work very hard unless it's for themselves."

Each of the sergeants was in charge of taking roll for his own company. Company 5 lined up farthest away, so their sergeant was last to get back to the gate after finishing his count; when he arrived, the ranks were dismissed and the men streamed back to their barracks.

Then came free time. Outdoors, in the lingering light of the courtyard, some of the men started a round of sumo while others played catch with a cloth ball. Others gathered in groups inside to sing or to play makeshift instruments. Each man enjoyed himself according to his own personal interests and how much energy he had left from the day's exertions.

The activity for which the prisoners showed the greatest zeal was gambling, the most popular mode being a card game called *kabu*. A few played mah-jongg with hand-carved tiles of bamboo, but ever since the PX distributions had made cigarettes readily available as a currency for betting, the vast majority had turned to the far less complicated and faster-moving card game. Typically each barracks had at least two such games going, and depending on how lucky or cautious they felt, players could choose between low stakes games in which bets were one or two cigarettes at a time and high stakes games where the betting was by the pack.

There were even some professional gamblers among the prisoners, though the gambling spots controlled by such men were relatively few—perhaps one per unit. Since the stakes were on the order of ten and twenty packs at a time, these spots drew more spectators than players.

The gamblers were all very serious. They wore masks of ardent disinterest and affected a deliberate offhandedness in their motions as they examined their own cards and eyed the others'. Then the victor would rake in his winnings with untoward swiftness.

The gambling bosses soon acquired underlings, who crouched diagonally behind them at the games. As the packs of cigarettes at the bosses' knees piled higher, their henchmen reached in from the side to gather in the surplus and add it neatly to their reserves; when their luck soured and

the piles in front of them vanished, the henchmen replenished their supplies from the stockpiles.

I have little doubt that cheating occurred. The supply of playing cards
depended entirely on the Americans, so starting with a fresh deck every day
was out of the question. There was nothing to keep the professionals from
marking the cards with their fingernails. As a result, most of the cigarettes
each gambler received from the PX every month found their way into the
hands of two or three bosses within the span of ten days or so.

The bosses kept their games going until after midnight and were in no
shape to participate in outwork the next day, so they sent underlings in their
stead. The platoon leaders disapproved of this practice, but the bosses regularly bribed them with cigarettes to gain their silence.

The sleepy-faced bosses spent their days wandering about camp like
somnambulists, visiting the various companies on which they had previously
bestowed their largess. In their bearing they exuded a feeling of independence and self-satisfaction not seen among the others. These men were
indeed living.

The most infamous among them went by the name of Sama, written
with the characters for "left" and "horse." The name came from the character for horse tattooed backwards on his left arm. His detractors claimed
that this backwards character was traditionally inscribed on the back of a
geisha's three-stringed *shamisen* when she engaged in illicit prostitution, so
in Sama's case it must mean that he had stabbed his friends in the back.
No one said this to his face, of course.

The man was tall, with large eyes, and he had a gold-crowned canine
tooth on the right. He spoke slowly, in a deep voice. When he stopped by
my company's office he spoke only with Hiwatashi, paying no attention to
the rest of us. He never came on any particular business; he was merely
dropping in to pass the time.

Another boss, with a little less sway, started out as one of the camp's
barbers. After establishing himself in gambling, however, he resigned from
this post. He was a small, dark-skinned man with a slender face. Instead of
swaggering around self-importantly like Sama, he stole about camp quite
unobtrusively—though still with the dauntless air of a boss.

I witnessed one diffident young man grow suddenly into an inveterate
gambler. Conscripted while a student of economics at a private university
in Tokyo, he had become a gunnery sergeant in the Sasebo Marines. I first
got to know him in the hospital, where we shared books as well as discussed
the progress of the war and debated strategy. Light-skinned and well-
favored, he had the mien of a pampered heir. His father owned a trucking
company in a city in northern Kyushu.

He had recovered his health and moved from the hospital to the old camp before me, and when I arrived some while later he was spending his days as an "office boy" in the American camp office. Though not unprecedented, it was unusual for the Americans to employ prisoners in this manner. The POW brass believed he was writing up some kind of report on the current state of the Imperial Navy since that had been the case with another man of similar background.

I once overheard the man heatedly arguing with Imamoto's staff about naval law. I gathered from what he told me later that it involved accusations of aiding the enemy, but he refused to recount the details.

Whether because the staff intervened or because his work had come to an end, he was eventually excused from his duties and rejoined the rest of the prisoners. The Japanese leadership would have nothing to do with him, however, and he received no new post in camp in spite of his language skills.

Not long after that, I noticed that he had begun playing flower cards. This was during the period when cigarettes were still in short supply, and the stakes never exceeded one or two cigarettes, but since he was learning from his opponents as he went, he had no chance of winning. Though I urged him to stay away from such foolishness, he paid no attention.

When the big-time gambling at *kabu* commenced, I looked in on a game one night to find him faced off with the bosses and, with a mountain of cigarette packs piled high at his knees, quite clearly holding his own. To my astonishment, he even had a lackey attending him.

He smiled sheepishly when he saw me and pressed an entire carton of cigarettes into my hands. I was happy to accept his generosity but declined his invitation to join the game. Though I was regarded as a skillful gambler among my friends back home, I could muster no interest in gambling as a POW.

It saddened me to witness this young man's corruption, and it puzzled me as well. His decision to provide information to the Americans (though it could hardly have been information of any great significance) must have come from a deep hatred for the Japanese military, which had been fostered by his experience in the marines. Yet even such a hatred could not have displaced his patriotism without well-reasoned cause. The intellectualism that could be glimpsed here simply did not fit with his newfound fondness for gambling—at least not in my way of thinking.

In the end I could but conclude that the monotony of prison life had led him astray. Men will sink to anything, it seems, in their efforts to stave off boredom.

I do not know when and for what purpose humankind invented gambling. One theory apparently has it evolving from divinations conducted before the gods, but such an evolution could not have taken place without the existence, first of all, of private property. Furthermore, the idea of hinging an exchange of personal property, the crystallization of one's labors, on the whims of some silly rules of chance, could have come only to someone with an excess of leisure on his hands. When lives have purpose and present their own occasions for divining and taking risks, people have no need to immerse themselves in such meaningless games of chance.

I suppose it is because their lives have no purpose that POWs and soldiers are so fond of gambling. Both live lives of captivity. Their possessions represent an illusory wealth that cannot be spent, so perhaps it feels more refreshing to simply stake it all on some accidental chance. Or perhaps because their lives are already so completely controlled by chance, they take it in their minds to play games with it as well.

The reason I had no desire to join in the gambling was that I found a great deal to observe and think about in the camp, and I never experienced the same degree of boredom as the others.

The inmates had one other great pleasure besides their gambling games: drinking. The cookshacks maintained a constant supply of wine made from raisins and yeast included in our rations. Some of the prisoners also made their own in five-gallon cans (the tall and skinny rectangular kind with special seals you see attached to the back of jeeps) buried under their beds. In every barracks, the boisterous singing of drunken POWs would go on deep into the night.

Eventually the clamor drew the attention of the Americans, and one day the sergeants conducted a sweep in which they not only dumped out all the five-gallon containers in the cookshacks but also dug up the ones buried under prisoners' beds. Hissing sounds came from every direction as the pressure inside the cans was released. Our punishment was to spend half the night in cleanup details.

The regular ration of raisins came to a halt, but the men often managed to obtain some at their labor sites, either by pilfering or by having their leaders make special requests to the officers in charge. When these means proved unsuccessful, other sweets like sugar, honey, and jam provided easy substitutes. It is impossible to prevent bored men from discovering a means to fulfill their desires.

When I asked myself what had caused our fall into corruption, the primary answer seemed to be the boredom of captivity. However, if we had been held as true prisoners, locked up in individual prison cells, there could have been no such fall from grace no matter what the desires. By the same token, without the plentiful supply of food and the PX distributions, neither the drinking nor the gambling could have taken place.

Around then I read an article in *Time* magazine about Charlie Chaplin's new divorce trial. At issue was how much alimony his estranged wife

should receive. Side-by-side photos accompanying the article showed a
dutiful-looking middle-aged woman sitting on a courtroom bench with a child
on her lap, and a grimacing, white-haired Chaplin with chin cupped in hand.
The caption beneath the first picture read "Underpaid?"; beneath the second,
"Overacting?" It struck me that perhaps we prisoners were overpaid.

The food, clothing, and shelter we received, along with the three dollars' worth of PX goods distributed in lieu of a stipend, were based on standards set by international conventions on the treatment of soldiers taken
prisoner. Granting such provisions to prisoners was essentially a direct extension of granting them to soldiers.

As POWs, however, we no longer had the obligation to do battle. Our
only obligation was to remain inside a fenced compound. This represented
a severe physical restraint on our liberty, but it was made necessary by the
fact that the country to which we belonged and the country that had erected
a fence to contain us remained in a state of war, and our continued liberty
would pose a distinct hazard to the latter. Be that as it may, the occasion
for overpayment arose from the mismatch between the passive nature of
our obligation and the active generosity with which the Americans rewarded
our fulfillment of those obligations.

To be sure, even men deprived of liberty and suffering from extreme
boredom must go on living, but the specific nature of our remunerations
went well beyond the simple necessities of survival.

Food equivalent to 2,700 calories per day proved too heavy on our
stomachs in this tropical clime; large quantities had to be thrown away. The
indiscriminate distribution of 400 cigarettes per month to all prisoners regardless of whether they smoked led to such a glut of cigarettes in the camp
that they became currency for gambling. These amenities of civilization
obviously exceeded the due of our loss of liberty, and it was probably this
excess that led to our corruption.

The remuneration we received as soldiers had been commensurate
with the lifestyle we had been accustomed to, and with the domestically
produced goods available to us for consumption back home in Japan. However, when as an extension of our duties as soldiers we became POWs, the
remuneration we received from the enemy was commensurate with their
lifestyle and productive capacity rather than our own.

Laboring eight hours a day for a mere eight cents represented our current
productivity, and given the undemanding nature of the work, it seemed ques-
tionable whether we even deserved to receive the full eight cents. The work
left us not the least bit fatigued and failed to dispel our boredom. Perhaps we
would have been saved from falling into corruption if the Americans had
worked us as hard as we had previously had to work as soldiers.

After taking the outwork documents to the battalion office, I carried a chair outside. Lamps burned in the barracks, and the boisterous singing of groups far and near mingled together in the night. The moon shone through the clear tropical air, high and cool over the palm canopy, illumining the brittle leaves. The compound had been carved out of a palm forest; the scattered trees left standing after felling those needed for the fences and barracks cast dark shadows here and there.

East of the compound a small, dome-shaped hill rose over the otherwise flat terrain. The Japanese garrison at Tacloban had apparently dubbed this hill Cross Mountain. On its summit I could see the lights of an American antiaircraft lookout. An entire battalion of the Imperial Army's Sixteenth Division had perished in the area spanning from this hill, through where our camp now stood, to a river two kilometers west, and the men who had helped level the site for our camp spoke of unearthing a number of skeletons. Some of the younger men still trembled in fear when they saw will-o'-the-wisps light up in the bottom of the drainage ditches.

It felt exceedingly strange to be spending our days and nights in dissipation at a time when our homeland was on the verge of collapse. True, we were powerless to do anything about it, and for that matter, our captivity made us still a part of the war. Even so, there was something hard to swallow about the conditions under which we lived.

It is doubtless a civilized practice for warring nations to mutually succor their prisoners of war, but war itself is a barbaric act. Succoring prisoners while refusing to abandon war is a contradiction for which there can be no redemption. I can but hope that the things we had to witness and endure among ourselves as POWs need never be repeated again.

In the end I, too, became bored, so I asked Wally to let me go with the outworkers as an interpreter. I joined about thirty men led by the burly Kamimura of our fourth platoon on a work party assigned to an open-air supply dump located on a stretch of the Tacloban coast known as White Beach.

Exiting the gate at 7:00 A.M., we waited briefly for our truck to arrive and then leapt aboard. The truck lurched into motion, turned onto a road that cut between the east side of the camp and the foot of Cross Mountain, and proceeded along the marshland bordering the back of the camp. We crossed a murky river where we saw some elderly women busying themselves at laundry.

The truck passed through the town of Palo. The shabby rectangular church building there had lost most of its windows. Townspeople chased after the truck, screaming and making cutting gestures with their hands across their throats. Emerging from the town, we sped forward along a dusty road with jungle pressing in on both sides. A colorful array of English signs dotted the way. After turning several times, the road proceeded straight again for some distance, and then we came out on the coast.

Boats bobbed here and there in the offing. A stout woman wearing a gaudy swimming suit lay on the rocky beach, and a man dragged himself languidly from the water. A coastal highway with scraggly looking palms lining the ocean side of the road stretched as far as we could see. We drove past a seemingly endless bank of resplendent fuel tanks. After turning away from the coast for a time and bouncing roughly around several corners, we came back out on the oceanfront and, moments later, pulled to a halt in front of a barbed-wire fence surrounding huge mountains of boxes and crates.

Two guards sat in the shade of a dusty tent inside the gate. Dropping our lunches and a five-gallon can containing tea in the tent, we lined up out front for the guards to count us off. One of them recorded the number in a notebook as we returned to the shade of the tent to await further orders.

Suddenly a GI appeared with his hand held up and his fingers spread. "Okay, I need this many. Follow me," he said. That is to say, he wanted five men to go with him.

Other soldiers came and took ten men, three men, five men, and so on. Soon only Kamimura and I remained. We each lit up a cigarette.

"Do you speak English?" one of the guards asked—a jowly, black-haired corporal.

"Yes," I said.

"About how much does a geesha girl cost?"

I smiled and stated a figure about twice the going rate for a common "tumbling geisha" around the time I departed for the front.

"What's that in dollars?"

"I don't know. There's no current exchange rate, is there?"

"Is it more than the girls here?"

"I should think so. You have to remember," I said with particular emphasis, "a geisha's primary job is to entertain at banquets, and they're not so quick to tumble into bed."

"So I suppose we're talkin' at least five bucks, then," he said, looking a little disappointed. He gazed at the ocean spreading out on the other side of the fence.

"Do you like the local girls?" I asked.

"They're not deep enough."

The other guard was a young private with a prodigious nose. His face suddenly started into a strange contortion, with the corners of his mouth slowly turning up, his cheeks breaking into a profusion of wrinkles, and his eyes narrowing to mere slits. It almost looked like he was crying.

"American girls, very good," he said, pretending to take a girl in his arms and opening his mouth. We all laughed.

"Hey! Better go take a look around," the sergeant said.

"Okay. Come on," the private motioned to us as he stood up, his voice almost like a song.

The three of us walked between huge piles of crates. Working under the hot sun, most of the groups were restacking boxes that had been un-loaded in a hurry and left in disarray.

"Please be sure to give them a five-minute break every half hour," I reminded one of the GIs in charge.

"I know, I know."

A little farther on, we saw five or six prisoners dash off behind a moun-tain of crates.

"Hey, what's up?" Kamimura yelled.

"We're moving to a new job," the last man called back as he disap-peared after the others.

A GI wearing glasses came running out of a side alley among the crates.

"They got away from me," he said as he tried to catch his breath.

"So the good-for-nothings were actually running away," Kamimura said. "Hey, you bums!" he shouted, and raced toward the spot where they had disappeared.

I was left behind with the two Americans. The one in glasses rattled off something I could not catch. The private from the gate merely shrugged.

"This guy speaks English," he said, pointing his chin my way, but the other man was not listening. He kept glowering in the direction Kamimura had gone, and then, with an even fiercer scowl, he, too, dashed off. Kami-mura had reappeared farther up the drive with the fugitives in tow.

The private and I ambled slowly in their direction. Just as we came up to them, the bespectacled supervisor started the men down a side alley at double time and disappeared.

"Heh heh," Kamimura chuckled as we joined him. "What can you do with guys like that? They know an easy mark, and they'll make a fool of him every time."

The main driveway for the supply dump was very wide; a truck was parked with its nose sticking straight out into the road and its tail backed up against a mountain of boxes. About ten men in a line were passing cartons from the truck up to the top of the mountain.

"We haven't had any breaks since we started, sir," one of the men yelled to Kamimura. "It's been one truck after another."

I went up to the supervisor and asked him to give the men a break.

He looked at his watch but said, "I can't give them a break until the truck's unloaded."

"No, no, that's ridiculous," Kamimura said. "Tell him the men need a five-minute break every half hour."

I spoke to the supervisor again. He looked sympathetic but insisted that their rules said no breaks until the cargo was completely unloaded. All I could do was relay his words to Kamimura.

"That can't be right," he said. "Tell him again, and be more insistent. Hey, everyone," he called, "take a break until we get this settled."

The men halted their work, and the GI in charge flew into a dither. "No, no. Keep working. Keep working," he yelled to the men. He repeated the same words to me.

A jeep carrying an officer drove up, so we decided to negotiate with him. He was a first lieutenant, with big eyes and a square jaw.

"No," he said, casting a disapproving glance at the foot I had placed on the jeep's step. "No breaks until the truck is empty."

It flashed through my mind that I did not want to jeopardize the negotiations just because of that foot, but I was too vexed to withdraw it. I explained how hard the heat was on the men and that they had been working for hours without a break. It made no difference what I said, however—with or without my foot on the step.

"Those're the rules," the lieutenant said, and his jeep drove off.

Kamimura reluctantly turned to the workers. "Sorry, but I guess you'll have to continue." Trying to offer some comfort, he added, "This is probably the last truck."

We moved away. Our escort spoke up in his singsong voice. "I'm sorry, but there's nothing I can do. I wish I could give them a break, but I'm just a private and he's an officer."

I shrugged.

"Hey, this guy speaks English," he said to a GI coming the other way. The GI smiled vaguely and passed on by.

Back at the entrance, the private reported to the sergeant on what had happened in that same singsong voice.

"Hrumph," the sergeant grunted, but said nothing more. Moments later a truck rumbled in. "They sure keep comin' today," he said.

We stayed at the tent. Kamimura egged me to resume our earlier off-color conversation, but I declined.

Noon came, and the workers returned clamorously to the tent. They groused about the work as they opened their lunches from camp. The labor site provided some additional cans of food for us to share.

After an hour-long lunch break, the men scattered to resume their work, grousing about the day's heat.

Kamimura and I headed out for another look around—this time just the two of us. Most of the groups had moved to new locations. The men unloading trucks on the main drive had disappeared, and we walked on through the maze of stacked crates with no idea where they might be working.

"Let's take a breather," Kamimura said, sitting down in the shade between piles. It was not much cooler there. No matter which way we turned, boxes, boxes, and more boxes sat silently in the beating sun.

We heard a man laughing somewhere in the distance. "Haaah haaah," came the voice in long guffaws. It did not sound like a Japanese laugh. Since we had nothing else to do, we got to our feet and started threading our way toward the voice between the mountains of boxes.

After zigzagging through some narrow alleys, we came to a clearing with a small tent. Two black GIs sat under the tent with three POWs. The laugh belonged to one of the GIs.

The heavyset black man laughed with his mouth wide open. The prisoner seated in front of him was making the shape of a vagina with his fingers. The black man imitated him and then burst out with more peals of laughter. The two other POWs laughed along under their breath.

"What's going on here?" Kamimura demanded.

"We're on break," one of the prisoners replied.

The other black man said something to me, but he had a thick accent and I failed to catch his words. After asking him to repeat it, I finally understood that he was suggesting we make the rounds. He was a small man with a soft-spoken manner. Since he was relatively light-skinned, I guessed that he must be of mixed blood.

The two of us started off, leaving Kamimura behind. The black man said something to me, but once again I could not understand. I covered up with a little laugh. We found seven or eight prisoners at work transferring cartons by sliding them across a board from the top of one pile to the top of another. A slight incline worked in their favor, but they still had to hang onto the cartons all the way across to keep them from falling.

The black man said something again. It took me a moment, but I finally realized he had said, "They're working hard." I smiled.

We walked some more. Behind one stack of crates we found four or five prisoners sitting in a ring around a young, blond-haired GI, drinking something. The color on their faces made it obvious what that something was. Smiling vaguely, we passed on by.

"They're working hard," I said, and my companion smiled.

Back at the tent we found Kamimura sitting beside the larger black man, gazing dully into space. The laborers had returned to work, and the black man had dozed off.

Starting out from the tent again, Kamimura and I had gone only a short distance when we heard a shout, and a young prisoner leapt out from behind some crates. He saw us and stopped short. Behind him came the bespectacled GI of that morning, the one with the five fugitives.

"He stole! He stole!" the American yelled, pointing at the young prisoner.

Kamimura went up to the man. "Did you take something?" he demanded.

"Yes sir," he said, holding out two candy bars. He snapped to attention to take his punishment military style as Kamimura slapped him across the face.

"Don't hold this against me, now," Kamimura said. "You know I have to do it." He slapped the man a second time.

"That's enough. That's enough," the GI said, extending a trembling hand to stop him. Retrieving the candy bars from the ground, he put his arm around the prisoner's shoulder and led him away.

Kamimura and I sat down for another rest. A figure emerged from the other side of the main drive some distance away. It was the blond-haired fellow we had seen a short while ago, drinking with four or five of our men. His gait was distinctly unsteady.

"Stop it! Stop it!" he shouted as he hurled something from his hands first in one direction, then another. Even from where we sat, we could tell they were candy bars. We worried that he might come all the way up the drive to where we were, but he turned down a side alley before reaching us.

The day's work was through. The men lined up in front of the tent at the entrance to count heads and be searched for stolen goods, then climbed into the truck. The time was 3:30. As usual, the supply dump lacked sufficient work to keep the men occupied until the stipulated 4:00 P.M. quitting time.

The truck started up. Kamimura remarked that our return journey would take us over a different route from that morning's. We would pass in front of a prison camp by the beach, where some Japanese women were interned.

Sure enough, we soon came to a compound surrounded by barbed wire exactly like our own. Many of the women ran up to the fence to wave at us as we drove by. I must confess that this, my first glimpse of women from home in a year, failed to generate any impression of beauty. In their shiftlike dresses and unusually dark tans, I would have taken them for Filipino women if I had not already been informed otherwise.

As the truck raced by, Kamimura swept his arm in a big arc over his head. At first I thought he was merely waving, but then I realized he had thrown the women some candy bars. Knowing that the women there received no PX distributions, he had made plans to do this the night before, as soon as he learned that he would be coming to this labor site. He had a soft spot for the ladies.

The truck drove on along the coast, then turned onto the road that cut through the jungle. Traffic there was heavy, and the vehicles poked along bumper to bumper. Two black men rode in the cab of the truck behind us. They stared blankly in our direction, their faces frozen in expressionless masks.

The more I saw these people, the more extraordinary I found the color of their skin. Underneath the blackness lay a certain bluish glow—a quality that simply did not fit our usual conception of human skin. I also found it impossible to fathom what they might be thinking.

I must stop being so vainglorious, however. White people no doubt feel the same way when they see yellow people; they probably find the color of our skin just as inexplicable. And I know that the inscrutability of East Asians, with our own masklike expressionlessness, is legendary among them.

For what seemed like an eternity, we continued to crawl slowly forward with their truck practically right on top of ours, as if coupled together. The two masklike black faces stayed right there behind us all the while, their blankness never changing.

9

August 10

It is virtually impossible to remember precise dates when living in a prison camp, but these ten days in August were the exception.

On the night of August 6, 1945, Battalion Clerk Nakagawa came into our company office to report that a devastating new bomb had been dropped on Hiroshima. "They're saying it's unbelievably powerful," he exclaimed. "Just one bomb levels an area ten miles wide in a single blow."

He had come to spout off the latest information he had picked up at the American camp office on his nightly visit. It had long annoyed me how he effused about enemy weapons as though he were bragging about his own side. When he recounted his experiences defending a Leyte beach, it sounded more like an American account of their glorious landing.

An area ten miles across would encompass the entire city of Hiroshima. I could not bear hearing him rave on and on about such an immense calamity in his usual manner. When he started to repeat what he had already said, I cut him off. "Why don't you just shut up, Mr. Nakagawa? Does it really make you so happy for Japan to get pounded?"

I could see the color rising in his face. At an earlier date I would most certainly have suffered several indignant blows, but by this time the authority of the battalion staff had declined quite dramatically, and he had had to learn to exercise restraint even with a lowly company interpreter like myself. Besides, from a patriotic standpoint, I clearly had the advantage.

He managed to control his rage. "I didn't mean it that way," he muttered, and stalked off toward Company 3. He would no doubt crow about the news in exactly the same manner there.

Hiwatashi had been listening in silence nearby. "Ha ha ha, Ōoka, you really blew your stack," he chortled. It brought him great glee to see the battalion clerk cut down to size while on his turf.

Everyone joined in bad-mouthing Nakagawa for a spell, and then talk turned to the power of the new bomb. In fact, the detached, sensational tone of the ensuing discussion did not differ a great deal from the curiosity seeker's ravings to which Nakagawa had treated us.

Nakagawa had heard nothing about the particular nature of the bomb. I envisioned some kind of a two-stage device similar to a Molotov's Breadbasket: The huge new bomb would explode high in the sky and rain countless smaller bombs down on the city below. Whether the bomb could level an area ten miles across or twenty made little difference, though, so long as the Americans had the capacity to produce as many explosives and B-29s as they wanted. When Wally came the next day and boasted that the single bomb had been equivalent to ten thousand tons of TNT, I cited this reason to let him know I was not impressed.

"Of course," I added, "if you can get by with one B-29 where you used to have to send fifty, you'll be able to save some of the precious fuel your country has such an endless supply of."

Tilting his head in disbelief, Wally eyed me pityingly out of the corner of his eye.

I soon learned I had been mistaken. When Wally brought in a copy of the *Stars and Stripes* that afternoon, the word ATOMIC in the headline immediately caught my eye. Wally had probably used the same term that morning, but my limited vocabulary and lack of imagination had prevented me from fully comprehending what he was telling me.

If I confess that my first reaction was one of thrill, my readers may think me a traitor. Nonetheless, that is the truth. I had long held an avid interest in modern theoretical physics and had followed recent developments in research on subatomic phenomena. I was irked when I learned that the communists had dismissed the extraordinary theories being advanced as nothing more than a reflection of stage three capitalist decline. If a bomb based on those theories had now actually been exploded, then they could no longer scorn them as mere bourgeois fantasies. I believed this represented the most epochal advance in human civilization since the discovery of fire.

In the next instant, however, a chill gripped my spine as it suddenly struck home that my own countrymen had become the first victims of the unleashed atom. My vision of a two-stage device now seemed a joke. In a note of menacing overstatement, the article in the *Stars and Stripes* predicted that no living thing could grow in the ruins for twenty years. I shuddered in horror as I thought of the countless victims who would die in protracted agony from the terrible complications brought by the radiation that had penetrated their bodies.

In all my months as a POW, this was the first time I became seriously shaken by news of a catastrophe befalling my homeland. It had certainly distressed me to learn about the sinking of the battleship *Yamato*, or about Prime Minister Suzuki's declaration that Japan would prosecute the war to the bitter end. But as a POW I could accomplish nothing by fretting about such things, and in that sense they never loomed very large in my consciousness. Of course I could accomplish nothing by dwelling on the atomic bomb, either. What made the difference and left me so shaken, I think, was that I had long regarded the energy of an atom's nucleus with a kind of superstitious awe.

"Do you know what 'atomic' means?" Wally asked me.

"I think I do. I know we are talking about a truly historic invention."

"What kind of crazy fools are you guys, anyway? Why won't you surrender? We've already offered you very generous terms."

"I told you the other day why you can't expect our militarists to accept the Potsdam Declaration."

"It's crazy."

"But let me ask you, what's your opinion of the atomic bomb?"

"It's too damned destructive. I think we will come to regret that we used it," Wally said bleakly.

I stood up and yelled to the others. "Hey, listen up! They say the bomb they dropped on Hiroshima was an atomic bomb." Everybody gathered around.

Hiwatashi had heard that Japan was working on such a weapon as well. "It's a bomb that's about as big as a matchbox and can blow a whole fleet of warships out of the water," he said. "So they beat us to it, did they? That sure puts a damper on any hopes I had."

"The Yanks can throw all the money they want at something like that," one of the platoon leaders lamented. "I guess we're really done for now."

I found myself becoming more and more agitated. "It's crazy," Wally had said, and obviously he was right. Still, it would be just like the madmen directing the war effort back home to refuse to give in. No matter how many atomic strikes the general population suffered, they would sit tight in the safety of their underground bunkers dreaming of Oda Nobunaga's victory against impossible odds at Okehazama.

I was in no mood for reading detective stories, nor for continuing the screenplay I had started, and I hardly felt like sitting there exchanging pleasantries with the good Wally. I roved about the compound restlessly, anxiously, finding a small measure of comfort in agitated discussion of the atomic bomb with friends I had made in camp.

Such a state of agitation was a new experience for me as a POW. I contemplated its genesis.

Speaking from the perspective of a common citizen, the people of Hiroshima, or of any other city that might be hit by atomic bombs in the future, were no concern of mine. As a simple man who made his living in service to a business enterprise, my concerns extended only as far as my own family and friends. My family had almost certainly evacuated from the city, and I assumed that my friends, with their characteristic acumen, would know how to stay out of harm's way.

I had only very vague feelings of patriotism toward my country. "My country," in this case, signified the government that permitted my employer just enough prosperity to keep me in its employ. In wartime, it was of course the same government that prosecuted the war. In order to pay the costs of that war, the government demanded that I remit a sizable portion of my income as taxes and that I be prepared, if called, to go to my death on the front lines as a common soldier. My happiness during the war hinged solely on the accident of not being called up. Nothing else mattered.

Unhappily, that accidental circumstance did not last, but I was blessed instead by an accident on the battlefield—which made me prisoner of war to a civilized nation and allowed me to enjoy far better living conditions than the people back home or the soldiers still fighting in the field. Living under these conditions, patriotism could be nothing more than sentimentalism.

My country would eventually go down to defeat. The reports I had heard made it painfully impossible to believe otherwise even before the calamity that had now befallen the people of Hiroshima. An end to the war would surely cast my future livelihood into a panoply of difficulties, but as one whose livelihood had been sustained by the war I was in no position to complain. Without the war, a useless intellectual like myself would long since have joined the ranks of the unemployed.

My agitation upon hearing of the atomic catastrophe must have come from the novelty of a weapon that released the power of the atom—and from that weapon being "too damned destructive," as one common citizen of the country that used the weapon had remarked.

A hundred thousand human lives had been snuffed out in a single flash, and perhaps an equal number would continue to die slowly over time. It was a horror of unprecedented proportions. On further contemplation, though, except for a difference in degree, the medievals who first witnessed the carnage made possible by the cannon must have felt this same horror. To go back even further, the primitive who first witnessed his neighbor pierced with an arrow or cut apart by a metal sword—would he not have experienced it, too? Every new form of slaughter leaves witnesses shaken with horror, but for the victims, the ones who actually lose their lives, forms of slaughter would seem to be six of one and half a dozen of another.

Erich Maria Remarque luridly described a man who walked three steps spurting blood from the stump of his neck after having his head blown off by a shell. Norman Mailer, too, has given us grisly descriptions of decapitated corpses on the field of combat. But to find tragedy only in gruesome battle scenes of this kind is pure sentimentalism. The tragedy of war lies in the simple fact that so many must die unwillingly; precisely how they are killed is of no importance.

Furthermore, the majority of those who die are people who happily accepted the benefits bestowed by their governments during the war or during preparations for war. In truth, they are merely reaping what they have sown.

I had without doubt reaped what I had sown, and now the citizens of Hiroshima had done the same. Since becoming a soldier, I had lost all sympathy for those who died for the same reason I expected to die.

I finally concluded that the agitation I was experiencing represented my heart's response to the image of such massive numbers dying in a single instant. As a common citizen whose heart does not normally have room for social sentiment, I can but assume that my herd instincts as a human being had made my heart respond this way to the numbers. It was a purely visceral reaction.

From this visceral reaction arose a fierce hatred for the General Staff. These military experts could not possibly be unaware of how hopeless the war had become. They had to know, too, that no such thing as the "one-hundred million fight to the finish" they trumpeted could actually take place in modern warfare. For these men to persist in their refusal to surrender even after witnessing the power of the atomic bomb could be explained only by a purely selfish desire to escape punishment as war criminals. I was quite cognizant that their reasons for starting this war had been complex, and much had taken place that was beyond their control, but for them to go on passing the days without action at this juncture represented a purely visceral self-preservation instinct on their part. I had every right to experience a visceral hatred for them.

I spent the next two days roving about camp as aimlessly as an animal.

On August 9, the Stars and Stripes reported the Soviet Union's declaration of war against Japan along with the Soviet Far Eastern Army's invasion of Manchuria. Having seen the pick of the Guandong Army transferred to the Philippines, I knew that only inexperienced replacements remained on the continent. Manchuria would be conquered in a single sweep. Since this news could help spur the General Staff to surrender, I did not regard it as so terribly bad.

More bad news did arrive on August 10, however. An atomic bomb had now been dropped on Nagasaki—apparently a device even more powerful than the one dropped on Hiroshima.

"It's just insane!" Wally shrieked. "I mean, Christ! Isn't there some special order that emperor of yours can give to make the military surrender?"

"They'd probably kill him if he tried," I spat out, turning away.

Taken aback by my vehemence, so uncharacteristic of me as an interpreter, Wally let out a dyspeptic snort of a laugh and walked away.

———

At about nine o'clock that evening, the sky over Tacloban to the northeast lit up with countless searchlights sweeping back and forth through the darkness. The ships anchored in the bay sounded a protracted cacophony of whistles and horns and sent up red and green flares.

My first thought was of a Japanese air raid, but there had been none of those for several months, and the recent war situation positively ruled it out. Next I wondered if it might be an air defense drill, but in that case the flares seemed out of place.

A sudden premonition propelled me out onto Main Street and toward the gate, fifty meters away. A single guard stood on duty in the brightness of the floodlights illuminating the gate area. I saw another GI come running out of the darkness beyond, shouting something as he came. When he reached the guard a moment later, the two men pounded each other on the shoulders, clasped arms, and began dancing around and around.

I had seen enough American movies about the First World War to immediately apprehend the significance of this scene. I scarcely needed to ask.

I halted my steps. In the meantime, Imamoto and Oda had come charging out of battalion HQ. The professional soldiers could muster greater speed than the rest of us when the occasion demanded, and they had already reached the gate by the time I came to a stop. After exchanging a word or two with the guard, they dashed off toward the American camp office outside. Commandant Li from the Taiwanese sector also arrived at the gate, threw both arms in the air, and raced back toward his sector shouting at the top of his lungs. The situation could not have been clearer.

I turned around. As I retraced my steps, sounds of jubilation erupted across the fence among the Taiwanese: banging on wood, pounding on metal, ecstatic whoops of joy. Headquarters staff from other companies came running.

"What the blazes is going on?" they demanded.

"Imamoto just went up to the office. It looks like the war's over."

"What?" they said, and ran on by.

Anxious prisoners milled about in front of our company office. Hiwatashi had gone to battalion HQ. Searchlights still crisscrossed the sky to the northeast, and the cacophony of ships' whistles continued.

"What's going on, Ōoka?"

"I'm not sure, but it looks like the war's over. We'll know when Hiwatashi gets back."

"So Japan's been beaten?"

"What did you expect?" someone said in the darkness.

"Who said that?" demanded Kamimura. "Who's talking crap like that? Step out front!"

The crowd wavered vaguely, but no one came forward. Kamimura, for his part, was not so riled up as to step in and drag the culprit out.

"Shit! Listen to them kicking up their heels," Kamimura said, looking across at the Taiwanese sector where the clamor was growing louder and louder. I do not know what they could have been burning, but bonfires flared up here and there to light the tops of the palm trees.

Hiwatashi returned. He went up to Kamimura and spat out, "Japan threw up her hands. On the radio, apparently."

A murmur went through the crowd.

"Really? Are you sure?" Kamimura said. "I've got to get this straight from Imamoto." He took off at a run.

"You'll get the same answer no matter who you ask," Hiwatashi muttered under his breath.

The men who had gathered silently dispersed. Within moments the barracks were abuzz, mixed with occasional wails of lamentation. The commotion gradually spread through all of the units. Voices rose from the entire camp as one.

A young prisoner barged into our building in tears and caught hold of Hiwatashi.

"It can't be true, can it, sir?" he sobbed. "Tell me that it's not. Tell me it's not true. We didn't lose yet, did we? We can't have lost, can we? Please sir."

"Look, I don't know the whole story yet myself," Hiwatashi said, casting a glance my way. "But whatever the case may be, it doesn't do you any good to go around bawling like that. Pull yourself together."

One of the prisoners who dabbled in traditional poetry composed a tanka poem:

Exhausted of words
To raise in tearful lament,
The gallant braves
Cast themselves upon the ground,
Collapsing in heartsick silence.

The poem contains some exaggeration, but it is true that tearful figures could be seen embracing and comforting one another throughout the camp.

In time the searchlights weaving across the sky began to go out, and the ships' whistles fell quiet, but the clamor inside the camp showed no signs of abating. The banging on tin in the Taiwanese sector continued as the whoops and shouts gradually gave way to a chorus of song.

The third platoon's Hirota, one of our most rabid patriots, came running in.

"Sir, they're getting out of control!" he cried to Hiwatashi. "Some of the men are getting together in the courtyard, and they say they're gonna raid the Taiwanese." He glared in the direction of the Taiwanese sector. "Just listen to those bastards whooping it up!"

"They're 'getting together'? Isn't it that you got them together yourself?" Hiwatashi shouted.

"Not at all, sir. They say they're going over the fence on a raid. Right now they're rounding up all the bolos they can find."

"Bolos?" Hiwatashi screamed, leaping to his feet.

Bolos could be turned to deadly use, and prisoners were not permitted to keep them in camp. They had to be checked out from the warehouse in the morning and duly returned in the evening. Over the course of the months, however, the men had on occasion managed to smuggle out extra bolos not included in the official count, and each of the barracks had about two of them hidden away in case of emergencies.

"Did they get the ones from your barracks yet?" Hiwatashi asked.

"No, not yet. We still have ours."

"Then bring them here, now!" Hiwatashi demanded. When Hirota started to mumble something in protest, he repeated, "Just bring them here, and I'll take care of the hotheads!" He turned to one of the cooks at the back of the hut and said, "You there! Go get the leaders of the other platoons." Then he headed out to the courtyard where Hirota had said the raiding party was gathering.

Sure enough, about twenty dim figures milled about in the darkness in the middle of the courtyard. I watched Hiwatashi from where I stood. I did not need to follow; I already knew exactly what would happen. Climbing over the fence would be no easy feat to begin with, and they all knew very well the guards would shoot. I did not believe anyone in camp was actually willing to risk his life just because the Taiwanese were celebrating with so much ado.

Hiwatashi railed at the men for a time and then came back with a big smile on his face. "That Hirota," he said. "The damn harebrain. They were all his own men. If he didn't intend to go through with it, he should never have started shooting off his mouth in the first place."

The platoon leaders soon arrived. Their eyes were all bloodshot.

"Kimura's such a dear, bawling and clinging to me like a little boy. He's a good fellow, he is." The first platoon's Yoshioka had always taken a personal interest in his men, and he seemed genuinely touched. Kimura was the youngster who had come bawling to Hiwatashi earlier. Apparently he had done the same with several of the leaders.

Hirota appeared carrying two bolos.

"Here they are, sir," he said. He handed them to Hiwatashi, who immediately tossed them under his bed.

"I want all of you to hand over your smuggled bolos. Even if no one tries to raid the Taiwanese, there's no telling what else some of these guys might try."

"My men are fine. And we don't have any bolos," Yoshioka declared coolly.

"Same here," the second platoon's Okada mumbled.

"I heard you had two," Hirota broke in. He was no doubt beginning to regret that he had been so quick to yield up his own platoon's bolos.

"It's not true."

"We don't have any either," Kamimura joined in. "You'll just have to trust us on this one."

Hirota flopped down on a bed nearby. "Cripes, why did we have to give up? What's His Imperial Majesty doing, anyway? If he had prayed at Ise Shrine for Japan to be saved and offered his own life in return, I'll bet the divine wind wouldn't have stayed away then."

The other men exchanged strained looks. Even those who had been career soldiers found themselves hard put to respond to Hirota's fanaticism.

"In any case, I'll have to be excused from tomorrow's outwork. I'm in no mood to work."

This time he did not seem to be saying it just for show.

"You may say that now, but if you're ordered to go, you'll do as you're told," Hiwatashi said stonily.

Imamoto came in. He, too, showed his agitation.

"Gentlemen," he said. "I don't want to see any rash behavior. Japan has not surrendered. We have not yet lost. We've merely announced that we're willing to accept the Potsdam Declaration. That definitely does not mean we've lost, so go tell that to your men and make sure they keep their cool."

He headed for the next company.

"Actually, it's basically the same thing as surrender," Hiwatashi said to the four platoon leaders. "But be a little careful what you say."

"I wish I could be as composed as you are," Kamimura said with a touch of sarcasm. Then the platoon leaders departed in their several directions.

The din from the Taiwanese sector continued, but the commotion on the Japanese side gradually died down. The company clerk and cooks went to visit friends and discuss the big news, leaving only Hiwatashi and myself at headquarters. Neither he nor I had any particularly close friends with whom to share our thoughts at moments like this. Nor, for that matter, did we have much to say to each other.

"I think I'll make some cocoa," I said, heading toward the cookshack for some hot water.

Normally one of the cooks always remained on duty, but tonight the cookshack was empty and dark. A heater with an immersion element kept a large pot of hot water at the ready, mainly for headquarters staff. The light of its flames escaped through cracks here and there to reflect dimly off the surface of the water. As I dipped the cup from my U.S. Army mess kit into the pot, I resisted an impulse to scream.

We received cocoa every day with our rations, and I had accumulated a substantial stockpile. It came in the form of a small, hard tablet to be dissolved in a cup of hot water.

"Would you like some, too, sir?"

Hiwatashi had been sitting absently on his bed with nothing to do.

"Yeah, I guess maybe so," he said, and came to sit down across from me, bringing his cup. I poured half of the cocoa from my cup into his.

"You know, Ōoka," he said. "Everyone seems to be all upset about this, but I had actually been wishing we'd hurry up and surrender. At this point, it's only a question of sooner or later anyway, and I think everyone would agree that the sooner we can go home the better."

"Yeah, what it really means is that we can finally go home."

"I don't suppose we'll be going right away, but I'd think we could be home within a year." He gave a big sigh. "In any case, this finally brings things to a close." He forlornly gulped down the rest of his cocoa.

A runner came from battalion HQ summoning all of the company leaders.

"Shit, why don't they leave us alone? It's not as if we can change anything by meeting about it now," he muttered, but he went anyway.

I was left by myself. Quiet tears began to overflow my eyes. I had always been slow to react emotionally, not crying until after everyone else. I blew out the candle and sat in the dark, letting the tears flow freely down my cheeks.

So my homeland had been defeated. The grand achievements of our Meiji forebears had been undone by the third generation. In my relative ignorance of history, I had long believed that culture prospers when the nation prospers. In a Japan freed from the grip of those madmen, all would become rational and, we could hope, democratic, but also diminished—much diminished. We would lose touch with adjectives like "grand," "magnificent," and "sublime."

Midway along the path of my life, I had seen my homeland brought to its knees in war, and I felt a deep sense of personal loss. Back when I first departed for the front, I had resigned myself to death, telling myself that a defeated Japan offered nothing worth living for anyway. Now, having regained my life through captivity, I would have to live in just such a Japan.

I saw no need to panic, however. Without a doubt, my country's prosperity over the last fifty years had come almost exclusively from war. What the militarists gave, they had now taken away—defeat meant nothing more than that. Our great Meiji ancestors sixty and seventy years ago had labored tirelessly to better themselves under a standard of living so far below our own it could not even be compared. What was there to prevent us from returning to the spirit of that era and doing the same now?

It felt good to cry, but after a while I could no longer bear to sit there alone in the dark. I went in search of company and entered one of the barracks more or less at random. Complete quiet reigned inside. In two neat rows on either side, stretching to the far end of the building some sixty feet away, the men lay silently on their bunks, gazing endlessly up at the roof.

What they may have been thinking, each in his own world, I can hardly say; I was but a passerby. For the most part, in fact, I believe that they were not really thinking of anything at all. For example, I could tell that only a small minority of sentimentalists among them had shed any tears—and even those few tears probably would not have flowed but for a certain emotional latitude the men's state of captivity had given them.

Barely an hour after learning of Japan's surrender, these former members of the Imperial Army had, in essence, already lost interest. Compared to these men lying silently on their bunks, all my ruminations over "my homeland" and its former "grandness" were pure abstraction.

I cannot determine whether this was the natural response that one should expect from the masses everywhere or if it was the result of the year these men had spent living in captivity. I prefer to believe it was the latter.

As I walked up the center aisle my eyes met those of one of the men. In his otherwise expressionless eyes, I thought I saw a note of sheepishness like that of a child caught red-handed in some mischief, but it may have been only my imagination.

The clamor in the Taiwanese sector finally subsided, the last of the searchlights disappeared, and the camp returned to its usual nighttime tranquility. Hiwatashi came back late from battalion HQ with a list of three special instructions to relay to the men:

1. Pending confirmation of the reports, refrain from any rash behavior.
2. In particular, any kind of unified action is strictly forbidden.
3. No suicides.

We had a hearty laugh over the last.

Hirota's wish came true when more than half of the next day's scheduled outwork was canceled. The cancellations came partly out of consideration for our feelings, no doubt, but mainly they owed to the celebrating going on at the American labor sites.

"Did you hear the big news?" Wally asked.

"Yes, it's good news for us all."

When I read in the *Stars and Stripes* that Japan had demanded preservation of the emperor's sovereignty as a condition of surrender, I could not suppress a laugh. No matter what kind of face you might put on it, the fact remained that in one way or another the defeated country would fall under the control of the victorious.

"I regard this condition as the final stupidity of our military leaders," I told Wally. "I hope the broad-mindedness your country has demonstrated in the past will allow your government to accept it."

"That condition got a lot of heat last night in my barracks, too," Wally said. "But we're all anxious for the fighting to end. Like you, we hope the government accepts it."

It was a quiet morning in the compound. The prisoners lay motionless on their beds, their varicolored hand towels hanging unkemptly from the wires overhead.

I noticed Wally eyeing the towels through the window.

"I'm at my wits' end about those towels," I said. "I don't know why the men can't see how unsightly they are."

"Let it go today. Think of their despair."

My face burned, less from the shame of having my obsequious remark brushed aside than from knowing the truth about the despair for which Wally showed such sympathy. The men might indeed be feeling a measure of despair, but far more than that, I knew, they were luxuriating in the respite their supposed despair had won them: release from outwork and the chance to just take it easy for a day.

On August 12, we learned that the Allies had agreed to let the emperor stay—with the condition that his authority would be subject to the Supreme Commander for the Allied Powers. Now it was Japan's turn to show some broad-mindedness. I believed the military would ultimately accept the condition. Reality compelled it.

The American sergeants all seemed more relaxed now that peace was in hand. Instead of going on their usual rounds, they wandered about talking amongst themselves. Eventually they ended up leaning against the waist-high wall at the entrance to our building, carrying on about their impending release from the army.

I have written previously of Odaka, an eccentric and sometimes unruly fellow in our unit. His cocky assertiveness had put him on joking terms with Wally.

Once before, as he passed by our building, he had without provocation called out to Wally, "You, *kiring kiring.*"

Kiring kiring was apparently a colloquialism for "crazy" in Tagalog. Odaka twirled his right index finger next to his temple as he said it.

Failing to comprehend, Wally turned to me. I forced a smile and explained.

"He's saying you're crazy. *Kiring kiring* means 'crazy' in Tagalog."

"Ask him why he thinks I'm crazy."

"He wants to know why you say he's crazy."

"You, *kiring kiring,*" Odaka simply repeated.

Lest our supervising officer's feelings be hurt, I provided my own commentary.

"He's calling you crazy because he's actually a little crazy himself."

"You, *kiring kiring,*" Wally said to Odaka.

"You, *kiring kiring.* Give me cigarette."

"Sorry. No can do. I'm *kiring kiring.*"

Odaka happened by again when the whole group of sergeants was gathered out front. He approached Wally.

"War is over," he said, extending his hand for a handshake. He had learned this English phrase from a propaganda balloon the Imperial Army had raised over Manila when they occupied the city in 1942.

"No, not yet," Wally said with a grin as he deliberately hid his hand behind his back.

"Hey, you better not do that," the sergeant standing next to him cautioned. "You might make them angry."

"What do you mean? It's just a joke," Wally bristled.

The mild-mannered, middle-aged sergeant who cautioned him had received his discharge notice a few days before. It gave Wally cause for considerable disgruntlement, since he had earned more points than the other man, and it seemed to have created something of a sore spot between them.

"It's not formally over yet. The Japs haven't transmitted their answer."

"Ohh, I amu so-o-olly," Odaka said in heavily accented English, with his usual cocky smile; then he walked away. He was just about the only rank-and-filer I knew who was willing to strike up a conversation with the Americans in his broken English the same way he had done with Filipinos in broken Tagalog.

Wally turned to me. "We're all hoping your government doesn't keep us waiting too long," he said.

On the thirteenth, the *Stars and Stripes* reported with a tone of impatience that the Japanese response had not yet arrived. When Wally asked about it, I told him that the war criminals were probably making a last ditch effort to prolong their lives and save face by using the emperor as an excuse to refuse surrender.

Worse news came on the fourteenth. The *Stars and Stripes* reported in a more menacing tone that the Soviets continued their shelling of Japanese troops in Manchuria and that planes from the aircraft carrier Nimitz had bombed several Japanese cities "to keep the pressure on for a decision."

I was outraged. While our leaders quibbled over the formal status of the emperor, soldiers continued to die meaningless deaths in Manchuria and civilians senselessly went on losing their homes in our cities. The indignation I felt on behalf of these fellow citizens was, once again, visceral.

I know little about the lofty debates surrounding the economic foundations of the emperor system or notions of a human emperor that smiles on his people, but based on the visceral indignation I experienced as a POW, and in the name of all those people who died purposeless deaths between August 11 and August 14, I would conclude that the continuing existence of the emperor system is harmful.

Late that night Battalion Clerk Nakagawa went from unit to unit spreading the word that our government had finally accepted the terms of the Potsdam Declaration. As always, he sounded like he was reporting a victory, but just this once I was grateful for his timely performance of the town crier role he undertook with such seeming relish.

The news drew no reaction from the men. For all of us in the prison camp, the date of Japan's surrender was August 10, not August 15.

————

At noon on August 15, Imamoto and Oda went to the American camp office to hear the emperor's surrender broadcast. They came back saying they could not understand a word of it. Sometime later, Oda went around to each company reading a version of the broadcast rescript he had translated back into Japanese from an English translation. Not everyone gathered around to listen, and some of those who did neglected to bow their heads—a reception undoubtedly attributable to having lived so long in a prison camp.

The translation was obviously flawed, but quite apart from that, the rescript itself struck me as rather comical. It represented the final shame of militarist Japan, hung out by the emperor's closest advisors for all the world to see. In what must actually have been sour grapes, they had by pure chance hit one nail on the head when they inserted a line declaring that the atomic bomb "could in turn destroy all of human civilization."

"Our heart is torn asunder thinking of those who died untimely deaths, sacrificing themselves in the line of duty on the battlefield, and of their grieving families," the rescript should have read, but Oda had mistranslated the last phrase as simply "and of others." I overheard one of the detachment leaders assuring his men that that part referred to us POWs.

Wally asked me to go with him to visit Odaka. I gathered that he wanted to extend the hand he had withheld several days before.

We found Odaka lying on his bed, but he rose radiantly to clasp the hand Wally proffered.

"Tell him I want America and Japan to be friends from now on," Wally said.

When I relayed this to Odaka, he first turned to Wally to utter a heavily accented "Sank-yoo" in English, then added to me, "Thank him for his kindness, and tell him I plan to go home and live a quiet life with my wife and children."

Hopping from one job to another as a miner and a construction worker, Odaka's earlier years had apparently been quite turbulent, but he claimed that by the time the war started he was living a more settled life as a tinsmith in Tokyo's Asakusa district.

"That guy's not really crazy at all," Wally said, as we walked back toward headquarters together.

～ 10 ～

New Prisoners
and Old

According to popular perception, the reason so many men in the old Imperial Army remained faithful to the Army Combatant's Code, which instructed them to choose death over the shame of capture, is that they had been duped. When it comes to matters as weighty as death, however, one does not easily remain a dupe. If the act of bowing in submission before another man did not inherently entail feelings of personal humiliation, few men would have adhered to such a code. In the course of their daily work, whether as tradesmen, physical laborers, or corporate managers, all men, no matter how powerless or insignificant, develop a sense of personal pride and honor.

Montesquieu spoke of honor as the mainspring of monarchy. He was referring to the effect decorations and other public awards for meritorious service have on the subjects, but it seems to me that we must distinguish between pride that seeks honor and that which preserves it. Even wild savages know the latter form of pride, and when untold numbers of old Imperial Japan's subjects found themselves alone in the wilderness, no longer able to walk, it was this pride that made them kill themselves even though they had no hope of gaining public acclaim for their deed.

We must acknowledge, too, that such pride was often buttressed by terror. A proud man fears everything beyond his own self. The Imperial Army brass knew what they were doing when they propagandized so relentlessly that Americans executed their captives.

At the same time, such pride can be sustained only so long as the physical, and therefore mental, health of the man who finds himself in the wilderness remains stable. When wandering through the dense jungle for weeks on end without food has reduced a man to the merest animal existence, and when this human animal then sees an enemy leaflet or hears an enemy announcement persuading him that, in their hands, even if he ultimately will be killed, he can at least live without starving until the fateful moment arrives—under such circumstances, nothing can stop him, assuming he still has the strength to walk, from turning his steps toward the enemy camp and presenting himself there with his hands in the air.

The fact that nothing discernibly "human" remains in this response is consistent with the lack of the same in any act of war.

American records inform us that the dozen or so Japanese troops captured on Attu had all suffered wounds rendering them immobile. By contrast, a number of ambulatory surrenders took place on Guadalcanal.

Half of the prisoners in the Leyte camp had been captured after being wounded, but many of those making up the other half had probably surrendered voluntarily. As I have described, first conversations between inmates invariably began with accounts of how they had been taken prisoner, and as a rule, the more detailed the account, the more suspect its veracity. I believe the men actually saw through one another's falsehoods, but by unspoken mutual consent, they maintained a pretense of credence. Several candid confessions I have heard since my repatriation lead me to this conclusion.

There is a subcategory of these voluntary surrenders that I will provisionally call "ideological surrenders." Actually, so far as my own experience is concerned, it is a category of one, since I met only a single such prisoner among the hundreds I encountered in the camp on Leyte; further, it remains unclear whether he was in reality as much of an activist as I imagined him to be. I lack any straightforward confession from him that would verify the category. Nevertheless, based both on the rumors that circulated among the inmates and on what I myself directly observed, I am quite certain that the appellation I have chosen is fitting.

Ayano was about thirty, a graduate of a commercial college in western Honshū. Though deeply tanned by the tropical sun, his face had the hollowed out appearance of a man suffering from tuberculosis. He had been stationed with the garrison on Marinduque Island but disappeared shortly after the Americans landed. Those taken prisoner in the aftermath of the garrison's demise found him already in the hands of the Americans, speaking English with them and passing his days in comfortable captivity. These men believed he simply waited for the Americans to land and promptly gave himself up.

I sensed in these allegations a good deal of latent antipathy built up from before, and indeed, Ayano's words and actions while in the Leyte camp served to intensify the ill feelings. For several hours each day, he went to work in the American camp office as an "office boy." This meant he could obtain cigarettes from the Americans at will, even during the early period when cigarettes were in short supply, so its most direct consequence was to earn him the intense jealousy of his fellow inmates. As with another prisoner who had worked as an "office boy," they believed he was supplying the enemy with information useful to them in some way.

It was whispered about that Ayano had belonged to the Communist Party. I had no means of confirming the veracity of this rumor, but at the time I found it easiest just to accept it as true—which is essentially what I had always done in civilian life with rumors about things not directly related to myself. Eventually he stopped going to the camp office, but because of his "prior record," the POW brass deliberately passed over him when interpreters were appointed at the time the camp was reorganized.

Ostracized by those around him, Ayano spent his days in self-satisfied isolation, reading English-language magazines and such until the end of the war. Then he spearheaded the formation of a "Democracy Group," which banded together a number of like-minded prisoners.

This Democracy Group drafted a document called "Outline for the Construction of a New Democratic Japan" and held gatherings for interested young prisoners each night. This was precisely the kind of activity the Japanese brass, with their old military ways, abhorred, and at an earlier time they would most certainly have suppressed it. Now, however, they were too disheartened by defeat to do anything—especially after the group's "Outline" received an enthusiastic review from the commandant when they translated it into English for him. The commandant had even asked the group to prepare a cover letter so it could be sent to General MacArthur.

The sharply right-leaning Hirota found it all exceedingly deplorable. "Those guys can go around saying whatever they want," he said, "but what I can't stand is seeing more and more of the younger guys listening to their tripe and taking them seriously. It really hurts to see them forming bad opinions of the emperor. I mean, cripes, don't they know Ayano turned himself over to the enemy voluntarily?"

My own sentiments on the matter roughly paralleled those of the career army men in the prison leadership. Though I believed that the principles the Democracy Group espoused were well reasoned and worthy, I could see no need for them to flaunt their ideology at a time when we all shared our captivity with militant fanatics of every stripe. Their real motives, I suspected, went no further than extracting revenge for past insults, or perhaps savoring the feeling of superiority they got from holding forth in front of an audience. Either that, or they were engaging in pseudointellectual philosophizing merely to beguile the tedium.

Hirota brought a copy of the "Outline" to show me. It proved to be an outline in form as well as name, with about fifty headings and subheadings listing such things as "Rationalization of Industry" and "Limitation of Profits" in language that actually seemed rather reminiscent of wartime economic slogans. I noted that the emphasis fell entirely on the production of wealth, while not a word addressed its distribution, which led me to conclude that the document was essentially a very clever way of licking American boots.

"You can relax," I told Hirota. "There's nothing Red here."

Because of the raisin wine available in camp, many of the men became quite drunk in the evenings, and one night a pack of besotted imbibers descended on the Democracy Group with their fists. The group immediately complained to the camp office. Since the commandant's foremost responsibility was to maintain peace and tranquility within the compound, he decided to first question Imamoto, who purportedly represented all of the POWs.

"Don't the majority have any desire to learn about democracy?"

Surrounded as he was by a clique of professional soldiers, Imamoto answered easily, "No, they don't."

The upshot was a directive enjoining the Democracy Group from holding meetings, and forbidding drunken rowdiness.

Later, when we landed in Hakata and were about to be discharged into the frigid December outdoors without any overcoats, it was Ayano who managed to obtain woolen blankets for us by negotiating with the demobilization office. He threatened that we would band together and refuse to leave the elementary school serving as our temporary quarters—a negotiation tactic that would never have occurred to any of the other men.

In the train on the way home to Osaka after we had been demobilized, I complimented him on his clever move. "I'm sure you'll have a lot to offer in the changes that lie ahead for the country."

"Hardly," he said. "I'm one of the fallen."

These words complete the basis on which I have called him an "ideological surrender."

I do not think the act of surrendering is as easy as many Japanese today seem to imagine. Besides the problem of how to traverse the distance separating the two opposing sides in combat, any such attempt is naturally attended by fear that the enemy might fail to recognize your white flag or raised hands. You must assume that soldiers engaged in combat, even democratic-thinking American GIs, will be in a highly belligerent state of mind.

In my own case, I had lost the ability to walk and I lay sleeping in the jungle underbrush when the Americans found me. Even so, if they had found me sleeping with rifle in hand, as the more seasoned soldiers made a habit of doing, they might well have started by pumping a bullet into me. The story on Leyte was that the Americans shot anything holding a weapon, including corpses. The GIs who found me treated me courteously the entire time they were with me, but I know that it must have taken a considerable effort for them to hold their hostility in check.

Even if Ayano was indeed a communist opposed to Japanese war objectives, and even if he had made a deliberate, "ideological" decision to give himself up to the Allies, it still required enormous courage for him to actually cross through the jungle between the opposing forces and present himself before the enemy. One might question whether ideology alone would be sufficient to inspire courage of this kind on the battlefield. On the other hand, if Ayano had previously experienced another conversion in which he had turned his back on one ideological camp to surrender to another, then it becomes a distinct possibility.

When Ayano told me on the train after demobilization that he was one of "the fallen"—which is to say, one of those who had recanted their belief in communism and broken ties with the Communist Party—it finally confirmed what rumor had led me to believe: that he was indeed an ideological surrender.

———

A somewhat more complicated relative of ideological surrender was group surrender. The possibilities here include a single leader who has won over a number of adherents, as well as groups formed of several like-minded individuals banding together as equals. In either case, one of the general requirements seems to be that something approaching a common ideology binds the men together.

The first group surrenders I became aware of in the Philippines took place in May 1945. They were concentrated on islands like Cebu, Negros, and Palawan, where little serious fighting took place. In the majority of cases, an army surgeon led the way.

Toward the end of the war, Japanese medical corpsmen no longer wore red-cross arm bands, and even conscripted surgeons had been inculcated with the same militarist ideals as career army men. Nevertheless, since looking after the sick and wounded was work of a gentle nature, and principally of the mind, both their appraisal of the war situation and their conduct in the field lacked the fierce, uncompromising militancy shown by combat troops.

Medical Cadet Asai, who arrived at the camp with a group of corpsmen from Cebu, was a graduate of the medical school at Kyoto University, which happened to be my own alma mater. Though I am not, as a rule, easily moved to benevolence solely on the basis of school ties, it was so rare for us in the prison camp to discover real-world social connections among ourselves that even something like this aroused feelings of commonality. When Asai was assigned to my company and I learned of our school ties, I used my position on staff to expedite the issuing of full uniform and rations for him. When we met in the showers, we exchanged stories about our graduating classes and compared notes on various rooming houses and watering holes we had known near the university.

His age was thirty-eight, making him two years my senior. He told me he had worked at a hospital in a small Hokuriku town. Though it was true that his short height, broad forehead, and restless goggle-eyes did not exactly make him the picture of success, it surprised me when he remarked that he had never completed his doctorate. Later, when I saw him join the Democracy Group and speak out strongly on the benefits of communism, I suspected that the real reason he had ended up as only a bachelor of medicine had to do with some such ideological impediment.

When the Americans landed on Cebu at the end of March, the field hospital Asai had been working at evacuated into the mountains, where they attempted to maintain services at an elevation of two thousand feet. Ultimately, though, he and a number of the medics working under him could no longer endure the cold or shortage of food. Descending from the mountain, they were discovered and taken prisoner by the Americans.

"You left others behind in the mountains, then," I said.

"Yes, we did. But I met one of them later at the prison camp on Cebu—he had finally decided to come down from the mountain, too—and he told me I had been right all along and thanked me for saving his life." A proud glint came into his eyes as he said this. He rattled off the last part rapidly, and it did not immediately register with me what the other man might have been referring to as being "right all along." At any rate, it hardly mattered in the camp; I continued to look after his comfort on the basis of our old school ties.

After August 15, soldiers who had laid down their arms began arriving in large numbers from all across the Visayan Islands. In essence, the Americans had chosen our location on Leyte as the place to gather all Japanese troops who surrendered anywhere in the southern Philippines. A second and third POW camp absorbed most of these new arrivals, but some came to our camp as well.

An entire new platoon assigned to our company was made up of men from the garrison on Cebu Island. One day the sergeant major acting as their leader approached Hiwatashi with an appeal: Members of the platoon were complaining that they could not tolerate being in the same unit as Asai. Would it be possible either for Asai to be sent elsewhere or for the unit to swap places with a platoon from another company?

"That bastard turned his back on patients in critical condition to go down the mountain on his own and give himself up," he said. "And to add insult to injury, he took the sick men's rations with him. There's no telling how many men starved to death because of him. One of the guys he abandoned is with us now only because he finally mustered the strength to walk and managed to get himself to another unit. We're all prisoners now, so we know we can't really pass judgment on him, but having to be in the same company and run into him all the time is just too much."

Hiwatashi summoned Asai to question him.

"I admit that I surrendered voluntarily," he said, "together with a number of corpsmen and patients who embraced my assessment of the situation and came down the mountain with me. It wouldn't do any good to list my reasons for you now, since I doubt you would really understand, but (at this point he let out a little laugh) the charge that I stole food from the sick and wounded is patently untrue. Several of the corpsmen disagreed with my intentions and chose to remain behind, and I'm sure they divided the food up fairly. You can think what you like, but I firmly believe that I saved the lives of the men who came with me. Of the sick who chose to remain behind at that time, I know at least one who later changed his mind and came down the mountain by himself to surrender (this was the man he had spoken to me about before). Still, even though I never had any direct contact with the men in that platoon, I guess I can understand how they might feel. I don't mind being the one to leave."

He had begun helping in the infirmary shortly after arriving in camp, and he now wasted no time in moving his things there. Apparently he had seen it coming and had already made arrangements. In his new quarters, too, he commenced lectures on communism and gained the attentive ears of the easygoing medics.

I could find nothing to censure in his behavior. Bystanders are in no position to judge the egotism that rears its head when a man finds himself on the boundary between life and death. Nevertheless, I stopped speaking to him after that. To be sure, he may indeed have saved several other lives along with his own, but when you considered the men in critical condition who might have survived if he had stayed at his post, he had just as surely caused several deaths as well.

Two years after his return home, Asai ran for political office as a member of the Japan Communist Party and lost.

I will write about one other prominent member of the Democracy Group. Sasaki had been a reporter for a small-town newspaper in northeastern Honshū and was stationed in Tacloban as a civilian employee of the army at the time of his capture. He was the first prisoner to start growing a mustache.

One morning he rushed into our company HQ and shrieked, "I stayed up all night thinking about it, and I've discovered the only path for Japan's reconstruction! We must adopt communism!"

"No POW is going to come up with the solution for Japan's reconstruction overnight," I retorted. "You'll have plenty of time to contemplate it after you get home. And the first thing you'll have to think about when you get there is how you're going to feed your face."

"I enjoy conversing with intelligent people," he said, and went out.

———

The title of this chapter, "New Prisoners and Old," refers respectively to those who were disarmed and taken into custody after the war ended and those who surrendered or were captured while the fighting was still in progress. When the hostilities ceased, Leyte POW Camp 1 held some two thousand "old" prisoners in seven companies. By mid-September every unit had gained a fifth platoon, increasing each company's strength to nearly three hundred, and the total number of units had increased to eleven as well.

The friction that arose between the new prisoners and the old must be considered one of the more bizarre effects wrought upon Japanese citizens by the Pacific War. Inasmuch as new and old alike now lived in the custody of American forces and were sustained by American provisions, both groups should have been equal. The new prisoners had a great deal of difficulty accepting this circumstance straightforwardly, however. Still under the sway of the Army Combatants' Code that declared the shame of capture a fate worse than death, they lost no opportunity to show their contempt for the old prisoners.

One night a former second lieutenant who had been stationed on Negros barged into one of our platoon barracks in violation of the prohibition against officers mixing with the rank and file.

"Why haven't you disemboweled yourselves?" he shouted. "How can you let yourselves be captured and then go on living? Cut open your bellies!"

The rowdy Odaka was always quick to speak up at times like this. "Oh yeah? You're a fine one to talk, when all you did was run around the mountains trying to keep out of harm's way. May I remind you that we're the ones who took the heat out front and got wounded and couldn't help getting captured? And incidentally, though they may choose to keep their mouths shut, we have some first lieutenants and captains in here, too, so a pipsqueak second lieutenant like you had better watch his tongue."

The claim that we had first lieutenants and captains among us was actually empty show. Some of the officers had claimed at first to be NCOs so as not to be held responsible, but in most cases they slipped up during their interrogations and got sent to the separate officers' sector of the camp. Nevertheless, the claim effectively parried the brunt of the lieutenant's attack.

"Hrumph," he grunted, and turned to leave, but Odaka was still steaming.

"Get outta here, you shithead!" he screamed after the lieutenant. "And don't come back, if you know what's good for you!"

The lieutenant spun on his heels. "What did you say?" he growled.

"Whatto isu whatto?" Odaka drawled in heavily accented English, and the onlookers burst out laughing. This was one of his favorite Japanese-English phrases—a literal English translation of the standard Japanese fighting retort to "What did you say?" The lieutenant stood there fuming for several moments but then disappeared into the darkness outside without saying another word.

For good measure, Odaka sought the lieutenant out in the officers' sector the next day and yelled at him some more. On his return, he seemed quite pleased with himself, noting that there had been quite a few colonels and lieutenant colonels in the tent. One of the leading colonels had spoken sympathetically: "What you say is true," he said, "but now that we've given up like this, it's all the same. There were a lot of things wrong with our armed forces, and that was why we lost. From here on out, we need to look to the future with an open mind and work together to rebuild our country." He then gave Odaka a cigar, saying it had been a special gift from the commandant.

"I guess colonels have more common sense," Odaka remarked to me. "Upstart lieutenants don't know what they're talking about. The S.O.B. turned out to be the colonel's orderly, serving him his meals and stuff like that."

In some ways I could understand why the newly arrived lieutenant might want to berate us. In March, when I first moved from the hospital to the old POW camp, the cheerful prisoners I met there hardly appeared human. They seemed like some other species, wearing nothing but loincloths and clamoring about like apes. The provision of clothing had soon improved, however, and now everyone actually went about looking quite dapper.

That the crisp new U.S. Army fatigues and caps had to have "PW" stamped all over them was something of a sticking point, of course, but otherwise they looked pretty sharp. On our feet we wore tall jungle boots that laced halfway up to our knees, leading some of the men to affect the chic look of golfers' plus fours by making their pants balloon out over the boot tops. Our generous daily rations had fattened everybody up, we had only light work to do during the day, and we spent our evenings getting drunk on bootleg wine, playing mah-jongg or cards, gambling at *kabu*, and raising our voices in song.

It was not difficult to imagine how all this must have appeared to young officers who arrived at the camp still stinging from the shame of surrender after so long enduring severe privation in the mountains. One of them looked at us and cried: "You are the enemy!"

Those new platoons that had to merge into the established units gritted their teeth and submitted to the command of the old leaders, but the men in the newly formed Companies 8 through 11 resolutely maintained a separate world unto themselves. They even petitioned Imamoto to give them completely different outwork assignments, but being an old prisoner himself, Imamoto rejected the plea. Imamoto also refused to give any extra rations to the weak and emaciated newcomers.

On one occasion, a new prisoner had to be punished for breaking into our cookshack at night. The culprit was sneaking back outside with some canned goods when his luck ran out and he was apprehended. Since our cooks were mostly former seamen captured after the Battle of Leyte Gulf, he received a navy-style punishment.

"Are you army or navy? Army, you say? Well, then, we'll give you your first taste of the navy's pep stick."

The thief was stripped of his pants and told to stand with his hands in the air. The white triangle of loincloth covering his buttocks practically glowed in the dark. The cooks had made themselves a huge five-foot-long wooden ladle for dishing out rice, and the mess sergeant now lifted it diagonally over his head.

"Every chance you get, you bastards insult us for getting captured," he yelled, "but I'll bet all that time you were just messing around with the nurses in the mountains, weren't you?"

He delivered a powerful blow to the thief's rear with the wide end of the ladle.

"Aaaa!" the culprit screamed, staggering forward.

"I'm not finished yet! I'm not finished yet! Keep those hands in the air! Take that!"

"Aaaa!" the man fell to his knees.

"Cut the crap! We know you've still got legs. On your feet, I say!"

One of the younger cooks dragged him to his feet. Taking the ladle from the mess sergeant, he continued in an even shriller voice, "That was just a warm-up. Now's when the real pep stick starts. There!"

The man fell forward without uttering a sound.

I had become friends with this young cook and had spent many hours in good-natured conversation with him in the evenings after supper, so I was quite taken aback by this show of brutality. I edged up to him to urge restraint.

"Don't you think that's about enough?" I said in a low voice, but he was too worked up to listen to reason.

"This is no time for you to be butting in, Mr. Ōoka. Just leave him to us."

It was on his watch in the cookshack that the thief had managed to snatch what he came for and sneak all the way back outside before getting caught, and he took it as a personal affront. It saddened me to observe this streak of ruthlessness in him, so utterly out of keeping with his usual benign cheer. He remained, after all, a product of the Imperial Navy.

The only thing left for me to do was apprise the culprit's unit of the situation. As I hurried along the road through the darkness, several men came running toward me from the other direction.

"Are you from Company 11? One of your guys is getting beat up right now. At Company 2."

The pack of men slipped by without a word. They could see by the jungle boots I wore that I was an old prisoner and hence belonged to a kind that was beneath their notice.

"Listen here! Rations are divided up according to the number of men in each unit, so everyone gets the same," our mess sergeant told them. "So why should this guy have to steal? Are your cooks cheating you out of your fair portions? Pay a little attention!"

The men from Company 11 said nothing. They formed a protective phalanx around the tearful thief and withdrew.

———

The barbed-wire fence surrounding the camp had been built in a double layer, twelve feet apart, so as to thwart any attempt at escape. With the war over and escape no longer a concern, the outer fence of Camp 1 became the fence for Camp 3 constructed on immediately adjacent land.

As we have seen, new and old prisoners confined within the same compound were constantly at odds, but curiously enough, when they were in separate compounds and did not share from a common pot, so to speak, they developed an unusual fondness for one another. In time, however, even this mutual fondness was disrupted as a result of differences in conditions between the old and new prisoners.

Each night, old prisoners gathered along the fence to talk with new prisoners lined up on the other side of the twelve-foot space originally intended to expose any escapee who got through the first fence before he reached the second. Floodlights lit up the divide, and the two opposing rows of men often stretched a hundred meters from one end to the other.

Lacking the time to build nipa huts, the new prisoners lived in sweltering, low-roofed tents. They maintained the same units they had had in the field and wore their Japanese badges of rank on the front of their U.S. Army caps.

The primary topic of conversation at the fence was news about our old units and the men who had been in them. I recognized a fellow who had gone through the special code clerk's training with me at the Eastern District Army Second Command in Tokyo.

Tominaga was a twenty-two-year-old reservist drafted in 1943, the son of a tobacconist near Kototoi Bridge in old Tokyo. One day when we went to Sumida Park for a joint code drill, we passed right by where he lived. His house was only fifty feet or so down a side alley off the main avenue, and he would have liked to dash off to say hello to his family, but he knew it was out of the question.

"Did you live here at the time of the earthquake, too?"

"Uh-huh."

"Then your house must have burned down, I suppose."

"I was only two and my mom carried me to safety, but I don't remember it myself."

I was already fifteen in 1923, the year of the Great Tokyo Earthquake, and there I was, ranked equal to, and enduring the same training as, someone who had been only two. It was a humbling thought.

Both in the army and in captivity, I generally shied away from men my own age and preferred to pass the time in idle talk with youngsters like Tominaga. At home today, however, I feel more comfortable talking with friends my own age. I do not know why.

Tominaga and I traveled together as far as Manila, but from there he went with several other code clerks to the command center of the Sakura Group. Having been sent to the isolation of Mindoro with a small, independent garrison, I had always envied them their assignment to the safety of a command center, but as I listened to Tominaga, I discovered that I had been by far the luckier one.

Before long they had been transferred to the Thirty-fifth Army Command on Cebu and had to learn a new high-level code in a great hurry. To make things worse, all the high-ranking officers around them demanded strict adherence to military discipline and deportment, and the code clerks were constantly being slapped across the face for one infraction or another. In November, they crossed over to Leyte together with the entire command, and from then until mid-March when they fled Palompon in small boats and returned to Cebu, they had experienced the same hardships as everyone else on the losing side in the battle for control of Leyte.

Of the four young code clerks who had remained together after our training in Japan, only Tominaga had survived. One died from an improperly treated bullet wound to his ankle, and one starved to death. The third suffered from advancing tuberculosis and had his rations cut off in the face of a mounting food shortage; when repeated pleas to both the command staff and the hospital fell on deaf ears, he blew himself up with a hand grenade in the command center kitchen.

Tominaga was short and on the chubby side, not exactly handsome but kind of cute. He was not a particularly good code clerk (I knew this from his performance during our training back home), so I supposed that he alone had survived the terrible adversities of Leyte because he had a quiet, companionable nature that endeared him to his superiors. I asked him about it.

"Yeah, I feel a bit funny saying so myself," he answered, "but my squad leader sneaked me extra food. Also, I only got the slap once, at the very beginning."

The fact was, I liked him, too. Since even the well-supplied Americans were unable to provide the huge influx of disarmed soldiers after the war with the ample rations they had been giving us old prisoners, the inmates of the new camps received only two meals and one cigarette per day. I took some cans of food and cigarettes from my own stockpiles and tossed them to Tominaga through the fence.

"Thank you very much," he said rather formally. "I'll share them with the rest of my squad."

Canned food and cigarettes were being tossed across all up and down the fence. Mostly, however, they were not for free, but in exchange for personal items the new prisoners had managed to hang onto until the end— whatever the old prisoners demanded. In the main, this meant watches.

These pocket and wristwatches had with few exceptions rusted to a halt in the mountains, but the old prisoners knew they would work just fine again once they had been repaired back in Japan. The going rate for Swiss or Seiko watches averaged about ten packs of cigarettes or fifteen cans of food. In the space of about ten days, all of the new prisoners' watches passed into the hands of old prisoners.

Now many of the old-timers proudly strutted about wearing motionless watches on their wrists. Gambling boss Sama's winnings had by this time reached several hundred packs of cigarettes. He exchanged them all and became the owner of enough broken watches to overflow both his arms. He also dangled a gold pocket watch on a chain—this one actually keeping time. He boasted of paying thirty packs of cigarettes for it.

Subsequently, as the population of prisoners in the other camps continued to increase, the supply of cigarettes for our own camp declined, which then led the old prisoners to begin accepting cigarettes in exchange for canned food. The new prisoners were still starving, so they chose to cut back on smoking in order to supplement their food rations. Since the cigarettes they now traded were the ones they had acquired from the old-timers in exchange for their watches, in the final analysis you could say they traded everything they had for food.

Neither before nor since have I ever witnessed such ignoble behavior, and I found it exceedingly painful to watch. I do not mean to sound holier-than-thou for giving things freely to Tominaga without coveting his broken timepiece, but all of these men had only recently been brothers in arms fighting a common enemy, and I could not help feeling that if some had a surplus while others had nothing, the haves ought to have been generous enough to provide for the have-nots without charge. After all, every item the haves proffered had been given them without cost by the Americans— at least without any direct cost to them in their capacity as POWs.

It saddened me further to see that it was not only men like Sama who engaged in this cruel trade but also a majority of the otherwise genial and warmhearted ordinary prisoners.

I blurted out my disgust one day in the company office.

"Say what you will, Ōoka, I really don't think it can be helped," Hiwatashi retorted. "Besides, a lot of these watches they have are pretty suspicious to begin with. I doubt very many of them actually put up their own watches for trade. I mean, look at how some of the NCOs had five and six watches. One way or another you have to figure they were stolen, either from the personal effects of soldiers who died or from the locals."

"And you think that absolves them?"

"At least I don't think our men are the only thieves. Anyway, that's the military for you."

He seemed a bit uncomfortable during this exchange, and I later discovered why. Though he was discreet enough not to personally go to the fence himself, he had in fact managed to acquire three watches by sending others to trade on his behalf. In November, when word came down that we would be permitted to carry only a single watch each on our trip home, I saw him carefully hollowing out bars of soap in order to hide his extra watches. His years as a petty officer in the navy had given him a good deal of experience smuggling ashore gifts from distant ports.

He was right that "that's the military for you." As commentators have found frequent occasion to remark, when military men are anywhere but in the midst of combat, they display markedly more egotistic behavior than civilians. I was apparently witnessing that principle at work among the POWs.

For immediate purposes, being able to walk around wearing a fancy watch that happened to be broken served in a small way to ease the monotony of life in camp, but I doubt such a trivial objective could, in itself, have sustained the watch trade. Had the men not envisioned those watches benefiting them after repatriation, the pleasure of ownership would surely have been much reduced. That is to say, the trading occurred only in anticipation of repatriation and could not have occurred otherwise; it had its roots in the common civilian desire for possession rather than in anything associated with the condition of being a prisoner. The winds of ordinary society had begun to blow among the POWs now that the war had ended.

I realized I had spoken out of turn. Though I myself had no desire to obtain a watch, the fact of the matter was that I belonged to the class of citizens who could expect to find two or three modest watches safely preserved at home upon my return. Had I not had that expectation, I seriously doubt that I could have remained untempted by the trade. Many of those who engaged in the cruel commerce had most likely never owned a Swiss watch before, and for some, the life they anticipated for themselves after repatriation may have loomed far more dismal than I could ever imagine.

If so, "that's the military for you" was not right after all; it should have been "that's human nature for you." The NCOs who took custody of their dead subordinates' personal effects and plundered the locals—they, too, had no doubt acted with a view to the value that the items would have after their return home. The winds of ordinary society had been blowing through the ranks of the military all along, just as they now blew through the ranks of the POWs.

So the winds of ordinary society gathered force among the men, and as they say, "Shame's unknown to the man far from home." To take advantage of their temporary condition as POWs and in great haste fill their pockets with items of value by whatever means—this was the underlying aim that had brought the majority into the despicable and cruel commerce.

Human nature cannot be changed. Two thousand years have passed since religion began attempting to transform morality from a set of socially imposed norms into a set of disciplines to be embraced from within, and yet there are still no signs of a change in human nature. This solution has already been tested.

It would seem that the only course of action is to transform the social conditions that permit such unconscionable behavior to arise.

The victimized new prisoners grew indignant. "You are our enemy," one of them spat out after giving up his last cigarettes in trade, echoing the voice heard earlier among the newcomers within our own camp. "Demons! Beasts!" he added.

The several old-timers who were the direct object of his rage wrapped the ends of some sticks with cloth, dipped them in gasoline, set them ablaze, and flung them over the fences. The new prisoners leapt aside, so no one was hurt, but the flames drew the attention of the American guards, and the men involved were sent to the brig. The previously tolerated contacts between the new and old prisoners were banned, and guards now paced the area between the fences at night.

After that I could no longer meet with Tominaga, of whom I was so fond. About a month later, however, when a limited amount of movement between the camps was authorized, he came to visit me. He was still starving, and I asked one of the cooks to open a can of corned beef for him. He ate it as though he had never tasted anything so good.

We sat at a table in our company office and chatted for about two hours. In the course of the conversation, I learned a good deal more about how this innocent youngster had survived the experience of military debacle. I gained the impression that he had passed through it all with no more trauma than he might have had getting over a fever.

He had known his first woman while on Cebu. Nurses accompanying the command center also served as comfort women for the soldiers. Though not subject to the appalling conditions endured by professional comfort women, these nurses were required to service one soldier each day, ostensibly to maintain the men's fighting spirit amidst the hardships of life in the mountains. If they refused, their rations were cut off. The head nurse, long monopolized by one of the officers, had chosen to come to Tominaga one night.

"So, what did you think?" I asked, unable to suppress a smile.

He blushed slightly and squirmed in his seat for a moment before answering. "When I was done, she said, 'Pardon my rudeness.' "

The cook, who had sat down beside us to listen, burst out laughing. Then he said, "And I suppose you saluted her and said, 'Thank you for your trouble.' "

Tominaga opened his eyes wide in amazement. "How did you know?" he said. "That's exactly what I did."

————

In spite of the account I have thus far given, I must refrain from making too much of the friction between the new and old prisoners. The shame worse than death of being captured was in the end merely an implanted idea, which at worst manifested itself as self-righteousness among the new prisoners and as an inferiority complex among the old, and it did not take long before whatever friction it caused was wiped away by the practical necessities of daily life—which is to say, the performance of labor duties. Once the fighting had ended, the work schedule demanded by the Americans in order to cover the now gratuitous expense of feeding us gradually grew heavier, and it was not long before, at least among prisoners within the same camp, the new and old no longer had the time to get at one another's throats. And besides, with the war over, the foremost concern on everyone's mind was the question of when we would get to go home, so the issue of whether one had become a prisoner during the war or had laid down arms only after its end receded into the past.

To us the most tangible evidence of the war's conclusion was that the antiaircraft lookout on the summit of Cross Mountain no longer lit up at night after August 15.

As the days passed, we learned little by little how things were progressing with Japan's surrender through articles in *Time* and photographs in *Life:*

One picture showed a member of the Japanese delegation that flew into Manila to arrange a date for formally signing the documents of surrender. He stood awkwardly with his hand extended in midair while his American counterpart made a diversionary gesture to avoid taking it. A later issue covered the arrival of air transports at the Atsugi airfield. A statement by MacArthur about there being surprisingly few rapes brought a sour smile to my lips.

We laughed with scorn when we heard about Tōjō Hideki's unsuccessful suicide attempt.

"You know he could have done a whole lot better than shooting himself in the chest," Hiwatashi said. "And the way he did it just as the MPs arrived makes him look like some small-time crook who bungled a burglary. It's hardly what you'd expect from the leader of a country."

It infuriated us when General Yamashita Tomoyuki declared in court that he knew nothing about atrocities committed by troops under his command in the Philippines.

"Since he knows he can't get off anyway, you'd think he could act more like a general and take responsibility for the crimes of his subordinates."

The "Malay Tiger," as he was popularly known, had remained the hope and pride of retreating troops throughout the Philippines to the very last. It is of course the standard practice in court to deny one's guilt, but this single sentence spoken in accordance with that standard instantly toppled him from the status of hero.

Japanese newspapers printed in special quarter-sized editions for overseas prisoners arrived. On the front page they carried a copy of the Imperial Rescript proclaiming Japan's surrender together with a photograph of General MacArthur and the emperor standing side by side. The general stood at ease, with one foot slightly forward, while the emperor stood at attention with his heels together and his feet at right angles.

One of the newspapers was from western Honshū. It displayed a picture of the aircraft carrier *Amagi* under bombardment at the naval station in Kure, and the accompanying article gave a blow-by-blow account of the scene in exactly the same style used to describe the sinking of enemy warships during the war.

"Like fish gathering to the bait, first one hit, then another, until soon the *Amagi* was wrapped in a billowing cloud of smoke . . ."

It seemed odd to me that the reporter possessed only a single idiom for describing a given situation.

We learned that Japan's surrender had merely been "the end of the war," not "defeat," and that the foreign troops landing in Japan as a result were not "occupying" our country but merely "being stationed" there.

Word reached the Philippines about how inhumanely American POWs in Japan had been treated. I did not notice any particular change in the attitudes of the men directly connected with our camp, but guards at the labor sites apparently found occasion to vent their personal fury on the outworkers.

Wally finally received his discharge papers. That night he borrowed a civilian suit-jacket, pants, and tie from his buddies, and he wore the entire outfit to bed.

"No more Sergeant Walsdorf," he said. "From now on it's *Mister* Walsdorf."

When he departed for a base on the coast to wait for his boat home, he left his address with me. He was a bachelor and would be staying at his sister's house for a while. I promised to send him a folding fan from Kyoto when I got back to Japan, but restrictions on foreign mail prevented me from fulfilling my promise. Then, by the time the restrictions were finally lifted, I thought he probably would have gotten married and moved, so I never even sent him a letter. I still feel a little miffed that he did not shake my hand when we parted.

Almost all of the sergeant liaisons were replaced. The new "sergeants" were actually privates—some of them boys of only eighteen, with pimples all over their faces. They loved to sing and boasted a lot about their girl-friends.

My company's new supervisor was a thirty-five-year-old farmer from Florida named North. He was dark-skinned and over six feet tall, with a rather gangly build. He showed me a picture of his family in front of his house. The yard was filled with large cacti, and an amazingly stout woman stood beside five skinny children as gangly as he was.

He was not as bright as Wally. He appeared somewhat bewildered by his new job of overseeing POWs and went out of his way to humor me.

"I bet you can't do this," he said one time when we ran out of things to talk about in the office. Then suddenly his teeth came loose inside his mouth, both top and bottom. He had a full set of false teeth.

Once we had a severe storm warning. Leyte Island lay in the path of a typhoon gathering force near the equator in the Pacific. In great haste ropes were distributed to all units, and we tied down our nipa huts, post by post. We worried about what might happen to the roofs if the typhoon actually hit. Even if the roofs held, there was little to keep the rain from blowing into the huts, whose waist-high walls left us quite exposed to the elements. All of our beds and clothing were sure to get soaked. At least we were in the tropics, we reassured ourselves. Anything that got wet would dry in a day. And we had no need to worry about our food supplies, since everything was canned.

Fortunately, the typhoon veered away, but in October the rainy season began—the first rainy season since we had moved to this camp in June. The clay soil quickly turned to mire and swallowed up truckload after truckload of fresh gravel no matter how many the Americans hauled in.

We received dapper new rain ponchos—dark green rectangles of rubberized fabric with holes in the middle. When you put your head through the hole, the fabric naturally draped down to cover your front and back as well as both arms. They had an almost forbidding aspect, and donning them made us feel like policemen or soldiers instead of POWs.

It made quite a magnificent sight when three thousand prisoners lined up for roll call on Main Street all wearing these identical ponchos. A sodden sash of dark green, undulating like waves, stretched out as far as one could see, its other end disappearing into the mist.

We were only marking time now—waiting for the day of our repatriation. That day, however, was not one that our own government could determine at will, for our country no longer had a merchant marine; everything depended on loans of Liberty ships and landing craft from the United States. The Americans understandably wanted to send their own demobilized troops home first.

Judging from descriptions the newspapers gave of conditions back home, there was in any case little to be gained by an early repatriation. Meals equivalent to the 2,700 calories per day we now received would be beyond all possibility. We were better off staying where we were, fulfilling our relatively nominal labor obligations during the day and enjoying ourselves in drink and song at night.

Of course, we were all anxious to see our families again, but in the course of our long separation as soldiers, even the love we sustained for our families had turned into a kind of abstraction—abstract and attenuated enough that six months or a year sooner or later made little difference.

Our existential condition remained that of prisoner. As such, we all inevitably took on the same coloration whether we were new prisoners or old.

The two-hundred-meter-square compound might have seemed ample room for three thousand men, but the fact remained that, no matter which way we turned, we would soon come to a fence. As we moved about within that enclosure, we could slip past one another or bump head on, we could stop to talk with one another or pass in silence, but we had no choice about encountering the same faces day in and day out from one week to the next.

We pretended to be anxiously waiting to go home, because, after all, what else could we do? In truth, we were enjoying ourselves quite nicely right where we were.

And the result was an inexorable slide into decadence and corruption.

~ 11 ~

Theatricals

Blue is the skin of mackerel, and black the heart of man.
—Ozaki Shirō

As time passed, the inmates lapsed rapidly into decadence.

The end of the war removed the last moral thorn prickling at the consciences of the prisoners in Leyte POW Camp 1. Suddenly gone were the pangs of guilt we had experienced from living comfortably in the midst of the enemy while untold numbers of our compatriots continued to lay down their lives across the Pacific. In their place came a new view: We had been lucky, and the dead had not—pure and simple. All that remained now was to pass the days until we could go home. The Americans continued to provide us with everything we could possibly need.

One of the ironic effects of this life of ease was that it aroused feelings of nostalgia for the war among some of the men. A man named Tsukamoto, for example, was a suicide attack pilot shot down over the sea east of Leyte on October 24, 1944. As the anniversary of the Battle of Leyte Gulf approached, he spent his evenings writing a memoir of sorts and intoning it to himself in solemn voice: "Indeed does the fate of all East Asia's multitudes lie in the balance at this moment of decisive battle!"

Hiwatashi snickered. "We lost the war long ago," he said. "Don't you think it's a tad late for decisive battles?"

Tsukamoto was one of our young cooks. A small-framed fellow, light-skinned and handsome, he was self-possessed and hard-working beyond his years. As leader of one of the two cooking squads that worked in shifts, he had acquired the nickname of Chief. I humored him one night when we

257

were having a private party in our company office, getting drunk on some raisin wine: "You know, Chief, I don't think any of us'll ever want to go geisha-partying with you. You'd get all the attention, and the rest of us'd get nothing but the clown treatment."

A while later, about the time he started writing his battle memoirs, Tsukamoto came into the office one evening when I was having a smoke after finishing the day's paperwork.

Sliding up to my desk he said, "Say, Mr. Ōoka, how about we go get us some geisha sometime?"

I knew very well what he wanted me to say. "Forget it," I retorted. "If I went with you, I'd just be the clown."

I was still quite willing to humor him this second time, but when he started coming in every night fishing for the same response, it quickly grew tiresome. Hiwatashi finally lost his patience.

"Hey, Chief. Ōoka is one of our busy clerks. He doesn't have time to be fooling around with you, so stop bugging him all the time."

I was a clerk, all right, but the job did not really amount to that much work. Though I did spend a great deal of time at my desk, in many cases I was merely whiling away the hours working on one of my treacly screenplays. Still, I did not enjoy having this diversion of mine interrupted to feed Chief's vanity. When he continually needed to confirm his own charm by comparing himself with someone like me, whatever charm he had quickly dissipated.

In fact, Chief's initial popularity had faded significantly by this time. This owed in part to how he vented his lack of freedom as a prisoner by expressing the kind of nationalistic fervor and nostalgia for combat I noted above; it owed also to the way he vented his lack of sexual outlet in open coquetry.

The Americans had given us a white powder to prevent athlete's foot, directing us to sprinkle it between our toes every day after our showers. This precaution was universally regarded as too much bother, however, and everyone waited for the little blisters to show up before applying the powder to just the affected areas. This left us with large stores of the stuff on hand, and Chief started powdering his face with it. In the dim shadows under the nipa roof at dusk, with his already light skin made even whiter by this powder, his face stood out as eerie as a ghost.

Having made himself up in this manner, he would repair to Company 5 in pursuit of Shindō, our famous female impersonator. Shindō was a young reservist who landed on Leyte's western shore with a unit of reinforcements in November 1944. He arrived at the POW camp quite late, after a long sojourn in the mountains during which he had been favored with the affections of his commanding officer.

Shindō's name became known throughout the camp a short time before the war ended, when the companies started holding weekly talent shows. On one such night, after our own men had performed their favorite pop songs and hometown ballads and such, Shindō jumped in with a rendition of the "Chinese Maid's Song." His falsetto had considerable range, and to the prisoners he sounded exactly like a woman.

"Hey hey, my poker's starting to squirm," someone in the audience yelled.

From that day forward, all of the companies fought to get Shindō in their talent shows. After the war was over, when these company-sponsored talent shows gave way to camp-wide stage shows, the organizers decided it would make an even greater impression on the audience if they dressed him up as a woman.

For a wig, they unraveled a burlap bag and dyed the threads with black draftsman's ink. Our tailor altered a white undershirt for a blouse and made him a skirt out of a flour bag dyed with blue ink. Our *geta* craftsman contributed a pair of sandals. For face powder, he needed something that would last longer than Chief's improvisation, so Imamoto put in a special request to the commandant and obtained some facial cream and powder from a WAC. He also acquired some lipstick and rouge.

On the night of the show, as I sat before the stage in front of battalion HQ waiting for the performance to begin, I saw Shindō being led by one of his attendants across the rocky open lot into the dressing room area backstage, and I could hardly believe my eyes. I knew, of course, that this was merely a man dressed up in women's clothing; but he looked every bit the woman, from his hair, face, and chest (he wore falsies, like many young women today) down to the curve of his hips and the way he walked. Even the little mannerisms that showed his self-consciousness before the ogling eyes of so many men, including myself, gave the impression of a genuine woman.

Ever since that experience, I have begun to suspect that what we men ordinarily see when we look at a woman is not really the woman at all, but rather some kind of a doll decked out and made up in accordance with our male preconceptions of what a woman should be. An oft-repeated commonplace among theater-goers is that the actors who play women in kabuki are more feminine than women themselves are.

From the man's perspective, all that really matters in a woman is that he can hold her hand, caress her breasts, kiss her, and generally do with her as he pleases, and the image of the woman projected upon his retina in no way reflects the real woman. The various movements of the heart that produce love at first sight, or perceive beauty in a sweetheart, or lead us to attribute all manner of inner qualities to a woman merely from observing the actions of the muscles on her face would seem to be nothing more than delusions of our eyes.

The very fact that women endure a lengthy process of making themselves up each morning, affixing a layer of plant and animal fats to their faces to be left in place throughout the day, shows us something about their strength of will. We must not forget this.

In order to truly know his lover, a man must touch her both outside and in, both physically and spiritually. And it is not necessarily clear even then that his delusions will disappear, for it is the both wondrous and troublous way of nature that touching arouses passion.

On the other hand, perhaps these thoughts of mine were themselves only the delusions of a mind befuddled by prison life. What made a man in a burlap wig wearing a flour bag look so much like a woman to me may actually have been nothing more than an excess of imagination, deriving ultimately from the repressed sexual desire that is inevitably part of a prisoner's condition. If so, all the speculations that that image gave rise to in my mind were false.

I have no desire to call the general population to task for taking pleasure in messy love scandals and tangled romance novels. I merely feel compelled, in my own imperfect way, to puzzle out the generalized implications of something I experienced during my days as a POW, now receded into the distant past.

Shindō excelled at impersonating and singing like a woman but proved himself quite inept at any other kind of stage business. Still, he was the first "female" to appear in camp, and "she" attracted a whole gaggle of suitors who vied for "her" attention.

When our own Tsukamoto began powdering his face, it was to join in this contest. He had acquired an American sergeant major's armband from somewhere and wore it proudly on his belt. Given the utter uniformity of the U.S. Army–issue fatigues and hats that made up our prison garb, literally anything could serve as an adornment. He did not appear to have very much success, however.

Besides making one segment of the POW population act unduly masculine, Shindō the singing princess made another segment of the population act unduly feminine. As the performances expanded and talent shows gave way to fully staged plays, the actors who took the female roles all followed Shindō's lead in trying to make themselves seductive to men. Shindō had taken to going about in drag all evening even on ordinary nights, and these other female impersonators used the apparel they had gained through their performances to do the same. They played the bar girl at drinking parties, speaking in falsetto squeals as they poured wine or fell playfully against their neighbors' knees. Some who lacked the looks or gift for a complete makeover chose instead to wrap lengths of cloth they had dyed red or yellow around their heads like turbans—a fashion they continued to affect clear until they were on the train home after demobilization in Japan.

The vast majority of prisoners endured their sexual isolation by themselves, but from time to time one of these female impersonators would enter into a steady relationship with a suitor, and it would lead to a great to-do with passionate love letters flying back and forth. In spite of the many exaggerated accounts that have appeared in the documentary literature, however, I was not personally aware of any such relationships that involved sodomitic behavior.

In recalling these developments, I find myself wondering whether there can be any true basis for the arguments advanced by proponents of homosexual love. André Gide's *Corydon,* perhaps the only truly honest book this great twentieth-century master of invention has penned, argues for the social legitimation of homosexual love from a biological standpoint, but so long as society is not itself built upon love, we have no chance of bringing social legitimacy to any variety of love. At present, society recognizes minimally the love found in marriage, and in the parent-child or brother-sister relationships deriving from marriage. However, the simple fact that marriage was not originally a unit of love leaves society and love in an adversary relationship where, when love exists, it is forever being betrayed by society, and vice versa, whenever society attempts to stifle love, love insists on gaining its way. Christianity proposed a kind of universal love in an effort to mitigate this dramatic conflict, but the reason this has had relatively little effect in spite of monumental efforts to spread the word is that Christian love could never actually replace any other kind of love, only dilute it. And so the drama continues to play out, forever and ever.

Every individual who pursues love must construct his own personal morality, and no matter how highly he may refine his arguments in support of that morality, it remains ultimately founded on egotistic self-interest. In this sense, Stendhal was correct to stand on the principle of egotism throughout his life, never asking to be accepted by society, whereas the arguments for moral legitimation made in D. H. Lawrence's *Lady Chatterley's Lover* and Gide's *Corydon* constitute nothing more than sentimental whining.

Aware of his abnormality, Gide falls back on the words of an eighteenth-century monk, who asserted that it was better to simply learn to live with one's affliction than to become fixated on ridding oneself of it. "Whatever I may be, I still wish to live!"—this has become the common cry of all those who dwell in the "basement"; underlying this cry is the advance of civilization to a stage where society grants all persons, no matter how fiendish, the right to live—including those sentenced to life imprisonment at hard labor. The basement-dwellers know their welfare is utterly dependent on the magnanimity of a society at peace. That is why they go so willingly, like sheep to the slaughter, when their society convulses and orders its citizens to lay down their lives in battle; they raise no cries of "I want to live!" then. It is also the reason why most of them align themselves with the conservative party in politics.

We POWs were the product of exactly such a social convulsion, but the quality of life we experienced during our imprisonment proved to be far more "magnanimous" than the lives we had experienced as civilians in peacetime. For example, there were no punishable crimes so long as our actions caused no injury to the enemy nation that sustained us. At worst, we worried about the arbitrary actions of our own Japanese bosses in camp, or the possibility of private lynchings. Thus, even though homosexuality is not accepted in Japanese society at large, it became a viable means of asserting one's individuality in the prison camp, owing to the simple fact that our population consisted solely of men.

Another simple fact—that prison life offered no privacy—introduced some measure of constraint. As one might expect, homosexual love between prisoners was expressed by sleeping together at night—naturally at considerable annoyance to the lonely man in the next bed who wished to get some sleep. One day, the detachment leaders from all the platoons came to Hiwatashi as a group to protest what was taking place. They went over the heads of their immediate superiors, the platoon leaders, in doing this because they were convinced that the platoon leaders would merely squelch the protest on the spot.

The protest did not directly address the problem of homosexual lovers but rather aimed at reforming the behavior of the cooking staff. As it happened, most of the men making nocturnal visits to the beds of female impersonators were cooks. Among the several demands listed by the detachment leaders was an item that read as follows: "The cooking staff's practice of entering the platoon barracks at night to engage in behavior of a homosexual nature must be halted."

In homosexual relationships among the prisoners, the initiative generally came from whichever party possessed superior status within the camp, and the cooks were like nobility among the prisoners because they could bring gifts of special delicacies to their partners. It is the same in any society: The powerful are the ones who assert their love. In writing about the "unjust" lawsuits brought against men like Oscar Wilde and an army general whose name I no longer recall, Gide would have done well to also point out that in each case the plaintiffs brought suit partly out of jealousy toward the defendant's social position.

When the sixteen detachment leaders from our four platoons appeared out of the blue one night with their list of demands, it represented the first time that any of the prisoners had turned to democratic activism. (I regret to say it was also the last, since violent force became more and more the preferred mode of control as our period of captivity dragged on.) Their inspiration had come from militarist Japan's defeat by the democratic United States.

I have already written several times of the high-handedness displayed by cooks both in the military and in the POW camps, so I will not detail the rest of the demands. In any event, Hiwatashi was forced to promise reform not only of the cooks' "behavior of a homosexual nature" but of their many other egregious abuses as well.

The general behavior of the cooks did indeed show improvement—in limited measure and for a limited time. With regard to the "behavior of a homosexual nature" however, the only change was that the female impersonators now came to visit the cooks.

———

Aristotle said that tragedy depicts superior men, and comedy, inferior. Since no one can be lower in station than a prisoner, the plays produced by camp inmates must be classed as tragedies. Whether they were dramas about the sad and fleeting lives of gambling toughs on the old post roads, or scenes from the ever-popular vendetta tale of the loyal retainers, or contemporary family tragedies about war veterans trying to cope with the humiliation of defeat, they all depicted persons and things "superior" to anything in our lives as POWs. The ever-indolent prisoners showed no sign of seeking catharsis, however, and none of the plays ever really went beyond the realm of spectacle.

The prisoners' first recreation had been sumo wrestling. They liked this sport in particular because it offered an outlet for the aggressive instincts they had nurtured as soldiers. Then, as our POW careers progressed, the more passive entertainment of listening to others sing had gained favor. Singing stars were born, a few from each company, and the fact that from the beginning their excellent voices tended to be quite feminine in tone can be thought of as prefiguring the appearance of someone like Shindō. One of those early singers, a young PFC named Hanai, was Imamoto's pet and had been given the feminine nickname of Hanako. When Shindō appeared and started dressing as a woman, Hanai followed suit, but he was a little too tall and chunky for the part and Imamoto soon made him desist.

The development of these simple prison pastimes into full-blown theatrical productions may be attributed to American curiosity. One day while the war was still in progress, Oda organized a sumo tournament to entertain the Americans and opened the festivities with a rousing speech:

"I know some of you consider it demeaning to make yourselves into a spectacle for American troops, but I'd like you to take the broad view and not let such feelings prevent you from giving us your very best effort. The commandant has been gracious enough to donate some special prizes for the winners, and he has said that if friendlier relations between Americans and Japanese can be promoted through events like this, he'll be willing to arrange a film show for us sometime."

As you might expect, it became a competition among the companies, and cheerleading squads in all manner of dress danced about, enlivening the performance for the spectators. During the intermission, two of the inmates gave a judo demonstration and drew a huge round of applause when one flipped the other over his head with a *tomoe* throw.

One evening not long after that, we were treated to a showing of a Technicolor film starring the figure skater Sonja Henie on a screen set up in front of battalion HQ. The close-ups in the kissing scenes brought hoots and catcalls from the audience. Though some film critics insist that the medium is meant to be viewed privately in a dark room, I realized this was another way to enjoy a motion picture. I should note that the picture did not have Japanese subtitles, so the audience could respond only to the visual images on the screen.

Once the war was over and the mood in camp grew more relaxed, these experiences with large-scale entertainments led some of the inmates to propose an evening of stage plays. The organizers set up an open-air theater in front of battalion HQ, laying boards out for a stage, enclosing the stage on three sides with old tents, and supplying it with electricity for lights. This time, too, the companies would compete with one another for the best performance. Prisoners with a penchant for showing off stepped forward to fill the roles. The writers drew on dim recollections of plays or movies they had seen in the past to come up with ideas for plots that could be resolved in one or two relatively simple acts.

All of the plays in this first show were period dramas, and in fact, most were about vagabond gamblers who lived outside the law. Though they bore different titles—*Spring Showers on the Old Post Road, Wayfarer in the Autumn Rain,* and so forth—their plots resembled one another to an uncanny degree, almost without exception centering on a gambler who hears the dying wish of a man he has cut down on behalf of a benefactor, seeks out the dead man's sweetheart or younger sister or someone, and falls in love with her. The organizers of the show balked at performing these all at once and decided to have the sponsors draw lots, but then the losers complained that they had already expended a great deal of time and effort in preparations and were in no position to change their entries at the last minute. In the end, three virtually identical dramas were performed on the same night, differing by little more than whether the heroine was the dead man's sweetheart or sister.

If I am not mistaken, this plot formula for films about roving gamblers was inspired by the American picture called *The Broken Lullaby*. In that case, the killing took place on the field of war, but it is not difficult to see the resemblance between the battlefield and the gambling underworld. In both cases, strangers who have no personal quarrel or debt seek to kill one another out of loyalty to higher benefactors. The notion of love blossoming from antihuman acts apparently appeals to our sense of romance. Could this link between antihuman stimulus and love tell us that love is itself, in some sense, antihuman?

The denouement of these plays was utterly predictable: The killer cuts down a band of villains who attack the sister or sweetheart of his victim, then ultimately reveals that he is the mortal enemy of her brother or sweetheart—which is to say, he is the object of her vengeance—and sadly but gallantly sets out on the road once again. So the resolution, too, is entirely antihuman.

Behind the popularity of these fugitive gambler dramas, I believe, lies an idealization of this kind of antihuman circumstance. I suppose it is because in our daily lives as ordinary citizens we are forever being tormented by all-too-human hardships.

In my unit's offering, the killer was played by a gym teacher from a girls' school in Osaka. Not long after repatriation, he was fired for battering one of his students. The man who played the victim was a sailor from Kobe. A little over a year after repatriation, his mug shot appeared in newspapers throughout the country as a burglary and murder suspect wanted by police. By whatever odd coincidence, the two leading actors in my unit's antihuman theatrical offering both ended up as criminals.

Company 1 performed *The Treasury of Loyal Retainers*, beginning with En'ya Hangan's intemperate attack and going as far as his disembowelment. Not surprisingly, these episodes from the famous vendetta play won the most enthusiastic applause of all the shows. A Buddhist monk of the Pure Land sect played Lord Hangan, and afterward he presented himself before the curtain still wearing his white death robes. Kneeling and bowing deeply, he said:

"We chose to present this humble rendition of the well-known classical drama, *The Treasury of Loyal Retainers*, because we believed it would speak to you anew at this time of national defeat. I come before you now on behalf of the entire cast to urge you to remember the spirit of the loyal retainers as you devote yourselves to the reconstruction of our homeland."

Only in a POW camp is one likely to hear such words from the mouth of a religious priest—words, in effect, promoting vengeance.

This man was head priest of a prominent temple in western Japan. A short but portly man, he invariably wore a cheerful smile on his well-rounded face. Being a priest, he was an accomplished speaker and always had four or five eager listeners gathered around him in the evenings. He knew it would be foolish to overtly proselytize among the prisoners and refrained from doing so, but he did have a way of drawing words of wisdom out of mundane stories in the midst of general chitchat. He also had a good many amorous tales to share.

Apparently having smelled an intellectual in me, he gave me a recognizing look. As an avid reader of Stendhal, however, I had developed an aversion to religious men. I recalled a remark I had overheard in a conversation between some local fellows on the pier at Lake Nojiri, when I visited there once as a student: "So-and-so from Such-and-such Village is really good at telling fables," one of them said. "I figure he should become a priest."

This had always struck me as an apt expression of the low expectations we Japanese hold for men of the cloth. One day I related this experience and my thoughts about it to the POW priest. Normally he listened to my atheist views without losing his perpetual cheer, but just that once he made a sour face.

Much as he preached vengeance to the prisoners in camp, I suppose he is preaching democracy and the all-volunteer army to the general populace today.

———

The prisoners loved the performances, and similar evenings were planned at a frequency of about two per month. In time, men with a certain amount of prior acting experience stepped forward, and a unified troupe of players selected from all the companies was organized; they undertook to perform longer plays with highly complex plots, such as *The Wooden Clog from Higo*. They also managed to borrow some real Japanese kimonos from the civilian camp on the coast—though, unfortunately, the woman's kimono had a red stain on its backside.

Along with the birth of this theatrical troupe came the birth of a "tattoo syndicate," which eventually established itself as a separate power within the camp. The first sign was when a man with a dragon tattooed on his upper arm began loitering about the stage and dressing room areas for no discernible reason. Somewhere along the line this fellow had moved in with the battalion staff.

In the real world, thugs of this kind seem to appear spontaneously wherever public entertainments are found, and our prison camp proved no different. By the time the great majority of us gained release from the camp in December 1945, the thugs had not yet made themselves intolerable. But among the inmates detained after that as suspected war criminals, they gradually expanded their organization and influence, and apparently all members of the syndicate were compelled to draw tattoos of dragons on their arms in ink.

The camp commandant noticed these dragons, and knowing a little about the ultranationalist Black Dragon Society, he had the group's boss brought in for questioning. When it became clear that the man was merely a small-time contractor, however, he immediately let him go.

The quality of the new troupe's acting—imitations and exaggerations of kabuki styles—was at best on a par with what you might find at remote country playhouses, but the shows nevertheless aroused the curiosity of the Americans, and arrangements were made one night for troops from all U.S. Army facilities in the area to come and see them. Even better, a group of Japanese nurses was to come as well.

About one month after the end of the war, nurses from Imperial Army medical units began arriving from across the Philippines and were assigned to duties in the POW hospital located across the road from Camp 1. They came in WAC uniforms, and from our distant vantage point we ogled at their wide wagging behinds as they climbed clumsily down from the trucks that brought them.

From then on, the outworkers fought over every chance to go on labor detail to the hospital. Some came back happy, others indignant. Needless to say, they would like to have sat down face-to-face with the nurses for a leisurely chat, but they had no such luck. The nurses kept busy inside the tents, tidying up supply shelves and such, while the men were outside laying walkways or digging rain channels, so at most they could exchange a few quick words from a distance when the guards were looking the other way.

One man reported that a nurse spoke first. "How are you guys doing over there in the camp?" she asked politely.

"What can I say?" he replied. "We just hang our heads in shame for letting ourselves be captured."

I should note that none of these nurses were old prisoners from during the war. They had all been taken into custody after the war was over.

"Goodness, there's no need for you to feel that way," she came back. "This whole war was the fault of the militarists, and you have no reason at all to think ill of yourself."

Another man exchanged words with a different nurse, who was considerably less sympathetic. "Prisoner, prisoner," she needled.

"Oh yeah?" he retorted. "Let me remind you that we were on the front lines risking our lives, while you were up in the hills playing hanky-panky with the officers. You're in no position to be calling us names."

The nurse's response was to throw a stone at him. Even so, this man had to be counted among the fortunate, for he had at least had the chance to see and speak with a Japanese member of the opposite sex. As interpreter,

I always had to remain in our company HQ, which meant no such opportunity could come my way. Now, though, a whole bevy of fresh young maidens from the homeland would be coming to visit us in the camp. My heart danced with joy.

More than twenty of them pressed tightly together in their special front-row seats. Except for one thirtyish woman—no doubt her unit's head nurse—they were all young girls in their early twenties.

Frankly, however, I was disappointed. Even when I discounted for the fact that they came with their sun-darkened faces au naturel, lacking the benefit of powder or makeup, I could not efface the letdown I felt upon seeing their flat faces with tiny eyes and broad cheeks.

I hasten to add, lest I alienate my female readers, that today, five years after my return home, I do not regard these typical features of Japanese women unattractive in the least. In fact, quite the contrary, I find them exceedingly beautiful. There was, however, good reason for my disappointment with these women after a year of living in American captivity.

The only females any of us had seen up close while in the POW camp were those featured in American magazines. For the most part this meant pinup girls, pictured in provocative poses intended to ease the loneliness of men away from home. The GIs liked to hang such pictures on the wall next to their pillows. From maidenly bathing beauties in coquettish poses to more mature women draped shamelessly across a bed and gazing seductively into the camera—whatever your age or taste might be, there was a pinup girl to suit, and many of them had even gained a measure of celebrity.

These same pinup girls had become the sole feminine comfort of the camp inmates as well. Following the Americans' lead, we cut out the girls' pictures and hung them by our pillows. Then one day, after an officer came for inspection, we were ordered to take them all down. Were they implying that the men of the defeated nation had no right to look at the women of the victorious? we fumed indignantly. We had jumped to the wrong conclusion, however: When we raised the issue with Wally, he informed us that even the Americans had to take the pictures down when officers came on inspection—whereupon we persuaded him to let us put the pictures back up once the inspection was through.

The American beauties all wore faces put on for display. Some arched their eyebrows with an empty look of ecstasy in their eyes, others turned up the corners of their mouths in vacuous smiles. It is interesting to note that the faces we don for display like this all involve upward movements of the facial muscles. I suppose the ideal type for this kind of face is the Hannya demoness's mask.

What is it that constitutes beauty in a woman? What makes us think one woman beautiful and another ugly? Those who study the matter point to the elevation of the subject's nose or the balance between her forehead and her cheeks, and they speak of such things as symmetry and golden mean, but if we lived in a country where none of the women fit their principles, I doubt we would judge them all to be ugly.

In other words, our conception of feminine beauty is a product of culture, and it essentially springs from a taste for self-indulgence. The desire to win a paragon of beauty for oneself is probably common to all males of our day, and this situation most likely owes in large part to advances in printing technology that have made possible the mass dissemination of *bijinga*-style paintings of beautiful women and photographs of glamour girls. In the olden days, a man's only contemplation of superior beauty was through rumors about the peerless young maiden in the neighboring village, and he would not actually have a chance to see that beauty unless he made a point of traveling to the village for a firsthand glimpse. All of which is to say that, unless he had the travel funds and a lot of time on his hands, a man did best to simply think of his own wife as the most beautiful woman in the world.

I am not familiar with precisely how the artistic genre of *bijinga* developed, but it stands to reason that if an artist working at the cultural center of a society produces a painting according to his own ideals of beauty, and reproductions of this painting become universally available, then men will begin comparing their wives and sweethearts with the painting and will find them wanting. That is to say, the ultimate effect of these paintings of pretty women may be to place men in a constant state of dissatisfaction.

The same would hold for photographs of glamour girls. Techniques of photography have now advanced well beyond merely "capturing the true image." Through tricks of lighting that could not possibly occur naturally, or by touching up the picture to remove blemishes and lend it an ethereal coloring, today's photographer can create an idealized impression of the subject. Furthermore, he builds on the foundation of a special face the model puts on for display—a face she would never wear in actual daily life.

So the reason the maidens from home failed to impress me was, in essence, that I had grown addicted to American girlie pictures. Based on this experience, I can only hope that couples enchanted by American movie stars today will refrain from gainless comparisons that could lead to mutual disappointment.

With these young women from home in the audience, the performance took on a special flavor. The hero was played by an exceptionally handsome man, and by this time the wigs and makeup had advanced enough that you could truly say he overflowed with manliness. When he made his entrance by way of the elevated "flower path" leading through the audience to the stage, the women turned that way as one, leaving only the backs of their heads visible from where I sat. Risking the ire of my female readers once again, I might note what a magnificent sight it was to watch these twenty-some orbs of black hair moving back and forth in mechanical precision throughout the performance. They turned in concert with the movements of the actors on stage. I suppose there is little difference between these women being enchanted by the costumed actors and men being enchanted by paintings of beautiful women.

Shindō and several other female impersonators performed popular songs during the intermissions. Their costumes had also seen improvement, and on this day they wore bloomers of the kind strippers wear under ankle-length gossamer skirts. Nothing could be done about their bulging crotches, however.

"Shindō's big jigger spoils the whole effect," one of the homosexual gallants said loud enough for everyone to hear.

The false women danced for the real women, kicking up their heels and lifting their skirts. The real women broke up with laughter and buried their faces in one another's shoulders. They did not return for any more of our shows.

————

Some regard drama and dance as the fountainhead of all the arts. I do not know enough about such theories, but without question these were the two art forms that flourished most under the relatively primitive conditions of prison-camp life. I should note that this did not include participant dancing, however, which ended after only a single session of *Bon*[1] festivities. Our lives as POWs contained no grounds for festive dancing.

Our condition of captivity naturally influenced every genre of art the men took up in their search for ways to beguile the tedium. For example, it prevented anyone from adopting realism as his mode of artistic expression. It is my belief, for reasons too complex to delineate here, that realism fundamentally underlies all pictorial art, yet none of our painters saw fit to render images of prison life in their works. Neither the artists nor anyone else had the remotest desire to reexamine our present reality by contemplating it on a painted panel.

Our painters devoted themselves mostly to pictures of Mt. Fuji and geishas and dragons, which they produced not for their fellow prisoners but to sell to the souvenir-loving Americans. For their fellow inmates, they

---

1 The Bon Festival, taking place in mid-July or mid-August (today, mostly the latter), is a Buddhist observance in which family ancestors are honored by welcoming their spirits back home for a few days. The festivities usually include community *Bon* dances, with people of all ages dancing in circles around a platform or scaffold holding festival drummers and musicians (or a sound system).

painted erotic pictures—a genre of painting that has been among the far-thest removed from realism since Utamaro in the eighteenth century. Given the explicit nature of these pictures, we could not hang them on the wall for permanent display where they could be viewed at will, as works of pic-torial art are intended to be.

Architectural design was perhaps the art form most constrained by our condition, for the building materials and basic structures were all prede-termined. Even so, the small shelter constructed for the Lister bag managed to recall some of the characteristics of an old-fashioned well shed. Beneath it, the foot-square split-bamboo frame filled with small stones to catch water spillage also offered a distant echo of the aesthetic sensibilities displayed in Japanese gardens.

The condition of the POW afforded nothing to commemorate, so it need be no surprise that not a single sculpture was produced.

Music, with its fluid cadences, suited the inmates' temperament best, and the only tool anyone needed to participate was his own voice. Though none of the old military songs or pop tunes we knew had anything to do with our present lives, the melancholy tones of many such melodies fit the moods of our captivity.

"The Snow on Mt. Fuji, Hey!" was virtually the only cheerful tune we sang, and even this was almost entirely limited to when we broke out a new batch of bootleg wine. Even the doleful primitive must have a drinking song. When I unconsciously started into the old "Toasting Song" one day, the prisoners who were with me spent a long time learning its difficult chro-matic phrasings, and in almost no time at all it was being sung throughout the camp.

I learned several new pop tunes from others as well. The melodies were invariably sad—that seemed to be part of the definition of such music. We Japanese are apparently a melancholy people even when we are not POWs. I decided that to simply dismiss this music as uncultivated was to miss an important point. In "The Kuroda Ballad" I discovered traces of the ancient *gagaku* music of the imperial court, and in "The Mango Vendor of Java" I recognized the influence of Rimsky-Korsakov. If I were more learned, I believe I could explain the popularity of songs such as these entirely on the basis of their roots in more serious music.

Not to be overlooked among the art forms practiced by the prisoners was the recitation of old narrative ballads. It started with a small number of "gramophone masters" intoning a few (supposedly) climactic passages for their barracks neighbors, but as the talent shows got under way, reciters with enough proper training to have entered regional contests began to come forward one after another.

The tales of duty and sentiment that unfold in these old ballads are highly feudalistic, and they have virtually nothing in common with modern society. Yet they possessed a veritably magical power to hold the POWs in rapt silence, surpassing all other forms of performance. I recall that these ballads used to be promoted as "inspiring the way of the samurai," and I am aware that some observers fear their continued popularity may presage a reactionary trend. In my view, however, the real reason for their popularity most likely has to do less with the samurai spirit than with the epic quality of their narrative progress, which is consonant with the fascination we Japanese have shown for external incident ever since wandering minstrels carried *The Tales of the Heike* throughout the country in the twelfth and thirteenth centuries.

The last forty years have produced no great novels that might compete with *The Life and Times of Jirochō of Shimizu.* In this narrative ballad, Jirochō's Zeus, embodying wisdom, benevolence, and courage, heads up a plentiful cast of colorful characters, from the hot-tempered Ōmasa and cool-thinking Komasa, to the tragic Kira no Nikichi and the comical Mori no Ishimatsu. Including myself, the world teems with characters of the kind described in this ballad as "fools who can't be cured except by death." Why is it that contemporary novels fail to portray them? Our novelists seem to have lost what it takes to create a fool who retorts, "Then I'll take the cure by dying, boss."

In listening to these narrative ballads, I also observed how deftly they wove together story incident and natural setting. For example, the opening lines of Tamagawa Katsutarō's *Water Margin Tale of the Tenpō Years,* which I learned from my neighbor, go as follows:

> Between lofty Fuji and Tsukuba,
> Peaks ancient as the raging gods,
> Roved a rogue called Bandō Tarō,
> Who for ten tempestuous years,
> Turbulent as the Toné River
> Spanned by a rainbow bridge,
> In the name of manly honor,
> Washed blood with blood;
> And so from our own Tenpō Era,
> We have this "Water Margin Tale."

The style is not especially distinguished, and the pairing of Mount Fuji and Mount Tsukuba is even a little bit comical, but in any case we can see how nature and human deed are apprehended together. The disappearance of this quality ever since Shimazaki Tōson published *The Broken Commandment* in 1906 is, to my mind, the greatest loss our serious literary fiction has suffered in recent times. I would say, in fact, that the success popular fiction has enjoyed since Nakazato Kaizan's *The Great Bodhisattva Pass* won such acclaim in the 1920s owes precisely to effective use of the wide outdoors as backdrop.

According to John Ruskin, the Western enchantment with nature that began with Jean-Jacques Rousseau exhibits a tendency toward what he calls the pathetic fallacy. If we Japanese traditionally possess a unique, more sensuous and less sentimental mode of apprehending nature, unlike what is found in either the Greek or the Christian traditions, then is it not truly deplorable that our serious literature fails to make use of that rare treasure? Such were my thoughts as my neighbor taught me this ballad.

Having spoken of the arts, I must now speak of the artists. I have already said a good deal about the singers and actors. In essence, the singers attempted to mimic professional singers who were popular, while the actors attempted to mimic what they thought of as characteristically human. The prisoners in the audience, wishing only to be spectators, were satisfied no matter what they got.

Among us was a playwright named Sakoda, a proponent of the "New Theater" movement, who had belonged to a traveling stage troupe during the war. A small man with puffy cheeks, he claimed to have been pursued relentlessly by the beautiful proprietress of a coffeehouse near Nakano station on Tokyo's Chūō train line. He said she looked a lot like Higuchi Ichiyō, the famous authoress, but what I found most intriguing was that the war-time love story he told differed not one iota from a story that had made the rounds when I was a student fifteen years before, about the madame of a coffee shop along the same transit line.

Sakoda wrote plays in which he anticipated some of the social turmoil our defeated country would have to grapple with. Of all the plays produced by the prisoners, his plays and *The Loyal Retainers* of the Buddhist priest were the only ones that showed any seriousness of purpose.

His first play was entitled *The Heron*, and it told the tale of a lieutenant colonel from the General Staff Office who reluctantly acquiesces in the marriage of his daughter to a libertarian young man back from the war, then kills himself. As the happy lovers stroll along the beach that same night, the cry of a heron gives them a foreboding of her father's suicide and brings the curtain down.

Two other partisans of the New Theater style joined Sakoda in filling the play's three roles. Watari, the man who taught me so much about film, played the lieutenant colonel. Having been a student of progressive cinema theory in college, he had long been planning a screenplay called *Windows*. The picture would have four separate episodes linked by the camera sliding from one window to the next at an apartment house, unfolding at each stop a history of the occupants' lives. Although this idea had been incubating in his mind for ten years, he had yet to commit anything to paper.

Sakoda himself played the daughter. I do not believe his experience with the traveling stage troupe included opportunities for training in the techniques of playing female roles, but no one else was willing to take the part. Through tireless experimentation and practice, he managed to capture at least the general feeling of the passive sex. I suppose he was aided by the passive role he had played in the affair with the coffeehouse madame in Nakano.

Performing this serious drama before an audience of mere curiosity seekers was a thankless endeavor. The spectators talked constantly, making it impossible to hear the dialogue. Even so, the play made something of an impression: The actors wore costumes that resembled, if somewhat crudely, everyday clothing back home, and they sat properly on their knees on a tatami-like floor, with a low table between them.

"It sure makes me wish I were home," someone in the audience said.

The characters on stage were the only ones in the entire camp with serious things to say and do. I would like to believe that the thankless endeavor was, in its own way, a success.

We also had a songwriter in our midst. He had worked as a musician for a dance troupe in Tokyo, and his dream was to write a major hit. He could turn anything into a song. At the old camp, when four airmen had tried to escape and failed, he promptly wrote a song extolling their courage and deaths, but it failed to gain popularity among the prisoners.

The song he wrote when the war ended went as follows:

Walking in the shade of the sidewalk palms
A furtive wink sets her face aglow.
So dapper and dashing, hand in hand,
The Yankee maid and her sergeant beau.
In ever good cheer, their lips repeat
This, their favorite melody.
La ta la ta la.

Like most pop songs, the lyrics are virtually devoid of meaning, but one thing that nevertheless comes through clearly is a tone of obsequiousness toward the Americans. Though he had set the lyrics to a gentle, flowing tune, this song, too, failed to catch on.

That we had no graphic artists trained in European styles of painting was pure accident, but the presence of not just one but two painters with a measure of experience in traditional Japanese styles owed to the fact that Leyte had been defended by the Sixteenth Division, made up principally of

Kyotoites. As I noted before, however, their skills were limited to what they had learned by copying from model pictures, and though they were able to please the Americans, they failed to win the favor of their fellow prisoners until they began producing erotic works.

Even those paintings were soon eclipsed by line drawings of the same genre that began to show up among the prisoners. Tracing them to their source revealed that they were being drawn by a construction worker, the tailor, and several others like them who had never had anything to do with art. My guess is that they were men with a particular fondness for the genre, who had over the years developed a set repertoire of erotic drawings they could reproduce at will so long as they had paper and pencil in hand—even in the isolation of a prison camp. They were a curiously arrogant lot.

I myself became the first author among the prisoners when, with Watari's help, I began filling the empty hours by writing screenplays. I started out with crude adaptations of detective stories I had read in the Armed Services Edition series but eventually decided to resurrect some of the ideas I had had for novels as a literary youth and try setting them down in this new medium.

The stories were all trifling romances. Selecting various complications from my old love affairs, I lay in the dark each night humming to myself and developing scenes in my mind, then the next day I would write them out. Such stories appealed to me as well as to my fellow inmates because they had absolutely nothing to do with the lives we were then living. Within our bounteous prison camp we had time even to dream of love.

My screenplays initially started circulating while the war still raged, about the same time as Hanako started crooning songs in front of Headquarters in elegant feminine voice. Thinking back on it now, it seems clear that this was the first sign of our impending corruption.

When the erotic pictures appeared after Japan's surrender, I began receiving numerous requests to write erotic stories as well. The man of letters willingly complied. I had read a French translation of *Lady Chatterley's Lover* when I was in school; recalling Lawrence's highly figured description of the lovers' union in the woods, I wrote a story called "Pastoral Symphony."

It proved to be a great success. With the screenplays, I had occasionally failed to collect the one cigarette rental fee, but the men fought with one another to pay five cigarettes in advance for the opportunity to read an erotic story. Unfortunately, although the screenplays always came back and remained a continuous source of profit for me, the new book soon disappeared, so in the final analysis my gains were more limited.

The proud owner of a male organ that drove even professional comfort women wild (so he said) told me he became so aroused that he could not sleep. Of course, the credit for this tremendous response to the story must by rights go to the original author, D. H. Lawrence.

To fill the continuing demand, I next expanded the climactic love scene in Pierre Louÿs's *Aphrodite,* attempting to link a woman's moment of ecstasy with the pain of childbirth, but this interpretation failed to go over so well. Of course, I would like Louÿs to bear the blame in this case.

Some of my readers may regard me as a debauched man for having written such stories, even if only while a POW. For all they know, however, I may be a debauched man quite apart from having written erotic stories under those conditions. Before they pass judgment, I would ask them to first try eating corned beef for a year in an American prison camp.

———

The theatrical productions thrived, notching up one success after another. The gleeful Imamoto decided single-night shows were no longer enough and began planning for a huge performing arts festival that would span three full nights. It quickly became clear that the space we had been using would be too cramped, so the stage was moved to a larger open area at the back of the compound.

This time each unit had to come up with three separate entries for the program. When the mess sergeant, my company's artistic director, asked me to write a play, I wrote a sex comedy called *Carrots.* I will refrain from outlining the plot here, but it turned out to be a great success, and I take considerable pride in the fact that it remained an active part of the camp's repertoire long after I had been repatriated. This proved to be the only comedy performed in the camp, down to the very end.

The new stage was larger and the lights brighter. We even had a microphone for the singers now. A scatterbrained character in the mold of Matsui Suisei came out and introduced a female impersonator dressed as a Polish maiden. One of the new arrivals in Company 10, a former corporal, clicked castanets and sang "Habanera" from *Carmen.* Even an American GI, no longer satisfied just to sit and watch, climbed onto the stage to play his accordion and sing a doleful tune about longing for home.

One of the three nights was taken up by a single full-length drama performed by our "country players." The boss of the tattoo syndicate signaled the beginning and end of each act with a police whistle he had gotten hold of somewhere. It was bruited about that the man who played the female lead was his exclusive property. Several of the actors had learned to do handsprings and flips, which made the climactic fight scene more spectacular than ever.

Sakoda had written a new three-act play called *Crows.* A demobilized soldier visits the families of his fallen comrades one after another, learning about their checkered lives. The plot obviously drew on Watari's unrealized conception for *Windows*. Every time the former soldier enters one of his buddies' homes, he hears crows cawing on the roof, and this was what gave the play its title.

As the sex comedy I wrote got under way, I decided to return to my quarters. I had quite had my fill of these performances, and I certainly did not feel like staying to watch an off-color play I had written myself. The periodic swells of laughter I heard were, I knew, in response to my work. I somehow felt as though they were laughing at me, so in the emptiness of my company office, I laughed right back.

I went to get some bootleg wine from the cookshack. As I sat sipping it, I was startled by a figure that rose from a bed in the darkness at the far end of the building. I soon saw it was Yoshida.

"What's with you?" I asked. "Why aren't you at the show?"

"It's such a load of crap," he said. "You'd have to be a complete idiot to go to those things. Do they really think it's so amusing being a POW?"

To hear a seventeen-year-old kid ridiculing them made me want to take the audience's side.

"It's because they don't find it amusing that they're out there trying to enjoy themselves. Don't be such a smart aleck."

"Sure, call me a smart aleck if you want, but what's true is true."

He had a cup in his hand, too, and I realized that he was drunk.

"Well, I suppose you're basically right," I returned benignly. "I cut out because I thought it was pretty stupid, too." I raised my cup. "Shall we tip together?"

I was quite fond of this melancholy youth from a farm village in Nagano Prefecture. Orphaned and raised by relatives from a young age, he had been through a lot. On this night, too, he repeated his favorite dictum: "Take your meals with the same strangers for three years, and you're no longer taking meals with strangers." We both got very drunk.

The man who played the female lead in my play came back gushing with excitement.

"They really loved me! I've never seen them the way they were tonight!"

In *Spring Showers on the Old Post Road* he had played the man who got cut down. Though he lacked the good looks of our female impersonators, he had wanted very much to play a woman on stage, and tonight was his debut. It had gone over well, and he was elated, but I should note that for the female role in my comedy it did not really matter how feminine the actor looked.

I cannot recall what sparked the outburst—suddenly a screaming Yoshida was being restrained by the actor dressed in drag.

"Don't give me that crap!" he screamed at me. "You wanna fight? Come on, you can't scare me! I already died once!"

Too late I realized that this unfortunate youth was the kind who got violent when drunk. I had no desire to fight him. We were of exactly the same mind in our low opinion of the shows. I had no idea why two men of thirty-six and seventeen who agreed with each other should have to fight, even if we were drunk.

I suppose you could say that, in our state of confinement, once we ran out of amusements, we were left with little else to do but fight.

In the distance, that night's entries for the performing arts festival went on and on. Like the sound of a distant surf, waves of applause rolled through the sky into the darkness of the office.

⌣ 12 ⌣

Going Home

Prophets are a ubiquitous presence, whatever the time, wherever the place, and the POW camp was no exception. According to our own camp prophet, the war was supposed to end on August 17, so he missed the mark by a mere two days. There was just one problem: He had the victor and the vanquished reversed. He had predicted Japan would continue to be pushed back by the Americans, but then at the last possible moment, when we had no more ground to give, the tables would turn and we would emerge victorious.

Once the war had ended, the prisoners' concern shifted to when they would get to go home. Our prophet predicted October 28. By the time that date rolled around, everyone had given up on this forecast, but it ultimately came true in a way no one had expected: On the night of October 28, we received notice from the commandant that our repatriation date had been set for November 15.

I doubt any words committed to paper could express the extent of our joy. This goes hand in hand with the impossibility of expressing the true nature of our suffering as prisoners. Since there was nothing romantic about this joy, it would do no good for me to wax lyrical about what we thought or how we felt. The best I can do is to describe what we did.

First of all, on the night of the announcement, we broke out the boot-leg wine and held a huge celebration. Lights continued to burn in all of the barracks until after 1:00 A.M., with boisterous song echoing throughout the compound. The next morning some of the men cut the English letters GO HOME out of cardboard, colored them with red pencils, and hung them from the shelves over their pillows. Then they flopped down on their beds and lay gazing up at the letters all day long.

Preparations began immediately. The transport groups would be dis-

279

tinct from our existing companies, whose membership had been left up to the Japanese leadership. The new units went strictly according to ID numbers assigned at the time each man became a prisoner, and the size of each unit depended entirely on the designated ship's capacity. No consideration could be given to intimacies and friendships among the men.

We received large duffle bags, the kind the GIs carried, for packing our belongings. The camp administration directed us to have our uniforms stamped one last time with the letters PW. Hoping to use the high-quality U.S. Army–issue fatigues after returning home, the inmates did their best to avoid this.

The clothing already issued to each prisoner included two sets of cotton fatigues, top and bottom, T-shirts, underwear, four pairs of woolen socks, a hat, a poncho, boots, and an Australian blanket. Since we would be traveling from the tropics to the temperate zone in winter, each man now received a jacket and a jungle camouflage suit—the latter presumably because the end of the war had made them useless to the Americans. More than anything else, it was the jacket that the prisoners wanted to avoid having stamped PW. Imamoto tried to terrorize them with dire warnings of what could happen if they got caught in an inspection, but no one was inclined to place much store in anything he said. They were too attached to their American-made clothes.

The men had also accumulated numerous extra items of clothing from their bluebottling. This included sweaters, gloves, shoes, and the like—sundry items not included in the standard prison issue. Quite understandably, the POWs did not have the nerve to face the inspecting officers bearing this kind of contraband.

The Americans were quite aware of the presence of these stolen articles. One day Mr. North broached the subject. "We know you people have in your possession a number of articles stolen from our supply dumps. We'd like you to surrender them, no questions asked. We'll send them as relief supplies to Japan."

When I relayed this message to Hiwatashi, he laughed scornfully. "Oh, right, likely story. There's no telling what they'll really do. We'll just burn the stuff."

"But surely there's no need to burn the things," I protested. "Even if they gave them to the local population here instead of sending them to Japan, whoever gets them will be that much better off. If we burn them, all kinds of perfectly good stuff turns to ashes, and everybody loses."

Ignoring my protest, Hiwatashi immediately issued orders for the platoon leaders to gather all contraband clothing in a pile behind our latrines, then sprinkled the pile with gasoline and set it ablaze. The other company leaders apparently felt the same way. Fires burned at the back of each tract for the next three days and three nights. That was the military for you.

In spite of Hiwatashi's orders, I know one man who managed to smuggle a sweater and some gloves onto the ship. I saw another exchanging his stock of cigarettes for a blanket at the last minute. We were told we would have to return the major items when we landed in Japan, but those in charge in the Philippines and those in charge in Japan apparently had different views of the matter, and it ultimately depended on where you landed whether you got to keep them or not.

The impending separation colored our personal relationships with new sentiments. As we went about the customary routines we had established over the course of our long captivity, we could hear a different note creeping into our conversations, and we could see a different light in one another's glances when our eyes chanced to meet.

It would be going too far to say we were loath to part. We knew from the time we first became prisoners that our condition, however long it might last, was temporary; we knew we would each go back to our separate lives in the end. Because of this, when the moment of separation actually arrived, we were prepared to accept it simply as the inevitable coming to pass. Even so, when the routine activities we had grown accustomed to were suddenly disturbed by a flurry of preparations for going home, the feeling that everyone had already begun to withdraw into his own shell brought us a measure of heartache.

Like everyone else, I had made some friends during my ten months of captivity: Watari, who taught me about film and screen writing; Hirano, the medic, who kept me supplied with cigarettes; the happy-go-lucky young cooks with whom I got along so well. Each of them would now return to the life he had had before, as a simple city dweller or farmer, but in the tedium of camp life, if only for a passing moment, we had by our most basic instincts sought out one another's friendship.

"You know, Mr. Ōoka," one of the young cooks said, "you're always being such a kidder, but actually, I bet you think a lot more seriously about things than you let on."

I laughed at his flattery.

"Don't be silly," I said. "When a person makes a joke, he's really not thinking any farther than the joke. It's only in kabuki that you have characters who pass as jokers but are actually something else. If a guy spends more of his time laughing every day, it just means he's catching that much more fun on his way through this fleeting world; if he spends all his time getting drunk, he's really nothing but a drunk."

As I was saying good-bye to these fellows before we were transferred to separate camps to await the arrival of our respective ships, one of them declared, "The way I see it, Mr. Ōoka, you'll probably go back to being some big-shot manager or board member when you get home. I hope you won't stick up your nose at the people you met here and just have us turned away at the front door, because we certainly intend to come and look you up sometime."

"Well I'm not a manager, and I'm certainly no board member," I said. "To begin with, there's a huge difference between a manager and a board member. At any rate, you have my word. Assuming I even have a proper front door, I promise I won't turn you away, so just drop by any time you please. What I want to know is whether I can really be so sure you'll ever come. You better not forget."

"We'll come. We won't forget."

"I'll be expecting you then. Hah hah, what're you standing there looking so damn calm and collected for anyway? You should be crying. Don't you know tears are meant for times like this?"

"Waahhh, waahhh," they all pretended to cry. One of them had extended the ends of his skimpy eyebrows with tattoos. I have no idea what could have possessed him to adopt this cosmetic measure.

None of the young cooks ever came to visit.

———

Some men wished they did not have to part with friends; others wanted desperately not to part with the Philippines. Old man Soejima, a sixty-two-year-old corn farmer from Mindanao, had lived in the Philippines for forty years; he had a Filipino wife, five children, and even some grandchildren there.

Born in Fukushima Prefecture but orphaned at a young age, he had no home to return to in Japan. His only relations had long since left his native village for parts unknown.

Old man Soejima ended up in a POW camp with the rest of us former servicemen because he had helped the Imperial Army obtain food locally and had chosen to cast his lot in with Japanese forces after the American landing. Since a separate camp existed for Japanese civilians, he repeatedly sought to be transferred there after being brought to our camp in May. But once the Americans had recorded him as affiliated with the military, it proved impossible to have his status changed. They essentially had no means of investigating the matter.

Old man Soejima's anxiety deepened the moment we learned we were to go home. He begged Hiwatashi to explain his situation to the commandant and get the military affiliation removed from his name, and he even pleaded his case directly to Imamoto. Unfortunately, Hiwatashi and Imamoto were mentally halfway home already, and their minds were no longer on faithfully carrying out their leadership responsibilities in the camp. They made no effort to help him.

This man had been kind enough to give me some Spanish lessons (indeed, I would try anything to fill the empty hours, but lacking a text and with his Spanish limited to common phrases used by the islanders in their daily lives, systematic lessons were impossible; I abandoned the endeavor almost right away), and I also felt sorry for him when I spied him sitting dejectedly by himself, the lone man over sixty in a group otherwise under forty, getting his things in order with that just-so meticulousness that seems to come with age. I offered to go with him to speak directly with the American commandant.

"What does he expect to come of transferring to the civilian camp?" the commandant wanted to know.

"He thinks that there he'll be able to find some way to remain in the Philippines. His home and his family and all his possessions are in Mindanao, and he has nothing in Japan."

"Well, I'm sorry, but please tell him that there's no chance he'll be waived from repatriation even at the civilian camp. Tell him he'll first have to go home to Japan, and then, after a peace treaty is signed, if he still wants to come back to Mindanao and has the means to do so, that'll be a different matter."

Old man Soejima mumbled a sunken "I see" and said nothing more. He was a broad-shouldered, barrel-chested man of medium height, with thickset features and sun-toughened skin.

One of the interpreters for the Sixteenth Division Command Center at Tacloban had been a thirty-two-year-old Japanese expatriate named Aizawa, who had lived in Tacloban ever since graduating from the Spanish Department at the Tokyo School of Foreign Languages. His wife was of mixed Filipino and American blood, and they had one child. Aizawa surrendered as soon as American forces landed and was imprisoned with us because of his previous employment with the Sixteenth Division. His wife went to work as a nurse for the U.S. Army.

Aizawa thought his wife might somehow be able to pull some strings for him, or more to the point, get him released from the camp, and time and again he sent letters to her by way of the commandant, but she never replied. He concluded that she was deliberately ignoring his pleas because she wanted to keep him locked up and intended to leave him. When our repatriation notice arrived, he became convinced she would now have her wish fulfilled.

His statements and behavior grew increasingly erratic. He was stopped and chewed out by the guards for wandering near the fence in the middle of the night. He marched into the company office and shouted, "I know you all think I'm crazy," then proceeded right on out the other end.

One night he remained up late in the barracks. He stopped me when I happened by. "I thought I'd give you these," he said, and handed me his entire stack of English magazines and books.

A certain amount of antagonism existed among the men in camp who knew English. I got to be the company's official interpreter, while he had to slave away as a rank-and-file member of one of the platoons, only occasionally getting called on to interpret at an outwork site. Though all of us who knew English had built up meager little libraries of books we had obtained from the Americans we came in contact with, we generally did not offer to share them with the others unless specifically asked. I therefore thought it rather odd when he told me he wanted to present me with his entire collection—especially since we were on the verge of repatriation. On the other hand, no particular reason to refuse the gift came to mind, so after setting aside a few titles I already owned, I thanked him and accepted the rest. I left him sitting at his little table, writing.

I could see the light at his bunk still on after 1:00 A.M. At dawn, the man in the next bed awakened to the sound of groans and found Aizawa clutching his stomach in agony. Aizawa apparently begged his neighbor not to call the medics.

When the medics came, however, he obediently submitted himself to their care. Large quantities of a sticky, yellow substance came out of his mouth. It turned out to be Atabrine, a substitute for quinine developed by U.S. forces, which reportedly will not kill you no matter how much you ingest.

In his suicide note, Aizawa rambled on for ten long pages, venting unbounded bitterness toward his wife, but the medics believed he had staged the entire episode just to give her a scare. Although his gift of reading materials to me seemed to run counter to this view, I ultimately concluded the medics were probably right. Aizawa did not bite the fingers that were thrust to the back of his throat to make him regurgitate what he had swallowed. Sometimes those least intent on dying do the best job of staging their preparations to create the appearance of a serious attempt.

Aizawa was transferred to the hospital. A rumor soon circulated that he had managed to escape, only to be shot while hiding in a small boat. But a medic whose repatriation was delayed for two or three months due to war crime allegations told me he took a message to the hospital one day and saw Aizawa completely recovered and in immensely good cheer. His wife had finally come to see him. Even so, in accordance with regulations, he had to return alone to Japan like everyone else.

Aizawa's attempted suicide was the sort of thing one might expect from a woman whose husband had left her. This filled me with contempt for him, but the truth of the matter is that no man can avoid taking on some of the characteristics of the weaker sex when he lives in captivity as a POW. Of the qualities conjured up in our minds by the words *masculine* and *feminine,* some of the differences certainly do derive from biological distinctions between the genders, but I suspect a good many of them should more accurately be attributed to social conditions.

———

The greatest weight upon the POWs' minds was the question of how the people back home would receive them. Though Japan's defeat should have voided the "choose death before capture" code, shedding the code's hold on their psyches was no simple matter for these former soldiers.

I knew something of the very different European attitudes toward POWs, so being taken prisoner had not left me with much of an inferiority complex. I lightly brushed aside the concerns of one of the men who fretted endlessly about how things would be when we got home.

"Look, to begin with, how'll anyone know you've been a POW? You'll just blend right in with the crowd."

"But I come from a tiny village in the mountains of Tanba."

"Now, that could be a problem. In the big city, like Tokyo or Osaka, no one could care less who lives in the next apartment, whether he was a POW or whatever, but if you're talking about a small country village, that's another story. Of course, most people would be fine. But suppose the lady next door lost her son in the war. It's not gonna make her feel too good to see you walking around."

"Maybe I'll go up to Kyoto and find a job there," he said.

"Yeah, that'd be better. I suppose the only place any of us'll feel very comfortable is in the cities."

So it seems I actually had a pretty bad case of paranoia, too.

When I got home to the farm village to which my wife had evacuated, I was surrounded by fathers who had lost their sons and wives who had lost their husbands, but not one of them expressed the slightest bitterness at my having made it home alive. To the contrary, they rejoiced over every precious survivor.

The POWs' inferiority complex and paranoia generated all manner of dire imaginings about their return home. One day a curious notice was posted at the battalion office.

"Since serious doubts exist about our prospects after repatriation, we have contrived a plan to restore our hopes. All interested persons should assemble in front of battalion HQ at 7:00 P.M. this evening."

Fifty men showed up that evening to find out what it was all about, but the number dropped to twenty at the second meeting. The prisoners' paranoia had indeed given them serious doubts, but the so-called plan that was offered to dispel that paranoia had struck most of the men as a wild flight of fancy.

Imamoto and Oda had called the meeting to form a group called "The

Restoration Association." Monthly dues would be ¥100, with membership divided into three classes: Class A members were those like Imamoto and Oda, men with leadership responsibilities; class B members were the rank and file; and class C members were men who had sustained permanent disabilities from war wounds.

The Association was founded on the premise that former POWs would not be accepted back into mainstream society after repatriation. Our families would most likely refuse us entry into the house, and even if they did not actually turn us away, it would be far better to go out and establish ourselves on our own rather than to spend our days wondering miserably what our families thought of us. After all, we had already been on our own for many years as soldiers and prisoners of war. By allowing our families to think we had died, we could go on living independently. Everyone of like mind could rally together and help each other out as we blazed a path into the future.

This was the overall gist of the speech Imamoto delivered to the group of curious who gathered. The specific plan emerged as follows:

According to information Imamoto had obtained, the port of disembarkation in Japan would be Ōtake. Former navy hand Oda knew an inn there where members of the Association could rendezvous instead of going home. Once all had assembled, Imamoto and Oda would go to the offices of the Supreme Commander for the Allied Powers in Tokyo to negotiate for work. They had already obtained a letter of introduction from the camp commandant.

With Allied troops stationed in Japan, there was bound to be lots of work needing done. They would subcontract construction work for the Americans. Building materials would be shipped specially from the United States.

Class B members would do the actual work. If, for example, they earned ¥30 for a day's work, ¥10 would go to Association expenses, ¥10 to the worker's own livelihood, and ¥10 would be given to the disabled.

A noble cause indeed. The spirit of mutual support among POWs could not have been more clearly expressed. For me as one of the bystanders, however, the fact that Imamoto would be calling the shots raised a huge flag of caution. This man had previously made his living in the freight business and was an old hand at exploiting common laborers. He seemed to think of everyone he met as someone he could exploit.

Another thing I did not like about the group was the involvement of the tattoo syndicate. A member of the syndicate claimed to be on close terms with the son of a major industrialist in the Osaka area, and if anyone gave them trouble, he could get in touch with this rich boy and see to it that nothing stood in their way. I gathered that they intended to use this tie much like Yui Shōsetsu used his ties to the Major Counselor from Kii in his abortive plot against the Shogunate.

"I'm a bit suspicious as to why they thought it necessary to bring up the industrialist," I told a friend who said he intended to join the group. At twenty-five, he would be one of the class B members, and he spoke idealistically of offering his labor as a service to others.

"A scheme where they start out by talking about 'if anyone gives us trouble' sounds pretty unpromising to me," I said. "Imamoto was in the freight business, and you can bet when he gets back to Japan he's not going to find his former territory just sitting there waiting for him. As I see it, he's looking to take advantage of the one connection he has right now—which is to say, the relationship he's developed with the Americans—and exploit the rest of you guys for everything you're worth."

"But we really want to help the disabled veterans."

"I doubt this group will have that kind of strength. I mean, think about it: How many class B members do you have? How many'll actually be working?"

"Seven. But I think the number will grow once people understand what we're trying to do."

"No way are seven men going to be able to carry twenty, especially when not all of them have self-sacrifice in mind like you do. Some of them probably figure they'll join for now but later go their own way."

My friend's face had turned increasingly cloudy.

"Well, we can at least try. We're all firmly united on this," he said with a note of finality.

The Restoration Association's solidarity began to crack when it turned out that the repatriation parties would be based on prisoner ID numbers, and it broke apart completely when each ship had a different port of disembarkation. Even without such factors to stymie the plan, the notion that they could in effect take over an entire inn and stay there indefinitely during the severe food shortages following the war had been nothing but a pipe dream.

Still, I must ask my readers not to ridicule these prisoners' plans. Though the Restoration Association may have been a preposterously fanciful scheme conceived by freight-man Imamoto to exploit his fellow POWs, the more important point here is that the prisoners remained in the clutches of an inferiority complex strong enough to nurture such fancies.

Our prophet had proved to be on the mark for the day we received notice of our repatriation date, but our actual departure was slightly delayed. Two days after the announced date, on November 17, we finally left POW Camp 1 for the camps where each transport party was to await the arrival of its ship. The several days leading up to the seventeenth were busy ones. The company-by-company clerical and cookshack staffs were disbanded, and everyone was reorganized strictly according to ID numbers. We were directed to dismantle the various fixtures and furnishings we had constructed to make our bunk areas more livable, and now we slept on plain, bare cots with our duffle bags as pillows.

The new transport units needed leaders and clerks just as before, but I declined. As it happened, Kamimura, the former leader of my company's fourth platoon, became the leader of my transport platoon, and he objected strenuously to my resignation.

"This is ridiculous, Mr. Ōoka. You can't quit on us now. Once you've come this far, the decent thing to do is to see it through to the end."

He had no idea how much I had grown to hate being caught in the middle between the Americans and the Japanese. We interpreters had to stand face-to-face with the Americans and experience the POW's inferiority more directly than anyone else. Then when we turned around we got bombarded with bumptious and resentful demands from our fellow inmates, who sought an outlet for their own inferiority complexes.

Those released at this time from Camp 1 of the sprawling POW facilities at the foot of Cross Mountain did not constitute the entire population of the camp. The names of men accused of war crimes had been pouring in from all over the Philippines, and everyone with a matching name had to stay behind. For those prisoners held back because they had assumed false names at the time of their capture, this was a terrible stroke of bad luck. I had given my true name, so I would not have had to suffer the kind of regrets they did in any case, but I trembled to think that, even though Ōoka is a relatively rare surname, if there had been even one other man named Ōoka accused of a crime anywhere in the Philippines, I would have been detained with the others.

Furuta is the name of the poet I have mentioned several times before— the one who wrote the comic poem "How magnificent / The generous benevolence / Of the United States: / Not once in all our lives / Have we ever been so fat." A former shipping engineer, he was the thirtyish son of a Shinto priest from Nagano Prefecture, with a dark complexion and a long nose. He went around wearing an old-fashioned hood he had sewn from a cut-up pair of pants. He and I spent time together trying to remember the *Hundred Poems by a Hundred Poets,* and we held little haiku contests of sorts. He was one of the most sensible and temperate men I met while a POW.

I would have assumed that the only reason for his inclusion among the alleged war criminals was that he had the same surname as someone else. I happened to be talking with him when he received the notice, however, and I remember well the awkward look that came over his face.

Among the principal duties of shipping engineers was the operation of motor launches for short-haul transport of men and equipment. Zigzagging back and forth among some three thousand Philippine islands, the engineers displayed a propensity to engage in acts of piracy at their various destinations because they knew they would never be back. Toward the end of the war, they also engaged in trade, taking advantage of disparities in the cost of goods from one island to another. Most of the engineer noncoms were moving commodities worth several thousand pesos.

I would like to believe that Furuta did not engage in acts of piracy, but there can be no telling what kind of incidents he might have been dragged into because of the men he was with. At any rate, the expression that crossed his face when he received the notice seemed clearly to state: "Guilty." Precisely because he was such a decent fellow, he could not hide his true feelings.

"I can say with good conscience that I have done nothing wrong," he declared.

"Of course, of course. They're holding people back just because some woman or kid vaguely recalls their name, so I'm sure you'll be cleared with just a simple lineup."

"But what if one of those women who can't really remember decides to say it was me?"

I had no further words of comfort to offer. In war there are times when your deeds may be judged criminal even if you have done nothing that weighs on your conscience, but I could not very well say this to him.

Approximately five hundred men learned they would have to remain behind. Most returned home safely between three months and a year later. I pray Furuta was among them.

———

The day finally arrived. On November 17, 1945, we left behind the nipa huts we had made our homes for half a year—huts we had built with our own hands while the war was still in progress. At the time, a groundless rumor made the rounds that we were actually being tricked into building barracks for Filipino troops, and one of the companies had gone so far as to deliberately delay construction. In retrospect it all seemed rather silly.

The accused war criminals stayed behind in those nipa huts built by the old-timers. They eventually had to move to a camp on the coast because of pressure from guerrillas who liked the Americans no better than they had liked the Japanese.

The rest of us heaved U.S. Army duffle bags onto shoulders clad in U.S. Army fatigues exactly like those the GIs wore. The only differences were that we carried no weapons and we had the letters PW stamped on our backs.

"Good-bye. Good-bye."

We marched off down Main Street shouting our farewells to the accused war criminals, who stood under the eaves of the nipa huts waving at us.

"Good-bye. Good-bye."

They were not what you could call heartfelt farewells. We were simply cutting forever our ties with the clay and gravel and palm trees of that prison camp—that was all. We felt sorry for those who had to stay behind, but parting was inevitable in any case.

A swallow streaked low over our marching column, flying far to the rear, then quickly reversing course and streaking back toward the front. His companions darted busily back and forth in the wide open sky overhead. Perhaps some of them had only that moment arrived from Japan, the homeland for which we were departing.

We marched out the gate and into Camp 2 across the road. Camp 1 had been completely flat, but here there were valleys and streams. The tents scattered handsomely about on knolls and in hollows brought to mind the campus of a suburban school or hospital. In fact, one fenced-off section of the compound did house a POW hospital—the one where the Japanese nurses worked.

My platoon was led to a tent pitched in a small hollow. The nearby tents were all populated with soldiers who had been disarmed after the end of the war. Many of them still showed the effects of privation in the mountains.

Their eyes were lifeless and dull. For them everything had happened too quickly, and they had not yet had time to mentally adapt to the new circumstances and overcome the shock of defeat. We had been more fortunate, I decided, because being captured during the war had given us ample time to prepare ourselves psychologically for the end.

These men still maintained the hierarchical structure of their units in the Imperial Army. The cessation of hostilities should have made this structure meaningless, but perhaps its persistence was inevitable so long as the soldiers continued to live together as a group. The subordinates assumed so and acquiesced; the superiors tenaciously clung to their prerogatives of rank by admonishing their men, "Just because we have lost the war doesn't mean you can forget your Japanese spirit."

Here, too, the cooks appeared well fed. Since we had sated our appetites with plentiful rations every day for six months, we asked only for enough food to assuage our immediate hunger, and this particularly pleased the cooks.

"You old-timers are so polite," they would say, as they stirred the leftover stew. "This'll help the sick to regain their strength."

We knew very well, however, that they actually divided the leftovers amongst themselves to further augment the meat on their own bones.

The latrines were filthy. When it rained, the drop-pits overflowed and excrement mixed with the mud all around. We who had become prisoners early had had both the time and the energy to build proper facilities, but the new prisoners, still dazed by surrender, lacked the will to make their surroundings better.

We finally received the wages that had been accumulating on account for each day we worked. Amounts in excess of ¥200, the maximum amount we were permitted to carry with us into Japan, were issued in the form of a bank bill or payment order (I do not recall the exact name) made out to the Bank of Japan. The American camp office had apparently labored around the clock for three full days calculating each man's earnings, but even so, a host of errors resulted in highly inequitable payments.

The prisoners lined up single file to receive their pay. This money was for each of us to use in whatever manner we chose, and receiving it transformed us from mere members of a group into independent individuals. The paymaster, who reminded me of Kaiser Wilhelm II, sent us on our way with a jaunty laugh.

We remained in Camp 2 for five days. During that time, a succession of couriers came to escort newly accused war crime suspects back to Camp 1. Naturally enough, it made us all very nervous. Some men were pulled from line to remain behind even after we had assembled at the main gate for transportation to the coast, so our anxiety did not ultimately abate until our ship was actually under way.

A wooden fence lined one side of the camp driveway, and on the other side, we knew, was the hospital where the Japanese nurses worked. Each knothole in the fence soon had a POW peering through it. I found one, too. They were there, all right. In the shade of a small tent directly ahead, two Japanese women wearing WAC uniforms sat talking in low voices.

"Cripes, just look at them sitting there putting on airs," one of the men said loud enough for the nurses to hear.

I suppose they were indeed "putting on airs"—the way they nonchalantly went on with their conversation right in front of a fence where curious eyes filled every knothole. We started pounding on the fence. They quickly rose to their feet and disappeared from sight.

A GI came running. "You fucking something-or-other," he shouted, waving his fist about and showing some of the men what his boot felt like. We scrambled to get back into our lines. Oh, well, so what's a little kick. They weren't very likely to take us off the repatriation list just for teasing some Japanese nurses. At this point, all that mattered was getting home.

Finally—it must have been nearly one o'clock by then—the gate opened. Our transport party of roughly a thousand men dispersed among the trucks lined up in front of the gate and leapt aboard from all sides. This method of mounting U.S. Army trucks had become a trademark of the prisoners.

The convoy moved out and drove along the road skirting the foot of Cross Mountain. The flatlands along this road had sprouted several more prison camps in the last few months. One of them held the other transport party from Camp 1, apparently still waiting for their ship to arrive. I spotted Hirota, the right-wing radical, waving at us. Also Akiyama, the clerk from Company 3. They all waved their hands high over their heads, around and around. Whadda ya know! Those guys have been cooling their heels right here, too.

This was the last time I would see the dilapidated Filipino houses next to the muddy river, or the women doing their laundry. The church in Palo remained unchanged, its rectangular, cream-colored walls splattered with mud. Barefoot residents in wide-brimmed hats came and went. Now that the war was over, they no longer jeered at us. In fact, we were the ones to hail them with raised arms.

The bell was ringing in the tower at the front of the church. It must have been a Sunday.

I do not remember any of the scenery along the road after that. My next recollection is of sitting on the beach in Tacloban, waiting to board our ship. They had told us to expect a final inspection of our belongings here, but the harbor sergeant who took charge of us from the camp sergeant apparently did not think it worth the trouble. All he cared about was getting his bothersome cargo of prisoners loaded onto their ship as quickly as possible so he could turn responsibility for them over to the ship's captain.

Clouds hung low over the ocean. Even without the light of the sun, the sky-blue hulls of American military vessels stood out brightly on the water. An array of black-hulled ships lay beyond them, farther out in the bay. Which one would be ours?

After a time we were led by way of a small pier to a barge perhaps sixty feet square. By sitting on top of our duffels, we all managed to squeeze onto the barge without an inch to spare. A tugboat that looked barely six feet long approached and moored itself to us, then slowly began pulling us away from shore.

The waves were calm. Islanders quietly maneuvered their banca outriggers across the water. An American seaman in a vibrant blue uniform crossed our path on a motor launch. We raised our arms in greeting, but his wave seemed more like a brush-off as he sped by. Having grown accustomed to Americans being friendly to us as part of their job at the prison camp, we had forgotten that they ultimately saw us as extensions of the "Japs" who attacked Pearl Harbor.

As the barge moved out into the bay, fewer and fewer craft surrounded us. We tried to guess which ship was ours from the tugboat's heading. Two Filipinos were handling the tug, and I decided to try asking them in English.

"Dat, over dere," one of them said, pointing to a ship not far away. Their native tongue has no *th* sound.

Of the ships out in this part of the bay, it obviously was not one of the nicer vessels. Having envisioned a Liberty ship, we felt a trifle disappointed.

As we slowly drew closer, we could finally see the flag waving at its stern: a wind-soiled white flag with red in the middle.

When a starving soldier on Okinawa picked up a leaflet urging surrender, he apparently did not recognize at first what the blotches of red and yellow printed on the page represented. He said it took him an hour to realize that the red was a slice of raw tuna and the yellow a slice of sweet omelet—in other words, that he was looking at a picture of sushi.

My reaction to the Japanese flag I saw at the stern of my repatriation ship was something like that.

The "red on white" standard—ten months after becoming a POW, neither I nor anyone else had expected to see this flag flying again under Philippine skies.

A murmur of amazement passed among the men packed tightly on the barge.

"Hey, it's a Japanese flag!"

"It's from Japan! It's a Japanese ship!"

Then someone said, "Cripes! Does this mean we get to be silkworms again?" and everyone burst out laughing.

Now we could see the name painted on the stern: *Shinano-maru.*

The name seemed familiar somehow. Where had we heard it before? Only after we were aboard did we realize it was the famous *Shinano-maru* from the Russo-Japanese war—the ship that had first spotted the Russian fleet and radioed "Enemy fleet sighted" on the eve of the decisive sea battle in Tsushima Strait.

This former hero of Tsushima was one of two Japanese vessels pressed into service as repatriation ships. Nichiro Fisheries had turned it into a salmon cannery boat some time ago, and it had continued to serve in that capacity throughout the hostilities, escaping destruction at the end of the war by virtue of being in the Sea of Japan. It had already transported one load of POWs home from the Kurils, and this was its second such mission—the first time a Japanese repatriation ship had descended into southern waters.

The figures of the men lined up on deck watching us approach gradually grew more distinct. They wore tattered old Imperial Army uniforms and looked pitifully emaciated. We presently learned they were men who had surrendered on Mindanao. The wretchedness of their condition shocked and saddened us, but on their part, too, the sight of a sixty-foot-square barge crammed full of Japanese men dressed sharply in U.S. Army fatigues and caps must have had quite a jarring effect.

It took a long time for us all to file up the stairs that clung to the side of the ship, lugging our heavy duffels. I suspected that the tugboat operators would probably be the last Filipinos I saw.

"What do you think of the Japanese people?" I asked.

"Some Japanese are good, and some are bad," the fortyish helmsman answered. He looked to be of mixed blood. I was grateful that a man who knew about the atrocities committed in Manila and Bataan would say this.

"You people are all good," I said ingratiatingly as I waved good-bye.

———

We lined up on deck, and the headman of the Mindanao group came to take roll.

"Attention! Right dress! Count off!"

His commands were crisp, but his appearance far from it—he wore some odd-looking, brown civilian clothes and a scraggly beard. We recognized right away that this man was an old-timer. Living so long in a POW camp might have dulled our senses in other respects, but one thing we could tell immediately was whether a man had been taken prisoner during the war or only after Japan's surrender. We could tell it from the rhythms of his speech and the characteristic little smile that came to his cheeks. We could smell the old-timer in him, so to speak.

The Mindanao party was assigned to the afterdeck, our party to the foredeck. To no one's surprise, we found the hold filled with what we sarcastically referred to as "silkworm shelves"—only this time, unlike on our way out, we were to sleep three instead of fifteen to a six-foot-square shelf, so we would be able to spread our blankets and stretch out much more comfortably. Wishing to get as many of us home as quickly as possible, the ship's captain had apparently declared a capacity of five thousand, but the Americans had limited him to two thousand. We were grateful.

The evening meal included a special treat: miso soup. Although the broth was weak and it had only a single piece of gluten puff floating in it, it was the closest thing to home cooking I had had in almost two years, and I savored it with delight. We received *Kinshi* cigarettes at the rate of three per day for the expected ten-day passage. I had not smoked a Japanese cigarette in nearly a year. One of the crew brought out a portable gramophone. The only music we had heard at the prison camp came from male voices and a crude guitar fashioned out of some boards and wire. We now listened raptly to "The Ballad of Nagasaki" sung by a wondrous female voice and accompanied by complex harmonies.

Our ration of rice was two cups a day, the same as for civilians back home. Since this alone could not possibly satisfy the needs even of the best-fed prisoners, the Americans had provided C rations as a supplement—one and a half cases per person, or enough for forty-five meals. These became a source of friction between the Mindanao and Leyte contingents.

The Mindanao party had arrived on board first, and the three or four men serving as their leaders had ensconced themselves comfortably in a stateroom at the back of the bridge, while the leaders of our Leyte group had to bunk with everyone else on the silkworm shelves. The Leyte brass were already disgruntled about this when they discovered that the Mindanao brass had intervened in the distribution of the C rations.

Since each man was supposed to get a case and a half, many of the cases had to be broken open and divided up. In the process, the Mindanao men had helped themselves to the thirty cigarettes that came in each box.

By the time the Leyte brass realized what had happened and went storming into the Mindanao stateroom to protest, it was too late.

"If there was a problem, you should've said something right away. We smoked them already."

"Don't give us that crap! Give 'em back!"

"Look, if you've been brass for very long, you know as well as we do how these things work, so stop being such boobs. You guys obviously enjoyed much better conditions than we did, and I'll bet you've got plenty of cigarettes stashed away anyway."

"What we may or may not have stashed away is none of your business. If it were only us, we could let it pass, but everyone knows about it. You're making us lose face with our men."

The ship's captain agreed to save face for them by issuing an additional thirty *Kinshi* to each of the Leyte men.

I also witnessed one of the ship's crewmen hauling a box of C rations into the crew lounge in the bow. These rations had been provided by the Americans for the exact number of POWs on board, and there should have been no extras, so I knew something fishy was going on.

"A lot of mysterious things happen on ships," a former seaman told me. "There's really nothing anyone can do about it."

Having already grown tired of C rations at the camp, we in the Leyte group did not rush to break them open. We figured we would eat just one set a day between our morning and evening allotments of rice. The rice tended to be skimpy, though, and we wound up opening more and more. Some of the men had counted on having some of the rations left over to take home with them, and they complained about the meager servings of rice. They charged the crew with holding rice back for themselves.

Some claimed the crew were doing even better for themselves than that, holding back miso and dried herring as well, and who knew what else.

My own advice was to just forget it. We had escaped with our lives and were now on our way home. The trip would last only ten days. It hardly mattered what the crew did so long as we had enough food to sustain us during those ten days. But it is apparently human nature to be bothered by others' gains regardless of whether those gains result in any actual harm to oneself.

The illustrious *Shinano-maru* though it was, boarding a Japanese ship meant being buffeted that much sooner by the winds of the real world back home in Japan.

With our arrival on board, the ship had reached capacity. Everyone was anxious to be under way, but the ship remained at rest. On the third day we finally weighed anchor, and soon both the Tacloban coast and the dome of Cross Mountain far beyond disappeared from view. We presently halted again, however, off the coast of what must have been Samar Island. They told us we had to wait there for water.

A mountain lush with vegetation thrust nearly straight up from the shoreline, and a thin white waterfall stood out high on its side. When I thought of it as my last chance to enjoy the soft beauty of the verdant Philippine landscape, a powerful wave of nostalgia came over me. By the time we had remained at rest there for several days, however, I grew tired of seeing the same scenery day after day.

The water did not come and it did not come. Instead, six large wooden boxes were loaded onto the foredeck. We learned that they were life rafts— not exactly the sort of thing to inspire confidence.

Though we had left the camp first, being on a Japanese vessel meant we received low priority for drawing water, and now it appeared a Liberty ship bearing the other transport party would pass us by. We began to wish we could have remained in American hands all the way back to Japan.

The Liberty ship approached, its deck jammed with Japanese men wearing nothing but green boxer shorts. The shorts confirmed that they were from Leyte, but as we were unable to make out any of their faces, we just waved our arms high over our heads while they did the same. The ship circled us once as if to mock our lack of motion and then headed out to sea. Ruefully, we watched it go.

I felt a little better when I found out afterward that the Liberty ship had called at a port in Okinawa to off-load some cargo and reached Uraga only one day before our own nonstop voyage brought us into Hakata. I also learned, however, that those disembarking in Uraga had been permitted to keep every article of their U.S. Army–issue clothing. In Hakata, much to our chagrin in light of the severe clothing shortage at the time, we had had to return it all.

At long last the water came. A launch that looked like nothing more than a water tank made seaworthy moored itself sideways to the stern of our ship and started pumping. We set sail in the evening on the next day—November 30, I believe. As we got under way, the captain did not yet know our destination port; he was to receive his orders by radio en route.

A seaman from a destroyer warned us, "It's pretty calm around here, but the northerly winds on the seas near Japan can be really rough in November."

The ship began to rock almost immediately, however. We were sailing into a head wind and continued to pitch and toss all night long. The *Shinano-maru*'s top speed was twelve knots, but her cruising speed was supposed to be only eight knots. With such a strong head wind, I doubted we could actually be making much progress. Again, the situation did not inspire confidence.

Clouds still filled the sky the next morning, but the waves had subsided. Though we were steaming northward on a course east of Luzon, no land ever came into sight—only the blue-black surface of the ocean as far as the eye could see.

A wire hung from a pole that extended from the port side of the bridge, reaching down to the water near the stern. A round disk spun around and around at the point where the wire was attached to the pole. It was the ship's speedometer, I learned. Even to a man as ignorant of ships and sailing as myself, it seemed an exceedingly primitive contraption. This did not inspire confidence, either.

The men roamed about the decks in twos and threes. Many from the Mindanao group joined us on the foredeck where there was more breeze. It was painful to look at their emaciated limbs. Three of their number were quite sick. They had originally been scheduled to go ashore at Tacloban for treatment in the hospital there, but for some reason the plans had changed and they were being sent straight back to Japan.

A brass plate on the bridge-front bulkhead bore in English the date of *Shinano-maru*'s completion. It had been built in 1900 at a shipyard in England. That made it nine years older than I was. I prayed that the vessel would not break up from the force of the rough seas near Japan.

On the bridge above this brass plate stood the captain, gazing steadily out over the bow. I guessed from his graying hair that he must be close to fifty. This affable gentleman had been the ship's captain ever since it was a cannery boat. He preferred to stay out of quarrels between the crew and prisoners but came asking to see the copies of *Time* and *Life* that some of us had brought with us. Less than four months had passed since Japan's defeat, and he said he was grateful for the chance to find out what had really happened in the war's final stages.

In the hold the men gambled at *kabu*, this time betting not cigarettes but the cash they had received just before our departure. During the ten-day span of our passage, there emerged a number of penniless paupers as well as a number of wealthy magnates.

Much of the time the prisoners simply talked. Once again they exchanged stories about how they came to be captured. At the camp I had had relatively little interest in such stories. They all covered essentially the same ground: the overwhelming superiority of American combat troops and ordnance; the lack of food on the Japanese side; and how refreshing the first cigarette after capture had tasted, or how delicious the first candy bar. Every story came out sounding pretty much the same.

Now, on the verge of farewells, however, I found myself very much wanting to hear the men's stories. I roved all around the silkworm shelves listening to men from each of the divisions give their accounts. Most of what I know now about the fighting on Leyte is information I obtained in the ship on my way home.

The men displayed exceedingly good spirits. The joy of knowing they would be reunited with their families in only a few short days tugged constantly at the corners of their mouths.

For several days I did nothing but gaze out across the water. One day an American destroyer appeared to starboard, bearing across our path. The *Shinano-maru* blasted its shrill whistle and came to a halt. Our captain was presumably in communication with the destroyer by radio, and we started up again just as it was crossing directly in front of us. All the while, the destroyer maintained a steady course; it eventually disappeared beyond the horizon to port.

Flying fish were our constant companions during the journey. Entire schools would leap into the air near the hull of the ship, always flying a little farther than I expected before dropping back into the water. A huge spindle-shaped fish at least six feet long, probably a tuna startled to see us, rose halfway out of the water on its tail about a hundred meters to port, then dropped back in and lifted itself again, over and over, always keeping one eye trained our way. It seemed he would follow us like that forever.

One day a plane flew overhead, approaching from behind and passing low to starboard, then reversing course and passing to port. The men on deck cheered and waved, but the American pilot gazed ahead as stiff as a mannequin as he flew by. We guessed he had come from a base on Okinawa.

The air felt cooler now, and the men began layering their summer clothes to keep warm.

Two of the three sick men in the Mindanao group died. They were to be buried at sea, and a notice went round asking their brothers in arms to gather on the afterdeck.

It did indeed seem a pity that these men had died just three days before reaching their homeland. Strictly speaking, however, their deaths were no more unfortunate than those who had died long before in combat. I could easily have died myself. I brought back from the battlefield a chilly lack of sympathy for anyone who died for the same reason I might have died.

One should not attend a funeral if one brings no feelings of sympathy. The curiosity seeker in me insisted I should not miss this once-in-a-lifetime chance to witness a burial at sea, yet the realities of the war had turned me into an inhuman wretch who had no pity for the dead. When I considered the feelings that arose from this darker side of my heart, it simply did not seem right for me to attend out of mere curiosity. In the end I decided to do what seemed most right to me at the time—which is to say, remain in the hold.

After a time, the ship blew its whistle and gently began to turn. We were apparently tracing a circle around the spot where the bodies had been released into the ocean. The patch of sky and clouds visible through the hatch slowly spun around. Then, after a higher and longer than normal blast from the ship's whistle, we started forward again.

I emerged onto the deck. The corpses had apparently gone right under, leaving no trace on the surface. Night was falling. To the south rose towers of cumulonimbus clouds illumined from the West by the setting sun, stretching on and on as though they were a massive spit of land. To the north, layers of gray stratus clouds extended over a string of tiny islands floating dimly on the water like something out of an ink painting—apparently part of the Ryukyu chain. I could feel the cold winds of December blowing beneath those clouds.

As always, scores of prisoners wandered vacantly about the deck.

Bearing a cargo of two thousand POWs, each carrying with him his own personal joy or indifference, the repatriation ship *Shinano-maru* steamed ever closer to Japan at a speed of eight knots.

Nishiya Company Chronicle

Philippine Expeditionary Force, Unit 10672, Nishiya Company (official designation: 359th Independent Infantry Battalion Provisional Infantry Company 1) was formally organized on July 25, 1944, at Batangas in southern Luzon. The company comprised a unit of the transport battalion formed at the Eastern District Army Third Command (Konoe Infantry Second Regiment) in Daikan-chō, Kōjimachi, Tokyo, on June 13, 1944. With the exception of twelve men reassigned to other units or hospitalized while we were at Batangas, the transport company proceeded intact to its station on Mindoro.

Commanding officer First Lieutenant Nishiya Masao and the unit's other commissioned and noncommissioned officers, all from Tokyo and surrounding prefectures, had been summoned in an emergency call-up. The enlisted men consisted of reservists who had received their training under the Eastern District Army Second Command (Konoe Infantry First Regiment) between March 18 and June 10, 1944. I was one of the enlisted men.

Departing Shinagawa by train at 3:00 P.M. on June 17, we arrived in Moji on the morning of June 18, where we were billeted in private homes within the city until boarding our transport ship, No. 2 *Tamatsu-maru*, on June 28. The convoy of nine ships, including four destroyers as escort, steamed out of port on the evening of July 2. We headed southward in a straight line through the East China Sea.

Near Okinawa, we learned of the enemy landing on Saipan.

On the morning of July 9, the mountains of Taiwan came into view. The convoy made way along the island's eastern coast until midday, when off on the horizon, one of the escort ships suddenly began dropping depth charges. We circled back northward and entered the port of Chilung that evening. The next day we resumed our southward journey, this time along the western coast, and when we awoke the third day, Taiwan was no longer in sight. The tall waves told us we had reached the Bashi Channel.

At 6:20 P.M. on July 12, black smoke rose from the stern of the *Nichiran-maru*, the vessel sailing behind us. All aboard prepared to abandon ship. As conflicting rumors flew about—"It was an onboard fire, not a torpedo"; "No, they radioed that they had taken a hit in the stern but could still make way"—the *Nichiran* and one other ship gradually fell behind. Then several minutes later the *Nichiran* suddenly thrust its bow high in the air and, in a matter of moments, disappeared under the sea. The ship had been torpedoed by the American submarine *Piranha*. Fewer than one thousand survived—barely one-sixth of the men on board.

Fortunately, the *Nichiran* was our only loss, and we reached Aparri on the northern coast of Luzon by evening. The wet season was upon the Philippines, and a steady rain put a chill in the air. We lay in port overnight, waiting for a ship to arrive for the survivors of the *Nichiran*. We sailed again in the morning.

Luzon's volcanic peaks towered above us. A verdant range of coastal mountains and a series of white lighthouses remained constantly within sight to port. We arrived in Manila before dawn on July 15, the city aglow with lights that had not been blacked out. A crimson sunrise soon greeted us.

The transport battalion was billeted at Alberto School on the outskirts of the city. We cooked with our mess kits in the school yard. Outside the fence, a throng of Filipino children held up bananas, mangoes, candy, and such, shouting "Change. Change." We had received no liberty, nor had we been issued any military scrip. Most of the men "changed" personal items in barter.

My company and one other from the transport group were assigned to the Ōyabu Battalion (official designation: 359th Independent Infantry Battalion) of the 105th Army Division (Lieutenant General Tsuda Yoshitake, commander), at that time occupying the southern portion of Luzon. We were charged with policing the island of Mindoro. On July 22, a convoy of trucks took us to Ōyabu Battalion Headquarters in the southwestern Luzon port town of Batangas. We were to cross over to Mindoro from there.

Until earlier that month, the battalion had been headquartered in an advanced position at the northern Mindoro town of Calapan, but as a step toward strengthening defenses on Luzon, it had drawn back to Batangas in conjunction with our arrival.

The men in our transport battalion had originally been scheduled to police Manila and its environs as reinforcements for the Watari Group of the Fourteenth Army. However, the command center in Manila disagreed with the General Staff in Tokyo on the matter (to put it more bluntly, they reportedly declared they had no use for minimally trained and poorly outfitted men like us), and though we had arrived to take up our assignment, they had no intention of using us locally as per the original plan. Instead, they sent us to patrol an outlying area without even issuing us the additional arms and ammunition we would need.

We gained one benefit from this mix-up, however. We had to answer only to officers (no warrant officers) and NCOs (no sergeant majors), and we were spared the trauma of abusive PFCs lording it over us at the squad level. Once we had reached our station, the NCOs lived in separate quarters, so within our squads we were all equal.

In addition, our company CO proved to be quite lenient in his training policies (even after reaching the front, we officially remained in training). Rarely did anyone get slapped, and exercises were never unreasonably grueling.

Two-thirds of our number were thirty-four- and thirty-five-year-old reservists originally drafted in 1932, and one-third were twenty-one-year-old reservists drafted in 1943, all only recently called into active duty. First Lieutenant Nishiya, the company CO, was a man of twenty-six from the town of Katsunuma in Yamanashi Prefecture. He had received his commission after graduating from the reserve officer training course and had seen action at Nomonhan on the continent. The noncoms were reservists as well, but all had seen action on the Chinese front. The three second lieutenants serving as platoon leaders were older men who had enlisted back in the 1920s and had risen through the ranks, and they were our only superiors who had never experienced combat.

At Batangas we saw the results of bombardments by Japanese artillery early in the war, and we discerned hostility in the eyes of the local population. For about one week, we remained billeted at the official residence of the chief of security police, conducting exercises. Between July 28 and 30, each of our three platoons was transported by small motor launch (a fishing vessel from back home that had been pressed into service here along with its crew) to separate stations on Mindoro.

The island of Mindoro is situated southwest of the island of Luzon. About 150 kilometers long and 70 kilometers across at its widest point, the island covers an area approximately half the size of our Shikoku. In essence, the mountain range running from the Lingayen Gulf to the Bataan Peninsula on Luzon drops into the sea at the mouth of Manila Bay and rises up again about 150 kilometers farther south at the northwest tip of Mindoro. The main range continues southwest from there to the Calamian Islands and Palawan, and then on to Borneo, thus forming a platform along the eastern edge of the South China Sea. A branch pointing south-southeast reaches a height of two thousand meters above sea level in the central mountain range that forms Mindoro's backbone. The eastern lowlands receive large amounts of rainfall and produce both rice and corn. The area around Calapan in the north produces copra, and the mountainous southern regions produce timber.

Nishiya Company was to patrol the west and the south. The company command post was located with our third platoon (Second Lieutenant Inoue Noboru, commander) in the town of San Jose, a short distance inland along the southwestern coast; our first platoon (Second Lieutenant Tanaka Tai'ichirō,[1] commander) was stationed at Bulalacao in the southeast; and our second platoon (Second Lieutenant Watanabe Masaru, commander) was stationed at Paluan in the northwest. Shiono Company (Provisional Infantry Company 2) was to patrol the remainder of the island as well as the island of Lubang sitting astride the entrance to the Verde Island Passage that separated Mindoro from Luzon. The Shiono command post was located along with that company's third platoon at the northern Mindoro town of Calapan; their second platoon was stationed at Pinamalayan, halfway down the eastern coast (with one squad posted at Bongabong still farther south); and their first platoon was stationed on Lubang.

We each carried a Model 38 infantry rifle and 180 rounds of ammunition brought with us from Japan. In Batangas we were issued a captured heavy machine gun, but with its front sight bent askew it was mostly a showpiece. Furthermore, since we received only this single gun for the entire company, the platoons stationed away from the company command post had no rapid-fire weapons at all. In Nishiya Company, we later salvaged some flexible machine guns from a plane that had crash-landed near San Jose, and we fashioned wooden stocks for them so that all three platoons could finally have a machine gun. Not until November did the troops each receive a single hand grenade.

Company staff and our third platoon, including myself, arrived in San Jose on the night of July 30. We came ashore at a fishing village called Caminawit, ten kilometers south of San Jose at the mouth of Mangarin Bay, and proceeded the rest of the way by railcar.

The town of San Jose was situated on the northern edge of a small plain. The population of seven hundred consisted mostly of men from Luzon and the Visayan Islands who had come to work at a locally owned sugar mill. The town was divided into several districts—Central, Mindoro, Lubang, etc.—containing row upon row of identical tin-roofed wooden huts constructed by the sugar company. With operations halted due to the war, many of the huts were now empty, and the rest were occupied by old-time farmers from the area or by mill workers turned farmers.

A number of fancier houses with red roofs, also erected by the sugar

---

1 Called Second Lieutenant Yamada in chapter 6.

company, dotted the edge of the jungle on a hill overlooking the town, and the company owner and upper managers remained in residence there. They spent their days playing mah-jongg and seldom ventured out-of-doors. The lower classes found recreation in wagering on cockfights or cards.

The U.S. Army had built an emergency landing strip and radio tower at San Jose before the war and had posted a platoon there. The Imperial Army had dispatched an entire company to the site in the early stages of the war, but once public peace was restored, they withdrew all but a single platoon. That platoon's principal responsibility was to secure the emergency landing strip.

Besides this platoon, a unit of six meteorologists belonging to the Imperial Army Air Corps was stationed there, having requisitioned the mill owner's house. Nishiya Company depended on the weather unit's radio equipment and operators for communicating with battalion command at Batangas.

Until our arrival, a nine-man unit of the Division Signal Corps (Unit 10664), commanded by Sergeant Adachi Michito, had been attached to the San Jose garrison, but these men were now reassigned to Bulalacao. This move was intended to strengthen communications at the southern tip of Mindoro as the war situation grew more acute.

The platoon we were replacing departed on July 31, and we formally took up our duties on August 1. One squad was posted to Caminawit, which was our seaport, and detachments of seven men were billeted at islanders' homes in weekly shifts to keep watch on the wreckage of a plane that had crash-landed on the grasslands outside San Jose—so as to prevent the locals from stripping it of parts. This practice was later abandoned when the number of wrecks in the vicinity began to grow.

I was the company's code clerk. Once a day, at 7:00 P.M., I visited the weather unit to communicate with Batangas.

A grade school erected by the Americans served as our barracks. Our predecessors had built a raised platform about a foot high against one wall in each classroom. At night we spread our blankets on these large beds—a squad of twelve to fifteen men to a room. In our lamps we burned coconut oil.

On Mindoro the wet season runs roughly from June to October. It rained incessantly, day in and day out, making the early morning and late evening hours quite chilly.

In front of the barracks an open moor spread out about half a kilometer to the edge of the jungle. Beyond some foothills rose a craggy range we dubbed "Sawtooth Ridge," and at its back towered the island's central mountain range stretching northward.

With their snug cover of cogon grasses, the nearby hills presented a picture of soft, verdant green. The road running past the west side of the barracks was a typical palm tree–lined tropical thoroughfare, and in the evenings we watched beautiful sunsets over those palms.

Across the road spread cornfields. Formerly planted in cane for the sugar mill, they had now been converted to supply a staple of the local people's diet. There were two harvests a year, one of which we witnessed in December, when tractors rolled out of a barn at the mill.

In September, far in the distance on the other side of the cornfield, the eulalia grass put on its plumes and glistened in the sunlight. Beyond that flowed the Bugsanga River, which emerged from the mountains at the extreme northwestern end of Sawtooth Ridge and poured into the sea at San Agustin six kilometers west of San Jose. It was a muddy, rapid-flowing river about as wide as the middle reaches of the Tama River in Tokyo.

Fireflies climbed as high as the tops of the coconut palms at night. They also invaded our squad rooms and wove back and forth over our mosquito nets—large fireflies glowing intensely enough for their afterimages to describe full circles.

The mill still had a stock of some five thousand bags of sugar on hand, which it rationed out to the local residents. We soldiers, however, could buy any amount we wished at 40 centavos per kilogram. When we had liberty on Sundays, we took sugar with us to private homes nearby and traded it for chicken or pig, or had our hosts make sweet bean soup for us out of mung beans, a kind of green adzuki bean. Our pay was 21 pesos per month. Since 5 pesos automatically went into savings, our actual cash-in-hand was only 16 pesos, but because of our sugar privileges, we never ran short of pocket money. Our unrestricted buying privileges were eventually cut back, however, when a large order from the battalion in Batangas drastically reduced the mill's stocks.

Between rice and corn, we generally managed to get enough to fill our stomachs. Besides these staples, we received beef or pork once a week, as well as papayas and a local wild green similar to parsley called *kangkong*. Our official ration of tobacco was only two Japanese cigarettes per day, but our sugar privileges gave us access to an unlimited supply of hand-rolled smokes sold by the locals.

One could say, then, that our lives in San Jose were considerably easier than life back home in Japan. No one anticipated that the Americans would choose such a peripheral island as their next objective after Leyte.

For the moment, our only enemies were local insurgents. Commander Nishiya had received a detailed briefing on the activities of the island's guerrillas from his predecessor: their whereabouts, their strength, names and descriptions of their officers, and so forth. Trouble spots in the San Jose vicinity apparently included the area east of Mangarin Bay, the other side of the Bugsanga River, and the triangular area formed by San Jose, San

Agustin, and Caminawit. Our post in San Jose itself never came under attack, but someone or other was always stealing the windsocks we raised on a hill overlooking the airstrip.

Exterminating the guerrillas was outside the scope of our orders. The men took to the field for containment purposes only when activity was detected.

Our first antiguerrilla foray took place at the end of August, in the Mansalay area north of Bulalacao. Members of the Tanaka Platoon had been fired on while scouting the area to familiarize themselves with the terrain. On August 27, with First Lieutenant Nishiya personally in command, a detachment from our platoon bearing the company's heavy machine gun, together with a squad from the Tanaka Platoon, approached the area by sea. As it happened, however, the Mindoro guerrillas began fighting with some other guerrillas from the island of Panay, and both groups moved farther and farther north as they battled each other; the punitive expedition returned to our garrison on September 4 without ever having engaged the insurgents.

At the beginning of September, the Navy established a seaplane base at Caminawit with a ground crew of ninety-six men.

On September 21, the first enemy air raid on Manila temporarily interrupted communications.

On September 24, a large squadron of enemy planes passed over San Jose. A Japanese warship hit by aerial torpedoes sank near Ilin Island, and the company received a call for assistance in rescuing the crew, but in the end all were taken aboard other navy vessels.

At the end of September, I went to battalion HQ in Batangas for code training. The value of our military scrip had plummeted, and I observed that the local populace was growing increasingly restless. Although air-raid sirens sounded from time to time, no enemy planes actually appeared overhead.

About this time, the battalion ordered First Lieutenant Nishiya to take three squads (one of them drawn from the Watanabe Platoon in Paluan) on a guerrilla pacification mission to Sablayan, midway up the island's west coast. The force was attacked by guerrillas during the night and suffered four casualties, including one dead. I was still in Batangas at the time, waiting for a boat to take me back to my unit. I ultimately returned with the noncom who had accompanied the wounded men to the field hospital there.

On the return journey, the boat circled west of the island and sailed south along the coast, stopping at Sablayan to gather the remaining members of the expedition. After backtracking to Paluan to drop off the squad from the Watanabe Platoon, we attacked an American motor sailer anchored near shore at Santa Cruz and captured some U.S. Army documents, including a diagram of the U.S. intelligence network on Mindoro. These documents were subsequently forwarded to Batangas, and on October 13, First Lieutenant Nishiya received a special commendation from the newly appointed Area Commander, General Yamashita.

According to the captured documents, an American intelligence unit affiliated directly with the Southwest Pacific GHQ and commanded by a major had established itself on Mindoro, and it was compiling intelligence primarily in the form of photographs. Many of the unit members apparently suffered from malaria—the CO referred to his men as the "malaria squad."

The members of the expedition had in their custody the mayor of Sablayan and one of his clerks, taken prisoner on suspicion of having instigated the guerrilla attack. It was a few days into October when we arrived back in San Jose.

In the middle of October, Imperial Headquarters broadcast over the radio its account of a massive air battle that had taken place near Taiwan. I translated it into English and posted it in the town square, but none of the locals stopped to read it. When the Americans attacked Leyte, several days passed before a wireless message from Batangas belatedly informed us that three U.S Marine battalions had landed on Leyte.

Effective October 15, two-thirds of the privates were promoted to senior grade. Effective November 1, the remainder of the men were promoted as well.

On the night we held a talent show to celebrate the air battle near Taiwan, one of our two prisoners escaped. The talent show got under way at seven o'clock and lasted until eleven, and apparently during this time the prisoner—the mayor, aged twenty-five or twenty-six, a man of bold countenance—who had been bound and secured at the top of the school building's front steps, managed to loosen the bindings around his ankles. At about one in the morning, after everyone had fallen sound asleep, the prisoner muttered "Piss on you" and skittered lightly down the steps. Two guards stood in the hallway just inside the front entrance where he had been tied. One of them immediately started after him but tumbled down the stairs and only barely managed to get off a shot from a prone position as the fleeing prisoner ran for the back gate (an open, barrier-free gate) on the left-hand side of the forecourt. The guard's aim was much too high, and the shot flew toward the meteorologists' quarters, where it pierced the wall and lodged in the ceiling. The meteorologists thought they were under enemy attack. Meanwhile, the sentry standing guard at the main gate to the right had heard the commotion and dashed up the driveway in front of the school building toward the back gate, but he threw himself on the ground the moment the other guard's shot rang out. Thus, the prisoner was freed of any immediate pursuers.

One of the meteorologists secretly revealed to me afterward that they had seen the figure of a man hide behind a tree on the grounds. Because the circumstances were by no means clear to them, however, their CO judged it best to avoid any risks not related to their own express duties.

We quickly fanned out to conduct a search in the dark, and the search continued even after daybreak, but we failed to find the escaped prisoner. Commander Nishiya reported to battalion HQ that one of the prisoners had been shot to death while attempting to escape.

We tightened the bindings and our watch on the remaining prisoner. He cursed his colleague's escape, and apparently more relaxed now that he was alone, he began to divulge great quantities of new information. The commander extracted details about the American intelligence unit's bivouac location and then released him.

On November 1, the Ōyabu Battalion drew back to central Luzon, and although our company nominally remained under its wing, we now came under the direct command of the Ichimura Battalion in the Eighth Division's Fuji Group, which replaced the Ōyabu Battalion in the Batangas area. This battalion, newly arrived from the Soviet-Manchurian border, proved to be more generous with provisions and armaments (this was when we received hand grenades), but it was also much less communicative and we seldom received messages from Batangas anymore. According to plans made at the end of the previous month, before the Ōyabu Battalion's move, a major, battalion-scale search-and-destroy operation was to be mounted based on the information we had obtained at Santa Cruz, and our company was to lead the way. However, the Ichimura Battalion repeatedly pushed back the scheduled date—never once offering any explanations for the delays.

Commander Nishiya fretted impatiently over the postponements, but as we learned later, not only had the tide turned badly against our forces on Leyte, but the entire Fourteenth Area Army had been put on the defensive, making any search-and-destroy mission entirely out of the question. The Ichimura Battalion had its hands full fortifying defensive positions in the Batangas area.

The situation deteriorated on Mindoro as well. B-24s repeatedly strafed the seaplane base at Caminawit. Ten planes parked on the water were destroyed, and one sentry was killed. American twin-fuselage P38s began to appear overhead much more frequently.

In early November, guerrillas attacked troops traveling by railcar from San Jose to Caminawit and killed a young medic named Kobayashi. The incident occurred when an NCO and four privates were on their way to our company's Caminawit outpost bearing a message. The medic went along to see about obtaining some medical supplies from the naval unit there. At a small station en route, the car unexpectedly shunted from the main line onto a siding. The driver got out to investigate and discovered that a small rock had been wedged into the switch. Sensing danger, he spun around and saw a dozen or more guerrillas kneeling below the rail embankment with their rifles poised.

The medic, standing on the deck at the end of the car, was hit by several rounds and tumbled to the ground. The other men inside the car scrambled out the windows and fled in the direction of the outpost.

The driver alone flattened himself on the other side of the embankment and returned fire. The guerrillas did not emerge from their position. The wounded medic managed to drag himself to the driver's side and began instructing the driver how to administer first aid to him. Then he noticed he had soiled his pants.

"I'm done for," he said. "Stick around while I say my 'Long lives,' will you?" He called out "Long live the emperor" three times and then died.

The driver leapt up onto the tracks in uncontainable fury and screamed, "Come on out, you bastards! Let me give you a taste of your own medicine!" The guerrillas had already withdrawn, however, and the embankment remained quiet.

Alerted by a telephone call from the Caminawit detachment, Commander Nishiya rushed to the scene with almost the full strength of our garrison to search the area. In their absence, an informer appeared, warning us that a force of 150 guerrillas was making its way toward San Jose along the northern shore of Mangarin Bay. The ten of us left behind to guard the command center took up our usual defensive positions and remained on alert until nightfall, but no attack came. It was apparently a hoax perpetrated by the guerrillas and intended to divert strength from our main force. The troops in the field spent the night at our outpost in Caminawit and returned the following day after further attempts to ferret out the enemy proved fruitless.

Several days later, the guerrillas kidnapped a young woman from the town's Mindoro district who had often entertained Japanese noncoms.

Malaria gradually began to spread among us. On December 15, when the Americans landed, five men suffered from the fever, including myself.

The rainy season ended, the blazing sun beat down day after day, and sitings of American planes became quite regular. Every evening we saw B-24s flying low over the sea to the west. Observing this, a man whose cousin was a navy officer predicted that the Americans were planning a landing.

An American reconnaissance plane once flew low over our barracks in San Jose. It did not strafe us. Its objective was photo reconnaissance.

The paymaster, who had been away at Batangas, returned on December 11 or 12. The motor launch that brought him back was strafed by a B-24, wounding one soldier. Our paymaster had learned from the battalion adjutant that the situation on Leyte was now hopeless and that the Americans' next landing would most likely be at San Jose. The adjutant had also informed him that even in the event of a landing, the battalion would not be able to send troops to our aid, so we were to use our own discretion in determining our response.

Our paymaster brought back with him the first delivery of mail from home. It proved to be our last as well.

That same day, one of the men died of malaria. His body was cremated in the schoolyard behind the barracks overnight. At about 4:00 A.M., the men in charge saw an illumination shell explode out toward the coast. They maintained a vigilant watch against guerrilla attack.

December 15, 6:30 A.M.: As we ate breakfast in our squad rooms, the sound of big guns suddenly erupted from the direction of the coast, and a patchwork of black smoke filled the sky. A moment later came the scream of shells flying through the air, followed by clouds of dust rising from the cornfield outside the window.

"All troops take immediate cover in the jungle," came the command, but this order was quickly rescinded and replaced by a second: "Gather your gear, fill your mess kits with rice, and assemble in the jungle." The storeroom was thrown open for us to help ourselves to army boots or *jikatabi*.[2]

A noncom climbed up to the lookout on top of the sugar mill and counted some sixty American warships and transports on the sea to the southwest.

As we were about to take cover in the jungle, we observed two friendly planes fleeing to the northeast pursued by ack-ack fire.

After a time the naval bombardment came to an end. None of the shells had approached any closer than the first shell we had seen from the window. Caminawit was also under attack, and the commander of the medical corps there called to say they intended to seek cover in the hills to the north. Then the line went dead.

The fifty-one men of the San Jose garrison, six meteorologists, and four resident Japanese civilians began marching northeast toward Sawtooth Ridge. The time was probably about 9:00 A.M.

After marching northward for a time along the Bugsanga River, we cut eastward and emerged into a valley filled with huge fields of grass. The fields had been freshly burned and a brisk breeze blew the lingering smoke along the ground. Gazing up at the jagged form of Sawtooth Ridge before us, we marched through the open valley for the rest of the day, and finally, as darkness was closing in, we came to an isolated hamlet at the foot of the mountain. We spent the night there keeping a close watch for guerrillas.

The next morning, Commander Nishiya assembled the troops and an-

2 A split-toed sock with a sturdy, high-traction rubber sole melded to the bottom.

nounced his decision. We would make our way through the mountains to Bulalacao on the east coast, where we would rendezvous with the Tanaka Platoon and jointly consider our next plans. He cautioned, however, that we had only a two-day supply of food with us and that the Americans might have come ashore at Bulalacao as well.

The weather unit's equipment would be too cumbersome to transport over the mountain, so they decided to incinerate it there. I sent a final report to our battalion HQ by way of the Army Air Corps Command Center at Lipa. I can still recall the bulk of the message:

"At 0600 hours on December 15, enemy troops from sixty-warship fleet offshore commenced landing at San Agustin, six kilometers west of San Jose. Nishiya Company now marching through mountains toward Bulalacao. Will rendezvous with Tanaka unit and plan subsequent action. Present location ten kilometers north of San Jose. Morale exceedingly high; entire company vows annihilation of enemy."

We moved out behind two local men we had brought with us from San Jose to act as our guides. I continued to suffer from malaria and, along with four other ailing troops, had been placed in the charge of a noncom. We marched six kilometers eastward along the Sawtooth range, then began ascending an adjacent ridge through dense jungle. Rain fell in the evening. We found a mountain hut and camped there for the night.

We continued our uphill march the following morning, December 17. On the way, we passed through sugar fields belonging to highland tribesmen known as Mangyans, and we cut some canes to chew on. It had an unforgettable sweetness.

The mountain crest was grassy and offered a spectacular view. Sawtooth Ridge now lay below us, and far in the distance we could see Caminawit and the smooth water of Mangarin Bay, crisscrossed by the wakes of speeding enemy launches.

We descended along a spur that stretched eastward, buffeted by strong winds. Some Mangyan tribesmen led the way. At dusk we came upon a small stream twisting through a canyon and made camp beside it. The column had made it through the longest leg of our four-day march without losing a man. Our supply of food from San Jose was now exhausted, but we had harvested some green bananas along the way in preparation for breakfast the next morning.

December 18: We continued our descent and came to a river that flowed out of the mountains west of Mansalay and emptied into Mangarin Bay. After walking upstream along the right bank for a time, we crossed over to the left bank and made our way up a long grassy ridge. Our guides informed us that this was Rutay Ridge, the last we would have to traverse on our way to the east coast. At noon, from the ridge's highest crest, we gazed down upon Bulalacao Bay far in the distance and saw no sign of enemy ships.

An advance party returned to report that they had made contact with men from the Tanaka unit. Even though there had been no enemy landing at Bulalacao, the platoon had heard the blasting at San Jose and had decided to take refuge in the mountains preemptively, bringing with them an ample supply of food as well as their communications equipment. They had taken shelter in a Mangyan hamlet not far ahead.

Arrival; exchange of greetings; rest.

We radioed battalion HQ that evening and received orders to maintain a watch on enemy activity at San Jose, as well as to obstruct any operations.

Commander Nishiya paid the men who had guided us from San Jose with rice and sent them home.

We had descended a short distance farther east from the summit of Rutay Ridge to a spot where the ridge split into three spurs and formed a small tableland. On this small plateau stood four Mangyan huts with about twenty highlanders living in them.

These people belonged to a different tribe and were darker-skinned than the Tagalog people who inhabited the coastal areas. They remained indifferent to the war. Commander Nishiya presented them with some bolts of cloth, plunder given him at Batangas for potential use in placating the locals, in exchange for the right to harvest food from their fields. After a few days, the tribespeople chose to move to another location.

The Tanaka Platoon had brought along enough rice and miso to sustain us all for three months, and we supplemented this by harvesting bananas and potatoes from the Mangyan fields. On occasion, hunting parties went down the mountain and shot free-roaming carabaos for meat.

We established separate quarters squad by squad. Squads that did not get Mangyan huts built crude structures of bamboo and topped them with thatched roofs. Fortunately we had now entered the dry season and there was little rain. So long as the huts sheltered us from the nighttime dew, their primitiveness brought us no particular discomfort.

The personnel assembled at this location were roughly as follows: company command plus Inoue Platoon, 61; Tanaka Platoon, 45; signal unit, 12; San Jose weather unit, 6; shipping engineers, including First Lieutenant Kakizaki, 23; noncombatants, 16 (San Jose, 4; Bulalacao, 12). Total: 163.

Bulalacao was a town of approximately three hundred situated on the coast ten kilometers to the southeast. The residents were occupied mainly in fishery and animal husbandry. Six kilometers inland at Iraya, the Chilung Coal Company (an affiliate of Mitsui Mining) had established a mine in response to the Imperial Army's call for development of resources in the southern territories, and it had just recently begun to produce, but the workforce comprised only seven office staff and fifteen Taiwanese miners. The mine had a single inclined shaft, sloped at forty degrees. Operating under a highly primitive arrangement in which harnessed carabaos winched up the coal wagons, the mine's daily output apparently never surpassed three tons. The coal was lignite. Mine Director Kōno Moriyoshi, together with Shimamura Tetsuo, Asada Goichi, and nine others, had just arrived there on October 25, replacing the previous staff scheduled to take up new posts at a Mitsubishi mining station on November 1.

The Tanaka Platoon's foremost duty was to ensure the security of this mine. The platoon command post had been set up in the mine barracks, while one squad billeted in the Bulalacao town hall to facilitate communication by sea.

On the eve of the American landing at San Jose, the Tanaka Platoon had received word from Batangas that an enemy task force was steaming northward at full speed off the western coast of Negros. (We in San Jose failed to receive this message because the weather unit's radio equipment broke down that day.) They began preparing to evacuate as soon as they heard the bombardment of San Jose begin on December 15, and they arrived at this previously selected evacuation site on December 17 with twenty food-laden carabao in tow.

Sergeant Hashimoto and eight members of our Caminawit detachment had escaped into the hills north of town and found their way to our location on December 20. Two others had been cut off from them during the bombardment and remained missing.

On December 21, in response to the order from Batangas to maintain a watch on enemy movements, a twelve-man reconnaissance patrol was organized under the command of Second Lieutenant Inoue and departed on a mission to one of the ridges overlooking San Jose. They expected to be away for a week but returned safely around December 25, reporting that the Americans had built a new airstrip near the coast where B-24s took off and landed constantly (the planes were in fact B-25s, but the patrol misidentified them). Penetrating into the valley at the base of Sawtooth Ridge, they had come upon a large array of tents.

Private Ichie Issei in the Inoue detachment had caught a cold while on this mission. The cold progressed to pneumonia and he died on January 3, our first casualty in the mountains.

Forty-eight survivors from the seaplane base at Caminawit had also joined us on December 19. Several days later, all forty-eight descended the mountain, intending to cross over to Luzon by repairing a damaged motor sailer anchored at the mouth of the Bulalacao River. They returned to our mountain base, however, after losing ten men in a guerrilla attack, including CO Ensign Ishizaki. Because they had also lost the entire supply of food our company had apportioned to them, they now had to scour the surrounding hills and meadows for food, and they were soon a wretched sight to behold. The superior officers assailed the sick with blows, screaming, "Go on! Die!"

Malaria became epidemic. The man who came to replace the young medic killed by guerrillas on the way to Caminawit had left our stock of quinine behind in San Jose, so we had no means to fight the spread of the disease. By the time the Americans launched their assault on our position on January 24, no more than thirty of our men remained unaffected.

The Inoue patrol had scouted for a lookout site, and now the entire Tanaka Platoon relocated to a spot on Ridge 517 overlooking Mangarin Bay four kilometers to the southwest—to provide daily reports on enemy activities in the area. As their main base, they erected a shelter where the ridge formed a saddle, and individual squads took turns camping on the nearby summit one day at a time, observing the San Jose area, including offshore activity, through telescopes. Twice each day, three runners were dispatched from both directions, meeting at 10:00 A.M. and 4:00 P.M. beside a small stream flowing midway between our positions, to relay scouting reports and any other messages. The signal unit then transmitted these reports to battalion HQ each evening.

The lookouts reported observing three newly constructed airstrips, one on the coast and two outside San Jose. Everyday, like clockwork, twenty-four B-24s (again, actually B-25s) took off from San Jose at noon and returned at 3:00 P.M.

On most days, they counted five destroyers, three tankers, and some fifty to eighty other watercraft of all sizes anchored in and around Mangarin Bay. Out past the coral reef directly opposite San Jose lay five to ten destroyers and five to ten cruisers. In the narrows between Mindoro and Ilin were five to ten flying boats and some two hundred small craft.

On January 4, they spied a massive fleet sailing northward, then heading south again on the high sea west of San Jose, circling twice, three times. This was the fleet that ultimately landed at Lingayen Gulf.

At a time when Japanese airpower on Luzon had been completely decimated, even such primitive reports apparently had some degree of usefulness.

From around this time, the code clerk who had been with the Tanaka Platoon took over all coding duties, and I reverted to being a common foot soldier.

On January 1 of the new year, the battalion command sent word that 150 shock troops were being dispatched to arrive in Bulalacao the next day. Before dawn on January 2, Commander Nishiya assembled an escort two-squads strong under his personal command and set out to meet them. Two were selected to go along from my squad—myself and one other man. By this time, malaria had struck everyone, and I, who had been hit first, could be counted among the more able-bodied soldiers.

According to scouting reports, the force of approximately a hundred guerrillas that had earlier attacked the seaplane base survivors still remained firmly entrenched in Bulalacao. We headed down the mountain expecting to see action.

Reaching the outskirts of Bulalacao at noon, we fanned out from the jungle behind the town but found no trace of the enemy. A pack of dogs was gathered in the town square and crows flocked overhead. As we approached, we saw that they were feeding on the corpses of the navy men killed in the guerrilla ambush. Bones were exposed where the flesh had been torn away. The town's residents were all gone, and the only sound we heard was the gurgling of water, piped in from a mountain spring, as it poured from a broken tap at the side of the road. An enemy patrol boat came into view in the offing. We gathered that an American task force was on the move.

The commando unit failed to appear, so we spent the night in town. After midnight, the sound of oars approached—a local resident returning by water, unaware that we were in town. When taken prisoner, he identified himself as the mayor's son and said he had come back to retrieve some household belongings.

We waited again the next day, but the commando unit still failed to appear. At about 3:00 P.M. we started back to our mountain encampment, taking the prisoner with us.

At the encampment, we learned American forces had landed that morning at Pinamalayan, halfway up the east coast. Our prospective path for retreat was now cut off, and a wave of despair swept through the ranks.

Enemy planes flew by overhead from morning to night. When we first arrived on Rutay Ridge, single Japanese planes had flown over at dawn or in the evening, headed toward San Jose, and we sometimes heard bombs exploding shortly after they passed over. In the new year, however, such planes became increasingly rare, and after the American landing on Luzon on January 9, they stopped appearing altogether.

Malaria continued to take its toll, killing an average of two navy men and one army man each day.

On January 13, we received new notice of the commando unit's impending arrival. Hampered by the presence of the American landing force in nearby waters, they had been casting about for an opening on the sea farther east. On January 14, a squad was sent to meet them, myself included. The commando unit failed to appear this time, too, and we returned directly to our mountain encampment after slaughtering a pig and robbing some private homes of salt, fabric, and sugar.

My fever flared up again on January 16. Day after day my temperature remained at 104 degrees. I could no longer get to my feet, and my speech became slurred.

The mayor's son escaped. The following day, a noncom and several troops went down to Bulalacao to set fire to his house as retribution.

In the evening on January 22, the lookout on the bluff where we could see Bulalacao observed three American warships entering the bay. The scouting party sent that night under the command of Second Lieutenant Inoue failed to return the next day. A second party sent out early on January 24 under the command of First Lieutenant Kakizaki, commanding officer of the shipping engineers, walked into an ambush at the foot of the mountain; the lieutenant was killed.

Commander Nishiya decided that the signal unit, noncombatants, and ambulatory ill should evacuate to the position of the Tanaka Platoon, and a total of sixty-one men moved out at about 10:00 A.M. under the command of Sergeant Adachi of the signal unit. They had marched only about two kilometers, however, when they were hit by machine-gun fire and were sent scattering in every direction. Nine stragglers (seven army, one navy, and one noncombatant) were later captured by guerrillas after wandering through the mountains for a month.

At 11:30 A.M., the vicinity of our company command post came under mortar attack from the south. An enemy reconnaissance plane circled overhead. A soldier wounded in the thigh ended his own life. Commander Nishiya strode forward to investigate the position of the mortar launchers, and a direct hit killed him instantly.

There was no one to take command of the remaining troops. All those who were ambulatory, some sixty to eighty men, descended into the canyon to the west and attempted to escape toward Ridge 517, but when gunfire erupted in that direction, they altered their course and headed northward toward Pinamalayan. The majority exhausted their strength and dropped from the column within a few kilometers, and only twenty-four men remained by the time they ran into the Tanaka Platoon in the mountains to the north on January 30.

An hour after the mortar bombardment commenced, American troops closed in on our position from all sides. For a time, I tried desperately to follow the men who had escaped northward, but my strength failed me. The next morning, American troops found me collapsed in the underbrush about a hundred yards from our erstwhile command post. I was the only man taken prisoner at that location. Some thirty to fifty other men had been unable to move at all, and they either died in the attack or committed suicide.

The American force I saw after my capture had the strength of about two armed companies. Since the commanding officer, a major, indicated his troops would be returning to San Jose on craft waiting directly south of our position, and since the shelling had come from the southwest, I concluded that our attackers had come from that direction, and that the troops we had seen landing at Bulalacao were a separate force.

Apparently, the Americans had first circled around to the west of our position on January 23, thus cutting off our route to the Tanaka Platoon. From there they had advanced eastward to launch their attack.

As soon as they heard the bombardment begin on January 24, the Tanaka Platoon dispatched a detachment of two squads to investigate our position. Spying a small group of troops gathered on top of a rise, they whooped for joy, thinking the troops must be from our company, but their whoops merely drew a spray of bullets in reply. In the face of unknown dangers, they beat a hasty retreat.

On the morning of January 25, a patrol of twelve scouts was sent out, which this time penetrated as far as the canyon west of our company command post, where they fired on some enemy troops and quickly withdrew. On their return, they came upon a large number of Japanese troops lying dead in the grass alongside the path (without doubt the evacuees) and found an empty trench littered with empty ration cans and cigarette butts. The also saw the Mangyan huts on Rutay Ridge go up in flames.

Meanwhile, back at the platoon, nearby gunfire had raised great alarm, and the remaining troops abandoned their position without waiting for the scouts to return. Fortunately, they crossed paths with the scouts on January 26, in the jungle north of the ridge. Taking advantage of the full moon, they moved out at 7:00 P.M. and continued their march until midnight, when they stopped to camp in a valley about two kilometers farther north.

Commander Tanaka addressed his men: Since the unit on Rutay Ridge had almost certainly been wiped out, they would march through the central mountain range to Calapan on the northern shore and cross over to Batangas to report Nishiya Company's demise and await further orders. Their number at the time was about forty-five, eight of whom suffered from malaria. A one-week supply of rice remained.

January 27, 6:00 A.M.: Platoon moves out. 1:00 P.M.: Guerrilla attack claims one casualty. 7:00 P.M.: Stumble across familiar path connecting San Jose and Bulalacao. Descend to large river and march along its bed. Hear the sound of artillery in direction of San Jose and hasten steps northward, casting off helmets and backpacks. 12:00 midnight: Emerge on plateau stretching several kilometers and stop for night.

January 28, 4:00 A.M.: Move out. Mangyan huts dot plateau, ten kilometers north of Bulalacao. 4:00 P.M.: Come upon empty Mangyan hut and find rice, corn.

January 29, 7:30 A.M.: Move out. 2:00 P.M.: Encounter four Mangyan men and capture as guides. 4:00 P.M.: One casualty while crossing river. 8:00 P.M.: Stop for night at Mangyan hut.

January 30, 7:00 A.M.: Move out in steady rain, which makes progress along mountain ridge exceedingly messy and difficult; many falter and drop from column. Noon: Rain turns to violent downpour; column halts for lengthy rest, warms up with bonfire. 2:00 P.M.: Rain finally ceases; move out. Arrive at Mangyan hut in evening and find twenty-four men led by Staff Sergeant Ogasawara, survivors of attack on Rutay Ridge. Tanaka party (forty-two men) designated first platoon; Ogasawara party (twenty-four men), second platoon. Second Lieutenant Tanaka assumes post of acting company commander.

January 31: A day of rest. Acting Commander Tanaka scouts surrounding area with Corporal Furukawa and a private.

February 1, 7:00 A.M.: Move out. Several in the second platoon falter and drop from column. 1:00 P.M.: Five die in guerrilla ambush, including privates Ōdoi and Okada of the first platoon and Petty Officer Akatsugi of the second. Capture Mangyan tribesman and impress as guide; he escapes at sundown. 8:00 P.M.: Stop for night on high plateau.

February 2, 8:30 A.M.: Move out in rain, which continues all day long. Corporal Furukawa captures three Mangyans to serve as guides.

February 3: Continue northward march. 3:00 P.M.: Guerrilla ambush claims Private Miyamoto Iichirō. Evening: Town of Bongabong comes into view far to the northeast. Position is now twenty kilometers north of Ridge 517.

February 4: Ford middle reaches of Bongabong River. Water is deep, above troops' chests, but all cross safely with mutual assistance. 2:00 P.M.: Come to Mangyan hut and stop for day.

February 5: Guerrilla attack before dawn claims Privates Araki Takehiko and Kojima Shigezaburō. 10:00 A.M.: Move out. 2:00 P.M.: Mangyan guides escape while leading column up steep slope. 5:00 P.M.: Find shelter and stop for night.

February 6, 9:00 A.M.: Move out. Path is finally level again, suggests human habitation nearby. Discover Mangyan hamlet, billet for the night in eight separate homes. Distance to Bongabong is several kilometers, Mangyans say.

Officers gather to discuss situation. Have managed to avoid starvation by appropriating rice, corn, potatoes from the Mangyans, but too many men have died from illness or faltered from exhaustion during hard march through mountains. In spite of greater danger, consensus reached to march on flat ground at night and return to mountains only during the day.

February 7, 8:00 A.M.: Move out. March northward along branch of

Bongabong River. 2:00 P.M.: Ambushed by guerrillas; Sergeant Wakaba-yashi Yukimasa killed. 3:00 P.M.: Encounter Mangyan tribesman, the last seen in this territory. Come to large lumber mill. The people are Tagalog, but they have identification cards showing former employment at Japanese lumber mill, so company billets in two of their homes. Position is three kilometers from Bongabong, where Americans landed at the turn of the year; Americans have now withdrawn to Calapan.

February 8: Intended morning departure delayed by sudden outbreak of fever among men, including leading noncoms Staff Sergeant Ogasawara, Sergeant Matsumoto, and Corporal Miyazaki along with PFC Mogi, Private Nakamura, and others. Heavy downpour also encourages decision to take full day of rest. Total strength now fifty-seven.

Give lumber mill owner 1,500 pesos and some all-cotton fabric as payment for lodging, and also purchase chickens and pig. 5:00 P.M.: While troops prepare these for evening meal, guerrillas launch large-scale attack from jungle to southwest and scatter troops in all directions. Those con-firmed dead by Second Lieutenant Tanaka: Privates Kawai Shingo, Hattori Hiroo, Mutō Kiyoshi, Fujisawa Tamao, Nakamura Shigeji.

February 9, early A.M.: A total of fifteen men remain under Lieutenant Tanaka's command (Staff Sergeant Ogasawara, Corporal Miyazaki, PFC Mogi Misao; Privates Nakamura Masayoshi, Sakaiji Takeo, Nishimura Sei-ichi, Sengoku Tomoshirō, Yamanaka Tarō, Saitō Eiichi, Hashimoto Ken-tarō, Toyoshita Satomi, Ōsawa Kikujirō; and Privates Kimura, Itaoka, and Akita). Strike westward into the mountains; find cabin belonging to lumber mill and stop to rest, eat. 4:00 P.M.: While crawling up side of steep prec-ipice, come under fire from directly above. Staff Sergeant Ogasawara, Cor-poral Miyazaki, PFC Mogi and Privates Nakamura, Nishimura, Sengoku, Yamanaka, and Saitō turn up missing after the attack.

With this day the activities of Nishiya Company as a unit came to a close. In the thirty-five days between February 9 and March 16, Second Lieutenant Tanaka and eighteen other men from the unit, as well as one shipping engineer, were captured by guerrillas, either alone or in small groups, as they straggled northward from the mountains behind Bongabong toward Calapan, surviving only on nuts, roots, tadpoles, and the like.

The Watanabe Platoon in Paluan left no survivors, and we lack any means of learning about their demise. Paluan is situated within a bay at the far northwest point of Mindoro. The peak rising over this cape offers a view of the mouth of Manila Bay, and the Americans had long maintained a lookout on its summit, monitoring the number of Japanese warships going in and out of the bay or passing through the Verde Island Passage and radioing the information to their submarines. The American officer in charge, a Major Philips, had been executed in April 1944, but the Paluan platoon remained responsible for guarding against any further enemy activity of this kind on the peak.

Among the platoons in the Mindoro garrison, the one at Paluan was most isolated and lived closest to nature. They swam and fished in the ocean every day. An equestrian NCO rode bareback onto the beach to welcome our interisland motor launch as it rounded the cape; then, as our boat proceeded along the coast toward the moorage, he rode up onto the road that wound along the shoreline bluff, disappearing and reappearing behind clumps of trees as he kept pace with the boat.

Of the 180 men in First Lieutenant Nishiya's transport unit when it departed from Tokyo, one officer, four NCOs, and sixteen privates, a total of twenty-one men, came to the POW camp on Leyte and subsequently returned home. Twelve men had remained behind on Luzon when we proceeded to Mindoro; four of these were taken by the Division Signal Corps, two volunteered for the Military Police, two were transferred to the Brigade Drill Team owing to weak constitution, and four had to be hospitalized. Four of the twelve survived and returned home by different routes.

INDEX